OFFICIAL COPY.

$$\frac{40}{\text{W.O.}}$$
$$2923$$

FIELD SERVICE POCKET BOOK.

1914.

(Reprinted, with Amendments, 1916.)

GENERAL STAFF, WAR OFFICE.

LONDON:
PUBLISHED BY HIS MAJESTY'S STATIONERY OFFICE.

To be purchased through any Bookseller or directly from
H.M. STATIONERY OFFICE at the following addresses:
IMPERIAL HOUSE, KINGSWAY, LONDON, W.C. 2, and 28, ABINGDON STREET, LONDON, S.W. 1;
37, PETER STREET, MANCHESTER; 1. ST. ANDREW'S CRESCENT, CARDIFF
23, FORTH STREET, EDINBURGH ;
or from E. PONSONBY, LTD., 116, GRAFTON STREET, DUBLIN:
or from the Agencies in the British Colonies and Dependencies,
the United States of America and other Foreign Countries of
T. FISHER UNWIN, LTD., LONDON, W.C. 2

(Reprinted, 1917.)

Price 1s. Net.

NOTE.

THIS BOOK IS SUBJECT TO PERIODICAL REVISION. IT IS ONLY INTENDED AS A HANDY AND CONCISE BOOK OF REFERENCE FOR USE ON ACTIVE SERVICE, AT MANŒUVRES, OR ON INSTRUCTIONAL EXERCISES. IT SHOULD NOT BE QUOTED AS AN AUTHORITY IN OFFICIAL CORRESPONDENCE, NOR SHOULD IT BE UTILIZED AS A TEXT-BOOK FOR THE STUDY OF MILITARY SUBJECTS.

OFFICERS ARE EXPECTED TO KEEP THE BOOK UP TO DATE BY AMENDING IT IN ACCORDANCE WITH ANY CHANGES THAT MAY APPEAR IN ARMY ORDERS AND OTHER OFFICIAL PUBLICATIONS.

(B 12937)   Wt. 63186—718   150M   4/17   H & S   P. 16/168   (S)

CONTENTS.

		PAGE
Abbreviations	.. ..	v
Definitions	.. ..	viii

Section   CHAPTER I.

1.	War Establishments	1
2.	System of Command in the Field	24
3.	General Organization and Functions of the Staff	25
4.	Distribution of Duties among Administrative Services and Departments	28
5.	Organization of the Executive on L: of C.	29

CHAPTER II.

6.	Marches and March Discipline	33
7.	Time and Space	37
8.	Quarters..	43
9.	Camp Cooking, etc.	49
10.	Sanitation of Camps and Bivouacs	51
11.	Water Supply	52

CHAPTER III.

12.	Orders	55
13.	Intercommunication	59
14.	Information	70
15.	Protection	76
16.	Oversea Operations	79
17.	Map Reading and Field Sketching	84

CHAPTER IV.

18.	Field Engineering	88
19.	Summary of Tools and Explosives	92
20.	Table of Time, Men and Tools required for certain work	97
21.	Defence of Localities, etc.	101
22.	Obstacles	104
23.	Working Parties and Tasks	104
24.	Knots, Cordage, Blocks and Tackles	106
25.	Bridges and Bridging Expedients	109
26.	Demolitions	116

CHAPTER V.

27.	Transport	120
28.	Details of Vehicles and Stores in common use	130
29.	Convoys	137
30.	Transport by Rail	138
31.	,, ,, Sea	155

iv

Section	CHAPTER VI.	PAGE
32.	Small Arms and Guns	159
33.	Supply of Ammunition	165
34.	Rations, Fuel and Forage	168
35.	Notes on Supplies	172
36.	Supply Arrangements	174

CHAPTER VII.

37.	Pay	179
38.	Clothing..	181
39.	Field Kits	182
40.	Medical Service	198
41.	Remount Service	205
42.	Veterinary Service	206

CHAPTER VIII.

43.	Office Work and Private Correspondence	210
44.	Discipline	216
45.	Courts-Martial ..	217
46.	Provost-Marshal and Military Police	225
47.	International Law	226

CHAPTER IX.

48.	The Army in India	235
49.	The Military Forces of the Oversea Dominions, Crown Colonies and Protectorates other than India	239
50.	Details of Foreign Armies	251
51.	Weights, Measures and Money (British, Indian and Foreign)	259
52.	Thermometer ..	268

APPENDIX I.

Points of the Compass 269

APPENDIX II.

Magnetic Variation 270

APPENDIX III.

Dates of the Full Moon, 1913–1915 271

APPENDIX IV.

Sunrise and Sunset 272

APPENDIX V.

Authorities to whom Indents should be addressed 274

APPENDIX VI.

(a) Billeting Demand 275
(b) Billeting Order 275

APPENDIX VII.

Private Post Card, A.F. A 2042 276

APPENDIX VIII.

Aeronautical Terms in Common Use .... 27?

INDEX .... 27?

LIST OF PLATES.

To face page

1. Type of Bivouac for a Cavalry Regiment or Battalion of Mounted Infantry 44
2. ,, ,, ,, a Battery 44
3. ,, ,, ,, an Ammunition Column 44
4. ,, ,, ,, an Infantry Battalion 44
5. Type of Perimeter Camp for a mixed force.. 44
6. Bivouacs and Destructor 46
7. Cooking in the Field 46
8. Latrines 50
9. Scales 84
10. Conventional Signs 84
11. Types of Cover 102
12. Fire Trenches 102
13. Cover for Guns.. 104
14. Raft and Bridge Details 110
15. Types of Bridges 110
16. Diagram of Ammunition Supply for a Division 165
17. Diagram of Ammunition Supply for a Cavalry Division 165
18. Supply Service in an Army of 4 Divisions, 1 Cavalry Division, 2 Mounted Brigades, and other Army Troops, when the Force is Marching 174
19. Supply Service for 3 Divisions and Army Troops when Stationary 174
20. Sliding Alphabet Cipher 212
21. Distinguishing Flags and Lamps .. .. .. at end of book

ABBREVIATIONS.

Abbreviations denoting names of corps such as R.H.A., A.S.C., &c., are omitted.

" A " before an abbreviation signifying a principal staff officer, or the head of a service or department, means Assistant, similarly " D " signifies Deputy.

A.A.	Army Act.
A.A.G. ..	Assistant Adjutant-General.
A.B. ..	Army Book.
A.F.	Army Form.
A.D.C. ..	Aide-de-Camp.
Admn. ..	Administration.
A.D. Sigs.	Assistant Director of Army Signals.
Adv. Gd...	Advanced guard.
A.G. ..	Adjutant-General.
Amm. ..	Ammunition.
A. and S.	Ammunition and Store.
A.D.M.S...	Assistant Director of Medical Services.
A.O. ..	Army Order.
A.P. ..	Armour Piercing.
A.P.M. ..	Assistant Provost-Marshal.
Art. ..	Artillery.
Batt. ..	Battery.
B.C. ..	Battery Commander.
Bde. ..	Brigade.
B.M. ..	Brigade Major.
Bn. ..	Battalion.
Br. ..	Bombardier or Bugler.
Brig.-Gen.	Brigadier-General.
Capt. ..	Captain.
Cav. ..	Cavalry.
C.B. ..	Confinement to Barracks.
C.C.D. ..	Commander of Coast Defences.
C.G.S. ..	Chief of the General Staff in the Field.
Col. ..	Colonel.
Coln. ..	Column.

Comdt.	.. ..	Commandant.
Comdr.	.. ..	Commander.
C.-in-C.	.. ..	Commander-in-Chief.
Comdng.	.. ..	Commanding.
C.O.	.. ..	Commanding Officer.
Co.	.. ..	Company.
Cpl.	.. ..	Corporal.
D.A.G.	.. ..	Deputy Adjutant-General.
D.D.M.S.	.. ..	Deputy Director of Medical Services.
D.J.A.G.	.. ..	Deputy Judge Advocate General.
Det.	.. ..	Detachment.
Dept.	.. ..	Department.
Dist.	.. ..	District.
Div.	.. ..	Division.
Dn.	.. ..	Dragoon.
D.G.	.. ..	Dragoon Guard.
Dr.	.. ..	Drummer or Driver.
D.R.F.	.. ..	Depression Range-Finder.
D.Sigs.	.. ..	Director of Army Signals.
D.M.S.	.. ..	Director of Medical Services.
D.O.S.	.. ..	Director of Ordnance Services.
D. Post.	.. ..	Director of Postal Services.
D.R.T.	.. ..	Director of Railway Transport.
D. Remounts	..	Director of Remounts.
D.S.	.. ..	Director of Supplies.
D.S.T.	.. ..	Director of Sea Transport.
D.T.	.. ..	Director of Transport.
D.V.S.	.. ..	Director of Veterinary Services.
D.W.	.. ..	Director of Works.
Est.	.. ..	Establishment.
F. Amb.	.. ..	Field Ambulance.
F.C.	.. ..	Fire Commander.
F. Co.	.. ..	Field Company.
F.G.C.M.	.. ..	Field General Court-Martial.
F. Imp.	.. ..	Field Imprisonment.
F.M.	.. ..	Field Marshal.
F.O.	.. ..	Field Officer.
F.S.M.	.. ..	Field Service Manual.
F.S.R.	.. ..	Field Service Regulations.
f.s.	.. ..	Feet per second.
G.C.	.. ..	Gun Captain.
G.C.M.	.. ..	General Court-Martial.
Gd.	.. ..	Guard.
G.G.C.	.. ..	Gun Group Commander.
G.H.Q.	.. ..	General Headquarters.
G.O.C.	.. ..	General Officer Commanding.
Gr.	.. ..	Gunner.
G.S.	.. ..	General Staff, also General Service.
Hd. Qrs.	..	Headquarters.
Hd. Qrs. Gen. Hd. Qrs. Sig. Co.		Headquarters of a General Headquarters Signal Company.
Hd. Qrs. Army Hd. Qrs. Sig. Co.		Headquarters of an Army Headquarters Signal Company.
H.E.	.. ..	Horizontal Equivalent, also High Explosive.
Howr.	.. ..	Howitzer.
Hosp.	.. ..	Hospital.
Hr.	.. ..	Hussar.
I.A.	.. ..	Indian Army.
i/c.	.. ..	In charge of.
I.G.C.	.. ..	Inspector-General of Communications.
Inf.	, ..	Infantry.
J.A.G.	, ..	Judge Advocate-General.

Lieut.	.. ..	Lieutenant.
Lt.-Gen.	.. ..	Lieutenant-General.
L. of C.	.. ..	Line of Communication.
Lr.	.. ..	Lancer.
M.G.	.. ..	Machine Gun.
Maj.-Gen.		Major-General.
Med.	.. ..	Medical.
M.F.P.	.. ..	Military Foot Police.
M.L.	.. ..	Muzzle Loader.
M.L.O.	.. ..	Military Landing Officer.
M.P.	.. ..	Military Police.
M.M.P.	.. ..	Military Mounted Police.
M.F.E.	.. ..	Manual of Field Engineering
M O	.. ..	Medical Officer.
Mtd.	.. ..	Mounted.
M.T.	.. ..	Mechanical Transport.
m.v.	.. ..	Muzzle Velocity.
m.p.h.	.. ..	Miles per hour.
N.C.O.	.. ..	Non-Commissioned Officer.
O.C.	.. ..	Officer Commanding.
Offr.	.. ..	Officer.
O.O.	.. ..	Ordnance Officer.
Ord.	.. ..	Ordnance.
O.R.S.	.. ..	Orderly room Serjeant.
P.C.	.. ..	Principal Chaplain.
Pl.	.. ..	Platoon.
P.M.	.. ..	Provost-Marshal.
Pmr.	.. ..	Paymaster.
P.O.	.. ..	Post Office.
Pte.	.. ..	Private.
P.W.	.. ..	Royal Warrant for Pay and Promotion.
Q.F.	.. ..	Quickfiring.
Qr.Mr.	.. ..	Quartermaster.
Q.M.G.	.. ..	Quartermaster-General.
Q.M.S.	.. ..	Quartermaster-Serjeant.
R.C.M.	.. ..	Regimental Court-Martial.
R.F.	.. ..	Representative Fraction.
R.T.O.	.. ..	Railway Transport Officer.
Rgt.	.. ..	Regiment.
R.M.	.. ..	Riding Master.
S.A.A.	.. ..	Small Arm Ammunition.
Sec.	.. ..	Section.
Sjt.	.. ..	Serjeant.
Sig. Sec. A.	..	Signal Section Air-line.
Sig. Sec. C.	..	Signal Section Cable.
Sig. Co. D.	..	Signal Company with Division.
Sig. Sec. W.	..	Signal Section Wireless.
Sig.O.	..	Signalling Officer.
Sig. Sqn.	..	Signal Squadron.
Sig. Tp.	..	Signal Troop.
S.M.	.. ..	Serjeant-Major.
S.O.	.. ..	Staff Officer.
Sqn.	.. ..	Squadron.
Sup.O.	.. ..	Supply Officer.
Tel.	.. ..	Telegraphs.
T.O.	.. ..	Transport Officer.
T. & S.	.. ..	Transport and Supply.
Tp.	.. ..	Troop.
Tpr.	.. ..	Trooper.
Tr.	.. ..	Trumpeter.
Vet.	..	Veterinary.

V.I.	..	..	Vertical Interval.
W.E.	..	..	War Establishments.
5° ..	..	..	5 degrees.
5′ ..	..	..	5 feet or 5 minutes (geographically only).
5″ ..	..	..	5 inches or 5 seconds.
5ˣ ..	..	..	5 yards.

DEFINITIONS.

(For special definitions of terms used in oversea expeditions *see* p. 80.)

ABATIS. An obstacle formed of trees or branches of trees picketed to the ground with their points towards the enemy.

ACCOUTREMENTS comprise belts, pouches, bandoliers, slings, mess tins, haversacks, water bottles, and similar articles (other than arms) carried outside the clothing.

ADMINISTRATIVE COMMANDER. An officer vested with the command of administrative troops only ; *e.g.*, administrative commandants, directors of administrative services and their representatives.

ADMINISTRATIVE DEPARTMENTS. The departments of the Judge Advocate-General, Principal Chaplain and Paymaster-in-Chief.

ADMINISTRATIVE SERVICES. Signal, medical, supplies, transport, ordnance, railways, works, remounts, veterinary, postal.

ADMINISTRATIVE TROOPS. Troops, combatant or otherwise, belonging to the administrative services, including R.E. other than those of field units ; A.S.C. ; R.A.M.C. ; A.O.C. ; A.V.C. ; A.P.C. ; A.P.O.C.

ADVANCED BASE. The area within which may be situated the advanced depots of ammunition, supplies, animals, and material, from which issues are made to field units.

ALIGNMENT. Any straight line on which a body of troops is formed, or is to form.

BANQUETTE. The place upon which men stand to fire over a parapet.

BASE. A place where the L. of C. originates, where magazines of stores for the forces in the field are situated and maintained under direct military management and control, and where the business of supplying these forces is located and organized under the military authorities.

BASIN. (i) A small area of level ground surrounded (or nearly so) by hills ; (ii) a district drained by a river and its tributaries.

BAULK. A road bearer in a military bridge.

BAY. The distance bridged by one set of baulks.

BEARING. True bearing is the angle a line makes with the true north line. Magnetic bearing is the angle a line makes with the magnetic north line. In each case the angle is measured from North by East and South.

BENCH MARK. A stone placed to mark a level accurately fixed by instruments.

BERM. A small space left between the parapet and excavations of a work.

BIGHT. A loop formed on a rope, the two parts of which lie alongside one another.

BIVOUAC. An encampment without tents or huts.

BOMB-PROOF. A shelter, proof against penetration by shells.

CALIBRE. The diameter of the bore of a gun in inches measured across the lands.

CAPONIER. A small chamber formed in the ditch of a work projecting from the escarp to give fire along the bottom of the ditch.

CASEMATE. A shell-proof chamber constructed for the accommodation of a garrison of a work or position.

CHESS. A plank forming a portion of the flooring of a bridge.

COL. A depression between two adjacent hills: a break in a ridge; the neck of land connecting an outlying feature with the main range.

COLUMN. Bodies of troops formed one in rear of another.

COMMAND (Mil. Eng.). Vertical height of the crest of a work above the natural surface of the ground.

COMMANDER. An officer vested with the command of a detachment, unit, or formation of fighting or administrative troops.

CONTOUR. A contour is the representation on a map of an imaginary line running along the surface of the ground at the same height above mean sea level throughout its length.

CONTRIBUTION. A levy made on a town or community (*see* Sec. 47 and F.S.R., Part II, Sec. 35).

COSSACK POST. A " group " in outpost mounted troops (*see* Group).

COUNTERSCARP. The side of the ditch of a work farthest from the parapet.

CREST (Mil. Eng.). The intersection of the interior and superior slopes of a parapet.

CREST (TOPO.). The edge of the top of a hill or mountain ; the position at which a gentle slope changes to an abrupt one.

CRIB-PIER. A support for a bridge formed of layers of baulks of wood laid alternately at right angles to each other.

DEAD GROUND. Ground which cannot be covered by fire.

DEFILE. A portion of the route which troops can only traverse on a narrow front, *e.g.*, a mountain pass, a bridge, an embankment.

DERRICK. A single spar held by four guys, used for lifting or moving weights.

DISTANCE. The space between men or bodies of troops from front to rear.

DIVISIONAL COLLECTING STATION. A place where slightly wounded men who are able to walk are collected.

DRESSING STATION. A place where wounded are collected and attended by the personnel of a field ambulance.

ECHELON. A formation of successive and parallel units facing in the same direction, each on a flank, and to the rear of, the unit in front of it.

EMBRASURE. A channel through the parapet of a work through which a gun is fired.

EPAULMENT. A small parapet to give cover to a gun and detachment in action.

ESCARP. The side of a ditch nearest the parapet.

FASCINE. A long bundle of brushwood used for revetting, roadmaking, &c.

FIELD ARMY. That portion of the forces in the field not allotted to fortresses, coast defences or garrisons.

FIELD DEPÔT. A small temporary depôt of supplies in the immediate vicinity of the field units.

FIELD UNITS. Mobile units of the field army allotted to divisions, cavalry divisions, brigades, army troops, or L. of C. defence troops.

FIGHTING TROOPS. Infantry, cavalry, artillery (including ammunition columns), flying corps and engineer field units. The headquarters of commanders of fighting troops are fighting units.

FIRE, ENFILADE. Fire the line of which sweeps troops or defences from flank.

FIRE, DIRECT LAYING. When the gun is laid by looking over or through the sights at the target.

FIRE, FRONTAL. Fire, the line of which is perpendicular to the front the target.

FIRE, HIGH ANGLE. Fire from all guns and howitzers at all angles of elevation exceeding 25°.

FIRE, INDIRECT LAYING. When the gun is laid for direction on an aiming point or on aiming posts and elevation adjusted by sight clinometer.

FIRE, OBLIQUE. Fire, the line of which is inclined to the front of the target.

FIRE, REVERSE. Fire, which is directed against the rear of a target.

FILE. A front rank man and his rear rank man.

FORCES IN THE FIELD. The whole of the military forces mobilized in the theatre of operations under the supreme command of the C. in C. Includes the field army or armies, fortress, coast defence and garrison troops, and L. of C. units and defence troops.

FORM LINE. An approximate contour; a sketch contour.

FOUGASSE. A small mine filled with stones which are projected towards the enemy on the mine being fired.

GABION. An open cylinder of brushwood, sheet iron, &c., used for revetting.

GLACIS. The ground round a work within close rifle range. Sometimes formed artificially.

GORGE (TOPO.). A rugged and deep ravine. (Mil. Eng.) The face of a work least prepared to receive frontal fire.

GRADIENT. A slope expressed by a fraction. $\frac{1}{30}$ represents a rise or fall of 1' in 30'.

GROUP. On outpost duty, a sentry post of from 3 to 8 men.

GUY. A rope fastened to the tip of a spar or frame, to support, raise, or lower it.

GYN. A tripod with tackle, used for raising weights.

HEADERS. Sods, sandbags, &c., placed so that the longest side is at right angles to the face of the structure.

HEADQUARTERS, ARMY CORPS. The headquarters of the commander of an army corps or group of divisions.

HEADQUARTERS, ARMY. The headquarters of the commander of an army or group of army corps. If army corps are not grouped in separate armies, army headquarters and general headquarters become identical, and the latter term will be used.

HEADQUARTERS, GENERAL. The headquarters of C. in C. of the forces in the field.

HORIZONTAL EQUIVALENT. The distance in plan between two adjacent contours measured in yards.

HORSE-LENGTH. 8 feet.

„ WIDTH. 3 feet, which includes 3 inches outside the rider's knee on either side.

INTERVAL. The lateral space between men, units or corps measured from flank to flank.

KNOLL. A low detached hill.

LINES OF COMMUNICATION. The systems of communication by rail, road and navigable waterways between the army and its base or bases inclusive, together with the district through which they pass, within such limits as the C. in C. may determine.

L. OF C. DEFENCES. The defences of that portion of the L. of C. for the security of which the commander of L. of C. defences is made responsible by the C. in C., together with all fortifications and defences in that area.

L. OF C. DEFENCE TROOPS. That portion of the field army which is detailed for the defence of the L. of C.

L. OF C. UNITS. Administrative units on the L. of C. and under the command of the I.G.C.

MAGNETIC MERIDIAN. A magnetic north and south line.

MAGNETIC VARIATION. The angle between the true north and magnetic north.

MERIDIAN. A true north and south line.

MOBILIZATION is the process by which an armed force passes from a peace to a war footing. The mobilization, therefore, of a unit means its completion for war in men, horses, and material.

ORDERS, OPERATION. Orders which deal with all strategical and tactical operations and which include such information regarding supply, transport, &c., as it is necessary to publish to the troops.

ORDERS, ROUTINE. Orders which deal with matters not concerned with operations such as discipline, interior economy.

ORDERS, STANDING. Orders issued to adapt existing regulations to local conditions and to save frequent repetitions in operation and routine orders.

PACE. The denomination of different degrees of speed ; also a measurement of distance (30 inches).

PARADOS. A traverse to give cover from reverse fire.

PATROL. A body of men sent out to reconnoitre, or to guard against surprise.

PLATOON. The quarter of an infantry company. Consists of four sections.

PLOTTING. The process of laying down on paper field observations and measurements.

POSITION OF OBSERVATION (artillery) implies batteries in action watching all ground in their field of fire and ready to open fire.

POSITION OF READINESS (artillery) implies batteries limbered up under cover with positions in the immediate neighbourhood reconnoitred and everything ready for their occupation.

PROFILE. The outline of the section of a parapet at right angles to the crest.

PRIMERS. Small discs of dry guncotton used to detonate wet guncotton (*see* page 117).

RAILHEAD. A locality on the railway where ammunition and supplies are transferred to ammunition parks and supply columns.

REDOUBT. A work entirely enclosed by a defensible parapet, which gives rifle fire all round.

RE-ENTRANT. A valley or depression running into a main feature.

REFILLING POINTS. Places where divisional ammunition columns and supply sections of trains are refilled from ammunition parks and supply columns respectively.

REGULATING STATION. A place where railway trains are marshalled, and whence they are despatched to railheads.

RELIEF. The length of time that men have to work before being relieved, or a number of men who work, or are on duty, for a given length of time.

RENDEZVOUS. Places where ammunition parks and supply columns are met by representatives of the headquarters concerned and directed to refilling points.

REQUISITION. A mode of making inhabitants of a district contribute supplies, &c., to an army. Must be paid for (*see* page 176), but a Requisition Receipt Note implies no promise to pay.

REVETMENT. Any material formed into a retaining wall to support earth at a steeper slope than the natural one.

RIBAND. A beam or spar fastened down on each side of a roadway to keep the chesses in place.

SADDLE. *See* COL.

SANGAR. A dry built stone wall to give protection against rifle fire.

SAP. A trench formed by constantly extending the end towards the enemy.

SCALE. The proportion which a distance between any two points on a map bears to the horizontal distance between the same points on the ground.

SECTION. Cavalry. 4 front rank men with their coverers.

    ,,   Artillery. 2 guns of a battery with their complement of men, horses and wagons.

    ,,   Infantry. The quarter of a platoon.

    ,,   Topography. The outline of the intersection of the surface of the ground by a vertical plane.

SECTION OF DEFENCE. A portion of a defensive position which is allotted to a distinct body of troops.

SERREFILE. Such officers, N.C.Os. or men, as may be detailed to ride in rear of the rear rank of a squadron when in line.

SHEERS. Two spars lashed together at the tip and raised to rest on their butts, which are separated. They are used to lift and move weights in one plane.

SIGNAL UNITS. Units employed on the service of intercommunication. They include signal squadrons and troops, divisional and L. of C. Sig. Cos. Hd. Qrs. of a Gen. Hd. Qrs. Sig. Co., Hd. Qrs. of an Army Hd. Qrs. Sig. Co., and airline, cable, and wireless sections, but do not include regimental signallers on the establishment of other units.

SLOPE. Exterior. The outside slope of a parapet extending downwards from the superior slope.

  ,, Interior. The inside slope of a parapet extending from the crest to the banquette.

  ,, Superior. The top of a parapet immediately forward from the crest·

SPAN. The horizontal distance between the centres of any two supports of a bridge.

SPLINTER-PROOF. A shelter, proof against splinters of shell.

SPOT LEVEL. The record on a map of the exact height of a particular point.

SPUR (TOPO.). A projection from the side of a hill or mountain running out from the main feature.

SQUAD. A small body of men formed for drill or for work.

SQUADRON. Tactical unit of cavalry, 3 or 4 troops.

STAFF, THE. Staff officers appointed to the General Staff, to the A.G.'s and Q.M.G.'s branches of the staff, or as brigade-majors and staff captains, to assist certain commanders in the discharge of their duties.

STRETCHERS (Mil. Eng.). Sods, sandbags, &c., placed so that their longest side is parallel to the face of the structure.

SUPPLIES. Food, forage, fuel, light and disinfectants.

TACKLE. Any system of blocks and ropes by which power is gained at the expense of time (i.e., more power, less speed).

TAMP, TO. To cover a charge over with earth or other material so as to confine the gases at the commencement of an explosion, and thus develop their forces more fully.

TASK. The amount of work to be executed by a man during a relief.

THEATRE OF OPERATIONS. The whole area of land or sea in which fighting may be expected or in which movements of troops are liable to interruption or interference by the enemy.

TRACE. The outline of a work in plan.

TRAIN. Transport allotted to fighting units for the conveyance of the baggage stores and supplies necessary for their subsistence.

TRAVERSE (Mil. Eng.). A bank of earth erected to give lateral cover.

TRAVERSE (TOPO.). The survey of a road, river, or track by measuring a continuous series of straight lines along its course and the angles at their junctions.

TROOP. A sub-division of a squadron, corresponding to a platoon in the infantry. Also used for certain units, e.g., field troop, signal troop.

VEDETTE. A sentry of mounted troops.

VERTICAL INTERVAL. The difference of level between two adjacent contours in feet.

WATERCOURSE. The line defining the lowest part of a valley whether occupied by a stream or not.

WATERSHED. A ridge of high land separating two drainage basins ; the summit of land from which water divides or flows in two directions. It does not necessarily include the highest points of a range.

WATTLE. Continuous brushwood hurdle work.

FIELD SERVICE POCKET BOOK,

1914.

CHAPTER I.

1. WAR ESTABLISHMENTS.*

1. Information regarding the war establishment and war outfit of regular units can be derived from the following sources :—

Men and animals	{ War Establishments. †Transport, Remount and †Veterinary Manuals, War. Field Service manuals.
Ordnance stores, i.e., arms, ammunition, vehicles, harness, tools, &c.	{ Equipment Regs. Mobilization Stores Tables. A.F. G 1098. Ordnance Manual, War. Field Service Manuals.
Clothing and necessaries ...	{ Clothing Regs., Part III. Field Service Manuals.
Stationery	{ Tables of books, &c., required on mobilization. A.F. L 1398 (Regs.); L 1399 (T.F.)
Medical stores...	{ †Medical Manual, War. Field Service Manuals. Regulations, A.M.S.
Veterinary stores	{ †Veterinary Manual, War. Field Service Manuals.
Food, forage and light	{ Supply Manual, War. War Establishments. Field Service Manuals.
Transport	{ War Establishments. †Transport, Remount and Veterinary Manuals, War. Field Service Manuals.

* War Establishments (Expeditionary Force) show the establishment on mobilization and are based on 1914 edition of War Establishments, Part I, Expeditionary Force.
† These books are in course of preparation.
NOTE.—There is a separate series of the above publications referring to India, except Equipment and Clothing Regulations.

2.—A CAVALRY DIVISION.*

Detail.	Personnel.		Horses.			Guns.		Vehicles (excluding gun carriages and limbers).							
	Officers.	Other Ranks.	Riding.	Draught.	Pack.	13-pr. Q.F.	Machine Guns.	2-horsed Carts.	2-horsed Wagons.	4-horsed Wagons.	6-horsed Wagons.	Motor Cars.	Bicycles.	Motor Cycles.	
Headquarters	15	81	53	10	1	..	..	1	..	2	..	16	..	..	
4 Cavalry Brigades ...	340	6,532	6,492	928	72	..	24	32	4	196	..	4	292	12	
Hdqrs. Cav. Div. Art. ...	3	17	14	4	..	24	..	..	..	1	..	..	3	..	
2 H.A. Brigades ...	38	1,324	554	1,004	..	..	..	8	12	14	112	..	24	..	
1 Field Squadron a ...	7	184	104	92	14	..	..	14b	..	6	4	..	44	..	
1 Signal Squadron... ...	8	198	80	70	..	..	..	2	9	3	5	2	34	6	
1 Hdqrs. Cav. Div. A.S.C.	4	22	5	6	..	..	..	1	..	1	..	1	7	..	
4 Cav. F. Amb. ...	24	472	48	264	..	..	..	16	24	16	16	..	8	..	
Total	439	8,830	7,350	2,378	87	24	24	74	49	239	137	23	412	18	

* Excluding details at base.
a For bridging material see p. 111.
b Includes the four double tool carts with each troop which are shown as two vehicles.

3.—HEADQUARTERS OF A CAVALRY DIVISION.
Commander.

Major-general.

Personal Appointments.

2 Aides-de-camp.

Staff.

1 General staff officer, 1st grade.
1   „   „   „   2nd „
1   „   „   „   3rd „
1 Asst. adj. and quartermaster-general.
1 Dep. asst. adj. and quartermaster-general.
1 Dep. asst. quartermaster-general.

Administrative Services.

1 Asst. director medical services.
1 Dep. asst. dir. of medical services.
1 Asst. director of veterinary services.
1 Dep. asst. director of ordnance services.
— Army postal service (3 clerks).

Special Appointment.

1 Asst. provost-marshal.

Police, clerks, &c.

4.—A CAVALRY BRIGADE (WITH CAV. DIV.).*

Detail.	Personnel.		Horses.			Machine Guns.	Vehicles.					
	Officers.	Other ranks.	Riding.	Draught.	Pack.		2-horsed carts.	2-horsed wagons.	4-horsed wagons.	Motor Cars.	Bicycles.	Motor Cycles.
Headquarters ...	6	41	25	8	...	...	2	...	1	1	7	...
3 Cav. Regiments	78	1,569	1,584	222	18	6	6	...	48	...	60	...
1 Signal Troop ...	1	23	14	2	...	...	...	1	...	...	6	3
	85	1,633	1,623	232	18	6	8	1	49	1	73	3

* Excluding details at the base.

5.—HEADQUARTERS OF A CAVALRY BRIGADE WITH CAV. DIV.
Commander.

Brigadier-general.

Personal Appointment.

1 Aide-de-camp.

Staff.

1 Brigade-major.
1 Staff captain.

Administrative Services.

-— Army postal service (3 clerks).

Police, clerks, &c

6.—A CAVALRY BRIGADE NOT ALLOTTED TO A CAVALRY DIVISION.*

Details.	Total Personnel.		Horses.			Guns.		Vehicles (excluding gun carriages and limbers).							
	Officers.	Other Ranks.	Riding.	Draught.	Pack.	13-prs.	Machine Guns.	2-horsed Carts.	Wagons. 2-horsed.	Wagons. 4-horsed.	Wagons. 6-horsed.	Motor Cars.	Bicycles.	Motor Cycles.
Headquarters	7	47	25	8	...	...	...	2	...	1	...	5	7	...
3 Cavalry Regiments ...	78	1,569	1,584	222	...	...	6	6	...	48	...	...	60	...
1 Horse Artillery Battery	7	215	108	132	18	6	...	2	...	2	12	...	3	...
1 Ammun. Col. ...	2	115	25	119	...	...	...	1	3	1	16	...	1	...
1 Field Troop (a) ...	3	74	42	28	...	...	...	6	...	1	1	...	15	...
1 Signal Troop ...	1	42	30	6	5	...	...	...	3	...	...	...	6	3
1 Cavalry Field Ambulance	6	118	12	66	9	...	...	4	6	4	4	...	2	...
Total in the field ...	104	2,180	1,826	581	32	6	6	21	12	57	33	5	94	3

* Excluding details at base.
(a) For bridging material see p. 111.

7.—Headquarters of a Cavalry Brigade not Allotted to a Cavalry Division.

Commander.

Brigadier-general.

Personal Appointment.

1 Aide-de-camp.

Staff.

1 Brigade-major.
1 Staff captain.

Administrative Services.

— Army postal service (3 clerks).

———

Police, clerks, &c.

2.—A DIVISION.*
(After Concentration.)

Detail.	Personnel.		Horses.				Guns.				Vehicles (excluding gun carriages and limbers).							
	Officers.	Other Ranks.	Riding.	Draught.	Heavy Draught.	Pack.	18-prs.	4.5-inch Howitzers.	60-pr.	Machine Guns.	Carts 1-horsed.	Carts 2-horsed.	Wagons 2-horsed.	Wagons 4-horsed.	Wagons 6-horsed.	Motor Cars.	Bicycles.	Motor Cycles.
1 Headquarters	15	67	49	2	2	1							1			5		
3 Infantry Brigades	372	11,793	195	336	102	108				24	12	99	84	6			108	
1 Headquarters Div. Art.	4	18	20														2	
3 Field Artillery Bdes.	69	2,316	594	1,644	6		54					36	3	12	174		15	
1 Field Art. (Howitzer) Bde.	22	733	195	500	2			18				5	1	1	55		5	
1 Heavy Bat. and Am. Col.	6	192	29	6	109				4			1	1	16			1	
1 Divisional Ammun. Col.	15	553	56	625	28							2	1	6	94		6	
1 Headquarters Div. Eng.	3	10	5	1							1	1					1	
2 Field Companies (a)	12	422	34	106	4						1	28	7		6		66	
1 Signal Company	5	157	33	37	2	8						2			3		32	
1 Cavalry Squadron	6	153	153	10	2	8						1		2		4	6	9
1 Divisional Train	26	402	66	38	274	2					1	16	125	2			30	
3 Field Ambulances	30	672	42	45	111							21	48				3	
Total in the Field	585	17,488	1,471	3,350	644	127	54	18	4	24	15	213	271	45	332	9	275	9

* Excluding details at base.
(a) For bridging material, see p. 111.

9.—HEADQUARTERS OF A DIVISION.

Commander.

Lieutenant or Major-General.

Personal Appointments.

2 Aides-de-camp.

Staff.

1 General staff officer, 1st grade.
1   ,,   ,,   ,,   2nd ,,
1   ,,   ,,   ,,   3rd ,,
1 Asst. adjt. and quartermaster-general.
1 Dep. asst. adjt. and quartermaster-general.
1 Dept. asst. quartermaster-general.

Administrative Services.

1 Asst. director of medical services.
1 Dep. asst. dir. of medical services.
1 Asst. director of veterinary services.
1 Dep. asst. director of ordnance services.
— Army postal service (3 clerks).

Special Appointment.

1 Asst. provost-marshal.

Police, clerks, &c.
Note.—(1) When a division is acting independently, 1 G.S.O., 3rd grade, with 3 horses and 2 bâtmen will be added.
(2) The asst. director medical services commands the R.A.M.C. of the division.

10.—AN INFANTRY BRIGADE.*

(After Concentration.)

Detail.	Personnel.		Horses.				Machine Guns.	Vehicles.					
								Carts.		Wagons.		
	Officers.	Other Ranks.	Riding.	Draught.	Heavy Draught.	Pack.		1-horsed.	2-horsed.	2-horsed.	4-horsed.	Bicycles.
Headquarters ...	4	23	13	8	2	...	...	...	1	...	2	...
4 Battalions ...	120	3,908	52	104	32	36	8	4	32	28	...	36
	124	3,931	65	112	34	36	8	4	33	28	2	36

11.—HEADQUARTERS OF AN INFANTRY BRIGADE.

Commander.

Brigadier-general.

Staff.

1 Brigade-major.
1 Staff captain.

Administrative Services

1 Veterinary officer.
— Army postal service (3 clerks).

Police, clerks, &c.

* Excluding details at base.

12.—War Establishment of Various Units.
(After Concentration.)
(Including attached but excluding details left at base.)
For details of transport see p. 120.

Unit	Personnel		Horses				Guns		Vehicles (excluding gun carriages and limbers).							
	Officers.	Other Ranks.	Riding.	Draught.	Heavy Draught.	Pack.	Guns.	Machine Guns.	Carts 1-horsed.	Carts 2-horsed.	Wagons 2-horsed.	Wagons 4-horsed.	Wagons 6-horsed.	Motor cars.	Bicycles.	Motor cycles.
Cavalry :—																
Regiment	23	523	528	74		6		2		2		16			20	
Hd. Qrs. and M.G. Section	8	67	69	32				2		2		7			3	
Squadron	6	152	153	14		2						3			4	
Squadron (Divisional Cavalry)	6	153	153	10	2	2				1		2			6	
Horse Artillery :—																
Brigade	19	662	277	502			12			4	6	7	56		12	
Battery	5	200	102	126			6			1		1	12		3	
Amm. Coln.	4	223	44	236						1	6	2	32		3	
Batty. for a Cav. Bde. not allotted to a Cav. Div.	7	215	108	132			6			2		2	12		3	
Amm. Coln. for a Cav. Bde. not allotted to a Cav. Div.	2	117	25	119	2					1	3	1	16		1	
Field Artillery :—																
18-pr. Brigade	23	772	198	548	2		18			12	1	4	58		5	
18-pr. Battery	5	193	50	122			6			1			12		1	
18-pr. Amm. Coln.	3	155	20	176						8		3	22		1	
4·5" Howr. Brigade	22	733	195	500	2		18			5	1	1	55		5	
4·5" Howr. Battery	5	192	50	122			6			1			12		1	
4·5" Howr. Amm. Coln.	2	119	17	128						1			19		1	

Heavy Artillery :—																
Heavy Artillery Batty. ..	5	163	26	6	86	..	4	..	..	1	1	11	..	..	1	..
Heavy Artillery Amm. Coln. ..	1	29	3	..	23	..	..	..	..	..	..	5	..	..	..	..
Divl. Amm. Coln.	15	553	56	625	28	..	..	..	1	2	1	6	94	..	6	..
1st, 2nd, or 3rd Section ..	3	148	12	178	..	..	..	..	..	..	..	..	27	..	1	..
4th Section	2	85	8	79	26	..	..	..	..	..	..	6	12	..	1	..
Transport and Supply :—																
Divisional Train	26	402	66	38	274	..	..	..	1	16	..	125	..	4	30	..
Divisional Train Hdqrs. ..	5	7	6	1	2	..	..	..	1	..	..	..	..	..	2	..
Divisional Train Hdqrs. Co. ..	6	155	18	16	128	..	..	..	..	7	58	..	..	1	7	..
Divisional Train, other Cos. ..	5	80	14	7	48	..	..	..	..	3	22	..	..	1	7	..
Army Troops Train	7	93	16	6	55	..	..	..	1	2	25	..	..	1	9	..
Field Ambulances :—																
Cav. Field Ambulance	6	118	12	66	..	..	..	..	..	4	6	4	4	..	2	..
Cav. Field Ambulance Sec. ..	3	57	6	29	..	..	..	..	..	2	3	1	2	..	1	..
Field Ambulance	10	224	14	15	37	..	..	..	..	7	16	..	..	..	1	..
Field Ambulance, Sec. A ..	4	77	6	5	13	..	..	..	..	2	6	..	..	..	..	..
Field Ambulance, Sec. B or C..	3	73	4	5	11	..	..	..	..	2	5	..	..	..	..	..
Siege Artillery :—																
6" Howr. Brigade	30	949	102	31	464	..	16	..	1	15	..	72	..	..	..	..
6" Howr. Battery	5	177	17	6	80	..	4	..	..	3	..	10	..	..	..	..
6" Howr. Amm. Coln.	3	104	13	2	72	..	..	..	..	1	..	16	..	..	..	..
Heavy Brigade	13	274	11	..	..	..	8	..	..	..	..	..	..	..	..	..
Heavy Battery	5	124	2	..	..	..	4	..	..	..	..	..	..	..	..	..
Engineers :—																
Field Squadron	7	184	104	92	..	..	..	..	..	6	..	6	8	..	44	..
Field Troop	3	74	42	28	..	5	..	..	..	2	..	1	3	..	15	..
Field Company	6	211	17	53	2	4	..	..	..	14	..	1	3	..	33	..
Field Company Section ..	1	43	2	6	..	1	..	..	..	3	..	..	..	..	8	..
Bridging Train	7	278	59	351	2	..	..	..	1	2	..	4	50	..	1	..
Signal Service :—																
Signal Squadron	8	198	80	70	..	14	..	..	..	2	9	3	5	2	34	6
Signal Squadron, A Troop ..	1	33	10	20	..	..	..	..	..	..	2	1	2	..	..	..
Signal Squadron, B Troop ..	1	36	12	20	..	..	..	..	..	..	2	1	2	..	..	..
Signal Squadron, C Troop ..	1	43	29	14	..	12	..	..	..	..	4	..	1	..	..	..
Signal Squadron, D Troop ..	2	53	16	2	..	..	..	..	..	..	1	..	..	2	28	6

12.—WAR ESTABLISHMENT OF VARIOUS UNITS—*continued.*

(Including attached but excluding details left at base.) For details of transport *see* p. 12).

| Unit. | Personnel | | Horses | | | | Guns | | Vehicles (excluding gun carriages and limbers). | | | | | | | |
	Officers.	Other ranks.	Riding.	Draught.	Heavy draught.	Pack.	Guns.	Machine Guns.	Carts 1-horsed.	Carts 2-horsed.	Wagons 2-horsed.	Wagons 4-horsed.	Wagons 6-horsed.	Motor cars.	Bicycles.	Motor cycles.
Signal Service—contd.																
Signal Troop with Cav. Bde. (Cavalry Division)	1	23	14	2	:	:	:	:	:	:	1	:	:	:	6	3
Signal Troop with a Cav. Bde. not allotted to a Cav. Div.	1	42	30	6	:	9	:	:	:	:	3	:	:	:	6	3
Divisional Signal Company	5	157	33	37	2	8	:	:	:	2	7	:	3	:	32	9
Signal Company, No. 1 Sec.	1	48	18	24	:	:	:	:	:	:	3	:	3	:	:	:
Signal Company, other Secs.	1	24	2	2	:	2	:	:	:	:	1	:	:	:	8	:
Hdqrs. G.H. Qrs. Signal Co.	5	81	12	8	2	:	:	:	:	2	:	1	:	3*	9	16
Hdqrs. A.H. Qrs. „ „	4	63	10	4	2	:	:	:	:	2	1	:	:	2†	6	12
An Air-line Section	1	57	13	24	:	:	:	:	:	:	2	:	2	1†	1	:
A Cable Section	1	35	12	18	:	:	:	:	:	:	2	:	3	:	1	:
A Wireless Section	1	52	13	26	:	:	:	:	:	:	3	:	:	:	6	:
Flying Corps:—																
Hdqrs. and Kite Squadron	6	99	13	40	:	:	:	:	:	2	:	2	4	3*	4	:
Aeroplane Squadron	19	135	:	:	:	:	:	:	:	:	:	:	:	32	:	6
Infantry:—																
Battalion	30	977	13	26	8	9	:	:	1	12†	3	:	:	:	9	:
Hdqrs. and M.G. Section	6	93	9	26	:	1	:	2	1	1‡	3	:	:	:	9	:
Company	6	221	1	:	2	2	:	2	:	:	:	:	:	:	:	:

* Includes lorries, &c.   † Lorries.   ‡ Includes travelling kitchens.

INDIA.

13.—CAVALRY BRIGADE.

War Establishment (winter scale without tents).

Detail.	Personnel								Animals						Rifles, Guns and Vehicles					Attached Transport				
	Fighting Men						Followers		Horses			Ponies	Riding camels	Mess transport	Rifles	Machine guns	13-pr. Q.F. guns and limbers	Ammunition wagons and limbers	G.S. war ns.	A.T. carts	Mules			Personnel
	British			Indian			Public	Private	Riding	Pack	Draught										Riding	Pack	Draught	
	Officers	Other ranks	Total	Officers	Other ranks	Total																		
Headquarters	6	7	13		6	6	1	22	28			1		2	12					3			6	3
1 British Cavalry Regiment	27	436	463				30	62	489	12		1		6	416	2				42		59	84	68
2 Indian Cavalry Regiments	25		25∶33		940	973	188	84	1,003	24		2	16	6	898	4				84		128*	168*	84
1 Horse Artillery Battery	5	171	176	1	15	15	19	15	98		132	1		2	48		6	12	2	13		6	26	16
1 Field Troop	2	2	4	1	54	55	9	6	61	6					56					6†			12†	6†
1 Cavalry Brigade, Ammunition Column	2	18	20	1	62	63	9	4	14		91				16			15	1	35		1	70	36
1 Section British Cavalry Field Ambulance	1	6	7		1	1	50	7	1			4								5	20	5	10	27
2 Sections Indian Cavalry Field Ambulance	2	1	3		10	10	78	12	2			6								10	40	10	20	53

* Government and regimental grass-cut mules.   † Approximate

INDIA.

13.—CAVALRY BRIGADE—continued.

Detail.	Personnel — Fighting Men — British — Officers	British Other ranks	British Total	Indian Officers	Indian Other ranks	Indian Total	Followers Public	Followers Private	Horses Riding	Horses Pack	Horses Draught	Ponies	Riding camels	Mess transport	Rifles	Machine guns	13-pr. Q.F. guns and limbers	Ammunition wagons and limbers	G.S. wagons	A.T. carts	Mules Riding	Mules Pack	Mules Draught	Attached Transport Personnel
1 Cavalry Brigade Supply Column (including Butchery and Bakery Sections)	1	4	5	...	5	5	53	9	4	...	...	4	...	...	...	...	...	...	...	93	...	...	186	93
Transport Headquarters ...	1	...	5	1	15	16	...	4	2	...	...	11	...	16	...	...	...	...	...	...	10	40	45	137
Total	72	649	721	36	1,108	1,144	437	225	1,702	422	6	30	16	16	1,446	6	6	27	3	291	70	249	627	523

Note.—The following deductions have been made:—

(a) For Provost Establishment (included in Headquarters).
British Cavalry 6 "other ranks," 6 riding horses.
Indian Cavalry 6 "other ranks," 6 riding horses.

(b) For Ammunition Column (included in Cavalry Brigade Ammunition Column).
Indian Cavalry, 1 British Officer, 1 Indian Officer, 6 other ranks, 9 riding horses.

INDIA.

13 (a).— HEADQUARTERS OF A CAVALRY BRIGADE.

Commander.

Major-general.

Staff.

1 Brigade-major.
1 Staff captain.

Administrative Services.

2 Veterinary officers.

Personal Appointment.

1 Orderly officer to commander.

———

1 Clerk.
12 Provost establishment.

INDIA.

14.—A DIVISION.

WAR ESTABLISHMENT (WINTER SCALE WITHOUT TENTS).

Detail.	Fighting Men. British.			Fighting Men. Indian.			Fol-lowers.		Horses.		
	Officers.	Other ranks.	Total.	Officers.	Other ranks.	Total.	Public.	Private.	Riding.	Pack.	Draught.
Headquarters	18	18	36	...	26	26	9	57	43	...	...
3 Infantry Bdes. (b)	209	2,439	2,648	151	6,596	6,747	582	465	177	...	...
1 Indian Cav. Regt. (c)	13	...	13	17	464	481	287	42	497	12	...
1 Pioneer Battalion	13	...	13	17	736	753	64	33	14	...	...
Hdqrs. of Div. Artillery	2	8	10	...	...	...	1	7	14	...	...
1 Field Artillery Bde.	17	525	542	...	36	36	58	49	163	...	384
1 British Mountain Art. Brigade, or	12	229	241	...	332	332	49	34	18	...	...
1 Indian Mountain Art. Brigade	12	...	12	6	557	563	58	34	18	...	...
1 Div. Ammun. Col.	5	71	76	2	227	229	31	15	20	...	316
Hdqrs. Div. Eng.	4	1	5	...	...	...	...	13	8	...	...
2 Field Companies	8	4	12	6	380	386	34	30	10	...	...
1 Signal Company	5	60	65	2	159	161	15	11	28	...	...
2 British Fd. Ambulances	8	42	50	...	4	4	382	44	8	...	...
3 Indian Fd. Ambulances	12	3	15	...	66	66	471	66	12	...	...
1 Div. Supply Column (a)	7	16	23	...	22	22	250	42	12	...	...
1 Div. Supply Park	1	5	6	...	3	3	33	7	2	...	...
Transport Headquarters	6	16	22	14	115	129	...	22	12	...	...
Total with British Mntain. Artillery Brigade	340	3,427	3,767	209	9,166	9,375	2,266	937	1,038	12	700
Total with Indian Mntain. Artillery Brigade	340	3,208	3,548	215	9,391	9,606	2,275	937	1,038	12	700

(a) Includes bakery and butchery sections.
(b) Less 12 British ranks for provost establishment and 1 British Officer, 30 non-commissioned officers and men for Divisional Ammunition Column.
(c) Less 12 ranks and 12 horses for provost establishment.

INDIA.

14.—A DIVISION.

WAR ESTABLISHMENT (WINTER SCALE WITHOUT TENTS).

	Animals.				Rifles, Guns and Vehicles.						Attached Transport.						
Ponies.	Pack mules.	Riding camels.	Mess transport.	Rifles.	Machine guns.	10-pr. B.L. guns.	18-pr. Q.F. guns and limbers.	Ammunition wagons and limbers.	G.S. wagons.	A.T. carts.	Ambulance tongas.	Pack mules.	Draught mules.	Camels.	Bullocks.	Personnel.
7	...	...	5	24	...	...	...	...	...	...	...	34	...	10	...	16
15	144	...	51	9,023	24	...	...	...	...	...	...	1,344	...	807	...	744
1	...	8	3	449	2	...	...	...	...	...	...	*299	...	...	...	x
1	42	...	3	735	2	...	...	...	...	...	...	143	...	70	...	75
...	...	...	...	...	...	...	...	...	...	2	...	...	4	...	...	2
3	...	...	6	144	...	...	18	36	6	38	...	20	76	...	...	48
16	328	...	4	164	...	12	...	...	...	...	...	...	...	52	...	19
16	328	...	4	216	...	12	...	...	...	...	...	...	...	50	...	9
1	...	...	2	80	...	...	...	54	3	234	...	4	468	40	...	250
1	...	...	1	...	...	...	...	...	...	...	...	...	...	3	...	1
6	36	...	4	324	...	...	...	...	...	...	...	104	...	...	...	60
...	40	...	3	118	...	...	...	...	...	...	...	109	...	...	...	45
20	...	...	...	...	...	...	...	...	...	...	16	32	...	86	32	38
30	...	...	...	...	...	...	...	...	...	...	24	48	...	120	48	84
8	...	...	...	...	...	...	...	...	...	...	...	...	...	636	...	235
5	...	...	...	...	...	...	...	...	...	...	...	...	...	1,215	...	425
36	...	...	...	...	...	...	...	...	...	...	...	362	47	111	20	471
150	590	8	82	11,111	28	12	18	90	9	274	40	2,499	595	3,182	100	2,532
150	590	8	82	11,163	28	12	18	90	9	274	40	2,499	595	3,180	100	2,532

* Regimental and Government grass-cut mules, 277. Supply and Transport Corps mules, 22.

INDIA.

14a.—Headquarters of a Division.

Commander.

Lieutenant or major-general.

Staff.

1 General staff officer, 1st grade.
1   ,,   ,,   ,,   2nd grade.
1   ,,   ,,   ,,   3rd grade.
1 Dep. assist. adjutant-general.
1 Asst. quartermaster-general.

Administrative Services and Departments.

1 Asst. director of medical services.
1 Dept. asst. dir of medical services.
1 Dep. asst. director of ordnance services.
1 Asst. director of veterinary services.
2 Veterinary officers.
1 Assistant director of supplies.
1 Assistant director of transport.
1 Chaplain (Church of England.   Other denominations will be attached if required).

Special Appointments.

- 1 Assistant provost marshal.
1 Treasure chest officer.

Personal Appointment.

1 Aide-de-camp.

———

17 Clerks.
27 Provost establishment, etc.

INDIA
15.—AN INFANTRY BRIGADE.
WAR ESTABLISHMENT (WINTER SCALE WITHOUT TENTS).

Detail.	British Officers	British Other ranks	British Total	Indian Officers	Indian Other ranks	Indian Total	Followers Public	Followers Private	Riding horses	Ponies	Pack mules	Mess animals	Rifles	Machine guns	Attached Pack mules	Camels	Personnel	Remarks
Headquarters ...	3	7	10	...	6	6	1	10	6	1	...	2	12	...	7	2	4	The following deductions have been made for Brigade provost establishment which is shown in Brigade Headquarters. British Infantry, 1 N.C.O. and 5 men. Indian Infantry, 1 N.C.O. and 5 men.
1 British Infantry Battalion	28	810	838	...	...	...	37	46	11	1	12	6	810	2	123	72	47	
3 Indian Infantry Battalions	39	...	39	51	2,202	2,253	156	99	42	3	36	9	2,199	6	318	195	77	
Total ...	70	817	887	51	2,208	2,259	194	155	59	5	48	17	3,021	8	448	269	248	
Add, if acting independently—																		
1 Brigade Section Divl. Signal Coy.	1	12	12	...	28	28	...	2	4	...	6	...	333	...	15	...	10	
1 Section British Field Ambu ance	1	6	7	...	4	4	47	7	1	4	...	...	...	...	5	10	6	

INDIA.

15.—AN INFANTRY BRIGADE.—WAR ESTABLISHMENT (WINTER SCALE WITHOUT TENTS)—continued.

Detail.	Personnel. Fighting Men. British.			Indian.			Followers.		Animals.				Rifles and Machine Guns.		Attached Transport.			Remarks.
	Officers.	Other ranks.	Total.	Officers.	Other ranks.	Total.	Public.	Private.	Riding horses.	Ponies.	Pack mules.	Mess animals.	Rifles.	Machine guns.	Pack mules.	Camels.	Personnel.	
Add, if acting independently—contd.																		(a) Sufficient for two days tinned supplies for men and grain for animals. If more days supplies are to be carried extra transport in proportion will be allotted.
3 Sections Indian Field Ambulance	3	1	4	...	15	15	118	17	3	8	...	...	...	...	10	17	10	
1 Bde. Sec. Supply Column Supply Establishment (b)	1	4	5	...	5	5	19	11	2	4	...	...	...	...	...	...	...	
1 Bde. Sec. Supply Column Transport Establishment	...	...	...	...	...	...	...	...	...	...	...	...	...	...	...	108(a)	38	(b) Includes Butchery and Bakery sections.
Transport Headquarters	1	2	3	2	10	12	...	4	2	14	...	...	...	...	95	27	103	
Total ...	77	842	919	53	2,270	2,323	378	196	71	35	54	17	3,354	8	573	431	415	

INDIA.

15 (a).—HEADQUARTERS OF AN INFANTRY BRIGADE.

Commander.

Major or brigadier-general.

Staff.

1 Brigade major.

Personal Appointment.

1 Orderly officer to commander.

———

1 Clerk.
12 Provost establishment.

INDIA.

16.—WAR ESTABLISHMENTS OF VARIOUS UNITS.

Detail.	British. Officers.	British. Other ranks.	British. Total.	Indian. Officers.	Indian. Other ranks.	Indian. Total.	Followers. Public.	Followers. Private.	Horses. Riding.	Horses. Pack.	Horses. Draught.
Cavalry:—											
British:—											
Regiment	27	442	460	...	...	...	30	62	495	12	...
Hdqrs. & M.G. Sec.	5	38	43	...	...	...	14	14	47	12	...
Squadron	6	101	107	...	...	...	4	13	113	...	...
Indian (a):—											
Regiment ...	13	...	13	17	476	493	94	42	509	12	...
Hdqrs. & M.G. Sec.	3	...	3	1	36	37	22	10	41	12	...
Squadron ...	3	...	3	4	110	114	18	8	118	...	...
Indian (b):—											
Regiment ...	13	...	13	17	476	493	287	42	509	12	...
Hdqrs. & M.G. Sec.	3	...	3	1	36	37	31	10	41	12	...
Squadron ...	3	...	3	4	110	114	64	8	118	...	...
Artillery:—											
Horse Battery ...	5	171	176	...	15	15	19	15	98	...	132
Horse Brigade (c) ...	12	354	366	...	30	30	39	34	209	...	264
Cav. Bde. Amn. Col.	2	18	20	1	62	63	9	4	14	...	94
Field Battery... ...	5	171	176	...	12	12	19	15	50	...	128
Field Brigade ...	17	525	542	...	36	36	58	49	163	...	384
Howitzer Battery (5″)	5	165	170	...	18	18	24	15	47	...	114
How. Bde. (5″) with Amm. Col.	21	547	568	...	187	187	96	62	167	...	546
Mountain Batt. (Brit.)	5	113	118	...	166	166	24	15	7	...	...
Mountain Batt. (Ind.)	5	...	5	3	277	280	29	15	7	...	...
Div. Amm. Col. ...	5	71	76	2	227	229	31	15	20	...	316
Engineers:—											
Field Troop (d) ...	2	2	4	1	54	55	9	6	61	6	...
Field Company ...	4	2	6	3	190	193	17	15	5	...	...
Bridging Train (d) ...	...	...	...	...	22	22	...	...	...	...	...
Printing Section ...	...	2	2	...	4	4	2	2	...	...	...
Litho. Section ...	...	2	2	...	4	4	2	2	...	...	...
Signal Service:—											
Wireless Squadron (d)	4	101	105	2	90	92	20	8	145	44	42
Signal Troop (d) ...	1	7	8	...	17	17	...	2	26	...	...
Div. Signal Co. (d) ...	5	60	65	2	159	161	15	11	28	...	...

(a) When mobilized with draught transport.
(b) When mobilized with pack transport.
(c) Brigade headquarters not yet sanctioned.
(d) Not yet sanctioned.

INDIA

16.—War Establishments of Various Units.

Animals				Rifles, guns, and vehicles							Attached transport					
Ponies	Pack mules	Riding camels	Mess transport	Rifles	Machine guns	10-pr. B.L. guns	13-pr. and 18-pr. Q.F. guns, and 5" howitzers	Ammunition wagons	G.S. wagons	A.T. carts	Ambulance tongas	Pack mules	Draught mules	Camels	Bullocks	Personnel
1	...	...	6	...	2	...	...	...	...	37	...	59	74	...	...	63
1	...	...	6	...	2	...	...	...	...	9	...	11	18	...	...	15
...	...	...	...	...	...	...	...	...	...	7	...	12	14	...	...	12
1	64	8	3	...	2	...	...	...	...	33	...	...	66	...	...	33
1	12	...	3	...	2	...	...	...	...	9	...	...	18	...	...	9
...	13	2	...	...	...	...	...	...	...	6	...	...	12	...	...	6
1	277	8	3	...	2	...	...	...	...	...	...	22	...	...	...	8
1	37	...	3	...	2	...	...	...	...	...	...	22	...	...	...	8
...	60	2	...	...	...	...	...	...	...	...	...	...	...	...	...	...
1	...	...	2	48	...	...	6	12	2	18	...	12	36	...	...	12
2	...	...	4	96	...	...	12	24	4	20	...	14	40	...	...	27
...	...	...	...	...	...	...	...	15	1	34	...	1	68	...	...	35
1	...	...	2	48	...	...	6	12	2	9	...	6	18	...	...	12
3	...	...	6	144	...	...	18	36	6	29	...	20	58	...	...	39
1	...	...	2	48	...	...	6	9	2	9	...	6	18	...	...	12
4	...	...	8	...	...	...	18	54	9	37	...	24	74	...	...	49
7	164	...	2	...	...	6	...	...	...	...	...	...	...	20	...	7
7	164	...	2	...	...	6	...	...	...	...	...	...	...	19	...	7
...	...	...	3	...	...	...	...	54	3	234	...	4	468	31	...	247
...	...	...	...	...	...	...	...	...	...	...	...	...	...	...	...	...
3	18	...	2	...	...	...	...	...	...	...	...	52	...	16	...	28
...	...	...	...	22	...	...	...	...	...	1	...	5	...	...	298	194
2	...	...	...	...	...	...	...	...	...	...	...	9	...	...	...	3
2	...	...	...	...	...	...	...	...	...	...	...	9	...	...	...	3
...	...	...	...	...	...	...	...	...	...	...	...	...	...	...	...	...
...	...	...	...	...	...	...	...	...	...	...	...	...	...	...	...	...
...	40	...	3	...	...	...	...	...	...	...	...	102	...	...	...	55

INDIA.

16.—War Establishments of Various Units—*continued*.

Detail.	British. Officers.	British. Other ranks.	British. Total.	Indian. Officers.	Indian. Other ranks.	Indian. Total.	Followers. Public.	Followers. Private.	Horses. Riding.	Horses. Pack.	Horses. Draught.
Infantry :—											
British :—											
Battalion	28	816	844	...	...	...	37	46	11	...	...
Hdqrs. & M.G. Sec.	5	45	50	...	...	...	13	20	8	...	...
Company	3	97	100	...	...	...	3	3	...	...	...
Indian :—											
Battalion	13	...	13	17	736	753	52	33	14	...	...
Hdqrs. & M.G. Sec.	5	...	5	1	36	37	12	17	6	...	...
Company	1	...	1	2	88	90	5	2	1	...	...
Indian (Pioneers) :—											
Battalion	13	...	13	17	736	753	64	33	14	...	...
Hdqrs. & M.G. Sec.	5	...	5	1	36	37	13	17	6	...	...
Company	1	...	1	2	88	90	6	2	1	...	...
Supply & Transport :—											
Cav. Bde. Supply Col.	1	4	5	...	9	9	109	11	2	...	...
Div. Supply Col. ...	7	16	23	...	22	22	300	53	14	...	...
Div. Supply Park ...	2	5	7	5	43	48	458	16	4	...	...
Coolie Corps	1	1	2	6	9	15	1,016	3	2	...	...
Carrier Corps... ...	1	...	1	...	1	1	630	2	2	...	...
Medical :—											
British Field Ambulance	4	21	25	...	2	2	191	22	4	...	...
British Cavalry Field Ambulance (*a*)	4	21	25	...	2	2	191	22	4	...	...
Indian Field Ambulance	4	1	5	...	14	14	16	22	4	...	...
Indian Cavalry Field Ambulance (*a*)	4	1	5	...	14	14	165	22	4	...	...
Veterinary :—											
Field Veterinary Section	1	3	4	...	2	2	111	2	2	...	...
Miscellaneous :—											
1st Class Field Post Office	...	1	1	...	2	2	4	1	...	...	...
2nd Class Field Post Office	...	...	...	...	1	1	2	...	...	...	...
A Survey Section ...	1	...	1	2	...	2	11	4	...	...	...

(*a*) Excluding ambulance riding animals.

INDIA.

16.—War Establishments of Various Units—*continued.*

Animals				Rifles, guns and vehicles						Attached transport						
Ponies.	Pack mules.	Riding camels.	Mess transport.	Rifles.	Machine guns.	10-pr. B.L. guns.	13-pr. and 15-pr. Q.F. guns.	Ammunition wagons.	G.S. wagons.	A.T. carts.	Ambulance tongas.	Pack mules.	Draught mules.	Camels.	Bullocks.	Personnel.
1	12	...	6	...	2	...	...	...	...	...	...	122	...	72	...	66
1	12	...	6	...	2	...	...	...	...	...	...	...	...	...	...	...
...	...	...	...	...	...	...	...	...	...	...	...	...	...	...	...	...
1	12	...	3	...	2	...	...	...	...	...	...	06	...	62	...	58
1	12	...	3	...	2	...	...	...	...	...	...	...	...	...	...	...
...	...	...	...	...	...	...	...	...	...	...	...	...	...	...	...	...
1	42	...	3	...	2	...	...	...	...	...	...	119	...	67	...	66
1	14	...	3	...	2	...	...	...	...	...	...	...	...	...	...	...
...	3	...	...	...	...	...	...	...	...	...	...	...	...	...	...	...
4	...	...	...	...	...	...	...	...	...	88	...	...	176	...	...	...
16	...	...	...	...	...	...	...	...	...	...	...	...	...	591	...	...
22	...	...	...	...	...	...	...	...	...	...	...	...	...	1,215	...	...
1	...	...	...	...	...	...	...	...	...	...	...	...	...	...	...	...
...	...	...	...	...	...	...	...	...	...	...	...	...	...	...	...	...
10	...	...	...	...	...	...	...	...	...	...	8	16	...	41	16	28
10	...	...	...	...	...	...	...	...	...	21	...	16	42	...	...	27
10	...	...	...	...	...	...	...	...	...	...	8	16	...	38	16	27
10	...	...	...	...	...	...	...	...	...	20	...	16	40	...	...	26
3	...	...	...	...	...	...	...	...	...	...	...	4	...	5	...	4
...	...	...	...	...	...	...	...	...	...	...	...	5	...	...	...	2
...	...	...	...	...	...	...	...	...	...	...	...	3	...	...	...	1
2	...	...	...	...	...	...	...	...	...	...	...	15	...	...	...	5

2. SYSTEM OF COMMAND IN THE FIELD.

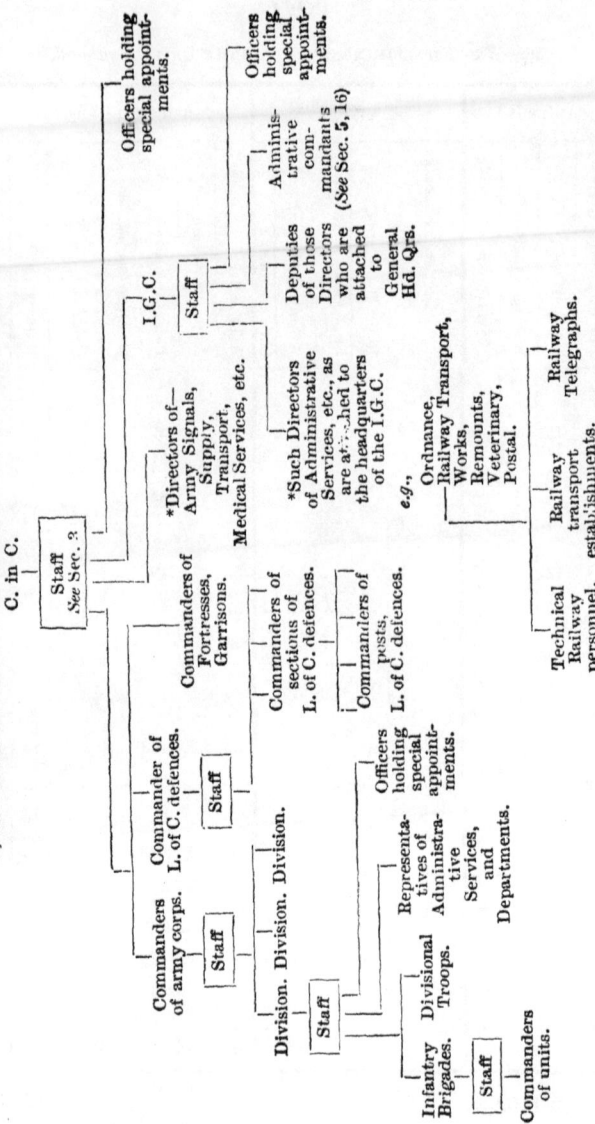

C. in C.

Staff
See Sec. 2.

Officers holding special appointments.

I.G.C.

Staff

Officers holding special appointments.

*Directors of—Army Signals, Supply, Transport, Medical Services, etc.

*Such Directors of Administrative Services, etc., as are attached to the headquarters of the I.G.C.

Administrative commandants (*See* Sec. 5, 16)

Deputies of those Directors who are attached to General Hd. Qrs.

Commanders of Fortresses, Garrisons.

Commanders of sections of L. of C. defences.

Commanders of posts, L. of C. defences.

e.g.,

Ordnance, Railway Transport, Works, Remounts, Veterinary, Postal.

Railway Transport.

Railway Telegraphs.

Technical Railway personnel.

Railway transport establishments.

Commander of L. of C. defences.

Staff

Commanders of army corps.

Staff

Division. Division. Division.

Staff

Officers holding special appointments.

Representatives of Administrative Services, and Departments.

Infantry Brigades.

Staff

Divisional Troops.

Commanders of units.

* The offices of directors of administrative services will be located as directed by the C. in C. *See* F.S. Regs.

3. GENERAL ORGANIZATION AND FUNCTIONS OF THE STAFF.

The Staff is organized in three branches :—

   i. The General Staff branch.
   ii. The A.G.'s branch.
   iii. The Q.M.G.'s branch.

For the efficient performance of staff duties all three branches must work in close co-operation.

The General Staff are responsible that, with due regard to secrecy, information as to situation and probable requirements of troops is furnished to the A.G.'s and Q.M.G.'s branches in sufficient time to enable these requirements to be met.

The following table shows the distribution of duties amongst the three branches :—

Chief of the General Staff* or
Senior General Staff Officer of a Command.

General Staff Branch.	Adjutant-General's Branch.†	Quartermaster-General's Branch.†
Co-ordination of staff work as far as this power is delegated by the Commander. Advice on all matters affecting military operations. Signing and issue of all orders, except routine orders and instructions, by the Commander.	The duties include :— Discipline. Military law. Administration of martial law, and compilation of regulations relating thereto. Executive duties connected with the appointment and promotion of officers.	The duties include :— Embarkations and landings within and if necessary outside the theatre of operations, subject to the general control of the C.G.S. Distribution, in detail, of quarters and buildings within the areas delimited by the General Staff.

* The power and responsibility of co-ordinating staff work at general headquarters is vested in the C.-in-C.; but he will delegate it as he may think fit to the C.G.S., who is his responsible adviser on all matters affecting military operations, through whom he exercises his functions of command, and by whom all orders issued to field units will be signed. Other commanders will exercise their functions of command and issue their orders through their senior general staff officer on similar principles.

† When certain staff officers of a headquarters are charged with duties appertaining both to the A.G.'s and Q.M.G.'s branches of the staff, e.g., A.A. and Q.M.G., D.A.A. and Q.M.G., the senior staff officer of these branches supervises the work of both, the respective duties of the two branches being distributed among the several staff officers as may be most convenient.

Responsibility for the working out of all arrangements, and for the drafting of detailed orders regarding :—

All military operations, including the general control, in co-operation with the Navy, of embarkations and landings within the theatre of operations.

War organization and efficiency of the troops.

Selection of lines of operations.

All plans for the concentration, distribution and movement of troops and materiel by rail, road or inland waterways in the theatre of operations

The general allotment of areas in which units or formations are to be quartered ; security, marches, and battle.

Intercommunication in the field.

Special reconnaissances.

Policy connected with raising new units.

Provision of guides and interpreters.

Acquisition and distribution of information about the enemy, the country and its resources.

Questions of policy in connection with international and martial law, including, in the case of martial law, advice as to the necessity for and scope of its enforcement.

Flags of truce and correspondence with the enemy.

Censorship over communications, i.e., the post, telegraphs, telephones and cables.

Questions relating to the supply of military personnel to the army; interior economy, personal services, pay, promotion, honours and rewards, enlistments and applications of all kinds concerning the fighting troops; spiritual welfare of the army.

Sanitation.

Provision of medical equipment.

Casualties and invaliding.

Mobilization of improvised units.

Police measures.

Disposal of prisoners of war.

Burying parties and places.

Routine garrison or camp duties.

Ceremonial.

Preparation of reports, despatches and diaries relative to the above.

Drafting all orders, regarding these duties, for insertion in orders issued over signature of C.G.S.

Signature and issue of all routine orders and instructions connected with above duties.

Questions concerning :—

Supplies.

Ammunition, equipment, clothing and stores of all kinds (except provision of medical equipment).

Land, inland water and sea transport.

Railway administration.

Remounts.

Veterinary.

Postal.

Rendering of proper accounts for expenditure of an abnormal character.

Preparation of reports, despatches and diaries relative to the above.

Subject to strategical and tactical considerations, the limitations of which are communicated by the G.S., the co-ordination of all administrative arrangements between the I.G.C. and commanders of field units or formations.

Drafting all orders regarding these duties for insertion in orders issued over signature of C.G.S.

Signature and issue of all routine orders and instructions connected with above duties.

Control of the press and press correspondents.

Secret services, ciphers, care and disposal of captured documents.

Provision, distribution and revision of maps.

Charge of foreign attachés.

Preparation of reports, despatches, and diaries relating to the above.

Advice as to movements or disposal of all impedimenta, including supply columns and parks and L. of C. units when the military situation requires it.

4. DISTRIBUTION OF DUTIES AMONG ADMINISTRATIVE SERVICES AND DEPARTMENTS, AND BRANCH OF THE STAFF RESPONSIBLE FOR THE ISSUE OF INSTRUCTIONS.

G.S. Branch ...	Director of Army Signals	Organization and maintenance of all means of intercommunication, including visual, electrical, and mechanical, and despatch riders in the theatre of operations. Administration and distribution of the signal troops, and for the employment of those not allotted to subordinate commands.
A.G.'s Branch..	Director of Medical Services	Care of sick and wounded. Provision and administration of hospitals and convalescent depôts. Provision of medical equipment. Recommendations for measures to preserve health and prevent disease in the army and civil population. Subject to naval arrangements, control of medical equipment and readiness of hospital ships for invalids. Medical services in regard to tactical dispositions are dealt with by the General Staff.
	Deputy Judge Advocate-General	Represents J.A.G. Advises a commander on matters of military, martial, and international law.
	Principal Chaplain ...	Spiritual administration and welfare of the army.
	Provost-Marshal ...	Commands the corps of military police and is responsible for their organization, efficiency and distribution.
Q.M.G.'s Branch	Director of Supplies...	Provision and administration of all food, forage, fuel, light and disinfectants.
	Director of Ordnance Services	Provision and administration of ammunition, equipment, clothing, and stores of all kinds other than medical and veterinary stores. Provision of technical vehicles of artillery and engineer units, and provision and administration of workshops on L. of C. for repair of all kinds.
	Director of Transport	Provision, administration and distribution of all transport (except technical vehicles under Director of Ordnance Services), excluding railway and sea transport, but including inland water transport.

Q.M.G.'s Branch	Director of Railway Transport	Provision and administration of railway transport. Control, construction, working and maintenance of all railways. Provision of telegraph operators for railway circuits. Control and working of telephones and telegraphs allotted to the railway service.
	Director of Works ...	Provision, construction and maintenance of buildings, offices, stores, camping grounds, roads, etc., on the L. of C. Provision of water supply, gas, electric lighting, or other technical plant required for military purposes on L. of C. and not provided by other services.
	Director of Remounts	Provision, administration, training and distribution of all animals.
	Director of Veterinary Services	Care of sick animals. Provision and adminstration of veterinary hospitals and advice as to their distribution. Provision of veterinary stores. Inspections and recommendations regarding health and efficiency of the animals of the forces.
	Director of Postal Services	Provision and administration of all postal communications.
	Paymaster-in-Chief ...	Supervision and control of all pay and cashiers' offices. Responsibility for bringing to account all moneys payable and receivable on public service.

5. ORGANIZATION OF THE EXECUTIVE ON LINES OF COMMUNICATION.

(*See* F.S.R., Part II, Secs. 10–13.)

COMMANDERS OF LINES OF COMMUNICATION DEFENCES.

1. Unless the L. of C. are very short, executive authority on them is usually organized in two separate branches :—

(i) Defence.
(ii) Administrative and traffic control.

2. The commander of the L. of C. defences is solely responsible to the C.-in-C. for the tactical security of the L. of C., including all personnel, animals and material comprised in them, throughout the area for which he is made responsible by the C.-in-C. and of which the limits will be notified from time to time in general orders. He is also responsible for the military government of that portion of the L. of C. which is under martial law. He is allotted a staff and a proportion of L. of C. defence troops, varying in number according to the length of the L. of C. and the military situation of the moment Officers and men detailed for duty under him will not be removed without the authority of the C.-in-C.

3. The L. of C. will usually be divided for purposes of defence into sections, each under a subordinate L. of C. defence commander, who will be responsible to the commander L. of C. defences for the security of his section. Each section may contain one or more posts. A base will usually be regarded as outside the sectional organization. Such L. of C. defence troops as are not allotted to commanders of sections or posts will be retained as a mobile

reserve at the immediate disposal of the commander of L. of C. defences,
and stationed at whatever point on the L. of C. is best situated to the needs
of the military situation.

4. The commander of L. of C. defences should be at all times in direct
telegraphic communication with the C.G.S., the I.G.C. and his own subordinates.

5. Every commander of section or post defences should have a map of the
country as far as the two adjoining sections or posts, on which should be
shown the position of the changing and passing places of convoys, the
position of the piquets, the place for the relief of escorts, and the places
where attacks are most likely.

6. A commander of L. of C. defences has, normally, no control over the
movement along the L. of C. of personnel, animals or material, other than
those of his own command, except in the face of imminent danger from the
enemy. In the latter event he is responsible that traffic is stopped until,
in his opinion, it may safely be resumed, or until orders from superior
authority are received. The action taken will in all cases be telegraphed
direct to the C.G.S. and to the I.G.C.

7. No troops or ammunition proceeding to the front are on any account
to be diverted for the defence of the L. of C. unless, in the opinion of the
commander of the L. of C. defences, or his subordinate on the spot, the force
at his disposal is insufficient to meet an impending attack by the enemy,
in which case traffic will be stopped as above mentioned, and the situation
reported by telegraph to the C.G.S. An officer will incur grave responsibility
in taking such a step, which only extreme emergency can justify.

8. Should an officer senior in rank to a commander or subordinate commander of L. of C. defences be temporarily detained at a post or section he
will in no case interfere with the defence commander of the section or post,
except in the event of actual attack by the enemy, in which case the senior
officer of fighting troops on the spot will assume command.

9. When armoured trains are used, their crews will form part of the troops
allotted to the L. of C. defences and will come under the orders of the subordinate defence commander of the section over which they run. Railway
traffic is not to be dislocated by the use of armoured trains, except in the
face of imminent danger from the enemy.

THE INSPECTOR-GENERAL OF COMMUNICATIONS.

10. Responsibility for the control and co-ordination of all traffic on the
L. of C. up to and including the rendezvous, or to localities fixed by general
(or army) headquarters, is vested in an officer styled the Inspector-General
of Communications, who receives the C.-in-C.'s instructions through the
General Staff, or the A.G.'s or Q.M.G.'s branch of the staff, according to the
approved distribution of staff duties. The I.G.C. is the commander of all
L. of C. units (exclusive of L. of C. defence troops), and regulates the
working of the administrative services and departments on the L. of C.
charged with transportation and with duties ancillary thereto. He is also
responsible for the disposition of all reinforcements, supplies, and stores on
the L. of C., and for sending up to within reach of field units all such requirements as are communicated to him from time to time. Similarly he arranges
for the evacuation of all that is superfluous.

11. He keeps the C.-in-C.'s staff informed as to the daily situation of all
base and other depôts, and depôts and stocks of ammunition, supplies, stores
and material on the L. of C. The General Staff are responsible for bringing
to the notice of the I.G.C. any changes in distribution rendered necessary by
impending operations.

12. In a friendly country, and when a short line of communication is
utilized, responsibility for the security of the line, and the area or district
through which it passes, as well as the control of the traffic on the L. of C.,
may be vested in the I.G.C.

13. The selection of the base or bases and the general direction of the
L. of C. is made when deciding on the plan of campaign. Subject to considerations of tactical security for which the commander of L. of C. defences
is responsible, the duties of the I.G.C. include the selection, appropriation,
and allotment of sites and buildings for depôts of all kinds, quarters, offices,

hospitals, plant and material of every description that may be required for the service of the L. of C.

He also arranges for the supply and maintenance of garrisons and posts on the L. of C., and for the supply and accommodation of all troops halting or moving within the area of his jurisdiction.

14. The method of transport by which requirements are forwarded is for the I.G.C. to decide. Should more demands be made on him at any time than the means of transport at his disposal can meet, he will report the situation to general headquarters. A ruling as to the precedence to be given to conflicting demands will then be obtained by the Q.M.G.'s branch in consultation with the General Staff and communicated to the I.G.C.

15. To assist the I.G.C. in performing his duties, he is allotted a suitable staff, and has under his orders subordinate commanders styled administrative commandants together with certain directors and representatives of administrative services and departments.

ADMINISTRATIVE COMMANDANTS.

16. For purposes of routine and administration the L. of C. are divided into bases, sections and posts, the boundaries of which will usually be the same as those organized for defence. For each base, section, or post an administrative commandant is appointed who is responsible to the I.G.C. for the discipline, sanitation, interior economy, and policing of the area within his jurisdiction.

17. He should be in direct telegraphic communication with the office of the commander of L. of C. defences and the latter's subordinates.

He transmits the orders of the I.G.C. for the movement of all personnel, animals, materials, mails, &c., to the commanders of units or representatives of administrative services and departments concerned, and facilitates their despatch by the railway transport establishment, communicating particulars to the adjoining commandants, if any, as to the time and place of the next halt. Except in urgent and unforeseen circumstances he will not, without the special authority of the I.G.C. or the commander of L. of C. defences, detain either personnel, animals, or material in transit. In all such cases the I.G.C. or his representative will be informed of the action taken.

18. He will detail such fatigue parties as the railway transport establishment may require for loading and unloading trains. Should he himself not dispose of sufficient troops for this purpose he may either apply to the defence commander of the section or post, who will furnish such fatigue parties as can be spared without prejudice to the safety of the command ; or with the approval of the I.G.C., may obtain the necessary labour from civilian sources.

19. He is responsible for the reception and accommodation of all personnel (including prisoners of war) and animals, on their way to or from the front. Any person arriving on his way to or from the front without proper authority will be detained and his case investigated.

20. No person, other than an officer or man officially borne on the strength of the forces in the field, is permitted to move on or in any way utilize a L. of C. without a written authority or pass signed by the I.G.C. or by one of his assistants.

21. In default of special instructions, a commandant includes within the limit of his command the area up to a line half-way to the two adjoining posts.

MILITARY LANDING OFFICER.

22. When a sea-base is used, a M.L.O. and one or more assistant M.L.Os. are appointed to the headquarters of the base commandant to supervise the embarkation and disembarkation of all personnel, animals and material. The M.L.O. works under the base commandant in communication with the I.G.C. and with the Director of Sea Transport (see para. 25). All details of embarkations and landings are arranged by the military landing officer in concert with this officer and the base commandant.

All communications with the naval transport authorities pass through him.

On the arrival of a ship, the M.L.O. boards her as soon as possible to verify her contents and hands the commander of the troops on board such copies of local orders as may be necessary.

23. Under instructions from the base commandant, the M.L.O. informs the director of sea transport when and where it is most convenient, from the military point of view, to receive the contents of the vessel. In consultation with the representatives of any services and departments concerned he then issues orders regarding the disembarkation of the contents of the ship and for forwarding them to their destination.

24. Similar arrangements are made by the M.L.O. and Director of Sea Transport in connection with the re-embarkation of men, animals, and stores.

DIRECTOR OF SEA TRANSPORT.

25. The Director of Sea Transport controls the arrangements in connection with the provision of sea transport on behalf of the Admiralty. The requirements of the C.-in-C. as regards sea transport for evacuation by sea of sick, wounded, prisoners, &c., are communicated to the I.G.C. and are forwarded by him through the M.L.O.

CHAPTER II.

6. MARCHES AND MARCH DISCIPLINE.

(See F.S.R., Part I, Secs. 21–33.)

GENERAL RULES.

1. The rate of marching throughout a column should be uniform. An irregular pace is most exhausting to the troops, especially to those in rear of the column.

No trumpet or bugle call is allowed on the march, and on service no compliments are to be paid.

2. Space must be left on the right flank of a column, both when marching and when halted, for the passage of officers and orderlies. In dusty and hot weather the column may be opened out on each side of the road, the centre being left clear.

3. An average march under normal conditions for a large column of all arms is 15 miles a day, with a rest at least once a week ; small commands of seasoned troops can cover 25 miles a day under favourable conditions.

4. To prevent minor checks in a column being felt throughout its length, the following distances will be maintained :—

In rear of a section of a field company or signal company	6 yards.
„ „ battalion, squadron, battery, or infantry company	10 „
„ „ cavalry regiment, artillery brigade or infantry battalion	20 „
„ cavalry or infantry brigade	30 „
„ „ division, according to circumstances.	

5. By order of the commander of the column, distances may be increased in dusty or hot weather, and reduced or omitted when marching by night and, by day, when an engagement is imminent.

6. When there is no possibility of meeting an enemy, the order of march of the main body will depend chiefly on the comfort of the troops, which in its turn depends largely upon convenience of supply.

When within reach of the enemy, units will usually march in the order in which they would come into action, but artillery must be preceded by sufficient infantry to afford it protection

7. *Cavalry.*—When marching along a road, not more than four horses if in sections (or groups), or not more than two horses if in half-sections (or files), should march abreast, including commanders, &c.

To avoid any increase in the length of columns, commanders, centre guides, &c., should march in the regulation distances between units, or fill up blank files.

8. *Artillery.*—Brigade signallers and range takers should ride three abreast at the head of the brigade to which they belong. The regulation distance between carriages should be strictly preserved.

Batteries should always march on the left of the road. When a halt is ordered each carriage must be drawn up at once by the roadside. Cross roads should be left clear.

Dismounted detachments should never march on the off-side of the carriages.

9. *Infantry.*—When marching in fours, not more than four men should march abreast, including commanders and supernumeraries. Bands and drums will conform.

Columns of fours will march on the left side of the road unless direct orders to the contrary are issued.

Exact distances and covering are to be maintained at all times when marching in fours ; the fact of marching at ease is not to affect the relative position of men in the ranks, or that of supernumeraries or commanders, unless orders to the contrary are issued.

10. *Transport.*—All vehicles should march on the left of the road, and when a halt is ordered each vehicle should be drawn up at once on that side of the road.   Cross roads should be left clear.   The regulation distance between vehicles should be strictly preserved, and no one, other than the driver, should be allowed to ride on any vehicle without a written order.

11. *Followers.*—Camp followers, sutlers, civilians, &c., who accompany croops or their transport on a line of march, must be marshalled and be made to observe the regulations laid down for infantry.

12. *Starting point.*—A point, termed the starting point, which the head of the main body is to pass at a certain time, is fixed in operation orders. If troops are not all quartered together, it may be necessary for the commander to fix more than one starting point, so as to enable subordinate commands to take their places in the column of march punctually without unnecessary fatigue to the troops, and without crossing the line of march of other commands.   In the absence of such orders, subordinate commands must arrange their own movements to the starting point.

13. *Halts.*—A short halt should be ordered soon after the column has started in the case of both mounted and dismounted troops, subsequent halts being arranged at regular intervals.   The notification of these arrangements should usually be arranged for in standing orders.

14. *Fords.*—The following depths are fordable :—

> For infantry, 3 feet.
> For cavalry, 4 feet.
> Wagons containing ammunition, 2 feet 4 inches.

Gravelly bottoms are best, sandy bottoms are bad, as the sand gets stirred up and the depth of water thus increases.

The depth of a river is generally most uniform in straight parts ; at bends the depth will generally be greater at the concave bank and less at the convex.

For this reason a river which is not anywhere fordable straight across may be found passable in a slanting direction between two bends.

The simplest plan for measuring the velocity of a stream is described in Section 11 (2).

All fords should be clearly marked by strong pickets driven into the river bed above and below the ford, their heads being connected by a strong rope which is securely anchored to holdfasts at each shore end.   Marks should be made on those pickets which stand in the deepest water, at a height of 3 feet and 4 feet above the bottom, in order that any rise of water above the fordable depth may be at once evident.

Marching in Frost and Snow.

15. *Cold.*—The most efficacious measure against cold is an increased issue of rations ; during halts the men should not be allowed to sit down, or to fall asleep.   It is best not to make long halts.   In the cavalry, men should dismount from time to time.

16. *Frostbite.*—To preserve the feet and limbs :—

> (a) Keep the feet clean, as dirty feet are more liable to perspire and are consequently more sensible to cold.
> (b) Wash the feet with soap and then smear them over with some greasy substance such as unsalted grease, kerosine, &c.
> (c) Wear stout roomy boots and woollen foot cloths or stockings, or the feet may be wrapped in a double set of linen foot cloths, the under pair being greased.

To protect the hands and face : smear them with one of the greasy substances referred to above, wear mits or woollen gloves and ear-flaps.   Men should be instructed, as soon as they feel frostbite anywhere, to rub the part with snow at once until the colour returns, but on no account to warm it near a fire.

17. *Snow blindness.*—To prevent snow blindness wear coloured glasses ; failing these, a mask with very small holes for the eyes, or the end of a pagri over them gives fair protection.

The cheeks and sides of the nose greased and covered with powdered charcoal also relieves the eyes.

18. *Face blister.*—The preventive for this is a mask of some sort or a pagri end.

GENERAL RULES FOR NIGHT MARCHES.

19.—(*a*) Local guides should be procured.

(*b*) Outposts should not be withdrawn till last moment.

(*c*) The march should generally be protected by small advanced and rear guards, usually composed of infantry only; flanks are best protected by piquets posted by the advanced guard. The distance of these bodies from the column should be small.

(*d*) All ranks must know what to do in case of an alarm.

(*e*) Every commander must have a fixed place in the column.

(*f*) Regulation distances between units should be reduced or omitted. An officer should invariably march in rear of each unit.

(*g*) Branch roads should be blocked by the advance guard to prevent troops going astray.

(*h*) Rifles should not be loaded, but magazines should be charged.

(*i*) Hours and periods of halts should be arranged beforehand. Men may lie down but must not leave the ranks during a halt.

20. *To silence the noises made by harness and vehicles at night.*—The chief causes of noise are: (*a*) in harness: mouthpieces of bits and links, spare and quick release; (*b*) in vehicles: play of pole supporting pole bar, swingletrees, wheels, trail-eye, and shield of gun.

No special stores are carried for the purpose of stopping the noises caused by the above. The following hints are given as a guide to the materials which may be made use of if obtainable.

To silence the noises caused by links of pole bar straps, breast collar, and quick release ends of traces they should be bound with strips of canvas and secured by stitching; bits should be bound with cord or twine between ring of side bar to stop the play of the bar; loops of bar supporting pole and swingletrees, with cord or sacking; pole, with sacking over the copper binding; trail-eye, with sacking, leather or rubber; drag washers, tied to a spoke or fitted with additional washers to a working fit. Wheels may be covered by motor tyres (eight to a gun and limber), leather belting 6 to 7 inches wide, 15 feet long laid along the tyre and tied across the felloes, or straw, hay, or rope bindings. To save the necessity of binding stirrup irons, spurs should not be worn.

CARE OF THE FEET.

21. The real causes of sore feet are ill-fitting boots and socks, combined with uncleanliness.

The feet should be washed at least once a day, and if this is impossible they should be wiped over with a damp cloth, especially about the toes.

Excessive sweating may be relieved by bathing the feet in water coloured a bright pink with permanganate of potash.

Socks when taken off should be stretched, well shaken, and placed on the opposite feet when next worn. Where the socks fit over tender parts of the feet they should be greased inside.

Blisters should be pricked with a clean needle and all tender parts smeared with some simple ointment or with soap.

A good ointment is one of vaseline with 2 per cent. of salicylic acid added, and various powders are in use for the same purpose.

CARE OF HORSES.

22. Nothing should be carried beyond the authorized articles.

Rise in the stirrups, do not lean on rifle (if carried), see that the load is evenly distributed on both sides of the saddle. If possible, at some halts off-saddle or loosen girths and shift the saddle. When saddles are removed slap the backs to promote circulation and allow the horses to roll.

On a night march, when hard work is expected, halt, water and feed an hour before dawn.

23. *Watering.*—Take every opportunity of watering on the march. Always water before feeding, never immediately after.

Dismount, remove bits and loosen girths before watering.

Do not allow horses to go further into a pool to drink than necessary, or the water will be fouled for those coming after.

Do not move at a fast pace immediately after watering.

Select watering place with sound bottom, good approach and water at least 4 inches deep. Running water with gravelly bottom is the best. Avoid dark-coloured water.

Animals do not drink well in the early morning. When an early start has been made, all animals should be watered after about 3 hours' march.

24. *Feeding.*—Give a small feed before a long march, however early the start may be.

Feed *en route* during marches over 5 hours. Remember that horses require a considerable time to consume their rations—not less than 5 hours in 24 should be allowed.

Remove nosebag when horse has done and let him graze if possible.

CARE OF TRANSPORT CAMELS.

25. Do not march in the heat of the day. Camels travel best, and with least fatigue, at night or the cool of the morning and evening. The whole of the marching should be done between 4 p.m. and 9 a.m.

Avoid keeping camels loaded up a moment longer than is necessary. Men should be trained to load and unload as quickly as possible. Loads should not be carried more than 4 hours at a stretch.

Great care is necessary in balancing loads carefully and packing them as securely as possible to avoid unnecessary swaying and fatigue to the animal.

26. Camels require 5–6 hours a day to graze and ruminate. Immediately after the morning march is the best time for this. The young shoots of the Camel Thorn are the best grazing. Care should be taken to detect and avoid poisonous plants, some of which are readily eaten by camels.

The grain ration should be given at night.

Camels bred in districts where water is plentiful require to be watered daily, but desert camels usually will not drink more than once in three days, and are best for fast work. Water should be given in the morning, before grazing, and no marching must be done for several hours afterwards with desert camels.

27. The backs and feet should be inspected daily after the morning march. Camelmen must do any repairs necessary to saddlery during midday halt.

Grooming is not usual, but camels thrive much better if they are rubbed over daily with a piece of sacking or a whisp.

Ticks must be carefully removed daily, after the animals come in from grazing.

Skin disease must be constantly guarded against, and any suspicious patches, particularly between the legs, should be periodically washed with soda or wood-ashes and dressed with a mixture of sulphur and oil, or fat, 1–4. This should be issued regularly to camelmen, and a little tar may be added, if available.

28. The pace of a baggage camel is $2\frac{1}{2}$, and of a trotting camel 5 miles an hour. They must not be pushed beyond these paces.

CARE OF TRANSPORT CATTLE.

29. Avoid travelling in the heat of the day. Cattle go better and with less fatigue at night. As far as possible, all journeys should be done between the hours of 4 p.m. and 9 a.m.

Cattle should never be driven beyond their natural, steady walk, but they will travel much faster at night than during the day, without pushing.

Do not march more than 4 hours at a stretch.

30. Cattle require at least 5–6 hours daily to graze and ruminate. After the morning march is the best time, or in the evening, if not marching.

Grain should be given at night mixed with some chaff or hay. A good man will get up once or twice during the night and give his cattle a small feed. Nothing helps so much to keep them in condition.

Water should be given after the morning march and in the evening before starting. If possible, cattle should be grazed near water, where they can drink at will, and where grass is luxurious.

31. Ticks should be removed daily after grazing. In a badly-infested country ticks are liable to collect in large numbers between the toes and

cause sores. This may be prevented by removing them and rubbing the skin with tar.

Wounds and sores are difficult to heal, and every effort should be made to prevent them, by careful attention to the fitting of the yoke, &c. The men should constantly look to this and make any small alterations which may be necessary at the mid-day halt.

7. TIME AND SPACE.

TIME.

1. In moving to a starting point it may be taken that all troops march at the rate of 100 yards a minute.

2. Rates of movement in the field are approximately as follows :—

Arm.	Yards per minute.	Minutes required to traverse 1 mile.	Miles per hour including short halts.
Infantry—			
Usual Pace	98	18	3
Mounted Troops—			
Walk	117	15	3½
Trot	235	8	7
Gallop	440	..	..
Trot and Walk	..	..	5

The length of a pace in slow and quick time is 30 inches.

			stepping out	,, 33	,,
,,	,,	,,	double time	,, 40	,,
,,	,,	,,	stepping shor	,, 21	,,
,,	,,	,,	side step	,, 14	,,

3. The rates of marching of transport on a level road are :—

Wheeled transport	..	..	..	..	2½	miles an hour.
Mule or pony cart, A.T.	..	..	.	..	2½	,,
Bullock cart, A.T.	..	..	..	..	1½	,,
Camel	..	..	..	. .	..	2	,,
Pack mule or pony	..	..	..	..	3	,,
Pack bullock	..	..	..	..	2	,,
Pack donkey	..	..	..	..	1½	,,
Coolie	..	..	..	..	..	2	,,
Tractors	..	..	..	..	3½	,,
Motor lorries	..	..	..	..	6	,,

These rates include short halts only.

SPACE.

4. In calculating the road space in tables given below it is assumed that :—

Cavalry and mounted infantry march in column of sections.
Artillery march in column of route.
Infantry   ,,   ,,   ,,   fours.
Vehicles   ,,   ,, single file.
Bicycles   ,,   ,, file.
Spare horses and pack animals march in file.

The distances enumerated in sec. 6 (4) are left between units.

5. The spaces allowed the various arms in column of route are :—

Headquarters of units	..	..	2 yards per riding horse.
Mounted troops in section	..	..	1 yard per horse in the ranks.
,, ,, half-sections	..	2 yards ,, ,,
Infantry in fours	..	..	½ yard per man ,,

```
Each pack animal (or pair)    ..      ..      ..     4 yards ⎫
     „    camel      ..      ..      ..      ..      ..    5   „  ⎪
     „    bicycle (or pair) ..      ..      ..      ..    6   „  ⎪
     „    2-muled or pony vehicle     ..      ..      ..    7   „  ⎪
     „    1- or 2-horsed     „        ..      ..      .. 10   „  ⎬ Including
     „    4-horsed vehicle ..      ..      ..      .. 15   „  ⎪    distances.
     „    6-horsed      „      ..      ..      ..      .. 20   „  ⎪
     „    2-bullock     „     (2-wheeled)    ..      .. 10   „  ⎪
     „    4-bullock     „         „        ..      .. 15   „  ⎪
     „         „        „     (4-wheeled)    ..      .. 20   „  ⎭
Light tractors  ..      ..      ..      ..      ..    5   „  ⎫
Lorries  ..      ..      ..      ..      ..      ..    6   „  ⎪
4-ton trucks    ..      ..      ..      ..      ..    6   „  ⎪
5-ton platform trucks ..      ..      ..      ..    6   „  ⎬ Actual.
Water-tanks     ..      ..      ..      ..      ..    5   „  ⎪
Travelling vans     ..      ..      ..      ..      ..    5   „  ⎪
Light tractor with 4-ton truck and G.S. wagon  16   „  ⎭
```

6. The minimum distance between lorries of a M.T. convoy is 15 yards, but when proceeding up and down hills distances should not be less than 40 yards.

In calculating the road space occupied by a M.T. convoy moving at full speed 100 yards per vehicle should be allowed.

ROAD SPACE TABLES.†

	Home Establishment.			Indian Establishment.			
						2nd Line Transport.	
	Fighting Portion.	1st Line Transport.	Ambulances and Trains.	Fighting Troops.	1st Line Transport.	Without Tents.	With Tents.
	Yds.	Yds.	Yds.	Yds.	Yds.	Yds.	Yds.
Headquarters :—							
Cavalry Division ..	30	100	..	100	..	105	120
Division ..	20	80	..	85	70	60	75
Cavalry Brigade ..	40	55	..	55	..	35	40
Infantry Brigade ..	15	50	..	20	15	20	25
Cavalry :—							
Regiment ..	570	480	..	555	215	380	440
Regiment Hd. Qrs. ..	50	115	..	55	10	90	95
Regiment M.G. Sec. ..	..	80	..	..	75	..	..
Squadron, or Squadron of Irish Horse	160	95	..	120	30	70	85
Silladar or Non-Silladar Regt.	..	..	..	540	215	445	470
Silladar or Non-Silladar Regt., Hd. Qrs.	..	..	..	40	10	90	95
Silladar or Non-Silladar Regt., M.G. Sec.	..	..	..	..	75	..	..
Silladar or Non-Silladar Regt., Squadron.	..	..	..	120	30	80	85

† No allowance is made for motor cars.

ROAD SPACE TABLES—*continued*.

	Home Establishment.			Indian Establishment.			
						2nd Line Transport.	
	Fighting Portion.	1st Line Transport.	Ambulances and Trains.	Fighting Troops.	1st Line Transport.	Without Tents.	With Tents.
Artillery :—	Yds.	Yds.	Yds.	Yds.	Yds.	Yds.	Yds.
Hd. Qrs. Cav. Divl. ..	15	35	..	..	..		
H.A. Brigade*	910	1,120	..	1,550	20	500	555
H.A. Brigade Hd. Qrs.	30	80	..	30	5	15	15
H.A. Batt.	440	90	..	445	15	155	180
H.A. Bde. Amm. Coln.	..	830	..	..	..	..	..
H.A. Bde. Amm. Coln. Sec.	..	395	..	..	..	..	..
H.A. Batt. with Cav. Bde. not allotted to Cav. Div.	445	120	..	..	..	..	..
H.A. Batt. Amm. Coln. with Cav. Bde. not allotted to Cav. Div.	..	425	..	..	..	..	..
Hd. Qrs. Divl. ..	20	25	..	30	..	20	20
F.A. Brigade (18-pr.)..	1,230	860	..	1,130	40	505	565
F.A. Brigade Hd. Qrs.	20	50	..	30	5	15	15
F.A. Batt.	390	65	..	360	15	165	185
F.A. Bde. Amm. Coln.	..	615	..	..	..	..	..
F.A. Brigade (4·5" Howr.)	1,230	675	..	1,850	50	450	535
F.A. Bde. (4·5" Howr.) Amm. Coln.	..	430	..	700	10	105	125
F.A. Brigade (4·5" Howr.) Hd. Qrs.	30	50	..	15	5	10	10
F.A. Batt. (4·5" Howr.)	390	65	..	365	10	115	135
Heavy Batt. (60-pr.)..	360	55	..	..	..	..	..
Heavy Batt. Amm. Coln.	..	95	..	..	..	..	..
Div. Amm. Coln. ..	..	2,400	..	1,125	1,615	170	200
Div. Amm. Coln. Nos. 1, 2 or 3 Secs.	..	615	..	..	..	..	..
Div. Amm. Coln. No. 4 Sec.	..	410	..	..	..	..	..
Div. Amm. Coln. F.A. Sec.	..	..	..	1,090	15	130	150
Div. Amm. Coln. M.A. Sec.	..	..	..	15	100	10	15
Div. Amm. Coln. S.A.A. Sec.	..	..	..	20	1,440	30	30
Cav. Bde. Amm. Coln.	..	..	..	330	200	125	140
Cav. Bde. Amm. Coln., H.A. Sec.	..	..	..	310	..	115	125
Cav. Bde. Amm. Coln., S.A.A. Sec.	..	..	..	20	200	10	15

* In the case of India 2 Batteries and 2 H.A. Sections of Cavalry Brigade Ammunition Column.

ROAD SPACE TABLES—*continued.*

	Home Establishment.			Indian Establishment.			
						2nd Line Transport.	
	Fighting Portion.	1st Line Transport.	Ambulances and Trains.	Fighting Troops.	1st Line Transport.	Without Tents.	With Tents.
	Yds.	Yds.	Yds.	Yds.	Yds.	Yds.	Yds.
Heavy Batt. (30-pr. or 4″)	..	..	..	180	100	70	85
Heavy Batt. (30-pr. or 4″) Amm. Coln.	..	..	..	..	320	25	30
Mountain Art. Bde. (British or Indian)	∴	..	..	665	..	305	345
Mountain Art. Bde.Hd. Qrs.	..	..	..	15	..	5	5
Mountain Batt. (British or Indian)	..	..	..	320	..	150	170
Engineers :—							
Field Squadron	450	110	..	..	..	..	..
Hd. Qrs. Cav. Divl.	..	..	..	10	10	20	20
Field Troop	170	30	..	60	..	..	..
Hd. Qrs. Divl.	10	30	..	10	10	20	20
Field Company	400	90	..	150	80	95	110
Field Company Sec.	80	..	..	..	..	..	..
Bridging Train	..	1,200	..	15	1,130	10	10
Field Co. of Sappers and Miners	..	..	..	130	225	135	165
Field Troop of Sappers and Miners	..	..	..	50	80	65	70
Pontoon Section	..	..	..	1,040	40	120	135
Signal Service :—							
Signal Squadron	..	625	..	..	..	..	..
Signal Squadron, A Troop	..	95	..	..	..	..	..
Signal Squadron, B Troop	..	100	..	..	..	..	..
Signal Squadron, C Troop	..	140	..	..	..	..	..
Signal Squadron, D Troop	..	160	..	..	..	..	..
Signal Troop with Cav. Bde.	..	75	..	50	..	..	..
Signal Troop with Cav. Bde. not allotted to Cav. Div.	..	135	..	..	..	..	..
Signal Co. with a Div.	..	420	..	..	..	..	..
Signal Co., No. 1 Sec.	..	125	..	..	..	..	..
Signal Co. Nos. 2, 3 or 4 Sec.	..	45	..	..	..	..	..
Hd. Qrs. of a Gen. Hd. Qrs. Signal Co.	..	226	..	..	..	..	..
Hd. Qrs. of an Army Hd. Qrs. Signal Co.	..	180	..	..	..	..	..

ROAD SPACE TABLES—*continued.*

| | Home Establishment. | | | Indian Establishment. | | | |
| | Fighting Portion. | 1st Line Transport. | Ambulances and Trains. | Fighting Troops. | 1st Line Transport. | 2nd Line Transport. | |
						Without Tents.	With Tents.
	Yds.	Yds.	Yds.	Yds.	Yds.	Yds.	Yds.
Signal Section (Airline)	..	150	..	..	..	..	..
Signal Section (Cable)	..	90	..	..	..	..	..
Signal Section (Wireless)	..	120	..	..	..	..	..
Wireless Signal Squadron	..	..	..	500	..	..	..
Wireless Signal Troop	..	..	..	150	..	..	..
Divl. Signal Co. ..	..	..	..	140	65	160	210
Divl. Signal Co.Hd.Qrs.	..	..	..	15	30	65	75
Divl.Signal Co.No.1Sec.	..	..	..	50	60	35	45
Divl. Signal Co. No. 2, 3 or 4 Sec.	..	..	..	25	25	20	30
Infantry :—							
Battalion	500	210	..	465	165	350	410
Battalion Hd. Qrs. ..	60	115	..	..	..	..	..
Battalion M.G. Sec. ..	..	30	..	..	..	..	..
Company	125	15	..	..	..	..	..
Indian Infantry Batt.	..	..	..	420	150	310	360
Pioneer Battalion ..	..	..	..	435	230	370	425
Medical :—							
Cav. Field Ambulance	..	..	290	..	..	490	510
Cav. Field Ambulance, A or B Sec.	..	..	125	..	..	..	..
Field Ambulance ..	..	..	380	..	..	375	390
Field Ambulance, A Sec.	..	..	140	..	..	..	..
Field Ambulance, B or C Sec.	..	..	110	..	..	..	..
Indian Cav., Field Ambulance	..	..	..	..	..	465	485
Indian Field Ambcc. ..	..	..	..	..	..	360	375
Transport and Supply :—							
Hd. Qrs. Cav. Divl. A.S.C.	..	60	..	..	..	..	..
Div. Train	..	..	1,755	..	..	..	..
Div. Train Hd. Qrs. ..	..	..	40	..	..	..	..
Div. Train Hd. Qrs. Co.	..	..	740	..	..	..	..
Div. Train Hd. Qrs. Co. (Baggage Sec.)	..	..	310	..	..	..	..
Div. Train Hd. Qrs. Co. (Supply Sec.)	..	..	285	..	..	..	..
Div. Train, other Cos...	..	..	310	..	..	..	..
Div. Train, other Cos. (Baggage Sec.)	..	..	90	..	..	..	..
Div. Train, other Cos. (Supply Sec.)	..	..	105	..	..	..	..

ROAD SPACE TABLES—*continued*.

| | Home Establishment. | | | Indian Establishment. | | | |
| | | | | | | 2nd Line Transport. | |
	Fighting Portion.	1st Line Transport.	Ambulances and Trains.	Fighting Troops.	1st Line Transport.	Without Tents.	With Tents.
	Yds.	Yds.	Yds.	Yds.	Yds.	Yds.	Yds.
Army Troops Train ..	..	..	355	..	..	..	..
Army Troops Train Hd. Qrs.	..	..	150	..	..	..	..
Army Troops Train (Baggage Sec.)	..	..	40	..	..	..	..
Army Troops Train (Supply Sec.)	..	..	165	..	..	..	..
Cav. Bde. Supply Coln.	..	..	..	..	..	650	650
Divl. Supply Coln. ..	..	..	..	..	..	1,600	1,600
Divl. Supply Coln. Hd. Qrs.	..	..	..	..	..	115	115
Divl. Supply Coln. Hd. Qrs. Sec.	..	..	..	..	..	605	605
Divl. Supply Coln. Sec. (for 1 Bde.)	..	..	..	..	..	295	295
Divl. Supply Park ..	..	..	..	..	..	3,140	3,140
Divl. Supply Park Hd. Qrs.	..	..	..	..	..	295	295
Divl. Supply Park Sec.	..	..	..	..	..	710	710
	Miles.	Miles.	Miles.	Miles.	Miles.	Miles.	Miles.
Higher Units :—							
Cavalry Division ..	6	$4\frac{2}{3}$	$\frac{5}{8}$	..	..	..	..
Cavalry Brigade (with Cav. Div.)	1	$\frac{7}{8}$	..	..	..	..	..
Cavalry Brigade (not allotted to Cav. Div.)	$1\frac{1}{4}$	$1\frac{1}{2}$	$\frac{1}{8}$	$1\frac{1}{2}$	$\frac{1}{2}$	$1\frac{2}{3}$	1
Division	8	5	$1\frac{2}{3}$	$5\frac{1}{4}$	$2\frac{1}{3}$	$7\frac{1}{4}$	$7\frac{7}{8}$
Infantry Brigade ..	$1\frac{1}{2}$	$\frac{3}{4}$	..	1	$\frac{3}{4}$	$\frac{3}{4}$	$\frac{7}{8}$
Divisional Troops ..	..	..	..	$2\frac{2}{3}$	$1\frac{1}{4}$	5	$5\frac{1}{4}$

NEW ARMIES.

Headquarters.--

	yards.
Division	210
Infantry Brigade	105

Artillery—

F.A. Brigade	2,210
F.A. Brigade Headquarters	90
F.A. Battery	365
F.A. Brigade Ammunition Column	615
F.A. Brigade, Howitzer	2,015
F.A. Brigade Howitzer Headquarters	90
F.A. Battery, Howitzer	365
F.A. Brigade Howitzer Ammunition Column ...	420
Divisional Ammunition Column	2,165
Divisional Ammunition Column Section	635
Motor Machine-Gun Battery	400 (approximate)

Mounted troops—

Cyclist Company (Mounted)	610 (approximate)
Cyclist Company (Wheeling)	300 (approximate)

Engineers—

Field Company	475
Divisional Signal Company	615
Divisional Signal Company Headquarters	210
Divisional Signal Company, No. 1 Section	180
Divisional Signal Company, Nos. 2, 3, 4 Sections each	70

Infantry—

Battalion	780
Battalion Headquarters	185
Battalion Machine-Gun Section	55
Company	130
Pioneer Battalion	895
Pioneer Battalion Headquarters...	185
Pioneer Battalion Machine-Gun Section	55
Pioneer Company	155

Transport and Supply—

Divisional Train	2,260
Divisional Train Headquarters	35
Divisional Train Headquarters Company	1,000
Divisional Train Headquarters Company, Baggage Section	340
Divisional Train Headquarters Company, Supply Section	510
Divisional Train, other Companies	400
Divisional Train, other Companies, Baggage Section	190
Divisional Train, other Companies, Supply Section.	100

Medical—

Field Ambulance	430 (approximate)
Field Ambulance, A Section	195 (approximate)
Field Ambulance, B or C Sections	120 (approximate)
Workshop A.S.C. for Motor Ambulance Cars ...	150 (approximate)

Veterinary—

Mobile Veterinary Section	60

Higher units—

Infantry Brigade	3,295
Division (less heavy battery)	15½ miles

NOTE.—Calculations will have to be made to meet special cases when road conditions do not permit of the formations laid down in Sec. 7 (4).

8. QUARTERS.

(See F.S.R., Part I, Chap. IV.)

GENERAL RULES.

1. In the presence of an enemy tactical considerations, *e.g.*, favourable ground for defence in case of attack, concealment, facilities for protection, and economy in outposts are of the first importance.

2. If an engagement is anticipated, the larger units should be distributed in the order from front to rear in which they will come into action, provided that when liable to attack, infantry is in the more exposed positions; cavalry and other mounted troops in the less exposed. Artillery, columns, and medical units should always be covered by the other arms.

3. The following rules must be observed in distributing troops :—

    (*a*) Depôts should be near good roads.

    (*b*) Dismounted units should be nearest the water supply.

    (*c*) Staffs and hospitals have the first claim on buildings.

    (*d*) When shelter is limited, cavalry and then other mounted troops have precedence of dismounted troops.

    (*e*) Hospitals should be given a quiet spot and the most sanitary position.

    (*f*) Staff and telegraph offices should adjoin, if possible, and should be clearly marked (*see* Plate 21).

    (*g*) Officers must be close to their men.

4. If a column is halted for a night only, the troops composing it should not be quartered more than from 1 to 2 miles from the next day's line of march.

5. Areas, termed *brigade areas*, will normally be allotted to each cavalry and infantry brigade or organization approximately equal to a brigade. The commander of a brigade area is responsible for all internal arrangements in his area, including the allotment of areas to units, selection of alarm post for his command, and measures regarding communications, police and sanitary matters.

BILLETS.

6. In allotting areas, units should be kept together under their own commanders as far as possible. To make full use of stabling, it may be necessary to mix the arms.

7. In the absence of data as to the capacity of an area, ordinary billets with subsistence should be possible for a force about twice the population for one week. Billets without subsistence can be provided at the rate of about 10 men per inhabitant in rich agricultural districts, and at the rate of about 5–6 men per inhabitant in town or industrial districts.

8. When time permits, billeting demands (*see* App. VI) are issued to representatives of units by brigade area commanders. The former, accompanied by a billeting party, consisting of an officer or N.C.O. and one rank and file per company, &c., proceeds to the mayor, or equivalent official in the area, presents the billeting demand, and obtains a billeting order (*see* App. VI) for each inhabitant on whom men and horses are to be quartered.

9. The men of the billeting party proceed to the houses allotted to them, inspect them and mark with chalk on the door the names of officers, the number of men and horses the building is to hold. The officer selects regimental headquarters, guard room, alarm post, sick inspection room, gun and transport parks, ascertains the best roads in and out of the area and informs the billeting party when reassembled. A rough sketch of the area should be made if possible.

10. In telling off troops to billets, the following points should be observed, in addition to those given in para. 3 :—

    (*a*) Regard should be paid both to the comfort of the men and the interests of the inhabitants.

    (*b*) Staff officers should be on main communications, and easily found.

    (*c*) Mounted men must be near their horses, guns, and wagons; and staff officers near their offices.

    (*d*) Both sides of a street should be allotted to the same unit, to prevent confusion in case of alarm.

    (*e*) Roads and communcations must never be blocked.

11. Close billets are adopted when a greater state of readiness is required than is possible in ordinary billets. Tactical considerations have precedence over considerations of comfort. As many men and animals as possible are billeted, and the remainder bivouac.

Billets may be of three descriptions, viz. :—

(a) Billets with full subsistence.
(b) Billets with partial subsistence.
(c) Billets without subsistence.

When billets with subsistence are provided, officers and others must be satisfied with the usual fare of the householder on whom they are billeted. Neither bedding nor furniture in billets can be demanded as a right. All billets will include attendance, and—when required—the use of ordinary cooking utensils belonging to the inhabitants.

CAMPS AND BIVOUACS.

12. The site should be dry and on grass if possible. Avoid steep slopes Large woods with undergrowth, low meadows, the bottoms of narrow valleys, and newly-turned soil are apt to be unhealthy. Ravines and watercourses are dangerous sites.

13. Good water supply is essential. Other points to be considered are the facilities offered for obtaining shelter, fuel, forage and straw.

14. On arriving within 2 or 3 miles of the site, staff officers of brigades ride ahead with representatives of units, receive instructions concerning arrangements for the night, lead their units to the ground allotted them, and explain arrangements.

15. Each commander must be informed of any localities or depôts outside his own area on which he may draw for water, fuel, forage, &c. ; also which roads he may use and any special defensive or other measures he is to take.

16. If grazing is necessary, the allotment and protection of grazing areas must be arranged for. The position to which dead animals are to be taken and method of disposal must be settled. The general position of latrines and kitchens in each area must be fixed.

17. Special care is necessary to prevent troops from the various areas crossing one another in proceeding to ground which they may have to occupy in case of attack.

18. When British and Indian troops camp together avoid putting slaughter places near Hindu troops. The slaughter places should be screened from view. British troops must not be allowed near native cooking places or watering places, nor must they touch their cooking utensils.

CAMPS IN MOUNTAIN WARFARE.

19. When selecting the site, the necessity for occupying the chief points from which snipers can fire into the camp and for forming a defensible perimeter round it should be borne in mind.

To adapt the site to the force lay out the longest diameter, then the cross diameter and allot space to units along these cross roads (which should be 15 yards wide, if possible). *See* Plate 5 for type of perimeter camp.

The following points should be attended to :—

(a) All troops fall in on their alarm posts as soon as possible after camp is laid out, and every evening at sundown.
(b) Prepare perimeter 5 yards clear of all shelters with breast work and entanglement.
(c) No cooking places or latrines inside camp.
(d) Camels should be in a zareba outside the camp.

CAMP AND BIVOUAC SPACES.

20. In the table below, units are taken as being at war establishment. When two numbers are given, *e.g.* 160 × 150, the first signifies the frontage, the second the depth that is required.

In bivouac it may sometimes be necessary to reduce the spaces given below for home establishment camps.

PLATE I

TYPE OF BIVOUAC FOR A CAVALRY REGIMENT
OR BATTALION OF M.I.

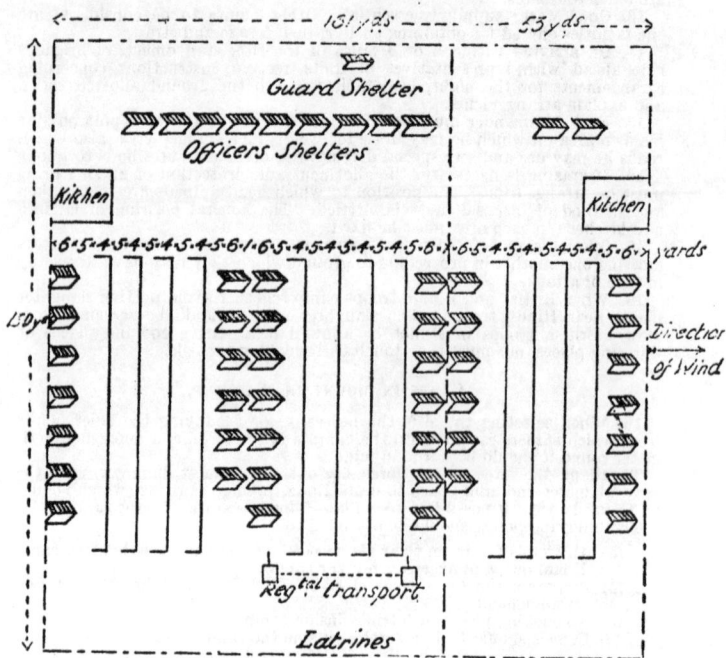

<--------- 131 yds ------ --- 53 yds ---->

Guard Shelter

Officers Shelters

| Kitchen | | Kitchen |

·6·5·4·5·4·5·4·5·4·5·6·|·6·5·4·5·4·5·4·5·4·5·6·|·6·5·4·5·4·5·4·5·6·> yards

150 yds

Direction of Wind

Reg^{tal} transport

Latrines

To face Plate II.

PLATE II.

TYPE OF BIVOUAC FOR A BATTERY OF HORSE OR FIELD ARTILLERY.

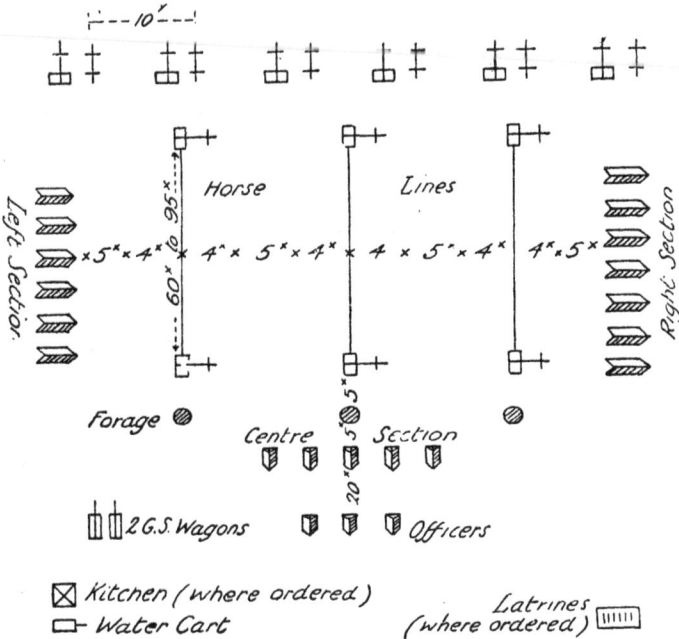

The horses of each section are fastened to one rope, using both sides of the rope. 5 feet between horses, and end horses 5 yards from vehicle.

To fo'low Plate I.

PLATE III

TYPE OF BIVOUAC FOR F.A. BDE. AMM. COLN.

Suitable for Field Ambulances or other units with
many vehicles.

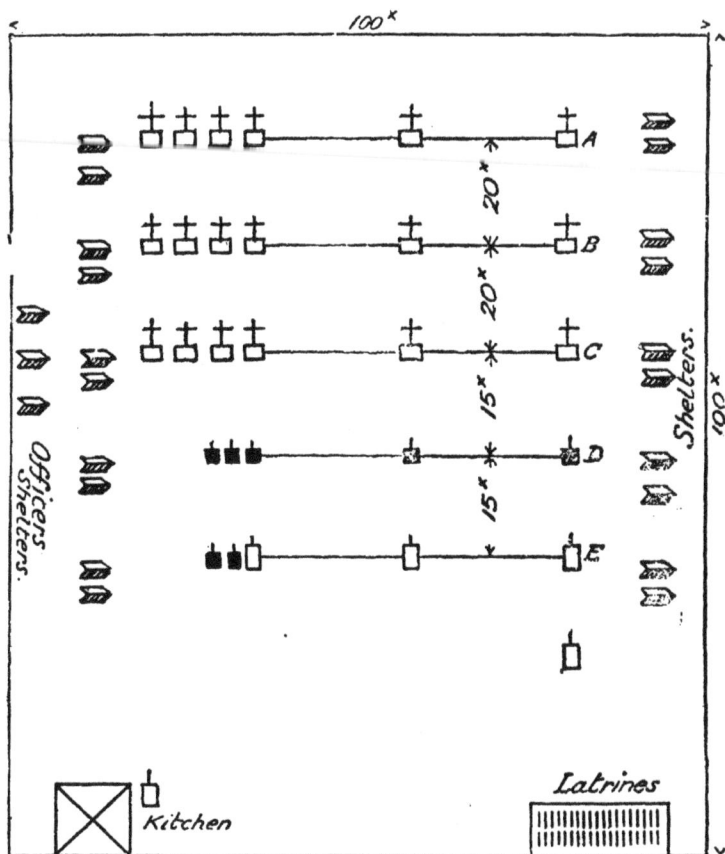

Horses tied on both sides of ropes stretched between Nos. 1, 2 and 3
Wagons of sub-sections. Remaining Wagons at close interval.

To follow Plate II.

PLATE IV.

TYPE OF BIVOUAC FOR AN INFANTRY BATTALION.

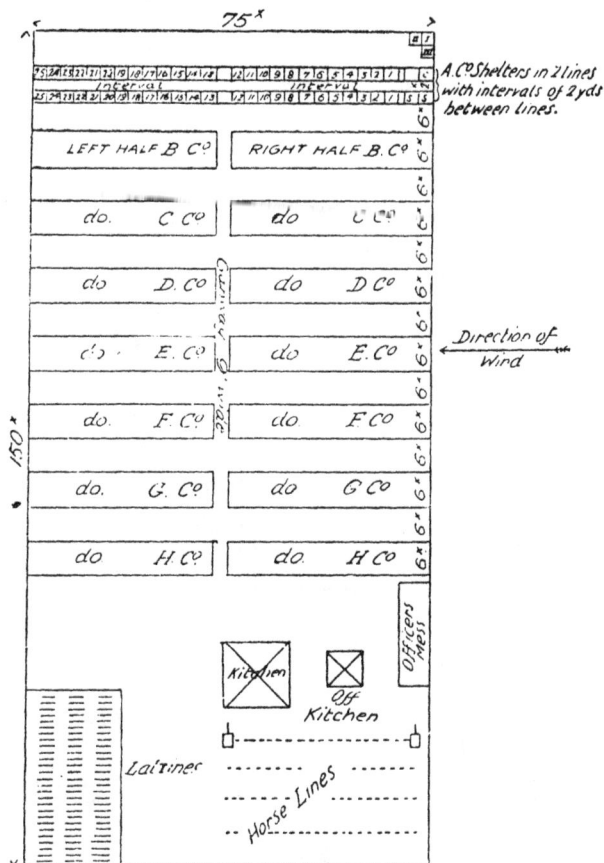

Notes.—(1) *Shelters marked* 1, 2 *and* 3 *for C.O., Adjutant and Senior Major.*
　　　　 ,, 　　 ,, 　　 C *for Company Commander.*
　　　　 ,, 　　 ,, 　　 S *for Subalterns.*
(2) *Every shelter end on to the front : heads of sleepers towards front : rifles at sides.*
(3) *The lateral space allowed is* 8 *ft. for each shelter If the company is over* 100 *strong, or if a frontage of* 75ˣ *is not available, the lateral space can be reduced to* 6 *ft.*
This plate does not apply to the four-company organization.

To follow Plate III.

PLATE V.

TYPE OF PERIMETER CAMP FOR A MIXED FORCE

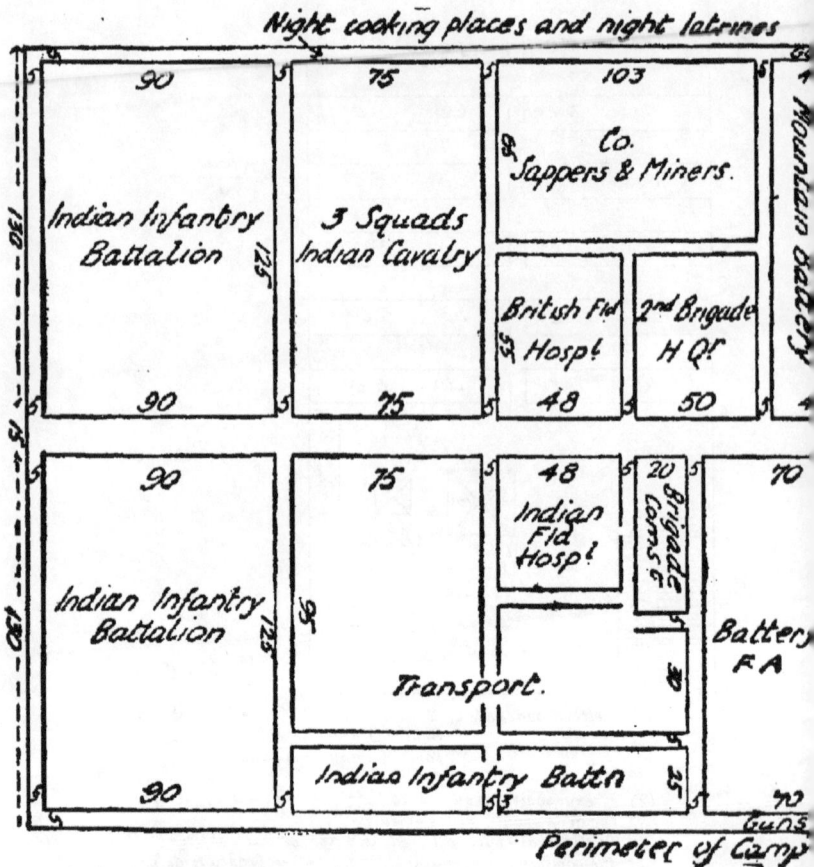

Night cooking places and night latrines

90	75	103	
Indian Infantry Battalion	3 Squads Indian Cavalry	Co. Sappers & Miners.	Mountain Battery
		British Fld Hospl	2nd Brigade HQrs
90	75	48	50
90	75	48	20 Brigade Comsgt	70
Indian Infantry Battalion		Indian Fld Hospl		Battery FA
	Transport.			
90	Indian Infantry Battn			70 Guns

Perimeter of Camp

To follow Plate IV.

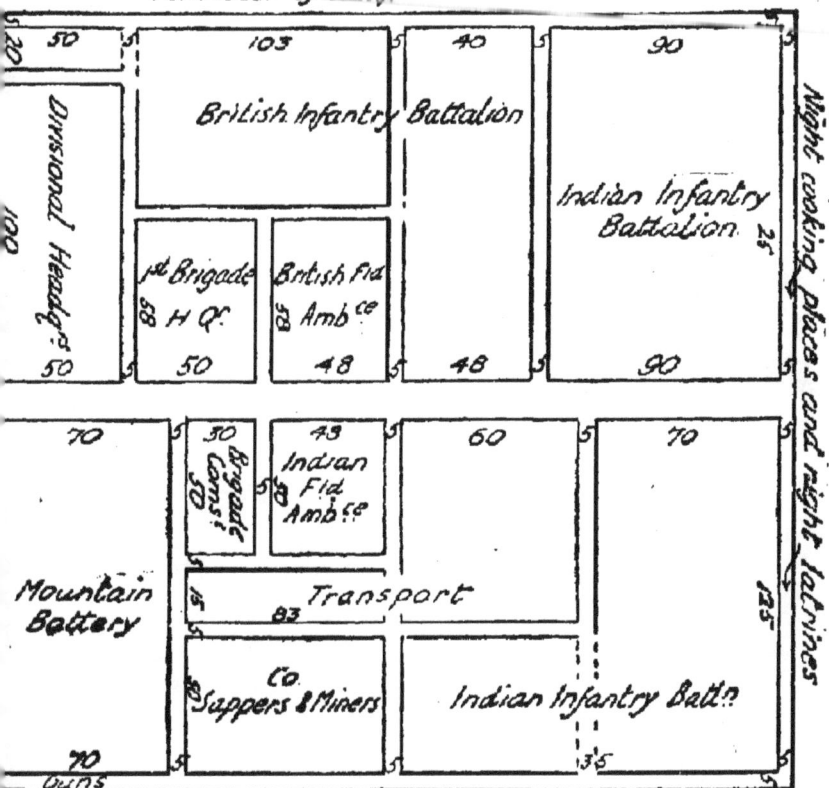

Perimeter of Camp

Night cooking places and night latrines

(B 11925)

Cavalry, mounted infantry and infantry require an alarm post of 60 yards depth in front of the camp or bivouac, in addition to the depth shown below. Other arms fall in on the ground where they camp or bivouac.

The following distances should be kept clear in front of guns or vehicles :—

Heavy gun (8 horses) .. .. 16 yards.
6-horsed gun or vehicle .. .. 12 ,,
4-horsed vehicle .. .. 8 ,,
1- or 2-horsed vehicle .. .. 5 ,,

Unit.	Home Est. Minimum Camping Space in yards.	Indian Est. Minimum Camping Space in yards.	
		With attached Transport.	Without attached Transport.*
Army Headquarters	100 × 150	100 × 150	..
Divisional Headquarters	50 × 100	40 × 66	..
Brigade Headquarters	30 × 50	30 × 40	..
Cavalry :—			
Regiment (British)	160 × 150	105 × 125	105 × 100
Squadron (British)	50 × 150	70 × 70	70 × 65
Regiment (Indian)	..	105 × 120	105 × 105
Squadron (Indian)	..	70 × 60	70 × 60
Artillery :—			
Battery (R.H. or R.F.A.) ..	75 × 150	70 × 95	70 × 90
Battery (Heavy)	60 × 150	60 × 70	60 × 60
Battery (Mountain)	..	70 × 130	80 × 70
H.A. Bde. Amm. Coln.	100 × 150	..	..
F.A. Bde. Amm. Coln.	100 × 100	..	..
Cav. Bde. Amm. Coln.	..	70 × 50	70 × 35
Divl. Amm. Coln.	400 × 100	265 × 70	155 × 70
F.A. Sec. Amm. Coln.	..	115 × 70	105 × 70
Mtn. Sec. Amm. Coln.	..	20 × 70	20 × 20
S.A.A. Sec. Amm. Coln.	..	130 × 70	30 × 70
Heavy Art. Amm. Coln.	..	70 × 30	70 × 30
Engineers :—			
Field Squadron	70 × 150	..	..
Field Troop	50 × 50	..	..
Field Company	35 × 150	40 × 80	40 × 55
Bridging Train	100 × 170	70 × 90	70 × 15
Signal Service :—			
Signal Squadron	75 × 175	..	..
Signal Troop	50 × 60	25 × 25	25 × 25
Signal Co. with Division ..	75 × 150	75 × 60	75 × 35
Signal Co. Hd. Qrs. and No. 1 Sec.	50 × 100	30 × 75	30 × 45
Hd. Qrs. of a Genl. Hd. Qrs. Signal Co.	40 × 80	..	..
Hd. Qrs. of an Army Hd. Qrs. Signal Co.	50 × 60	..	..
Signal Sec. (Airline)	40 × 80	..	..
Signal Sec. (Cable)	50 × 50	..	..
Signal Sec. (Wireless)	40 × 80	..	..
Signal Squadron (Wireless) ..	..	..	100 × 45
Signal Squadron (Wireless) less One Troop	..	..	45 × 30
Infantry :—			
Battalion (British)	75 × 150	105 × 105	105 × 75
Battalion (Indian)	..	105 × 90	105 × 70

* Transport vehicles remain in units' camps.

Unit.	Home Est.	Indian Est.	
	Minimum Camping Space in yards.	Minimum Camping Space in yards.	
		With attached Transport.	Without attached Transport.*
Medical :—			
Cavalry Field Ambulance ..	80 × 180	60 × 50	60 × 30
Field Ambulance (British) ..	120 × 200	60 × 50	60 × 30
Field Ambulance (Indian) ..	..	60 × 50	60 × 30
Supply :—			
Divl. Supply Coln.	..	100 × 115	..
Divl. Supply Coln. Hd. Qrs. ..	..	25 × 40	..
Divl. Supply Coln. Hd. Qrs. Sec.	..	100 × 45	..
Divl. Supply Coln. Sec.	..	100 × 25	..
Divl. Supply Park	..	220 × 100	..
Divl. Supply Park Hd. Qrs. ..	..	25 × 100	..
Divl. Supply Park Sec.	..	100 × 50	..
Cav. Bde. Supply Coln.	..	100 × 40	..

* Transport vehicles remain in units' camps.

21. For separate calculations the following spaces are required for animals, vehicles and tents :—

Horse, mule, pony or bullock	8′ × 15′
Camel	9′ × 15′
Elephant	9′ × 21′
13-pr. or 18-pr. gun or 4·5″ howr. and limber ..	7′ × 28′
Ammunition wagon and limber	7′ × 23′
Store cart, I.P.	7′ × 14′
Army transport cart..	5¼′ × 14′
G.S. wagon	6¼′ × 22½
Circular tent, single .. .. radius	9¾′
,, ,, double..	10′
E.P. ,, (peace only)	40′ × 36′
Hospital Marquee, large	80′ × 55′
,, ,, small	50′ × 36′
G.S. tent, India (160 lbs.)	22′ × 16′
,, ,, ,, (80 ,,)	16′ × 10′
,, ,, ,, (40 ,,)	12′ × 10′
,, ,, ,, (21 ,,)	9½′ × 7′
,, ,, ,, (officer's)	14′ × 9′
Operating tent	48′ × 40′
Shelter ,, ...	12′ × 7′
Staff Sjts. ,, ...	28′ × 28′
Store ,, ...	150′ × 40′
,, ,, ...	76′ × 60′

22. With circular tents, accommodation is allowed as follows :—

Generals, colonels and C.Os.	..	1 to a tent.	
Other officers	..	3 ,,	
W. officers	..	5 ,,	(1 W.O. = 3 men).
Serjeants	..	7 ,,	(1 Sjt. = 2 men).
Men	..	15 ,,	

Plate VI.

BIVOUACS.

Fig. 1.   *Fig.* 2.

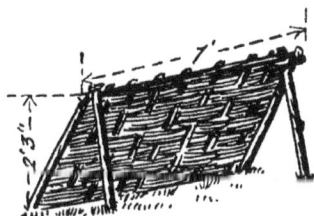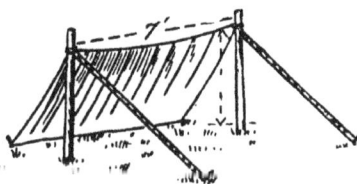

Shelter Tent.

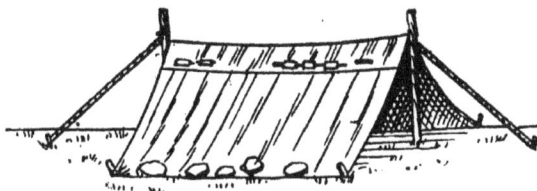

Fig. 3.

Refuse Destructor.
Fig. 4.

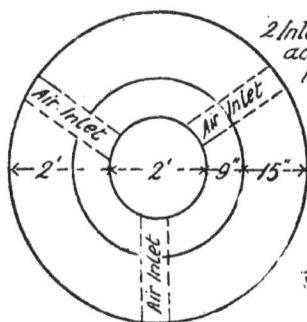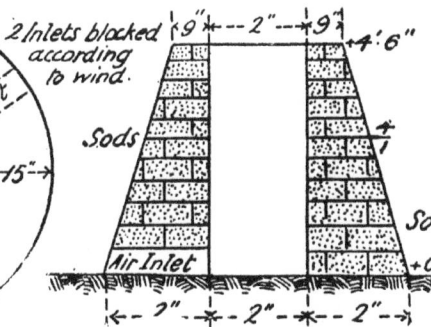

PLAN.   SECTION.

To face page 44.

PLATE VII.

Fig. 1.—COOKING IN THE FIELD.

Fig. 2.—OVEN BURROWED NEAR TOP OF A BANK.

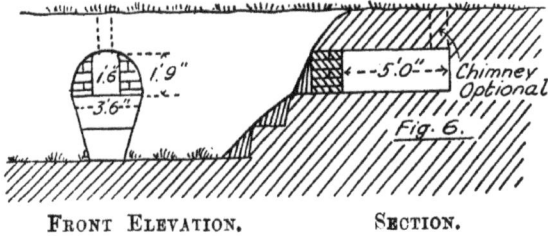

1.6" 1.9"
3.6"
5.0" Chimney Optional
Fig. 6.

FRONT ELEVATION.   SECTION.

Fig. 3.—KITCHENS.

SECTION OF COOKING TRENCH.

Length varies with No. of Kettles, allowing 8 per 10 ft.

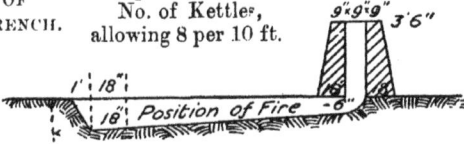

9"9"9" 3'6"

1' 18"
18" Position of Fire 6"

Fig. 5.

Raised Trench (wet weather).

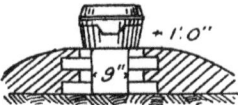

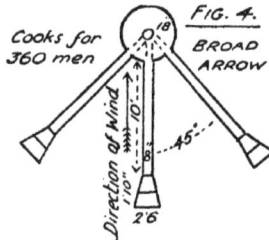

1'.0"

9"

FIG. 4.

Cooks for 360 men

BROAD ARROW

Direction of Wind

18
10"
8
45°
2'6"

Kettles measure :—
12 quarts 9" × 13½" × 11" high.
7 do. 8½" × 12¼" × 8" do.

The accommodation in other tents is as follows :—

E.P. tents accommodate 16 British.
G.S.   „   (160 lbs.) accommodate 16 British or 20 native soldiers.
  „   „   (80   „)   „   8   „   10   „
  „   „   (40   „)   „   1 Warrant or N.C.O.
  „   „   (officer's)   „   2 officers.
Shelter tent accommodates   2 men.
Staff Sjt's. tent   „.   2 Staff Serjeants.

DIRECTIONS FOR PITCHING TENTS (CIRCULAR).

23. Mark centre with peg. Describe a circle, with radius of 4 paces, on which the pegs will be. In this circle, drive in the two pegs opposite the door of the tent one pace apart. At 3 paces from these pegs, on either side of them, drive in pegs for guy ropes. The other guy rope pegs will be 5 paces from these and 5 paces from each other.

Put up tent, pole to be set and kept perfectly upright.

Drive in the other pegs, which should be one pace apart and in line with the seams of the tent.

Doors, if possible, point to leeward.

$7\frac{1}{2}$ yards from centre to centre of tents.

Cut drains round bottom of tent walls, and heap earth inside flap.

Dig a hole 6 inches deep close to tent pole, then if heavy rain comes on suddenly, the tent pole can be pushed into the hole and much strain is taken off the canvas, ropes and pegs.

Allow 1 yard between pegs of adjacent tents.
  „   1   „   „   tents of adjacent squadrons.
  „   3   „   „   „   „   „   companies.
  „ 10   „   „   „   „   „   units.

TYPES OF BIVOUAC SHELTERS.

24. Plate 6 suggests methods of forming simple shelters.

Fig. 1, two forked sticks driven into the ground with a pole resting on them ; branches are then laid resting on the pole, thick end uppermost, at an angle of about 45°, and the screen made good with smaller branches, ferns, &c.

A hurdle may be supported and treated in a similar way.

Fig. 2, a waterproof sheet, blanket, or piece of canvas secured by poles and string.

Fig. 3, a *tent d'abri* for four men, formed with two blankets or waterproof sheets laced together at the ridge, the remaining two blankets being available for cover inside.

Fig. 4, a wall of straw or reeds nipped between two pairs of sticks, tied together at intervals.

When no other materials than earth and brushwood are available, a comfortable bivouac for 12 men can be formed by excavating a circle with a diameter of 18 feet, or thereabouts, and piling up the earth to form a wall 2 feet or 3 feet high. The men lie down, like the spokes of a wheel, with their feet towards the centre. Branches of trees, or brushwood stuck into the wall, improve the shelter.

Huts can be made by thatching with stalks of any grain. In the absence of ropes, creepers can be used if available.

CARE OF HORSES IN CAMP OR BIVOUAC.

25. If possible choose ground flat enough to give a level standing to the horses, but with sufficient natural fall to carry away storm water ; sheltered by higher ground from the wind ; within easy reach of the water supply, but not draining into it. Shift after a wet night.

In very cold weather do not groom, but wisp and rub mud off legs. Put more covering on back. Do not let a horse stand in a hot sun with his back wet.

26. A horse when picketed requires 3 to 5 yards between picket line and heel pegs ; 5 feet between head ropes. The head rope should only be long enough to permit the horse to carry his head naturally when standing ; too long a rope permits him to get his leg over the rope and leads to heel galls.

In the case of a horse given to reining back, pass his head rope through a shackle on the forefoot. This soon tires him of reining back. Picket kickers separately. A gangway of 5 yards should be maintained between two horses' lines.

27. Horses require hay, grass or some substitute in addition to grain. Give a hungry horse some hay first, then his oats.

Scrub nose-bags frequently ; turn and dry them in sun. They should not be interchangeable to avoid risk of spreading infection. Avoid waste by keeping nose-bags in repair and by using hay nets when available.

28. Do not herd horses in mobs when grazing, but have guards out, who should only mount when rounding up. Keep kickers apart, or hobble their hind pasterns.

METHODS OF SECURING HORSES.

29. *Tying up a horse.*—The following is a useful method for securing a horse to a bush or small tree.

Fig. 1.   Fig. 2.

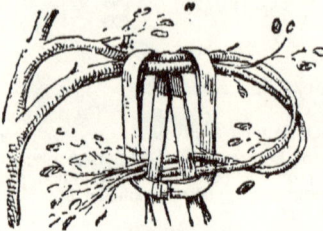
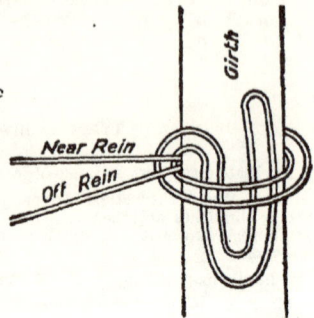

Take a suitable branch or bunch of branches, place the loop of the reins under and round it, then double back the end of the branch, breaking, if necessary, and pass it through the reins as shown in Fig. 1 and tighten up. A separate piece of stick will answer for the same purpose.

The more the horse pulls the tighter will the knot become, whereas the man can unfasten it very rapidly by simply pulling back the doubled end of the branch or piece of stick through the loop in the reins.

30. Single horses can also be kept from straying as follows :—

   (a) By knee-haltering.—The correct knot for knee-haltering is a clove
      hitch, fairly tight, above the knee, with a keeper knot (half-hitch)
      round the rope to prevent it from coming loose. The end should
      then be carried back to the head collar and so secured that the
      horse cannot tread on it. The rope should be from 1 foot to 1 foot
      6 inches from knee to lower ring of jowl piece of head-collar.

(b) By securing the bit to the stirrup iron by means of the rein or strap.

(c) By securing the bridoon rein to the girth on the rear side, as shown in Fig. 2. It should be drawn sufficiently tight to bend the horse's head to the left. When mounting in haste the rider can easily loosen the slip knot after mounting, and then pull the reins clear and pass them over the horse's head.

31. *Coupling horses.*—Horses can be securely coupled by turning them head to tail and tying each with the bridoon rein to the off back-strap or arch of the saddle of the other, taking care that the reins, when tied are not more than 6 to 8 inches long. (*See* Fig 3.)

Fig. 3.

32. *Linking horses.*—The head ropes are brought over the horses' heads clear of the reins, without unfastening the coil or knot. Each man hands his rope to the man on his right, who passes it through the upper ring of his own horse's head collar, and ties it with two half-hitches.

With three horses, one can be tied to the head collar of either of the two horses so coupled. Four horses are secured by tying a horse to each of the two originally coupled. No horse should have more than 1 foot length of rein, and the best knot to be used is a slip knot round the rein itself.

CARE OF HARNESS AND SADDLERY.

33. (a) The leather work of all saddlery should be kept soft and supple. Leather girths and breechings should be greased regularly. Steel work should be oiled.

(b) Stirrup leathers should occasionally be shortened or lengthened about an inch to bring the wear on fresh holes.

(c) Leather must not be washed with soda or hot water. Lukewarm water may be used, but leather should never be allowed to soak in any water.

(d) Saddlery should, if possible, always be hung up or raised off the ground.

9. CAMP COOKING.

1. Various types of field kitchen are shown on Plate 7. Camp kettles (large) will cook for 8 with, or 15 without vegetables; small kettles will cook for 5 men with, or 8 without vegetables. Fig. 1, Plate 7, shows how camp kettles can be arranged for cooking when time does not admit of a kitchen being made.

2. Cooking can also be done in mess tins. No trench is necessary. The mess tins should be arranged as shown in Plate 7, Fig. 1, with the opening facing the wind. Eight is a convenient number to form a " kitchen." The handles of the mess tins should be kept outside and the tins should be well greased on the outside before being placed on the fire. The position of the tins should be changed from time to time. Dinners can be cooked in from 1 to 1½ hours.

3. *Boiling.*—To boil a joint, place it in boiling water and allow it to boil quickly for 10 minutes, then bring it to a simmer by pouring in cold water

or reducing the fire.   The average loss by boiling is 15 to 20 per cent.   The time required to cook is about 15 minutes per pound of meat.

Vegetables should be placed in boiling water with a little salt and boiled quickly till tender.   Potatoes take from 20 to 30 minutes , carrots and parsnips 20 to 45 minutes.   Dried vegetables should be soaked for about 4 hours and then boiled slowly.

4. *Stewing.*—Stewing is not boiling. All that is required is a gradual simmering. This will make even tough meat tender and wholesome.

5. *Frying.*—Frying is cooking with the aid of fats ; in other words, frying is simply boiling in fat.   When possible cover the article to be cooked with fat.

6. Meat may be baked as follows : Dig in the ground a hole of sufficient size and build a fire in it.   After the fuel has become red-hot put in the meat, wrapped in paper in a clay case, or with the skin on, on a thick layer of green grass ; cover it with green grass, hot ashes and earth. Build a good fire over the meat and keep it burning for about 6 hours.   Unearth the meat and remove the skin.   Meat treated in this way at night will be found cooked in the morning.

7. When fuel is scarce, a good plan is to cook the meat partly in a kettle, and, when the contents are boiling, place the kettle in a box, surround it with hay or other non-conducting material, and close the lid tightly ; the contents will go on gently stewing, and should be fully cooked in three or four hours' time.

RECIPES.

8. *Kabobs.*—For a hurried meal the meat can be quickly prepared by cutting it into pieces about the size of a penny, but three or four times as thick.   These can then be skewered on a piece of wire or hard wood and roasted before the fire for a few minutes.

Stewed beef, mutton, or fowl.—Cut up the meat into thin slices or small pieces, the smaller the better. put a little fat into the bottom of the cooking pot, and when hot put in the meat, stir till brown, add a sliced onion, carrot, or turnip, season with pepper and salt, add a little flour and some hot water, stir well, and allow to simmer slowly till done.   Tomatoes, rice and powdered biscuit in lieu of flour may be added.

9. *Irish stew.*—Ingredients : meat, potatoes, onions, pepper, salt.   Peel, wash and slice the potatoes ; peel, clean and cut up the onions, cut up the meat into small pieces, place a little water in the kettle and a layer of potatoes at the bottom, then a layer of meat and onions ; season with pepper and salt, then add another layer of potatoes and so on to the top, potatoes forming the top layer.   Barely cover the whole with water and stew gently for about 2 hours.

10. *Sea pie.*—Ingredients as for Irish stew, with 5 lbs. of flour and 1½ lbs suet or dripping added for every 20 men.   Prepare ingredients as in case of stew, cutting the potatoes in slices lengthwise, and cover with paste, making a hole in the centre.   To make the paste, mix flour and water, roll or beat it out with the hands on a flat surface, adding a small teaspoonful of baking powder for each pound of flour.   The paste should be about ¼ inch thick. Time required to cook, about 2 hours.

11. *Mutton or beef soup.*—For 6 persons, 1½ lbs. of meat, 1 onion, 2 carrots, 1 turnip, 6 tablespoonfuls of rice or barley.   Cut the meat up into small pieces, peel and slice the onion, clean and cut up the other vegetables, put a little fat into the camp kettle, fry the meat and vegetables a light brown colour, add 5 pints of water and the rice or barley ; stew slowly for about 1½ hours. and take off the scum as it rises, season with pepper and salt, and serve.   When time does not admit, the frying of the meat and vegetables may be dispensed with.   Semolina, tapioca, sago, macaroni, tomatoes, green peas, beans, lentils, &c., can be substituted for the rice or barley.

12. *Beef tea.*—Cut up about 1 lb. of lean beef (no fat) into small pieces, put in a kettle, add 2 pints of cold water, boil slowly, removing the scum as it rises, cook for about 2 hours, or longer if time admits ; strain and serve.

PLATE VIII.

LATRINES.

Fig. 1. PLAN.

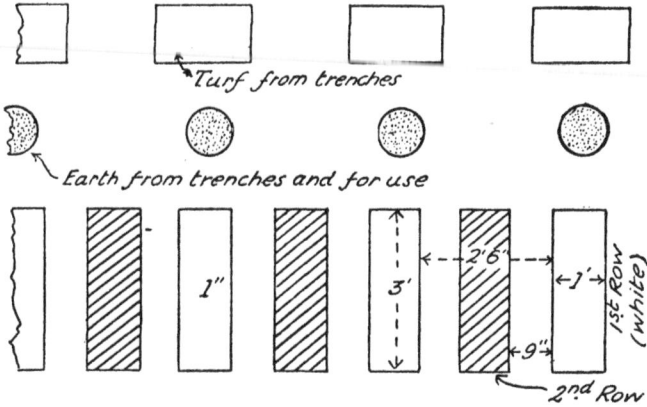

Turf from trenches

Earth from trenches and for use

1" 3' 2'6' 1' 1st Row (white)

9" 2nd Row

3rd Row

When filled in, the next series of trenches may be made
in the 2' 6" interspace if ground is limited. The turf
must be removed carefully and the excavated earth put
behind each trench—this earth must be well broken up.

Fig. 2. Fig. 3.

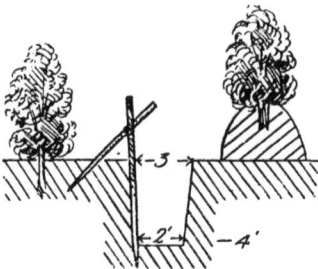
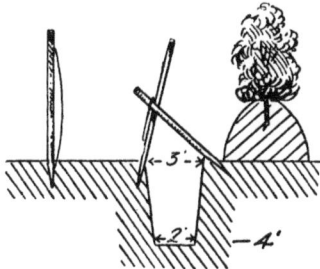

To face page 50.

13. *Salt meat*, when required hurriedly, should be cut into thin slices, placed in cold water, and brought to boiling point to extract the salt; this may be repeated until the meat is found palatable. Salt meat treated in this way may, if time will allow be used for stews in the same way as fresh meat.

14. *Stew made of preserved meat and vegetables.*—Cut up the meat, removing all fat and jelly, powder up the vegetables, and put them in a kettle or mess tin with water, cook until done, strain off most of the water, add meat and jelly, and season with pepper, salt, and a teaspoonful of brown sugar. Put on the lid, and allow to heat through, then serve. The secret of making palatable dishes with preserved meat is only to heat it through, as cooking spoils it.

If fresh vegetables are obtainable, they should be fried first, then stewed and added to the meat.

15. *Preserved meat soup.*—Take 4 ounces of meat and half a biscuit per man with his allowance of preserved vegetables, cut up the meat, and powder the biscuit and vegetables. Put the vegetables into a camp kettle containing ½ pint of cold water per man, boil slowly, and add the meat and biscuit, and continue the boiling for ½ hour, season with pepper and salt, if required, and serve; a quarter of a teaspoonful of brown sugar for each man may be added to improve the flavour.

16. *Plain rice pudding.*—Boil 1 lb. of rice in 6 quarts of water for 30 minutes, season with a pinch of salt, strain and save the water; put the rice into a dish, add 6 ounces of sugar, half a tin of condensed milk, a little of the water which has been strained off, stir well, and grate a little nutmeg or rind of a lemon on the top, place the dish on some embers, cover with a piece of tin, on this put some more embers, and bake for 20 minutes. If fresh milk is used, add 2 more ounces of sugar. If milk is not obtainable, the rice water alone may be used. If an egg is added, it should be beaten up with the milk or rice water; this is a great improvement.

17. *Chupatties.*—Mix some flour with water to make a stiff dough. Flatten a piece of the dough with both hands till it is about ¼ inch thick. Melt some fat in the cover of a mess tin and when quite hot place the chupattie in it and leave till it is brown on both sides On an average fire 1 lb. of flour can be made into chupatties in ½ hour.

18. *Bread made with baking powder.*—Spread the flour out evenly, sift the baking powder over it, taking care to break up any small lumps. Mix powder and flour thoroughly. Dissolve salt at the rate of 1 oz. to 7 lbs. flour in the softest water available. Mix with the flour and powder very thoroughly and place the loaves in a quick oven.

10. SANITATION OF CAMPS AND BIVOUACS.

(*See* Man. of Elem. Mil. Hygiene.)

1. The importance of prevention of disease on field service cannot be over-estimated. Neglect of sanitary measures inevitably results in great loss of life, and disease may assume such proportions as to paralyse the efficiency of a force. It is the duty of both officers and men to comply strictly with orders relating to the preservation of health. To keep himself healthy and fit is a duty that every soldier owes to his country, his comrades and himself.

2. In all camps the utmost care must be taken to prevent fouling of ground by excreta and refuse. Therefore urinals and latrines should be made immediately on arrival at a camp or bivouac, and should be filled in at the last possible moment.

3. Great attention must be paid to camp kitchens. Kitchen slop water should be disposed of in pits covered with brushwood, straw or any other material that will retain the grease. The brushwood, &c., should then be used as fuel in the kitchen fires. The habit of throwing kitchen water about to allay dust increases instead of diminishing discomfort in camp.

4. Food must be protected from dust and flies. To keep camps free from flies, horse dung, stable litter and other refuse, which form natural breeding places for those insects must be carefully disposed of.

Refuse of all descriptions should be burnt daily, and what cannot be burnt should be buried. The carcasses of dead animals should be removed from any ground likely to be wanted for camping, disembowelled and the viscera buried deeply. In standing camps the carcasses should be burnt or buried.

5. A drawing of an incinerator for disposal of camp refuse is shown on Plate 6.

Another effective incinerator consists of a circular, shallow, saucer-like depression, 10 feet in diameter, and not more than 2 feet deep in the centre, shelving gradually to the level of the ground at its edge. The whole of this hollow is lined with large stones or broken bricks, and a low wall built up round it, the excavated earth being packed against it to prevent surface water gaining access, and also to provide a sloping approach for tilting refuse into it. Next, a pyramid of large stones is built up in the centre of the basin; this pyramid should rise so as to have its top some 2 feet or more above the level of the rim or encircling wall. The object of the central cairn is to provide a steady draught through the centre of the burning material. Ordinary dry wood or brushwood must be used to start the fire, and after it is well burning it can be maintained by steadily adding refuse. The stones soon become intensely hot, and serve to dispose of liquid and damp stuff with rapidity. This incinerator is eminently adapted for stony or rocky country.

6. To keep tents dry they should be trenched; flies of tents should be rolled up daily, and blankets and kits aired.

7. Cleanliness both of person and clothing is of great importance. The feet should be washed or wiped at least once daily. The nails, mouth and hair require attention as well as the skin. Underclothing should be washed at least once a week.

8. Latrines, urinals, refuse pits, horse and cattle lines, and slaughtering places must be placed as far as possible from the kitchens, from any source of water supply, and to leeward if possible. They must never be placed in any gullies which, when it rains, may discharge into the water supply. A sanitary policeman should be placed in charge of each latrine, his duty being to see that every man covers up his excreta with earth. Failure to carry out this practice should be punished.

Slaughtering places should not be near horse lines.

9. In camps, short trench latrines should be dug. Each trench should be 3 feet long, 1 foot wide, and 1 foot deep, the interspace between each trench being 2½ feet; men should use these trenches straddlewise, and at once cover up their deposit with earth. Five trenches will suffice for 100 men for one day; they should then be filled in with earth and the turf replaced.

Trenches required for the second day of occupation will be dug in the spaces between the first row of trenches.

The method of preparing the short trench latrine is shown in Plate 8, Fig. 1.

If the area of ground be limited, the depth of the short trench may be increased to 2 feet; these deeper trenches should last 2 days.

In some cases, deep latrines may be necessary; they should be constructed to seat 5 per cent. of the troops, 1 yard per man being allowed. This type of latrine is shown in Plate 8.

The position of all old latrines should be marked with the letter L made with stones, &c.

10. *Disinfectants.*—For general use, cresol solution and chloride of lime are the most efficacious. To use cresol, mix 1½ ounces of cresol solution with 1 gallon of water.

Clothing may be disinfected by being plunged into boiling water, or by being baked in an oven heated from 210° to 250° Fahr.

11. WATER SUPPLY.

1. A daily average of 1 gallon per man is sufficient for drinking and cooking purposes. A horse, bullock, or mule drinks about 1½ gallons at a time. In standing camps, an average allowance of 5 gallons should be given for a man, and 10 gallons for a horse or a camel. An elephant drinks 25 gallons

each mule or ox drinks 6 to 8 gallons, each sheep or pig 6 to 8 pints. These are minimum quantities.

One cubic foot of water = 6¼ gallons (a gallon = 10 lbs.).

2. The rough average yield of a stream may be measured as follows :— Select some 12 or 15 yards of the stream where the channel is fairly uniform and there are no eddies. Take the breadth and average depth in feet in three or four places. Drop in a chip of wood and find the time it takes to travel, say, 30 feet. Thus obtain the surface velocity in feet per second. Four-fifths of this will give the mean velocity, and this multiplied by the sectional area will give the yield per second in cubic feet of water.

PURITY OF WATER.

3. As the health of a force depends largely on the purity of the water provided, everything possible must be done to ensure an ample supply of pure drinking water, and to keep it pure when obtained. It is mainly through drinking impure or contaminated water that cholera, dysentery, and enteric fever are contracted and spread. The water supply will always be selected in conjunction with the sanitary or other medical officer, who will satisfy himself as to its fitness for use. No water should be used for drinking purposes that has not been sterilized by filtration, by heating, or by chemical means.

4. Men must be prevented from drinking water from unauthorized sources, and they must be trained to economize the contents of their water bottles, which, before marching, should be filled with weak tea or sterilized water. Bad water drunk on an empty stomach is more dangerous than that drunk with a meal. Thirst is best assuaged by first moistening the lips and mouth, and only drinking a small quantity at a time. Large draughts of water should never be taken, as thirst is only increased thereby, and, if taken when the body is over-heated, bad effects may follow.

5. Muddy water should be cleared of suspended matter before being boiled or filtered. The following methods may be used :—

> (a) Alum (5 grains to the gallon, or 1 ounce, equal to a heaped up table-spoonful, to 100 gallons) stirred into the water and allowed to stand hastens the deposit of the suspended matter.
>
> (b) Tack a sheet on to a wooden frame so as to form a bag or basin ; put a couple of handfuls of wood ashes in the bottom and then pour on the water, placing a receptacle beneath to catch the water which percolates through.
>
> (c) Take 2 casks and place one inside the other, the outer cask pierced with holes at the bottom and the inner near the top ; the space between is filled with sand, or gravel ; when these are placed in a stream, the water rises through the filtering material between the barrels and flows into the inner one.

6. Filtration aims at purifying water by holding back suspended matter, including germs.

The filter usually provided is the filter water tank ; this will give about 200 gallons of filtered water in an hour. Another, the portable filter, capable of being carried on a pack saddle, will filter 60 gallons an hour. The filter candles should be boiled in water every fourth day.

7. There are two ways of killing germs in water, viz., by heat and by chemicals.

Purification of water by heat can be secured by either—(1) Boiling in an open vessel, in which case it will be sufficient to bring the water to the boiling point ; or (2) Heating in a special sterilizer, such as the "Griffith." The small type of these machines will sterilize 60 gallons an hour, the larger type 350 gallons in an hour. The average consumption of fuel for each is a gallon of oil for each 400 gallons of water.

The chemical substance chiefly employed for sterilizing water is chloride of lime.

This is employed as follows :—Take a teaspoonful of bleaching powder (chloride of lime) (containing about one-third available chlorine) and remove the excess of powder by rolling a pencil, &c., along the top of the spoon. Dissolve the bleaching powder in a cupful of water, making sure that all lumps are thoroughly broken up, and then add three more cupfuls of water to the solution. Stir up the mixture, allow it to stand for a few seconds to let any particles settle (this stock solution, if kept tightly stoppered, may be used for 4 or 5 days) and add *one teaspoonful* of this milky solution to 2 gallons of the water to be purified. Stir thoroughly and allow to stand for 10 minutes. This will give one-half part of free chlorine to 1,000,000 parts of water ; 1 lb. chloride is sufficient for 66,000 gallons.

Note.—Bleaching powder (chloride of lime) deteriorates rapidly when kept in cardboard packages or exposed to air.

8. Vessels or tanks in which drinking-water is stored, as well as being carefully covered, should be raised off the ground and provided with taps. Water-carts and barrels require frequent cleaning and periodical disinfection.

To clean water receptacles, dissolve 1 teaspoonful of permanganate of potash crystals in 3 gallons of water and rinse with this solution until a permanent pink colour remains.

9. Posts on the lines of communication should arrange to have enough sterilized water on hand to supply the wants of detachments passing through.

WATERING ARRANGEMENTS.

10. As a rule the military police, otherwise the first troops to arrive at a halting ground, will mount sentries on all water likely to be required for use, with such orders as will prevent any form of pollution. These sentries will not be withdrawn until permanent water guards are detailed.

11. The water supply should usually be marked with flags, as follows, by the advanced party of engineers :—

> White for drinking-water.
> Blue for watering places for animals.
> Red for washing or bathing places.

12. If water is obtained from a stream, horses will be watered below the place where troops obtain their drinking-water, but above bathing and washing places. Patrolling by mounted men will often be necessary for some distance above the spot where the drinking-water is drawn.

13. If running water is not available, the supply must be very strictly protected, a rough barbed wire fence if procurable, being run round it to keep animals out. Animals should, in this case, be watered by bucket or nosebag ; and washing should be allowed only at some distance from the water supply, empty biscuit tins or other receptacles being used to draw water for this purpose.

Similar precautions are often necessary with running water, if other bodies of troops are halted lower down the stream.

14. If many animals have to be watered and the frontage is small, times should be laid down for each corps to water. Five minutes may be taken as the average time for watering an animal.

An officer will invariably accompany watering parties of more than 20 animals .

15. A field squadron carries 1 lift and force pump per troop and a field company 1 per section, with suction and delivery hose. A lift and force pump can supply 600 gallons an hour at a combined lift and force of 60 feet, with 4 men at work, but twice that amount with 2 or 3 men if the height to which the water is to be raised is small. The following gear is carried for tapping water mains:—Field squadron, 2 sets ; field company, 1 set.

CHAPTER III.

12. ORDERS.

(See F.S.R., Part I, Secs. 8–20.)

GENERAL RULES REGARDING THE PREPARATION AND DESPATCH OF
ORDERS, REPORTS AND MESSAGES.

1. Communications in the field may be verbal or written, according to circumstances. The following general rules should be observed :—

(a) Orders issued by the higher commanders and reports will normally be prepared in writing. When issued verbally their substance should be recorded in writing by the recipient or his staff officer whenever it is practicable to do so. In war, verbal messages are often incorrectly delivered, especially in the excitement of an engagement.

(b) Orders and reports must be as concise as possible, consistent with clearness. They must be precise as regards time and place, the language should be simple and the handwriting easily legible. Anything of an indefinite or conditional nature such as " dawn," " dusk," " if possible," " should," is to be avoided.

(c) The hour of 12 will be followed by " noon " or " midnight " written in words.
A night will be described thus : Night 29/30 Sept. ; or Night 30 Sept./1 Oct.

(d) Names of places and persons will be written in block capitals, *e.g.*, LONDON or WELLINGTON. Names of places must be spelt exactly as given on the map in use. Only abbreviations about which there can be no doubt will be used.

(e) In naming units or formations from which a portion is excluded, the unit will be named and the words " less .... " appended, *e.g.*, 10th Hrs. less one sqn.

(f) If a map is referred to, the one used must be specified unless this is provided for in standing orders. The position of places will, as a rule, be denoted either by naming the map square, if any, on which they appear, or by the points of the compass, *e.g.*, " wood, 600 yards S.E. of TETSWORTH," or, when no points of reference are available, by actual compass bearings, *e.g.*, " hill, 1,500 yards true bearing 272° from CHOBHAM CHURCH," or by descriptions, *e.g.*, " cross roads ¼ mile S.W. of the second E in HASELEY," the letter indicated being underlined. A road is best indicated by the names of places on it, care being taken to name sufficient places to ensure that the road intended is followed. A position, whether occupied by hostile troops or not, will be described from right to left, looking in the direction of the enemy. The terms " right " and " left " are used in describing river banks, it being assumed that the writer is looking down stream. Except in the foregoing case, indefinite or ambiguous terms, such as right, left, before, beyond, front, on this side of, &c., must not be used, unless it is made clear to what force they refer.

(g) When bearings are given, they will invariably be true bearings, and this should be so stated. The variations of compasses must be checked before use.

(h) If the order, report or message refers to troops reaching a place at a certain time, it is assumed that the head of the main body is meant, unless otherwise stated.

(i) The writer, having finished his order or report, should read it through carefully at least once, and, if possible, get someone else to read it, in order to assure himself that it is clear, and, in the case of an order, that it is calculated to influence the recipient in the way only that it is intended.

(*k*) An order or report must be clearly signed, the rank of the sender, his appointment, and the force he is with being stated.

(*l*) A copy of all orders and messages sent will be kept by the sender, the copy and original being endorsed with the method and hour of issue or transmission, *e.g.*, " dictated to general staff officers of 1st and 2nd divisions at 11.20 a.m.," or " by signal to G.O.'s C. 2nd and 3rd cavalry brigades at 2.30 p.m."

2. Every precaution should be taken to assist the recipient of an order or report in grasping his instructions with a minimum of trouble and delay.

3. The authority who despatches a communication is responsible that proper steps are taken to ensure its safe and timely delivery. Important communications should be sent by more than one means, and acknowledgment of receipt should be obtained. Communications of a secret nature should usually be in cipher, but it must be remembered that enciphering and deciphering causes loss of time. One part of a message must not be enciphered and the remainder left in clear.

GENERAL ARRANGEMENT OF ORDERS.

4. The orders of a commander may be classified as follows :—

(*a*) Standing orders.
(*b*) Operation orders.
(*c*) Routine orders.

Special orders, such as " orders of the day," will occasionally be necessary and special instructions may be required in the case of detached forces, instead of operation orders.

5. Each class of order will be prepared and numbered separately. In the case of standing or routine orders the heading of the order should indicate the class to which it belongs.

6. It will usually be advisable to divide an order into numbered paragraphs.

STANDING ORDERS.

7. The object of standing orders is :—

(*a*) To adapt existing regulations to local conditions.
(*b*) To save frequent repetitions in operation and routine orders.

8. Unless carefully revised and kept up to date, standing orders may lead to misunderstanding. For this reason they should be confined to essentials, and added to as circumstances require.

9. The authority issuing standing orders is responsible that any alteration in them is notified to the troops, and that they are communicated to troops newly entering the command.

Repetition of existing regulations is to be avoided.

10. At least six copies of standing orders should be issued to each squadron, battery or company, and one to each officer.

OPERATION ORDERS.

11. Operation orders deal with all strategical and tactical operations, such as marches protection, occupation of quarters, reconnaissances, and battle. They include such information regarding supply, transport, ammunition, medical, and other services of maintenance, as it is necessary to publish to the troops ; but detailed orders for such services which it is not necessary for the troops to know, should be issued only to those directly concerned.

12. An operation order should contain just what a recipient requires to know and nothing more.

13. Definite rules as to the form in which operation orders should be drafted are not laid down. The object of an operation order is to bring about a course of action in accordance with the intentions of the commander, suited to the situation, and with full co-operation between all arms and units. So long as this object is fulfilled, the form of the order is of little importance.

Operation orders should, however, be arranged in logical sequence and should usually be framed on the following system :—

> The heading of the order will contain the name of the force to which it refers, the consecutive number of the order, the date, and, if necessary, the map to which references are made.
>
> For example :—
>
>
>
> 1st Division Order No. 23.
>
>
>
> Reference ¼″ Ordnance Map, No. 34.   10.3.11.

> The general situation should be given ; this will include such information about the enemy and other bodies of one's own troops as may affect the recipient of the order. If it is not desirable to mention the source, it should state the degree of credibility with which the issuer of the order regards the information.
> A brief summary of the intention of the officer issuing the orders, as far as it is advisable to make it known.
> After this should follow the necessary instructions for those to whom the order is issued. The actual arrangements of these paragraphs must vary with circumstances, but it should be clear, logical, and in order of importance, so that the chief essentials are brought to mind first.*
> Immediately above the signature should be stated the place to which reports are to be sent, and, when necessary, the position of the commander.
> . At the foot of the order, below the signature, should be noted the hour and mode of issue and the individuals to whom issued, as well as the number of the copy issued to each.

14. The information given regarding the enemy and other bodies of one's own troops should be strictly limited to what the recipients of the order require to know to assist them in carrying out their tasks.
Only so much of the intentions of the commander should be stated as it is really necessary for those to whom the order is issued to know for the purpose in view.
15. In the body of the order instructions to fighting troops should usually come first as being most important. Orders for supply, transport, medical, ammunition and other services should be limited, as defined in para. 11. Any necessary instructions as regards the maintenance of communication should be given.
16. The detail of troops, giving their order in the column of march or their allotment to sections of a position, will usually be given in the margin. If a separate commander is appointed, he should be left to arrange his own order of march. and the troops placed under his command will be named in order of seniority of arms and units. In allotting the rôles to the various units, the sequence for marches will usually be from front to rear, whilst in attack and defence. or outposts, it will be from right to left looking in the direction of the enemy.
If any portion of the force is to be detached for protective or other duties, its commander will, if possible, be named in the order.
17. Subordinate commanders in framing their orders will only embody so much of their superior's orders as is necessary. The distribution by a commander to his subordinates of copies of operation orders received by him from higher authority can seldom be justified.
18. Superior orders must be issued in sufficient time to enable subordinate commanders in turn to frame and distribute their own orders. If detailed orders cannot be issued till late in the evening, great inconvenience will be prevented by the issue of a preliminary order giving the time of assembly or of starting, and the issue of the detailed orders next morning. The pre-

---

* Particular points that should be mentioned in operation orders dealing with marches outposts, &c., are given under these headings.

liminary order should state when and where the complete order will be issued.

ROUTINE ORDERS.

19. Routine orders are of precisely the same nature in war as in peace. They deal with all matters not concerned with operations, such as discipline, interior economy, &c.

They will usually be issued daily at fixed hours—the earlier the better, and when stationary, never later than noon. At these hours commanders will ordinarily send an officer to the headquarters of their immediate superior. The officer will not only receive orders, but will also be prepared to give any information regarding the command to which he belongs, which the superior may require. Watches will be compared on this occasion.

20. Routine orders not being of a confidential nature may be freely distributed.

ORDERS FOR ATTACK.

21. Orders for an attack will be framed in accordance with the rules laid down for Operation Orders, and whenever possible should be in writing.

22. The commander of a force and subordinate commanders will be guided by the following principles in framing orders for an attack :—

    (a) A definite objective or task should be assigned to each body of troops, the actual limits of frontage being specified as far as possible. Each body of troops thus assigned to a distinct tactical operation should be placed under one commander.

    (b) The direction of the attack to be made by each body of troops should be distinctly stated.

    (c) Most careful arrangements should be made to ensure that attacks intended to be simultaneous should be so in reality.

    (d) The choice of the manner in which the task assigned to each body of troops is to be performed should be left to its commander.

23. Each commander who issues orders should assemble his subordinate commanders, if possible, in view of the ground over which the attack is to take place, explain his orders, and satisfy himself that they thoroughly understand their respective tasks.

ORDERS FOR NIGHT ATTACKS AND NIGHT ADVANCES.

24. In framing orders for night operations, it may be necessary to deal with the following points in addition to those dealt with under " Operation Orders " and " Orders for Attack " :—

    (a) Time of assembly at, departure from, and description of the position of assembly.

    (b) Order of march, and formations on leaving the position of assembly. Distances and intervals. Maintenance of communication.

    (c) Compass bearing of the route.

    (d) Time and duration of halts.

    (e) If possible, the position of the deployment should be described, and its distance from the position of assembly and from the point selected for attack notified.

    (f) Formation to be adopted at the position of deployment.

    (g) Special instructions for the assault and the signal for it.

    (h) Short description of the ground to be crossed.

    (j) Description of the position to be assaulted.

    (k) Conduct of troops during the advance.

    (l) Action in case the enemy opens fire.

    (m) Action, after the position is captured, to resist counter attack.

    (n) Extent to which the captured position is to be fortified, and the detail of troops who are to perform this duty.

    (o) Action of reserves or neighbouring troops against positions likely to enfilade the captured position.

    (p) Distinctive marks and watchword.

    (q) Place of the commander at the position of assembly, during the march thence and at the position of deployment.

25. Until the troops reach the position of assembly, no more should be made known to them than is absolutely necessary.

ORDERS FOR MOVEMENTS BY RAIL.

26. The following points should be observed in drawing up orders for the despatch of troops by rail, in addition to those mentioned under operation orders :—

(a) Date and place of entraining, destination and railway route to be followed.

(b) Schedule of trains and allotment of troops, hour at which troops are to reach the entraining place, and if necessary, the road they are to use.

(c) Special instructions regarding wheeled transport to be taken by rail, entraining and detraining.

(d) Arrangements for feeding troops and watering animals *en route*.

(e) Places of assembly near entraining and detraining stations,

(f) Special instructions regarding detrainment or off-loading.

(g) Steps to secure detrainment from surprise.

13. INTERCOMMUNICATION.

(See F.S.R., Part I.)

RESPONSIBILITY FOR MAINTAINING COMMUNICATION.

1. The means of communication must be carefully organized in each command, for the possibility of co-operation largely depends on constant maintenance of communication between various parts of an army.

2. All subordinate commanders are responsible for keeping their respective superiors, as well as neighbouring commanders, regularly informed of the progress of events. All commanders must arrange for communication with and between, their subordinates ; the subordinates must see that they are provided with the necessary means and must improvise the best arrangements when necessary.

3. Commanders of brigades and of larger formations, of detachments and of any other body of troops when advisable, will establish a headquarters where messages can be received and acted on even during their temporary absence, and will notify its position to all concerned. If a commander intends to leave his headquarters for any length of time, he should detail an officer to act for him in his absence.

4. All ranks are responsible for doing everything in their power to keep the means of communication intact.

5. Means of communication should not be used so as to cripple the initiative of subordinates by unnecessary interference.

Commanders in districts through which telegraph or telephone lines pass are responsible for their protection and the prevention of " tapping."

SERVICE OF INTERCOMMUNICATION.

6. The service of intercommunication is carried out by—

i. The units of the Army Signal Service.

ii. Intercommunication personnel forming part of other units.

iii. In India, telegraphs on the line of communication are worked by the Post and Telegraph Department, a civil department of the Government of India.

7. The units of the Army Signal Service are—

For a cavalry division	..	A signal squadron.*
For a cavalry brigade	..	A signal troop.
For an infantry division	..	A signal company.
With army troops ..	..	Headquarters of a general headquarters signal company.* 1 or more headquarters of an army headquarters signal company.* 1 or more air-line signal sections.* 1 or more cable signal sections.* 1 or more wireless signal sections.*
On lines of communication ..		1 or more lines of communication signal companies.

* In India these units are not yet organized.

8. The personnel and equipment provided for intercommunication purposes, and the duties on which these units will normally be employed, are
as follows :—

Unit.	Allotted to.	Means of signal communication available with unit.	Normal duties of unit.
Signal squadron— "A" troop		2 wireless (wagon) stations.	Intercommunication between cavalry divisional headquarters and general headquarters.
"B" troop	Cavalry division	2 cable detachments, having 28 miles of cable and 8 vibrator offices.	To keep divisional headquarters in touch with wireless stations serving it, or with the permanent telegraph system of the country; also can be used for general intercommunication within the division.
"C" troop		1 wireless (wagon) station. 3 wireless (pack) stations.	Intercommunication between divisional headquarters and brigades or reconnoitring detachments.
"D" troop		12 mounted men ... 28 bicyclists ... 6 motor cyclists ... 2 motor cars ...	For visual signalling and despatch riding purposes in conjunction with other means of intercommunication.
Signal troop with cavalry brigade (cavalry division).	Cavalry brigade	11 mounted men... 6 bicyclists... 3 motor cyclists ... 7½ miles of cable 8 portable telephones.	For visual signalling and despatch riding as required. For use when the brigade is at rest or employed in dismounted action, also for connecting with permanent lines in the theatre of operations.*
Signal troop with a cavalry brigade not allotted to a cavalry division.	Cavalry brigade not allotted to a cavalry division.	11 mounted men ... 6 bicyclists ... 3 motor cyclists ... 7½ miles of cable ... 8 portable telephones.	As for signal troop with cavalry brigade (cavalry division).
Divisional signal company Headquarters and No. 1 section.	A division.	2 wireless (pack) stations.	For intercommunication with general and cavalry divisional headquarters.
		3 cable detachments having 30 miles of cable and 9 vibrator offices.	For intercommunication within the division, or as required.
		4 mounted men 8 bicyclists ... 9 motor cyclists	For visual signalling or despatch riding in conjunction with, or alternative to, the cable communication.

* The signallers and despatch riders of the troop will lay and operate the
telephone lines when used. A separate telephone detachment is not
provided.

Unit.	Allotted to	Means of signal communication available with unit.	Normal duties of unit
Nos. 2, 3, and 4 sections.		Each section has 2 telephone detachments, having in all 8 miles of cable and 10 portable telephones.	For intercommunication within the infantry brigades, or between them and the artillery.
		8 bicyclists ...	For visual signalling or despatch riding as required.
A general headquarters signal company.		The headquarters contains 24 motor cyclists.	The company is completed by the addition of such air-line, cable and wireless sections as may be necessary for intercommunication between general headquarters and cavalry and army corps headquarters and headquarters of independent divisions or other forces.*
An army corps headquarters signal company.		The headquarters contains 18 motor cyclists.	The company is completed by the addition of such air-line and cable sections as may be necessary for intercommunication between army corps headquarters and the divisions, &c., composing the army corps.*
An air-line section.	Distributed to General and Army Corps Headquarters as may be required.	2 detachments, each of 1 air line wagon, with 5 miles of air-line and 1 second class office, and 1 light spring wagon, equipped with another second class office. The unit provides material for erection of 20 miles of air-line, instruments and operators for 4 second class offices, and linemen for the maintenance of 40 miles of line : it can also provide material, but no additional personnel, for laying 8 miles of cable, and instruments for 2 third class (vibrator) offices.	

* These units may also be required to link up general and army corps headquarters with the lines of communication signal system.

Unit.	Allotted to.	Means of signal communication available with unit.	Normal duties of unit.
A cable section		2 detachments, each with 1 cable wagon, and material for laying down and working a line of cable 10 miles long. Each line is equipped with 1 stationary office for the starting point and 1 movable office in the cable wagon. 2 additional stationary offices are carried in the R.E. limbered wagons.	
A wireless section.		3 wireless (wagon) stations.	
Signal company (lines of communication).	Head-quarters I.G.C.	Establishment and equipment may have to be varied to suit local conditions. Includes personnel to form nucleus of a signal clearing house on a L. of C.	For providing the army signal system within the limits of command of the I.G.C.

9. The intercommunication personnel, telephone equipment, and bicycles maintained in units other than Army Signal units are as follows :—

Unit*	Personnel.		Bicycles. (e)
Headquarters cavalry divisional artillery	7 rank and file (a)	..	3
Headquarters divisonal artillery ..	7 ,, (a)	..	2
Headquarters divisional engineers ..	.. ..	..	1
Cavalry regiment	{ 1 serjeant 14 rank and file (b) 27 rank and file (g)	..	} 15
Cavalry squadron with Division {	3 rank and file (b) 9 ,, (g)	..	4
A squadron of Irish Horse	6 rank and file (f)	..	8
Horse artillery brigade—			
Headquarters	9 rank and file (c), (d) ..		3
Battery	7 ,, (h)	..	3
Ammunition column ..	3 ,, (g)	..	3
Horse artillery battery* ..	9 ,, (c)	..	3
Ammunition column* ..	3 ,, (g)	..	1
Field artillery brigade—			
Headquarters	12 ,, (c), (d) ..		1
Battery	7 ,, (h)	..	1
Ammunition column	5 ,, (g)	..	1

* For a Cavalry Brigade not allotted to a Cavalry Division.

Unit.	Personnel.	Bicycles. (e)
Field artillery (howitzer) brigade—		
Headquarters	12 rank and file (c), (d) ..	1
Battery	7 ,, (h) ..	1
Ammunition Column	3 ,, (g) ..	1
Heavy artillery battery ..	8 ,, (c), (d) ..	1
Divisional ammunition column ..	6 ,, (g) ..	6
Field squadron	15 ,, (g) ..	..
Field troop	3 ,, (g) ..	..
Field company..	3 ,, (g) ..	1
Bridging train	.. .. ..	1
Infantry battalion	{ 1 serjeant .. 16 rank and file (b) .. 36 ,, (g) .. }	} 9
Divisional train	.. .. ..	2
Army troops train	.. .. ..	2
Cavalry field ambulance	4 rank and file (g) ..	2
Field ambulance	6 ,, (g) ..	1

(a) Includes 4 trained signallers.
(b) Trained signallers.
(c) Trained in signalling and telephonist's duties.
(d) Does not include drivers for telephone wagon.
(e) Provided for despatch riding and use of signallers as required.
(f) Despatch riders.
(g) Trained in semaphore signalling.
(h) Trained in semaphore signalling and telephonist's duties.

10. TELEPHONE EQUIPMENT.

	Telephones, Portable, D, Mk. II.	Cable, miles.	Remarks.
Horse Arty. Bde.—			
Headquarters .. .. {	4	4	Carried on wagons.
	..	$\frac{1}{3}$	Carried by mounted men.
Battery .. .. {	4	$\frac{5}{6}$	Carried by mounted men.
	..	1	Carried on wagons.
Horse Arty. Battery, with Cavalry Brigade not allotted to a Cavalry Division {	4	$\frac{3}{6}$	Carried by mounted men.
	..	1	Carried on wagons.
Field Arty. (gun or howitzer) Bde. :—			
Headquarters .. .. {	6	6	Carried on wagons.
	..	$\frac{1}{2}$	Carried on mounted men.
Battery .. .. {	4	$\frac{5}{6}$	Carried by mounted men.
	..	1	Carried on wagons.
Heavy Arty. :—			
Battery .. .. {	6	6	Carried on wagons.
	..	$\frac{1}{2}$	Carried by mounted men.
$\frac{1}{2}$ Battery .. .. {	4	$\frac{5}{6}$	Carried by mounted men.
	..	1	Carried on wagons.

11. *Administration of the Army Signal Service in war.*—The Army Signal Service is administered by the Director of Army Signals, who will have representatives at the following headquarters:—

At headquarters of Inspector-General of Communications	A Deputy Director of Army Signals.
At headquarters of an army	An officer i/c Army Signals.
At headquarters of a cavalry division	The Officer Commanding Signal Squadron.
At headquarters of a division ..	The Officer Commanding Signal Company.
At headquarters of a cavalry brigade not allotted to a cavalry division	The Officer Commanding Signal Troop.

12. Capabilities of methods of intercommunication employed by field units.

Field air-line.—Air-line is a bare wire erected on light poles. A detachment of 12 N.C.Os. and men should be able to erect at least 5 miles of line and do an average day's march.

Field cable.—Field cable is an insulated wire laid along the ground. A detachment of 8 N.C.Os. and men (including operators) can lay the cable at the rate of 1 to 6 miles per hour, depending on the nature of the country and for how long the cable is to remain down.

Wireless stations.—A wagon wireless station can maintain communication with another similar station at a maximum distance of 60 to 80 miles, and with a pack wireless station about 30 miles.

Two pack wireless stations can maintain communication with each other at a maximum distance of 20 to 30 miles.

Visual signalling.—Visual signalling is carried out by heliograph, flag, disc or lamp.

The range of visual signalling depends upon the nature of the country and state of the atmosphere.

A rough guide in suitable weather is :—

Heliograph.—In practice the limitation is the intervisibility of stations.
Flags.—3 to 7 miles.
Lamp.—Limelight, 10 to 15 miles.
       Begbie, 5 to 8 miles.

Despatch riding.—Horses, bicycles, motor cycles and motor cars may be used, the rate of travel depending on the nature of the roads and their freedom from traffic.

SIGNAL TRAFFIC IN THE FIELD.

13. No communication is to be sent by signal* or despatch rider when transmission by post would serve the purpose.

14. Signal messages are despatched in the order in which they are handed in, except that messages of special importance will be given precedence, if authorized by an officer who has power to do so. The order of precedence of messages is indicated to telegraphists and signallers by the " Prefix " which is written on each message at the " Office of origin."

15. The following is a list of the prefixes employed in all branches of the signal service :—

---

* The term signal includes telegraphs, telephones, and balloon or visual signals.

Messages to be Delivered at Receiving Station.	Messages to be Transmitted at Receiving Station.	Class.
D S ..	D X ..	Signal Service messages requiring immediate attention. (To be marked "Urgent Signal.")
S A ..	X A ..	Military Railway Service messages requiring immediate attention. (To be marked "Urgent Railway.")
S B ..	X B ..	Messages "O.H.M.S." marked "Priority."
S G ..	X G ..	Signal Service Messages.
S M ..	X M ..	Messages "O.H.M.S." not marked "Priority."
S	X	Private messages ⎫ Equal as
S R P ..	X R P ..	Reply paid messages ⎬ regards
S P ..	X P ..	Press messages ⎭ precedence.

16. Officers in charge of the signal arrangements are alone empowered to send "Signal Service messages requiring immediate attention." They should never do so unless such a course is absolutely necessary. Authority will be deputed to certain officers to send "Military railway messages requiring immediate attention."

17. No one but the commander on the spot, or an officer expressly authorized by him, is to frank a message, "Priority." Authority to frank a message will be sparingly delegated, and the number of "Priority" messages must be kept at a minimum. The names of officers having this authority will be supplied to the local signal stations and published in local orders. In these cases, the officer who authorizes the message will write the words "Urgent Signal," "Urgent Railway" or "Priority" as the case may be, in space Z, which must be signed.

In urgent circumstances any officer may send "Priority" messages but he will be held responsible that the urgency is sufficient to warrant such action.

18. Messages other than those referred to in the preceding para. must be franked by one of the following officers :—

(a) A commander.
(b) An officer of the staff.
(c) The head or representative of an administrative service or department.
(d) An officer holding a special appointment.

In the case of " Press Messages " special instructions will be issued.

19. A message in course of transmission will never be interrupted, if this can possibly be avoided. Telegraphists and signallers will use their discretion in stopping work on a message in order to deal with one of a higher prefix, taking the following points into consideration, viz. :—the lengths of the messages, their importance, and how near they are to the end of the message ; press and private messages must never be allowed to delay messages O.H.M.S. This applies to a message that is being received as well as to one being sent.

20. Officers only will be permitted to send messages in code or cipher, which must always bear their signature, rank and appointment.

21. Special arrangements will be made by the General Staff regulating the censorship and despatch of private or press messages. They will not be accepted unless the opening of the station for that purpose has been duly authorized and notified.

22. All signal stations should be in possession of copies of the following :—

(a) Order giving the names of officers entitled to send "Priority" messages, with any amendments, which may have been published.
(b) Order prohibiting unauthorized persons (officers or otherwise) loitering in the vicinity of stations.
(c) Order requiring all messages to be either written or dictated, and to bear the signature of the addressor or his deputy.

MESSAGES.

23. Messages intended for general headquarters, the headquarters of units or formations, or for administrative commanders or their representatives, will be addressed by the title of the unit or formation or administrative commander in an abbreviated form.

For this purpose the following abbreviations will be used and no others will be recognized :—

Full title.	Authorized abbreviation.
General headquarters	G.H.Q.
Headquarters, 1st (2nd, etc.) Army Corps ..	First (Second, etc.) Corps.
„ 1st (2nd, etc.) Division ..	First (Second, etc.) Div.
„ 1st (2nd, etc.) Cavalry Brigade	First (Second, etc.) Cav. Bde.
„ 1st (2nd, etc.) Infantry Brigade	First (Second, etc.) Inf. Bde.
„ 1st (2nd, etc.) Field Artillery Brigade	First (Second, etc.) F.A. Bde.
„ unit	Army List abbreviation of unit
„ Royal Flying Corps	Aeronautics
Inspector-General of Communications ..	Communications
Director of Army Signals	Signals
„ Supplies	Supplies
„ Ordnance Services	Ordnance
„ Transport	Transport
„ Railway	Railways
„ Works	Works
„ Remounts	Remounts
„ Veterinary Services	Vet.
„ Medical Services	Medical
„ Postal Services	Postal
Deputy Judge Advocate-General	Advocate
Principal Chaplain	Chaplain
Provost Marshal	Provost

The address will be followed, if necessary, by the name of the place to which the message is to be sent.

The foregoing abbreviations will similarly be used at the end of messages to indicate the authority from which they emanate.

24. After the address the number of the sender's message will be given followed by the day of the month.

If the message is in reply to or has reference to a message from the addressee the number of that message will then be quoted. The text of the message will come next. The message will end with the abbreviated title of the sender's unit or appointment, as in para. 23 above, followed by the place and time of despatch.

When the message is complete it will be signed, the rank, appointment and force being stated, in the right-hand bottom corner. If the message is despatched by signal this signature is not transmitted, but is the authority for despatch.

25. Messages will be written, whenever possible, on Army Form C 2121, which is provided with spaces for the particulars prescribed in the foregoing paragraphs.

26. If a signal message is to be delivered to more than one addressee it facilitates despatch if separate copies for each addressee should be handed into the signal office.

27. When the sender desires to inform different addressees that an order has been circulated, he will add this information at the end of the text of the message, thus—

Addressed (the unit or units to which the order is sent). Repeated (the units who are to be informed that above order is being given). When information has been sent to another unit the message will contain, at the end of the text—" (unit) informed."

28. In signal messages important numbers should be written in words. The use of Roman numerals in signal messages is forbidden. Complicated phrases are to be avoided. The letters AAA should be used for a full stop : the word " stop " should not be used to indicate punctuation as it may affect the sense of the message. Other ordinary signs of punctuation, inverted commas, brackets &c., can be signalled, and when used should be clearly shown in the message. Messages must be as short as possible consistent with clearness.

When letter ciphers or important words such as " not " are used they should be written in block letters, letter ciphers being arranged in groups of 5 letters.

29. The following special instructions apply to messages transmitted by wireless :—

i. Nearly all messages sent by wireless are from and to the headquarters to which the wireless stations are respectively attached. In these cases the addresses as written are not signalled, the station call signs taking their place. The message handed in by the signal service at the receiving end will, however, show the headquarters to and from which it is addressed and the time the message was written.

ii. When a message for transmission by wireless is to or from an address other than a headquarters to which a wireless station is attached, such address will, subject to the following sub-paragraph, be enciphered by the signal service at the transmitting end and deciphered by the signal service at the receiving end.

iii. An officer who drafts a message for transmission by wireless will complete the address to and address from, and will also state *in the body* of the message the place where it was written.

iv. Neither addresses "to" and "from" nor messages themselves are ever to be signalled in clear without the express order of the officer responsible for drafting the message.

The officer giving such order is to write the words "in clear" and put his initials on the message form in the space for " franking officer."

v. "Sender's number," "Day of month," "In reply to No." are never to be enciphered and will be signalled as written.

vi. All message forms and papers on which any work of enciphering or deciphering has been done will be burnt immediately the work is finished.

30.—SIGNALLING CODES.

Morse Alphabet.

A	.-		N	-.
B	-...		O	---
C	-.-.		P	.--.
D	-..		Q	--.-
E	.		R	.-.
F	..-.		S	...
G	--.		T	-
H	....		U	..-
I	..		V	...-
J	.---		W	.--
K	-.-		X	-..-
L	.-..		Y	-.--
M	--		Z	--..

NOTE.—There are certain technical differences in India, but these do not prevent signallers trained on the Indian system from working with those trained on the Home system

Numerals.

1 ▪ ▬ ▬		6 ▬ ▪ ▪ ▪ ▪
2 ▪ ▪ ▬ ▬		7 ▬ ▬ ▪ ▪ ▪
3 ▪ ▪ ▪ ▬ ▬		8 ▬ ▬ ▬ ▪ ▪
4 ▪ ▪ ▪ ▪ ▬		9 ▬ ▬ ▬ ▬ ▪
5 ▪		0 ▬

Long Numerals.*

1 ▪ ▬ ▬ ▬ ▬ .		6 ▬ ▬ ▪ ▪ ▪ ▪
2 ▪ ▪ ▬ ▬ ▬		7 ▬ ▬ ▬ ▪ ▪ ▪
3 ▪ ▪ ▪ ▬ ▬		8 ▬ ▬ ▬ ▬ ▪ ▪
4 ▪ ▪ ▪ ▪ ▬		9 ▬ ▬ ▬ ▬ ▬ ▪
5 ▪ ▪ ▪ ▪ ▪		0 ▬ ▬ ▬ ▬ ▬

Special Signals.

	Morse.	Semaphore.	
Full stop	▪ ▬ ▪ ▬ ▪ ▬	A A A	
Inverted commas	▪ ▬ ▬ ▪ ▪ ▬ ▬ ▪	R R	
Parenthesis or Brackets }	▬ ▪ ▬ ▬ ▪ ▬	K K	
Underline	▪ ▪ ▬ ▬ ▪ ▬	U K	
Oblique stroke	▪ ▬ ▬ ▪ ▬	L T	
Horizontal bar	▪ ▬ ▬ ▪ ▪ ▬ ▬	N R	⎧ Used to separate
Hyphen	▬ ▪ ▪ ▪ ▪ ▬	N V	⎪ the Sender's
Break	▬ ▪ ▪ ▪ ▬	i i	⎨ number, Date,
A A A	▪ ▬ ▬ ▪ ▬ ▪ ▬	A A A	⎪ and in reply to
			⎪ Number, from
			⎩ the text of a message.

31. Certain of the numerals have the same symbols as some of the letters of the alphabet. In order to distinguish between these, before signalling a numeral or group of numerals, the signal FI (figures intended) will be sent. For the same reason, on the conclusion of the numerals and before resuming letters, the signal FF (figures finished) will be sent.

32. When signalling words the context is, as a rule, a guide that the letters have been correctly read; but this is not the case with figures, and consequently it is necessary that they be verified. This is done by the " check," in which the figures 1 to 9 are denoted by the first nine letters of the alphabet, and 0 is denoted by K, thus :—

A for 1		F for 6
B „ 2		G „ 7
C „ 3		H „ 8
D „ 4		I „ 9
E „ 5		K „ 0

On receiving a group of numerals the corresponding letters are signalled back.

For example, 1 is checked by A.
12	„	„	AB.
123	„	„	ABC.
4210	„	„	DBAK.

33. In signalling (except when using the Semaphore system) each word or group is acknowledged before sending the next; with certain exceptions (as in the case of the numerals) the " general answer," i.e., one dash, is employed for this purpose.

---

* Long numerals are used when working with the Royal Navy, and in telegraphy.

34. SEMAPHORE ALPHABET, NUMERALS AND SPECIAL SIGNS.

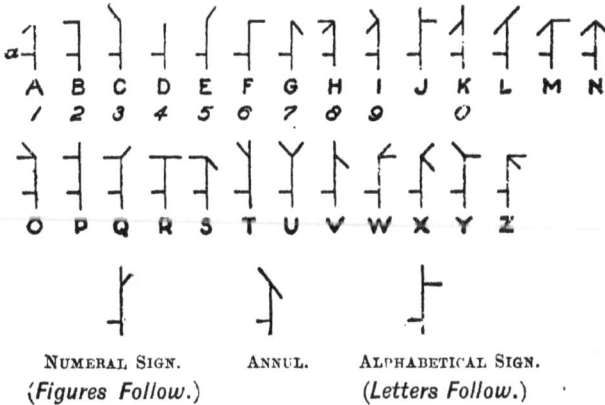

NUMERAL SIGN.   ANNUL.   ALPHABETICAL SIGN.

(*Figures Follow.*)   (*Letters Follow.*)

The small arm at *a* is called the "Indicator," and shows the side from which the Alphabet or signs commence ; the signaller, when working a fixed semaphore, is sometimes not visible, and the indicator is necessary because his back may be toward the reader. It also often happens on board ship that a semaphore signal is being read from both sides at the same time, and unless the indicator was used the reverse letters might be read, *e.g.*, K for V.

INTERCOMMUNICATION BETWEEN ARMY AND NAVY.

35. *Special signals for opening communication.*—Two special signals are established for distinguishing intercommunication between the two services when wishing to call one another up, viz. :—

(*a*) *By day.*—The "Naval and Military Pendant," which is white with 2 black crosses as shown below. This is always to be used by H.M. ships wishing to communicate with a shore station, or by a shore station equipped with a flagstaff and possessing this pendant, wishing to attract the attention of one of H.M. ships.

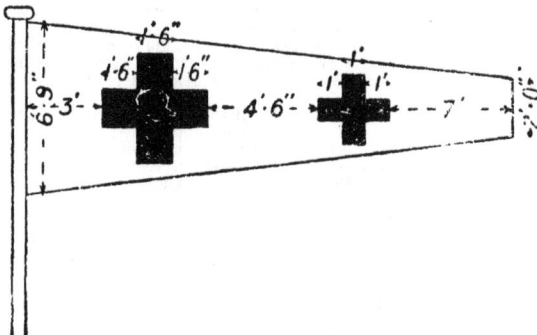

NAVAL AND MILITARY PENDANT.

The above must not be confused with the "Negative Flag," sometimes used by H.M. ships between themselves. The latter is a white square flag with five "black crosses on it."

(b) *By night or by day.*—The "Military Sign," which is the letter X made either by Morse or Semaphore. This sign is invariably to be used at night, and during daylight by stations which have no flagstaff or military pendant available.

14. INFORMATION.

(*See* F.S.R., Part I, Chap. VI.)

1. Timely information regarding the enemy's dispositions and the topographical features of the theatre of operations is an essential factor of success in war.

Information 's acquired principally by :—

(a) Reconnaissance.
(b) Examination of inhabitants, prisoners, deserters or papers
(c) Intercepting messages.
(d) Secret service.

Of these, reconnaissance is of most importance.

RECONNAISSANCE.

2. Reconnaissance is the service of obtaining information with regard to :—

(a) The topographical features and resources of a country.
(b) The movements and dispositions of an enemy.

In the latter case it may be strategical, tactical or protective.

Strategical reconnaissance is required before the opposing armies are within striking distance, to locate the hostile columns, and ascertain their strength and direction of march.

Tactical reconnaissance is required when two forces are within striking distance, to discover the tactical dispositions of the opposing force.

It is one of the most important duties of the protective cavalry, supported by the advanced guards of columns and sometimes by additional infantry and artillery.

3. While the advanced troops are engaged with the enemy, information may also be obtained :—

(a) By personal observation on the part of a commander.
(b) By general staff and other officers, patrols or scouts.
(c) By the air service.

4. Information may be gained by personal observation of the enemy ; by questioning the inhabitants, prisoners and others ; by reading signs, such as tracks, dust. fires, deserted camp-grounds, uniforms : or by tapping telegraph wires, taking letters and newspapers from post offices, telegrams and telegraph registers from telegraph offices, registers of despatches from railway stations, &c.

5. In questioning prisoners, or hostile inhabitants, it is well to take them separately out of hearing of others, to let them suppose that a great deal more is known by the questioner about the enemy than possibly is the case, and that questions are being put merely with a view to seeing whether they are speaking the truth or not, the answers being known. The examination should, if possible, be carried out by more than one person.

6. People not accustomed to seeing large numbers of troops are very apt to exaggerate their strength, a point which a scout should be careful to avoid. Information as to the uniforms of the enemy, number of regiment on the buttons or badges, &c., may be of great use.

A scout should know what are the usual formations of the enemy, and what are the usual strengths of his different organizations of troops.

7. If troops are moving along a road or defile, they may be timed while passing a certain point. For each minute, the following numbers would approximately go past :—

```
Cavalry, in sections, at a walk    ..    ..    ..    ..    120
    ,,         ,,      at a trot    ..    ..    ..    ..    240
Artillery, guns or wagons, at a walk ..    ..    ..    ..      5
    ,,         ,,      at a trot ..    ..    ..    ..     10
Infantry, in fours    ..    ..    ..    ..    ..    ..    200
```

8. The following signs should be noticed as affording information :—

(a) *Clouds of dust* show movements of troops or baggage, or cattle, &c. Cavalry raise a high light cloud. Infantry and vehicles a lower denser cloud. Motors, moving rapidly, a thick, high and continuous cloud. In some countries, it is customary to set fire to grass or bush so that the smoke may hide the dust of a movement.

(b) *Fires.*—In many countries it is customary to light signal fires, to send up a flare by night, or puffs of smoke by day. This latter is done by lighting a damp fire, and alternately covering it with a blanket and uncovering it.

The enemy's bivouac fires should be located, and counted in the evening or early morning. It is a common practice to light dummy fires to deceive the enemy's scouts.

(c) *Tracks.*—Much information can be gained by a good tracker from observing tracks on the ground.

Tracks give warning of enemy's patrols being about ; show the formation, direction and speed of his force, and almost the hour when the force passed by, by the marks of the feet, hoofs, wheels, &c.

(d) *Sounds.*—Since much of a scout's work has to be done at night, it is necessary that he should not fail to make every use of his senses of hearing and of smell, as well as of sight. Sound travels at the rate of about 380 yards per second. Four beats of the pulse to 1,000 yards is a fair rough calculation.

The sound of the explosion overtakes the modern pointed bullet at about 2,000 yards. A double report is heard when the bullet is fired by some one exactly facing the hearer.

9. In Egypt, Africa, India, &c., heat vapour often causes curious effects on the appearance of open country, lakes appear where there is no water, trees look like mountains, cattle like cavalry, and so on. These are very liable to deceive a scout who is not accustomed to them.

RECONNAISSANCE REPORTS.

10. To obtain satisfactory results it is essential that the reconnoitring officer should be given a clearly defined task, which should be within his powers to perform.

11. In drawing up his report the reconnoitring officer should be as concise as possible and should be careful to confine his information to what is relevant.

The most satisfactory method is to divide the report into two parts. The first part should contain a general description of the outstanding features of the reconnaissance, to enable the reader to get a grasp of the subject without having to wade through a mass of detail. The second part should contain the details in tabular form. For the same nature of reconnaissance (road report, river report, &c.) the headings in Part II should usually be the same : those in Part I, however, should be varied according to the tactical object of the reconnaissance. The disadvantages of a cut and dried form are counterbalanced by the greater ease with which items of information can be turned up or reports collated.

Care should be taken to distinguish between what are impressions or hearsay only, and what are facts

It is important to know the time of year when a reconnaissance is made.

12. Where the names of foreign places or towns are spelt in various ways, the anglicised form should be used, followed by the local form in brackets.

ROAD RECONNAISSANCE.

13. The information should supplement that given on maps, not merely repeating what is already shown, and it should be definite, *e.g.*, it is not enough to know that animals can be watered in a stream, but the numbers for which there is room, its depth, &c., must be given.

14. *Tactical information.*—Definite information is specially important when tactical questions are dealt with. Thus it is not sufficient to say that a certain ridge forms a defensive position. Information on the following is usually required : limits of the position and force required to hold it ; nature of ground in front and flanks, and of soil for digging ; localities which would form strong defensive points, artillery positions, own and enemy's ; what the view is like, points from which an extended view is obtainable and the average field of fire ; best lines of attack and counter-attack ; communications and water.

In order to make a good tactical reconnaissance it is advisable, before starting, to find out with what " special idea " the reconnaissance is to be undertaken.

15. *Road details.*—Roads with 14 feet or more of actual metalling or paving are classified as first class ; with less than 14 feet of metalling as second class. The surface condition and materials for repair should be mentioned. The ease with which troops can deploy from them is important. The nature of the fences or ditches enclosing the road should be mentioned.

Gradients.—Only such gradients should be mentioned as will affect the rate of marching.

16. *Bridges.*—It is not necessary to give details of every culvert, but bridges of any importance should be fully reported on. It is important to know if a bridge will bear mechanical transport. The type of bridge, material, length, width, height above ground or water, parapet and approaches should be noted.

17. *Turnings.*—Mention turnings only when they present some difficulty, *e.g.*, through a town where the names of the streets should be given.

18. *Observation points.*—Places from which a view can be obtained should be noted, with the direction and extent. The names of distant objects that can be identified should be mentioned, such as churches, country houses, &c.

19. *Local administration.*—System of local administration should be noted ; the identity of any individual who does all the work or wields all the power should be established.

20. *Supplies.*—For a thorough report on a district an expert is almost essential, but much useful information can be obtained by the non-expert without going into too great detail. Enquiries in the towns will produce better results in a shorter time than visiting a large number of farms.

In the former seek for flour mills and find out the normal amount of grain kept in stock. From the butchers ascertain if the locality is self-supporting, or if much frozen meat is brought in. For groceries find out the biggest firms and ascertain at what intervals of time stocks are renewed ; the date of the last order will show how long present stocks will last. Find out how many rations of tea expressed in ½ oz. and of sugar in 4 ozs. he has in hand ; the lower number of the two divided by the number of days the stock is estimated to last will give the approximate number of customers. This enables number of grocery rations obtainable to be estimated, as other groceries are usually present in sufficient quantities. The names of firms who sell petrol should be noted, stating amount of stock, quality of petrol, size of tins and price. For further notes on supplies *see* pp. 160, 162.

21.—*Headings for Part II :*—

Place.	Distance in Miles.		Details of Road.	Remarks.
	Intermediate.	From		

RIVER RECONNAISSANCE.

21. Owing to the variety of tactical uses to which a river may be put, the particular object of the reconnaissance should be ascertained before starting, and the report drawn up accordingly.

The headings in Part I will vary according to the tactical object; those in Part II, which contain nothing but facts about the river, need not vary.

22. The velocity of a river can be found by throwing a piece of wood well out and timing it over a measured number of feet. Mean velocity = $\frac{4}{5}$ surface velocity; $\frac{7}{10}$ mean velocity in feet per second = number of miles per hour.

23. Ice 3 inches thick will bear men in small detachments; 6 inches thick horses and carts; 9 to 12 inches thick, wagons and guns.

24.—*Headings for Part II:—*

Crossing.	Details.	Fit for Mechanical Transport.	River.			Quays.		Boats and barges usually available.	Approaches.		Remarks.
			Breadth yds.	Depth ft.	Velocity m. per hr.	Right bank.	Left bank.		Right bank.	Left bank.	

RAILWAY RECONNAISSANCE.

25. It should be borne in mind that an expert would be required to write an adequate report on which to work a railway.

26. *Stations.*—In ordinary circumstances a rough sketch of the stations on which the following information was shown, would suffice:—The approaches; number of lines; cross-overs; number, length, breadth and height of platforms; number and length of sidings; water turn-tables; end-loading and other ramps; goods sheds, lighting.

27. *Forming-up places.*—Places suitable for forming up troops before entraining or after detraining, with their area, approaches, water supply, &c., should be reported.

28. *Track.*—As regards the line itself, the gauge, any unusual gradients, type of fuel used, any triangles, and details of any bridges of importance, should be noted. In case of a single line the distance between crossing places.

BILLETING RECONNAISSANCE.

29. In reconnoitring areas for billeting purposes the population of the town, village or parish, whichever is available, must be taken as the basis of calculation. In addition to estimating the number of men per inhabitant that can be accommodated, the number of vehicles per inhabitant should also be given.

30. Billets without subsistence can be provided at varying rates.

The best class of village in a rich agricultural district will take up to 10 men per inhabitant; a residential town or village with good houses and wide streets about 5 men per inhabitant; while industrial towns with a dense population and a poor type of house will take still fewer. As regards horses a good agricultural village in Europe will provide accommodation for 3 horses per 4 inhabitants; this will entail using all barns, sheds and outhouses.

31. There are various questions affecting billeting, such as supplies, railways, &c., which should, as a rule, be treated generally in Part I of the report, details only being given when particularly required.

32. Particular care should be paid to giving details concerning the water supply, any large buildings, such as schools or country houses, which will accommodate a considerable number of troops, and any open spaces where troops can collect or vehicles be parked.

33. In many civilized countries chief officials of localities keep detailed lists showing billeting accommodation. Efforts should be made to obtain these lists.

34. In a billeting report based on the population of each parish, the small hamlets in each parish should be mentioned by name, as well as the parochial headquarters.

35. *Headings for Part II*:—

Name of Parish, Town or Village.	Pop.	Billets.			Nature of surrounding country.	Water Supply.	Railways.	P.O.		Supplies.	Remarks.
		Men.	4-horse vehicles.	6-horse vehicles.				Tel. O. Tph. O.			

HINTS FOR COMMANDERS OF PATROLS.

36. Make sure that you understand what you have to do, *i.e.*, how far you have to go, and what you are to look for. A patrol commander should, as far as possible, make up his mind beforehand what he will do in various circumstances.

37. Patrols are not sent out with the primary object of fighting. Therefore do not fight if you can gain your object without doing so, but remember that if you suddenly meet small parties of the enemy the assumption of a resolute offensive may be the best course of action.

38. Take precautions against surprise ; do not move or enter a village, copse, &c., in one compact body.

If your patrol is cut off, its members must make every effort to get away, so that at least one may arrive back with the information already gained. For this reason, every member of a patrol, while advancing in an enemy's country, must take notice of landmarks and distances as he goes along, so as to be able to find his way back. When advancing look behind you from time to time, so that the appearance of the country may be familiar to you.

39. When touch with the enemy is gained, do not be in too great a hurry to send back a man to report. Remember the number of messengers available is small and that as much information as possible must be conveyed by each man you send.

If the enemy is not found where he was expected, information to this effect should be sent back.

40. Avoid drawing attention to the movements of your patrol, *e.g.*, keep off the roads and in shadow as much as possible, cover up anything that will reflect the sun, avoid crest lines, &c.

Remember that to go and return by the same road may lead to being ambushed.

41. Do not halt all in one spot. Have men out watching the approaches. In the case of a mounted patrol the horses must not all be off-saddled at the same time.

42. In sending a written report think over what you want to send before commencing to write. Be accurate as regards your statements concerning places, hours, numbers. Do not waste time in writing a long story.

A verbal report should be as far as possible in the same form as a written report. Make your messenger repeat the message before he leaves.

RECONNAISSANCE OF A POSITION.

In the Attack.

43. In reconnoitring a position on which an attack is contemplated, definite information will rarely be obtained without fighting, except by special agents, since it will be necessary to drive in the enemy's covering troops. The troops engaged in this task will often have opportunities for acquiring information of value to the commander of the force and reconnoitring parties may be attached to them for this purpose. It will rarely be possible for one party to obtain all the information about a position which is wanted. Definite instructions should be issued by the commander of the force to each party employed on reconnaissance work.

44. In the future airships and aeroplanes may facilitate these reconnaissances ; but it must not be forgotten that the enemy will himself possess aircraft which must first be defeated and that aerial observers are liable to make mistakes, or to be misled by the enemy.

45. The following are the chief points on which information is desirable :—

(a) The general front of the position so far as it can be ascertained. The probability of advanced troops covering the real position will have to be considered.

(b) Points from which a good view of the country occupied by the enemy can be obtained.

(c) Localities to which the enemy is seen to be devoting attention, and any others which would appear likely to be of special tactical value to him. The position of any trenches, obstacles, &c., that can be located should be carefully noted.

(d) Lines which afford the attack most cover during their advance and which offer facilities for covering fire, both from guns and rifles, where it is exposed to hostile view and fire.

(e) Tactical points on the above lines of advance and elsewhere, the possession of which will favour the development of superiority of fire over portions of the enemy's position.

(f) The manner in which the flanks are secured, whether they rest on natural obstacles or whether there are any indications of supporting troops and works echeloned to the rear.

In the Defence.

46. When it is intended to occupy a defensive position, with a view to subsequent offensive action, the chief points to be noted are :—

(a) The extent of the position, the localities of special tactical importance in it and the means of securing the flanks.

(b) The minimum force necessary to occupy the position.

(c) The positions for the artillery and for the infantry firing lines. These should be considered together so that the best use of the ground may be made.

(d) The best line or lines for the counter-attack.

(e) The most favourable lines for the enemy to attack on, and positions from which his artillery can best support such attacks.

(f) Any tactical localities, the possession of which might enable the enemy to develop superiority of fire against some part of the position.

(g) Any advanced position, the occupation of which might have the effect of misleading the enemy and forcing him to a premature deployment.

15. PROTECTION.

(See F.S.R., Part I, Chap. V.)

1. Every commander is responsible for the protection of his command against surprise. A force can only be regarded as secure when protection is furnished in every direction from which attack is possible.

2. The commander of each protecting detachment, wherever situated, must keep his command in such readiness for action as the circumstances require.

In the absence of special orders a protective detachment is responsible that connection with the force protected is maintained. In the event of attack it must at any sacrifice gain time for the body which it protects to prepare to meet the attack.

3. Mounted troops are especially fitted for the service of protection on account of their mobility. Their duties when so employed may be grouped under three heads :—

    (*a*) Divisional duties.
    (*b*) General protective duties.
    (*c*) Special missions.

Mounted troops allotted to divisional duties usually form a permanent part of the division to which they belong. As a general principle a different body of troops should be detailed for general protective duties and for special missions, such grouping being varied by the C.-in-C. from time to time as the situation may demand.

4. Local protection on the march is afforded by *Advance, Rear* and *Flank Guards,* and when at rest by *Outposts.*

The strength of the Adv. Gd. of a force marching independently or covered by mounted troops only may vary from a fourth to an eighth of the whole force, and should be detailed as far as possible from a complete unit. It is divided into (*a*) Van Guard ; (*b*) Main Guard. As it has to reconnoitre and fight, it will usually be composed of all arms, the proportion of each depending chiefly on the character of the country. In an open country, the proportion of mounted troops and guns may be much greater than in a close or mountainous country.

The Adv. Gd. must protect the main body from the moment the march of the latter begins. It is the duty of the Adv. Gd. commander to decide the hour at which the Adv. Gd. will clear the starting point and the distance it will precede the main body.

OUTPOSTS.

5. Every body of troops when halted will be protected by outposts.

6. The duties of the outposts are :—

    (*a*) To provide protection against surprise.
    (*b*) In case of attack, to gain time for the commander of the force to put his plan of action into execution.

7. If an enemy is so continuously watched that he can make no movement without being observed, surprise will be impossible. The first duty, therefore, of the outposts is OBSERVATION OF THE ENEMY.

8. Should the enemy attack, he must be delayed until the commander of the main body has had time to carry out his plan of action and the enemy's troops must be prevented from approaching within effective field artillery range of the ground on which the main body will deploy. The second duty, therefore, is RESISTANCE.

Outpost troops will usually consist of cavalry or cyclists and infantry working in co-operation. The mounted troops will be responsible for the duties of observation at a distance from the outpost line ; the infantry for resistance and for their own immediate protection against surprise.

9. Three rules can be laid down as regards strength :—

    (*a*) Outpost duty is most exhausting. Not a man or horse more than is absolutely needed should be employed.
    (*b*) In enclosed country, the movements of troops being generally confined to the roads, it will usually be sufficient to hold the roads

by which the enemy may approach in strength, and to observe
the intervening country.
(c) The power of resistance of the outposts must be sufficient to delay
the enemy's attack until the main body has had time to get ready
to defend itself

THE OUTPOST COMMANDER.

The outpost commander should be told, before the force has halted :—

(a) What is known of the enemy, and of other bodies of our own troops.
(b) The intentions of the commander who appoints him, if the enemy
attacks.
(c) Where the force to be covered will halt.
(d) The general position to be occupied by the outpost troops under his
command, and if there are other outpost troops on his flanks the
limits of the line for which he is responsible.
(e) Detail of the troops allotted to him.
(f) The hour at which they will be relieved.
(g) Where reports are to be sent.

11. He will then give out such orders as are immediately necessary for
protection against surprise and will supplement this by detailed orders on the
following points :—
(a) Information of the enemy, and our own troops so far as they affect
the outposts.
(b) General line to be occupied by the outposts ; frontage, or number
of roads, allotted to each outpost company ; and situation of the
reserve.
(c) Disposition of the outpost mounted troops.
(d) Dispositions in case of attack. Generally the line of resistance
and the degree of resistance to be offered.
(e) Special arrangements by night.
(f) Smoking, lighting fires, and cooking.
(g) The hour at which the outposts will be relieved.
(h) His own position.

12. *Traffic through the outposts.*—No one other than troops on duty,
prisoners, deserters, and flags of truce will be allowed to pass through the
outposts, except with the authority of the commander who details the
outposts. Inhabitants with information will be blindfolded and detained at
the nearest piquet pending instructions, and their information sent to the
outpost commander. Only authorized commanders are allowed to speak to
persons presenting themselves at the outpost line. Prisoners and deserters
will be sent at once through the commander of the outpost company to
the outpost commander.
A flag of truce will be halted at a distance from the outpost line until
instructions are received from the commander of the outpost company.
If permitted to pass the outposts, the individuals must be blindfolded and
escorted to the outpost commander. If a letter or parcel is merely being
brought, the commander of the outpost company must instantly forward
it to headquarters, furnish a receipt and forthwith require the party to
depart. No conversation is to be allowed in the outpost line with the
bearers of a flag of truce.

DUTIES OF A COMMANDER OF AN OUTPOST COMPANY.

13. (a) Move his command to the ground covered by scouts.
(b) Halt under cover, holding a line in advance of the position for the
piquets.
(c) Examine the ground, decide on the number and position of the piquets,
and, if necessary, of detached posts, and the position of the support. Choose

the position primarily with a view to defence. The defensive line, corresponding if possible with piquet line, should support and be supported by adjoining companies.

(d) Move troops into position, withdraw covering troops and, if necessary, send out patrols. If advisable the patrols may be found from the supports.

(e) Give instructions to commanders of piquets and detached posts regarding action in case of attack, &c.

(f) Communicate with the companies on his flanks and ascertain their dispositions.

14. *Outpost squadrons* when employed follow the same principles as laid down for outpost companies.

Cossack posts are equivalent to sentry groups and consist of 3 to 6 men under a N.C.O. or senior soldier.

Vedettes take the place of sentries and should, as a rule, dismount.

When there is no danger of surprise feeding and watering should be carried out one-third at a time.

DUTIES OF A COMMANDER OF A PIQUET.

15. (a) Read orders to piquet, explain direction of enemy, position of support and of other piquets, action in case of attack by day or night, whether there is any cavalry in front.

(b) Tell off piquet and post sentry groups.

(c) Satisfy himself that group commanders know what is to be done with persons found entering or leaving the outpost line.

(d) Strengthen post as far as possible, make sanitary arrangements.

(e) Take ranges of important objects and lay out lines of fire.

(f) To avoid disturbing the men, arrange the piquet so that N.C.Os. and men of each relief of the various duties bivouac together.

(g) Not allow men to take off accoutrements by night. To avoid confusion in case of attack by night arrange that personnel lie head towards front and rifle at side.

16. *Sentries* are posted in groups, consisting of 3 to 8 men. Groups should be relieved every 8 or 12 hours. One or more sentries should be posted over the piquet to communicate with sentry groups and warn the piquet in case of attack.

A sentry must understand clearly :—

(a) The direction of the enemy.

(b) The situation of the sentries on his right and left.

(c) The situation of his piquet, of neighbouring piquets, and of any detached posts in the vicinity.

(d) The extent of ground and any special points he is to watch.

(e) How he is to deal with persons approaching his post.

(f) Whether any friendly patrols or scouts will return through his portion of the line and the signal by which they may be recognised.

(g) The names of villages, rivers, &c., in view ; and the places to which roads and railways lead.

17. *Detached posts* vary in strength from a section to a platoon according to the duty required of them. They are used to watch the flanks or places where the enemy might collect, but should not be employed except in case of necessity. They should act in the same manner as laid down for piquets.

18. *Outpost patrols* consist of 3 to 8 men under a N.C.O. They are sent out from the outposts to search the country in front of the outpost position or to watch the enemy if in close touch. They may consist of mounted men, cyclists or infantry. In normal circumstances a pair of *trained* scouts can perform this duty more efficiently than a strong patrol of men untrained in scout duties. By day, when cavalry or other mounted troops are attached to the outposts it will rarely be necessary to send out infantry patrols, unless the country is very close or the weather misty. By night the mounted troops will usually be withdrawn and infantry patrols will then be required.

19. *Standing patrols* consist of 2 to 8 mounted men or cyclists, under a N.C.O. sent well in advance to watch the principal approaches or points where the enemy might collect. Their positions are fixed and they are of special value at night. They are occasionally employed by infantry.

16. OVERSEA OPERATIONS.

(*See* F.S.R., Part I, Sec. 41, 42 and App. II.)

1. Oversea operations may be undertaken with a view to :—
(a) The establishment of a base for military operations either against the enemy's field armies or against a coast fortress.
(b) The establishment of a flying naval base.
(c) Raids against shipping, communications, &c.

2. Combined naval and military operations may be either offensive, when the navy assists the army in the capture of a fortress or locality near the sea, or when the navy secures and arranges the landing of a force in hostile territory ; or defensive, when for example, the navy secures the flanks of a position taken up by the army on an isthmus.

3. The success of oversea expeditions demands as a first postulate the command of the sea. In making use of this term it is not considered desirable to lay down any precise definition as to when this condition may be considered to have been obtained. It is sufficient to state that the naval situation will be such that the navy are willing to recommend the despatch of an expedition, and that such a decision on their part does not necessarily imply that the maritime communications would be absolutely secure against any interruption whatever.

4. The most important function of the navy in connection with a combined operation is the preservation of command of the sea, and whether it is preferable that the principal naval force shall be actually in company with the convoy or be disposed elsewhere is a matter for the decision of the navy having in view the general strategical situation afloat.

5. No standard can be laid down for the strength of the naval escort to the transport. The only essential is that the escort shall consist of sufficient ships to control the transports while in transit, and to provide the necessary boats and personnel for the conduct of the disembarkation.

6. The navy is responsible for the provision, despatch, and control of the sea transport of an army and for its security while at sea. The navy also maintains the communications of the army by sea.

7. The entire operations of landing and embarking troops, animals, guns, regimental stores and baggage, and stores (cargo), whether alongside wharves or piers (either government or mercantile), or to and from a beach, will be controlled by the navy, who will provide the boats, lighters and tugs, and any labour required in connection with same. All other necessary labour will be found by the army, except when circumstances render it desirable that the navy should provide some or all of the labour. The ultimate decision on this point will rest with the naval authorities.

8. The navy will be responsible for the berthing of all ships, lighters, tugs, and boats, but the convenience of the army must be considered, as far as practicable in the positions allotted. In landings and embarkations the navy will have full control of the entire beach up to high-water mark, and of such further portions of the same and of such piers and wharves as may be considered necessary to enable them to control the work of embarkation and disembarkation. Within these limits the military officers will carry out all instructions issued by the naval commander, but beyond them the responsibility for the safety and transportation of men, animals, guns, vehicles and stores on shore will rest with the army.

Should circumstances prevent the provision of the full naval personnel contemplated under the distribution of responsibility indicated above, the army will be prepared to undertake such duties as the respective naval and military commanders may arrange to allot to it, with the exception of control of movements when afloat.

9. While the foregoing are the general rules regarding the division of duties between the navy and army, it is to be understood that each service is working for a common object, and will render the other all the assistance that lies in its power. The complicated duties of embarking and landing troops and stores can only be carried out successfully so long as perfect harmony and co-operation exist between the naval and military authorities, and the staff duties devolving on both services have been carefully organized and adjusted.

10. When combined naval and military operations take place special duties, involving the use of unfamiliar titles, will devolve on officers of both services. These titles, &c., and the meaning to be attached to them are as follows :—

Principal Naval Transport Officer.—A flag officer or Captain Royal Navy appointed, in charge of Sea Transport duties, to assist the Senior Naval Officer in preparing the necessary naval orders and under his direction to conduct the disembarkation, &c.

Divisional Transport Officer.—A naval officer responsible for the efficient working of the transports and boats of the division under his charge.

Sub-Divisional Transport Officers.—Naval officers appointed to assist the Divisional Transport Officer.

Naval Transport Officer.—A naval officer responsible to the Divisional Transport Officer for the safe and rapid discharge of the transport to which he is appointed and the medium of all communications between the master of the ship and the officer commanding the troops on board.

Military Transport Officer.—A military officer appointed to co-operate with the Naval Transport Officer.

Principal Military Landing Officer.—An officer of the Q.M.G.'s branch of the Staff to assist the principal beach master in co-ordinating the work of the Army and Navy on the beaches, and to supervise the military beach control personnel.

Beach.—The stretch of shore allotted for the disembarkation of troops and material from one or more transports.

Principal Beach Master.—A senior naval officer who supervises and directs the work of landing on the whole of the beaches under his charge.

Beach Master.—A naval officer responsible for the rapid and safe clearing of the boats of the division of transport to which he is appointed.

Military Landing Officer.—A military officer appointed to assist the Beach Master.

Forming-up Place.—A place of assembly for the smaller units, clear of, but close to the beach, to which troops proceed directly they land.

Rendezvous.—A place of assembly for the larger units, to which the smaller units proceed from the " Forming-up Place."

Covering position.—A position to be occupied by an advanced detachment of troops at such distance from the selected landing that neither anchorage, beach, nor forming-up place are exposed to shell fire from the enemy's land forces.

A tow.—The number of boats, barges, or lighters, secured to one another, that can be towed by one steamboat.

A trip.—The passage of a tow from a transport to the landing place.

A round trip.—The time taken to load, tow ashore, and unload a tow as well as to return to the transport in readiness for the next trip.

11. When naval and military forces are associated in combined operations, all military ranks should be familiar with the meaning of the following expressions, naval terms and words of command :—

A ship or a boat is divided lengthwise into the *fore part*, or *bows* ; *midships*, or *waist* ; *after part*, or *stern*.

The right is the *starboard*, the left the *port side*, looking forward.

Forward.—Towards the bows.

Aft or abaft.—Towards the stern

Fore and aft.—Lengthways of the vessel.

Thwartships.—Across.

Alongside.—By the side.

Foc'sle.—In the fore part of the ship.

Quarter-deck.—A portion of the deck reserved for officers.

Accommodation ladder.—A ladder-way or staircase for entering a boat lying alongside a ship and *vice versa*.

Gangway.—A term indicating passage way.

Gang board or gang plank.—A special form of gangway for embarking or disembarking on or from a boat on an open beach.

Sea gangway.—The gangway used when the ship is at sea.

Gunwale.—A term used in a general way for the top of the sides of a boat.

Freeboard.—The distance between the water and the gunwale.

Lanyard.—A short piece of cord for tying on a knife, oar, &c.

Thwarts.—Seats for rowers in a boat.

Stretchers.—Rests for feet of rowers.

Stern sheets.—The space between the after thwart and the stern fitted with seats for passengers and steersman.

Rowlocks.—That part of a boat's gunwale in which the oar rests in rowing.

Poppits.—Pieces of wood which fit into the rowlocks when the boat is under sail.

Crutch.—A metal swivel rest for the oar to fit into when rowing; they are usually removable, but secured to the boat by a lanyard.

Halliards, stays, guys.—Names for ropes. *Halliards* are used for hoisting purposes; *stays* to support masts, &c.; *guys* for working derricks or other moving spars.

Purchase or tackle.—An arrangement of ropes and pulleys for raising or lowering weights.

Fall.—The rope of a purchase or tackle.

Cleats.—Pieces of wood or metal round which halliards, &c., are secured.

Painter.—A rope fastened to the bows of a boat with which to tow or fasten it.

Words of Command.

Ship or unship.—Fix or unfix; put into place or take out of place.

Back starboard.—Reverse the oars on the starboard side and back water.

Back port.—Reverse the oars on the port side and back water.

Lay on your oars, or Oars.—Cease rowing, place the oars in a horizontal position with blades feathered.

Toss your oars.—Lift oars to a perpendicular position and retain them there.

Boat your oars.—Place all oars inside the boat, blades forward.

Belay.—Make fast.

Ease off.—Slacken off.

Handsomely.—Gently, easily.

Stand by.—Be ready.

Walk back.—After hoisting a weight with a purchase, walk towards the weight with the fall of the purchase in hand to keep control over the weight when lowering.

Light to.—Let go the tail of the purchase.

When leaving a ship or pier :—

Shove off.—Push off from the ship's side.

Oars down.—Place oars in the water.

Give way together.—Commence rowing.

When approaching a ship or pier :—

Bows.—Bow oar " boats " his oar and prepares to use his boathook.

Way enough.—After the bow oars are laid in, this is the order given to the rowers at which they stop rowing, taking one stroke after the order, and toss and boat their oars; or in a gig or boat fitted with " crutches " (from which oars cannot conveniently be " tossed "), stop rowing and allow their oars to swing free, fore and aft.

12. The following tables give details of the boats in general use and of the numbers of each which form a tow.

(a) *Details of Boats.*

Rowing Boats.	Number that form a Tow.	Load.					Draught of Water.	Remarks.
		Men.	Horses.	Guns.	Vehicles.			
					4-wheeled.	2-wheeled.		
Lifeboats, 28' 0"	4	28	Nil	Nil	Nil	Nil	Mean, 1' 8" approx.	5 men in addition for working boat
Launch, 42' 0"	3	92	Nil	or 2	Nil	or 3	Mean, 2' 3" approx.	8 men in addition for working boat
Pinnace, 36' 0"	3	65	Nil	or 2	Nil	or 2	Mean, 2' 0" approx.	8 men in addition for working boat
Cutter, 30' 0", 1st class cruiser		32	Nil	or 1	Nil	or 1	Mean, 1' 8" approx.	6 men in addition for working boat
Cutter, 34' 0", 2nd class cruiser		42	Nil	or 1	Nil	or 1	Mean, 1' 9" approx.	6 men in addition for working boat
Horse-boats, 36' 3", includes 3" rubbers	2	110	or 12	or 2 field guns or 3 machine guns or 1 4·7 gun or 42 men with bicycles	or 2	or 4	Loaded, 2' 6" Light, 2' 0"	6 men in addition for working boat

NOTE.—Men in marching order. Vehicles fully equipped.

(b) *Details of Tows.*

Steamboats.	Life-boats.	Numbers that form a Tow.					Torpedo-Raft.	Draught of Water.	Remarks.
		Launch, 42' 0".	Pinnace, 36' 0".	Cutters, 1st class, cruiser, 30' 0".	Cutters, 2nd class, cruisers, 34' 0" and 30' 0".	Horse-boats.			
56' 0" steam pinnace picket boat	4	or 3	or 3	or 4	or 4	or 2	..	Forward 2' 8¼" Aft, 4' 8¼"	12 men's weight boat 1". sink
50' 0" steam pinnace	4	or 3	or 3	or 4	or 4	or 2	..	Forward, 2' 8¼" Aft, 4' 5¼"	10 men's weight boat 1". sink
40' 0" steam pinnace	4	or 2 and 1 cutter	or 2 and 1 cutter	or 4	or 4	or 1 and 1 pinnace or cutter or 1	..	Forward, 3' 3" Aft, 3' 10¼"	8 men's weight boat 1" sink
28' 0" transport steamboat	2	or 1	or 1 and 1 cutter	or 2	or 2	or 1	..	Mean, 2' 0" approx.	
30' 0" steam cutter (service)	2	or 1	or 1 and 1 cutter 30' 0"	or 3	or 2	or 1	..	Mean, 2' 0" approx.	

17. MAP READING AND FIELD SKETCHING.

1. *Scales.*—(a) Scales on maps of the United Kingdom, India and Canada are usually expressed in words, showing the relation between inches on the map and miles on the ground.

(b) Foreign maps and maps of British African Colonies and possessions are constructed on scales which bear the proportion of 1 to some multiple of 10.

The following examples explain the two methods :—

(a) Scale $\frac{1}{63360}$, or 1 inch to 1 mile.

(b) 1 : 100,000 (or $\frac{1}{100000}$), or on a foreign map 1 centimetre to 1 kilometre.

The fraction in each case is called the Representative Fraction or R.F., and means that 1 unit on the map (numerator) represents a certain number of the same units on the ground (denominator), thus from (a) above—

1 inch on the map represents 63,360 inches on the ground (= 1 mile)

from (b) 1 inch on the map represents 100,000 inches on the ground ; or 1 centimetre on the map represents 100,000 centimetres (= 1 kilometre) on the ground.

To find the number of English miles to the inch for any map that has a R.F., divide the denominator of the R.F. by 63,360 ; this gives the number of miles to the inch ; thus, if R.F. is $\frac{1}{50000}$, then $\frac{63360}{50000} = 1\cdot263$ miles to the inch.

To find the number of inches to the mile divide 63,360 by the denominator of the R.F. ; thus, if R.F. is $\frac{1}{80000}$, then $\frac{63360}{80000} = \cdot792$ inch to the mile.

A scale should usually be from 4 to 6 inches long (see Plate 9). The size of the scale depends on the object with which the sketch is made. Reconnaissance sketches of an area to explain a plan of attack, or to show lines of advance, of a road or river, or of a defensive or outpost position, are usually made on a scale of from 1 to 4 inches to 1 mile. Sketches for the defence of a village or town, or for the selection of a camp or billeting area, are generally on a scale of 4 inches to 1 mile.

TABLE OF BRITISH AND FOREIGN SCALES.

Representative Fraction (R.F.).	Approx. No. of Inches to 1 Mile.	Approx. No. of Miles to 1 Inch.	Where used.
1 over 10,000	6	$\frac{1}{6}$	Egypt.
,, 10,560			England.
,, 20,000	3	$\frac{1}{3}$	Belgium, Denmark, Japan.
,, 25,000	$2\frac{1}{2}$		Germany, Italy, Holland, Switzerland.
,, 31,680	2		England.
,, 40,000	$1\frac{3}{4}$		Belgium, Denmark.
,, 50,000	$1\frac{1}{4}$		France, Holland, Italy, Spain, Switzerland.
,, 62,500	1	1	U. S. A.
,, 63,360			England, India.
,, 75,000	$\frac{5}{6}$	$1\frac{1}{2}$	Austria, Italy.
,, 80,000	$\frac{3}{4}$	$1\frac{1}{4}$	France.
,, 100,000	$\frac{3}{5}$	$1\frac{3}{5}$	France, Germany, Italy, Norway, Spain.
,, 125,000		2	British African Colonies and Protectorates, U. S. A.
,, 126,000	$\frac{1}{2}$		Russia.
,, 126,720			England.
,, 160,000	$\frac{2}{5}$	$2\frac{1}{2}$	Belgium.
,, 200,000	$\frac{1}{3}$	3	Austria, France, Germany.
,, 250,000	$\frac{1}{4}$	4	British African Colonies and Protectorates, U. S. A.
,, 253,440			England, India.
,, 320,000	$\frac{1}{5}$	5	Belgium, France.
,, 420,000	$\frac{1}{7}$	$6\frac{5}{8}$	Russia.
,, 500,000	$\frac{1}{8}$	8	Egypt, France.
,, 1,000,000	$\frac{1}{16}$	16	International Map.

PLATE IX.

Scale 1/15840, or 4 inches to 1 mile.

Yards 500 400 300 200 100 0   500   1000   1500 Yards

Scale 1/31680, or 2 inches to 1 mile

Yards. 1000   500   0   1000   2000   3000   4000 Yards.

Scale 1/100000 or 1 inch to 1.58 miles

Mile 1 3/4 1/2 1/4 0   1   2   3   4   5   6   7   8   9 Miles

CONVENTIONAL SIGNS & LETTERING USED IN FIELD SKETCH

Note: Words which should appear on the Sketch are shown in black

Fields with walls, hedges, fences, ditches or any obstacle.

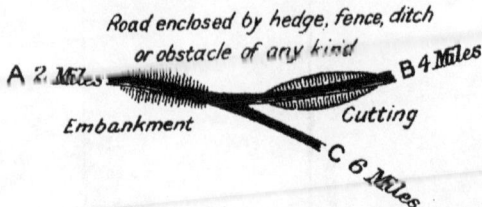

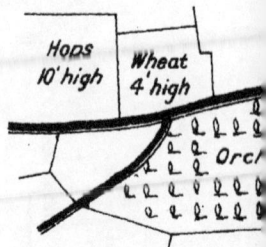

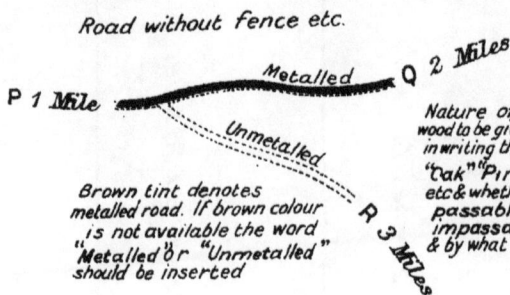

Road enclosed by hedge, fence, ditch
or obstacle of any kind

A 2 Miles   B 4 Miles

Embankment   Cutting

C 6 Miles

Hops
10' high

Wheat
4' high

Orch

Road without fence etc.

Metalled   Q 2 Miles

P 1 Mile

Unmetalled

R 3 Miles

Brown tint denotes
metalled road. If brown colour
is not available the word
"Metalled" or "Unmetalled"
should be inserted

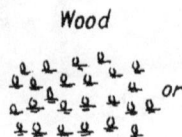

Nature of
wood to be given
in writing thus:-
"Oak" "Pine"
etc & whether
passable or
impassable
& by what arm

Wood

or

Footpath

Church or Ch

with Tower   with Spire   withou
or S

Embankment   Railway

Cutting

Single or Double

HAWLEY
4 Miles

Bridge
Brick
or
Stone

Tunnel

Sta.
Station
Level crossing

EYNSFORD
6 Miles

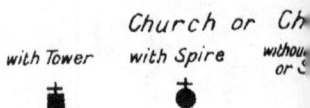

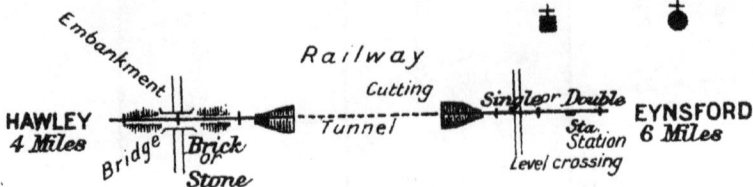

When there is not sufficient time to draw the cross-bars
a railway may be shewn by a broad black or red line with
the word "Railway" written along it.

entre

ABBREVIATIONS

P   Post Office

T   Telegraph Office

S.P. Sign Post

oW   Well

To follow plate 9.

6365. 63185.718. 150000.4.17.

Clearance or
Demolitions

Village
Scale 4 to 1 Mile

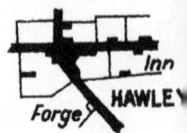

Inn

Forge   HAWLE

Plate 10

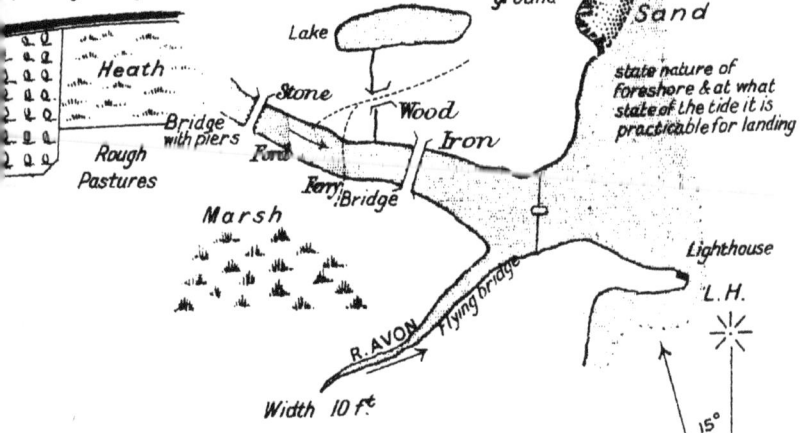

unnecessary to state the nature
he cultivation unless such information
quired by the object of the sketch.

Cliffs
Quarry or
precipitous
ground

Sand

Lake

Heath

Stone

Wood

Iron

state nature of
foreshore & at what
state of the tide it is
practicable for landing

Bridge
with piers
Ford

Ferry
Bridge

Rough
Pastures

Marsh

Lighthouse

R. AVON

Flying bridge

L.H.

Width 10 ft

15°

or

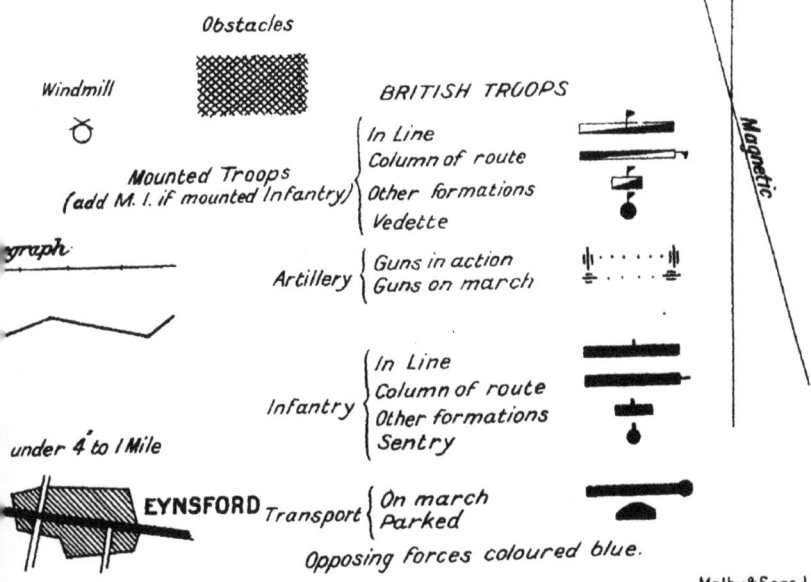

Obstacles

Windmill

Mounted Troops
(add M. I. if mounted Infantry)

graph

under 4' to 1 Mile

EYNSFORD

BRITISH TROOPS

In Line
Column of route
Other formations
Vedette

Artillery {
Guns in action
Guns on march

Infantry {
In Line
Column of route
Other formations
Sentry

Transport {
On march
Parked

Magnetic

Opposing forces coloured blue.

Malby & Sons, Lith.

2. *Conventional signs* enable information to be given on a sketch or map which could not otherwise be conveniently shown.

Plate 10 shows the approved conventional signs. In outpost sketches the letters P, S, R, may be written. nstead of piquet, support and reserve. The direction of a patrol is shown by an arrow. Whatever lettering appears on a sketch must be easily legible and should not interfere with the detail.

3. *Map enlarging.*—When it is required to enlarge a map squares of any convenient size should be drawn on the original, and the paper on which the new map is to be made ruled with squares, whose sides bear the required ratio to the sides of the squares on the original.

4. *Measurement of slopes.*—Slopes may be uniform, convex or concave, and may be expressed in degrees or as a gradient. Slopes are usually expressed in military terms by a fraction. Thus $\frac{1}{10}$ represents a rise or fall of the unit in 50. An approximate rule for expressing as a fraction a slope given in degrees is to divide the number of degrees by 60. Thus a slope of 3° is equivalent to $\frac{1}{20}$. This rule does not hold for steep slopes. Generally if the slope between two points is convex they are not visible from the other; if the slope is concave they are visible. Slopes are indicated on a sketch by means of " form lines." These are approximate contours sketched in by eye without accurate instruments. The level of a certain number of points is fixed and the shape and slope of the ground is shown by form lines arranged in accordance with these points.

5. *True and magnetic bearings.*—To convert from one to the other.

When the Variation is West.

To find true when given magnetic bearing. Subtract the variation; if the result is minus, subtract it from 360°.

To find magnetic when given true bearing. Add the variation; if the result is greater than 360°, subtract 360° from it.

When the Variation is East.

To find true when given magnetic bearing. Add the variation; if the result is greater than 360°, subtract 360° from it.

To find magnetic when given true bearing. Subtract the variation; if the result is minus, subtract it from 360°.

The most frequent error arises from forgetting that bearings are always given and measured through east by south, and not the shortest way when this is by west.

6. *Map reading.*—(a) Look at once for the scale; this is the key to distances.

(b) Note the vertical intervals used, and methods of showing form of ground.

(c) Note the position of ridges, hills and watercourses.

(d) Look for the direction of true or of magnetic north. If no north point is shown assume that its sides are true, north and south. In quoting a bearing the true bearing should be given.

(e) Note the character of the country and the effect this might have on operations carried out in it.

7. *Setting a map.*— A map is said to be " set " when it is laid out to correspond with the ground.

To set the map :—

(a) *With compass.*—If the magnetic north line is shown on the map, lay the compass over it (produced if necessary) and, without disturbing the compass, turn the map slowly round until the north end of the north point on the map is exactly under the north end of the needle. If the true north line only is shown, and you know the local variation of the compass, plot the magnetic north on the map with a protractor and proceed as before. If you have no protractor lay the compass on the true north line, and turn the map until this line makes with the needle an angle equal to the variation and on the correct side of it.

(b) *By objects.*—A map can be set by object on the ground without using the north point or compass.

(i) Identify the spot where you stand as some point marked on the map. Also identify on the map some distant object you can see. Join these two on the map by a straight line. Then turn the map about the point marking your position till this line points to the distant object.

(ii) When you do not know your position, place yourself between or in prolongation of a line joining any two points which can be identified. Revolve the map until the line joining the two points on the map points to the two places in the country.

A map can be set roughly for reading by identifying on the map several prominent objects that can be seen. The map is then held so that the directions between these objects as they appear on the ground and on the map are parallel to one another.

8. *The Service compass.*—The dial is graduated with two sets of figures which read like the hands of a watch. The inner set is for direct readings without the prism.

The compass gives "bearings" not "angles." The horizontal angles between any distant objects are found by taking the difference of their observed bearings.

To use the compass for night marching it has been constructed so that upon the black direction mark being turned to point to the required "bearing" as shown on the external ring and the arrow-head being made to correspond with it, the line between the luminous patches in the lid indicates the line of advance.

To prolong the line of advance, a stick painted white or prepared with luminous paint held at an angle of 45° to 60° with the horizontal in the direction indicated by the luminous patches will assist the operator to pick up some object to march on.

If no terrestrial objects are visible an assistant should be employed who notes the alignment of the stick and advances in that direction till halted by means of a low whistle. The operator then notes whether his assistant is on the true line of advance, and moves up on to what he judges the correct alignment, and again sends him forward. After a few advances the assistant should know how far he can go before being lost to sight and halt without waiting for the whistle.

9. Approximate methods of finding the true north :
(i) *With a compass.*—The magnetic variation can be obtained approximately from Appendix II.
(ii) *In the northern hemisphere.*—
(a) By the Pole star. In ordinary latitudes the bearing of the Pole star is always within 2° of North. To find the Pole star look for the Great Bear, which is like this :—

Fig. 1.

The two stars on the right in FIG. 1 point to the Pole star. As, however, the stars revolve round the Pole, the Great Bear is sometimes in the position shown in FIG. 2 :—

Fig. 2.

GREAT

BEAR.

N.
Pole Star.

(b) By a watch. Hold the watch face upwards point the hour hand at the sun, and bisect the angle between the hour hand and 12 o'clock. The line so found will point to south.

(iii) In the southern hemisphere :—

    (a) By the Southern Cross. Consider the Southern Cross as a kite ; prolong the greater axis $4\frac{1}{2}$ times in the direction of the tail, and the point reached will be approximately the South Pole. If a piece of paper marked along its edge with 12 equidistant lines and held so that the first and third coincide with the head and tail stars respectively, the twelfth line will give the approximate south point.

    (b) By a watch. Hold the watch face upwards, point the line from the centre of its dial to 12 o'clock at the sun and bisect the angle between this line and the hour hand. The line so found will point to north.

CHAPTER IV.

18. FIELD ENGINEERING.

(See also Manual of Field Engineering.)

1. No natural or artificial strength of position will of itself compensate for loss of initiative when an enemy has time and liberty to manœuvre. The choice of a position and its preparation must be made with a view to economizing the power expended on defence in order that the power of offence may be increased.

2. The influence of ground upon the effect of fire must be one of the first considerations in selecting a position. A clear field of fire, and ground on which artillery and infantry can act in combination, are of great importance, but this importance is relative to the ground over which the enemy must move ; thus it is better for the defence to have moderate facilities for the co-operation of infantry and artillery fire, and for the attack to have none, than for the defence to have good ground, but the attack better. The most favourable ground for the ultimate assumption of the offensive is that which lends itself most to *the co-operation of all arms*, and especially that which allows the advance to be covered by artillery and infantry fire. Ground from which any portion of the front or flanks of a position can be enfiladed is dangerous to the defence.

3. The troops will be divided into two main portions, one, known as the general reserve, to be held in readiness for the initiation of a general offensive when a favourable opportunity has been created, the other to create the desired opportunity by temporarily taking up a defensive position, and then to co-operate actively with the general reserve in its attack on the enemy.

4. When it is intended to occupy a defensive position, the chief points to be noted are :—

    (*a*) The best distribution of the infantry, and the means of protecting the flanks.

    (*b*) The positions for the artillery which should be posted so as to command—

        (i) The positions which the enemy may endeavour to seize in order to develop an effective fire against the position ; and

        (ii) The probable positions of the enemy's artillery.

    (*c*) Any points the possession of which might exert a decisive influence on the issue of the fight.

    (*d*) The most favourable lines of attack.

    (*e*) The most favourable ground for the counter-attack.

    (*f*) Ground to be occupied by the general reserve, by the cavalry, and by the other mounted troops.

    (*g*) Positions to be occupied in case of retreat.

5. A defensive position will normally include a number of localities of special tactical importance. The efforts of the defender will be directed in the first instance to occupying and securing these points, so that they may form pivots upon which to hinge the defence of the remainder of the position. The defences of these localities should be arranged so that they may give each other mutual support.

If these pivot points are naturally strong or can be made so artificially, and if they are adequately garrisoned, the defence of the intervening ground should not usually be arranged in a continuous line, the defence works being limited to ensuring that ground invisible to the defenders of the pivot points is swept by fire.

An extensive position is divided into sections to each of which a distinct unit is assigned. A section will usually include one or more tactical localities.

6. The infantry allotted to the defence of a position or section is divided into firing line, with supports if required, for garrisoning the tactical localities, and local reserves for the delivery of local counter-attacks over the intervening ground.

The supports should be close to the firing line, have covered communication with it, and be under cover from shrapnel fire ; if this is not possible the firing line should be self-supporting. The local reserves should be placed where they have good cover while awaiting occasions for the delivery of counter-attacks ; local reserves of flank sections should usually be écheloned in rear of the flanks.

The general reserve should generally be in rear of that portion of the position which offers the best line for the eventual advance. Its commander should be named in the orders for the occupation of the position and he must be provided with a sufficient staff.

7. Where a defensive position is to be held at night or during fog, it will usually be necessary to supplement the system of occupying localities, described above, by a more continuous line of defence in order to prevent the enemy from penetrating the position.

8. In order that field works may be designed to the best advantage the effect of rifle and gun fire at various ranges should be fully realized.

Rifle Fire.

9. Modern military rifles are sighted to about 2,800 yards. Their maximum range may be taken as about 3,700 yards. The slope of descent of the bullet varies from about $\frac{1}{15}$ at 600 yards and $\frac{1}{19}$ at 1,100 yards to $\frac{1}{5\cdot5}$ at 2,200 yards.

10. The heights over which an average man can fire on level ground, as adopted in various armies, are :—

		France.	Germany.	Russia.	Great Britain.
Lying down	..	..	11·8 in.	..	1 ft.
Kneeling ..	..	3 ft. 3·3 in.	2 ft. 11·4 in.	2 ft. 10·8 in.	3 ft.
Standing ..	..	4 ft. 7·1 in.	4 ft. 7·1 in.	4 ft. 8·0 in.	4 ft. 6 in.

A higher parapet can be used when firing uphill than downhill.

11. The following table gives the maximum penetration of the pointed bullet in various materials.

In order to obtain proof cover, a percentage must be added to these numbers, e.g., earth parapets should not be less than 3½ feet thick. If the soil is free from stones, a thickness of 4 feet is desirable :—

Material.	Maximum penetration.	Remarks.
Steel plate, best hard ..	$\frac{7}{16}$ in.	At 30 yards normal to plate; $\frac{3}{16}$ in. is proof at not less than 600 yards, unless the plate is set at a slope of $\frac{3}{4}$ when $\frac{3}{16}$ in. is proof at 250 yards.
,, ordinary mild or wrought iron	$\frac{3}{4}$ in.	
Shingle	6 ins.	Not larger than 1 in. ring gauge.
Coal, hard	6 ins.	
Brickwork, cement mortar	9 ins.	150 rounds concentrated on one spot will breach a 9-in. brick wall at 200 yards.
,, lime mortar ..	14 ins.	
Chalk	15 ins.	
Sand, confined between boards, or in sandbags	18 ins.	Very high velocity bullets have less penetration in sand at short than at medium ranges.
Sand, loose	30 ins.	
Hard wood, e.g., oak, with grain	38 ins.	
Earth, free from stones (unrammed)	40 ins.	Ramming earth reduces its resisting power.
Soft wood, e.g., fir, with grain	58 ins.	Penetration of brickwork and timber is less at short than at medium ranges.
Clay	60 ins.	Varies greatly. This is maximum for greasy clay.
Dry turf or peat	80 ins.	

NOTE.—Experiment has shown that—

    Walls of broken brick, 2 inches by 3 inches, between corrugated iron, are proof if 8 inches thick.

    Walls of road metal, 2 inches by 3 inches, between corrugated iron, are proof if 8 inches thick.

    Walls of screened gravel, $1\frac{1}{2}$ inches, between corrugated iron, are proof if 6 inches thick.

    Walls of hand-picked Thames ballast, $1\frac{1}{2}$ inches, between corrugated iron, are proof if 6 inches thick.

ARTILLERY FIRE.

    12. *Field guns.*—Both shrapnel shell and high explosive shell are fired by the field artillery of most foreign nations.

    Shrapnel with time fuzes can be used up to a range of about 6,000 yards. With percussion fuzes shrapnel can be used effectively against troops behind 14-inch (in the case of the 18-pr., 24-inch) brick or 2 feet thick mud walls, as they penetrate before bursting.

    High explosive shell are intended for use chiefly against troops under cover or against shielded guns.

    The angle of descent of the projectile varies from $\frac{1}{2}$ at 1,500 yards to $\frac{1}{4}$ at 4,000 yards.

    13. *Field howitzers* fire both shrapnel shell and high explosive shell. The chief difference between their fire and that of field guns is that the shell is heavier (varying from 30 to 45 lbs.), contains a larger bursting charge, and has a steeper angle of descent. Howitzer fire therefore possesses greater searching power than that of field guns. They can fire shrapnel shell up to a range of about 6,000 yards, while their extreme range is about 7,000 yards. The angle of descent of the projectile may be as steep as $\frac{1}{2}$.

    The amount of cover necessary to keep out the shell of a howitzer is described in M.E., Part II, Plate X, Fig. 3. The effect of the burst, though powerful is very local and 9 to 12 inches of earth or 3 to 4 inches of shingle supported by some suitable material suffices against splinters from the shell.

14. *Heavy guns* fire both shrapnel shell and high explosive shell of still greater weight at ranges up to 10,000 yards. These pieces are therefore specially useful for long-range enfilading fire.

15. The aim of field artillery in the attack of a position is to assist the advance of its own infantry by bursting its shell in such a position that the defenders will either be forced to keep under cover or be struck. No attempt is made to breach the parapets of the defence.

An occasional shell may strike and penetrate the parapet, but in the case of shrapnel the damage to the parapet will be trifling, while in the case of a shell filled with high explosive, the effect will be no worse on a thin parapet than on a thick one. It is, therefore, useless to spend time and labour on making a thick parapet simply to keep out shell.

16. Ranges.

Terms applied to Ranges.		Rifle.	Field Art.	Heavy Batteries.
		Yards.	Yards.	Yards.
Distant	.. ..	2,800 to 2,000	6,500 to 5,000	10,000 to 6,500
Long	.. ..	2,000 to 1,400	5,000 to 4,000	6,500 to 5,000
Effective	.. ..	1,400 to 600	4,000 to 2,500	5,000 to 2,500
Close	.. ..	600 and under	2,500 and under	2,500 and under

The extreme range of field artillery using percussion shell may be taken as 9,000 yards, and of heavy artillery as 10,000 yards.

The width of the area of ground struck by the bullets of an effective shrapnel is about 25 yards.

The distance effectively covered by shrapnel bullets varies from 100 yards at short ranges to 50 yards at long ranges.

The radius of the explosion of a high explosive shell is about 25 yards.

19. TOOLS AND EXPLOSIVES.

Wagon and Cart Equipment also tools issued with machine gun tripods are excluded from this table (*see* footnote).

Tools.	Weight. (lbs. ozs.)	Length. (ft. in.)	Cavalry regiment.	Horse artillery brigade.	Field artillery brigade, 18-pr.	Field artillery (Howitzer) brigade.	Horse artillery battery.	Field artillery battery 18-pr.	Field artillery (Howitzer) battery.	Heavy artillery battery.	Horse artillery battery ammunition column (?).	Heavy artillery battery ammunition column.	Field troop.	Field company.	Bridging train.	Infantry battalion.	Squadron of Irish Horse.	Headquarters infantry brigade.
Intrenching tools.																		
Shovels a	3 8	3 1	18	84	126	144	30	30	…	16	12	8	37	111	10	110	6	568
Spades	5 10	3 0	…	12	18	…	6	6	36	…	…	…	7	19	10	…	…	…
Pickaxes	8 0	3 0	12	48	72	72	18	18	18	8	6	4	39	107c	40	76	4	368
Intrenching implements d	…	…	…	…	…	…	…	…	…	…	…	…	…	…	…	937	…	…
Cutting tools.																		
Felling axes	6 7	2 8	13	12	18	27	6	6	6	…	…	…	25	47	40	16	4	…
Hand axes	2 3	1 4	7	…	…	…	…	…	…	…	…	…	14	28	…	8	2	1
Billhooks	1 13	1 3¼	12	48	72	72	18	18	18	8	6	4	18	39	40	40	4	…
Hand saws	5	1 2	4	36	54	54	12	12	12	8	6	4	16	27	4	1	2	…
Cross-cut saws	6 7	5 0	…	74	58	46	…	…	…	…	…	…	2	4	…	…	…	…
Reaping hooks	1	1 6¼	…	…	…	…	…	…	…	12	24	…	6	10	8	20	12	3
Folding saws (complete)	1 12	1	36	62	82	82	20	20	20	20	10	6	4	8	…	32	18	…
Wire cutte s d	…	…	3	…	…	…	…	…	…	…	…	…	18	41	44	24	…	…
Miscellaneous.																		
Crowbars	12 0	3 6	3	2	1	1	…	…	…	4	1	1	6	8	…	8	1	9
Guncotton (including primers) lbs	…	…	105	…	…	…	…	…	…	…	…	…	292¼	570	…	…	…	…
Sandbags	…	…	150	…	…	…	…	…	…	…	…	…	264	852	…	…	…	…
Mauls	…	…	3	…	…	…	…	…	…	8	…	1	3	5	40	…	1	…

a The weight and length given are those of G.S. shovel. The R.E. shovel weighs 5 lbs. and is 3 feet 4 inches long.
b For a cavalry brigade not allotted to a cavalry division.
c 88, with heads weighing 4½ lbs.; 19, with 8 lb. heads.
d Carried on the person.

Wagon and Cart Equipment.

NOTE.—

(i) 1 pickaxe, 1 felling axe, 1 billhook, and 2 shovels, in addition to the tools shown in the table, are carried as part of the
     wagon or cart equipment of all G.S. and G.S.R.E. wagons, and Maltese carts.
     These tools do not form part of the wagon equipment of R.E. technical vehicles.

(ii) 1 pickaxe, 1 shovel and 1 billhook are carried with each machine gun tripod as part of its equipment.

(iii) 20 sandbags per cavalry regiment and infantry battalion are carried for use with machine guns.

(iv) 1 pickaxe, 1 felling axe, 1 billhook and 1 spade are also carried as part of the wagon equipment of telephone wagons.

(B 11925)   I 2

INDIA.

Entrenching and Pioneer Tools and Explosives.

Articles.	British cavalry regiment.	Indian cavalry regiment.	Guides cavalry.	Horse artillery battery.	Field artillery battery.	Field artillery (howitzer) battery.	Field artillery (howitzer), A.C.	30-pr. or 4-inch battery.	6-inch battery, siege train (3 units).	Mountain artillery British battery.	Mountain artillery Indian battery.	Field troop.	Field company.	Field company (light hill equipment).	Pontoon section.	British infantry battalion.	Indian infantry battalion.	Pioneer battalion.
A. Entrenching Tools—																		
Spades, N.P. ...	8	…	…	…	…	…	…	…	…	…	…	…	…	…	…	…	…	…
Pickaxes ...	34	24	18	(b)36	(b)(l)36	(b)(r)39	(b)(s)60	24	78	24	24	24	(g)96	75	36	48	48	(m)144
Shovels, G.S. ...	80	80	60	…	…	…	…	…	153	6	6	…	…	…	8	160	160	…
Shovels, R.P. ...	…	…	…	36	36	30	60	24	…	…	…	24	92	92	36	…	…	…
Mamooties, G.S. ...	16	16	12	…	…	…	…	…	15	12	12	…	2	2	36	…	…	…
Sirhind entrenching tools	…	…	…	…	…	…	…	…	…	…	…	…	…	…	…	(p)606	(p)524	(n)32

Remarks.

(a) Aden Troop only (2 lbs. 2 ozs.)
(b) Eighteen 6½ lbs. heads and eighteen 3 lbs. heads.
(c) Three 5′ 6″ and three 3′ 6″.
(d) Burma only.

The footnote references used in the table below:

(e) One 4' 6" and four 2' 6".

(f) One hundred and twelve 2 oz. primers and one hundred and ninety-two 1 oz. primers.

(g) Ninety-two pickaxes (helved) 8 lbs. and four 3 lbs. heads for mining.

(h) Four 4' 6" and two 2' 6".

(i) Two hundred 2 oz. primers. Four hundred 1 oz. primers.

(k) In Assam and Burma (except Rangoon) only.

(l) For buglers of Gurkha Rifles.

(m) The number taken is settled by the O.C.

(n) Spare mamooties at discretion of O.C.

(o) Or 24 kukries in lieu.

(p) For units in the 1st, 2nd, 3rd, 4th, 5th and 7th Divisions only.

(q) Slabs.

B. Cutting Tools—																
Felling axes	32	8	8	36	18	18	8	6	6	39	16	17·31	20	20	3	4
Hand axes					30	30	6								12	1
Billhooks and switching bills	(m)	32	32	36	(o)24	24		12	12	39	24	17·31	20	20		16
Reaping hooks	16			36							16	36	6	6		
Gambion knives		32		36	24	24						65				
Knives		16						(d)18								20
Kukries		(l)32			(o)16	10				15						
Dahs	48														12	
Hand saws	16	16	30			10		18		15	4	9·27	12	12	12	4
Flexible saws	16	(k)4			4	4										
C. Miners' Tools—																
Miners' shovel (short)					6	8	2									4
Sledge hammers	32				4	18	2									
Boring hammers	48				4	6	3									
Jumping bars	8				3	2										
Tamping bars, I. P.	8				3	4										
Priming needles	8				4	8										
Scoops and scrapers	22				3	4										
Sawyers' wedges																
Miners' worms																
D. Miscellaneous—																
Platelayers' tools and sets of railway plant																8
Pliers (pairs)																4
Gun spikes	8														3	48
Spoke-shaves																4

INDIA.

ENTRENCHING AND PIONEER TOOLS AND EXPLOSIVES—*continued.*

Articles	British cavalry regiment	Indian cavalry regiment	Guides cavalry	Horse artillery battery	Field artillery battery	Field artillery (howitzer) battery	Field artillery (howitzer) A.O.	30-pr. or 4-inch battery	6-inch battery, siege train (3 units)	Mountain artillery, British battery	Mountain artillery, Indian battery	Field troop	Field company	Field company (light hill equipment)	Pontoon section	British infantry battalion	Indian infantry battalion	Pioneer battalion	Remarks
Nippers	4	...	...	...	...	...	...	...	...	...	...	...	...	...	...	...	...	...	
Crowbars	...	...	...	6	6	6	3	4	(c)6	3	3	(e)5	(h)6	5	2	...	...	48	(r) 24 6½-lb, and 15 3-lb. heads.
Sand bags	...	...	...	...	...	...	3	200	600	...	...	9	120	70	240	...	...	...	(s) 30 6½-lb. and 30 3-lb. heads.
Tracing tapes	...	...	...	...	...	...	...	...	...	...	...	...	8	...	...	...	...	8	
E. Explosives—																			
Gun cotton slabs (lbs.)	42	42	42	...	...	...	...	...	(g)21	...	...	115	219-12 oz.	90	...	...	...	160	
Dry primers	72	72	72	...	...	...	...	...	3	...	...	(f)304	(i)600	240	...	...	...	1232(t)	(t) Boxes.
Detonators	64	64	64	...	...	...	...	...	48	...	...	48	1,250	100	...	...	...	16	
Rectifiers	8	8	8	...	...	...	...	...	6	...	...	...	20	8	...	...	...	16	
Keys, plug, G. S.	...	...	...	...	...	...	...	...	3	...	...	...	1	...	...	...	...	8	
Boxes, vesuvian matches	4	4	4	...	...	...	...	...	...	...	...	...	200	100	...	...	...	64	
Safety fuzes, fathoms	...	...	...	...	...	...	...	...	...	...	...	...	...	...	...	...	...	400	

20. TABLE OF TIME, MEN AND TOOLS

REQUIRED FOR THE EXECUTION OF CERTAIN FIELD WORKS.

Except where otherwise stated the material and tools are assumed to be on the site of the work. All tracing and marking out is to be done before the distribution of the working parties at the sites. Not more than five minutes should be consumed in distributing the men, or in changing reliefs, if the men have been told off into suitable groups or parties under leaders previously instructed in the nature of the particular works in hand. One leader or foreman can conveniently supervise up to 20 unskilled men on earthwork.

No.	Nature of Work	Minutes of one Man.	Per Unit of Task.	Suitable Unit Party.	Tools per Party.	Remarks and Notes.
	ENTRENCHING.					
1	Excavation only ...	3	1 cubic ft.	1	1 shovel and 1 pick	{ Average over a relief of 4 hours in ordinary easy soil.
2	Fire trench, 1 rifle ...	100	2 paces or 45 cubic ft.	1	"	Including elbow rest and share of drain. If tools are double manned the time can be reduced to 70 minutes.
3	Fire trench, 1 rifle ...	300	2 paces or 90 cubic ft.	1 or 2	"	Earth removed or scattered by other men (see items Nos. 6 and 7). If tools are double manned and first pair relieved after 2 hours, time can be reduced to 150 mins.
4	Fire trench, 1 rifle ...	420	2 paces or 110 cubic ft.	1 or 2	"	This may also be taken as normal for 1 rifle entrenched as in Plate 12, Fig. 2, in a recess 3ft. 6in. wide. If tools are double manned and first pair relieved after 2 hours, time can be reduced to 180 mins.
5	Communication trench	240	2 paces or 80 cubic ft.	1	"	If tools are double manned and first pair relieved after 2 hours, time can be reduced to 135 mins.

Volume excavated in cubic feet : average hourly rates.

Tools used by	1st Hour.	2nd Hour.	3rd Hour.	4th to 8th Hour.
One Man :—	30	25	15	10
Too } Double Manned :—	40	33	20	13

TABLE OF TIME, MEN AND TOOLS—*continued.*

No.	Nature of work.	Minutes of One Man.	Per Unit of Task.	Suitable Unit Party.	Tools per Party.	Remarks and Notes.
6	Shovelling loose earth	1	1 cubic ft.	1	1 shovel	As into barrows, boxes, gabions, stretchers, sacks, &c., or cross lifting or spreading carefully. Averaged over 8 hours work.
7	Removing 50 yards (average) deposit, and return...	1 2	1 cubic ft. 1 cubic ft	1 2	1 barrow 1 stretcher	2 cubic feet per load. Average weight of earth or sand 1 cwt. per 1 cubic foot. Removing earth over 100 yards is usually more economical by horse and cart, or tram. Averaged over 2 hours work, i.e. 120 bags filled by 3 men. Size up to 20 in. × 10 in. × 5 in. Weight 60 lbs.
8	Filling sandbags ...	3	1 sandbag	3	2 shovels	For sacks use item No. 6. Corn sacks average 2 bushels = 2½ cubic feet when quite full. Allow 1 cubic foot only.
9	Head cover, sandbags or sods	60	1 loophole	1	1 shovel	Up to 12 (sandbags or sods), according to description. For spaces between loopholes calculate by items 13 or 15 below, if necessary.
10	Overhead cover, added to head cover ...	60	1 rifle	1	1 shovel, 1 hand axe	Allow for 25 square feet of roofing per rifle, in addition to necessary supports. Nails, &c., as obtainable.
	REVETMENTS.					
11	Brushwood, rough or planks as hurdle	1½	1 sq. ft.	2	1 billhook, 1 mallet	Allow 4 lbs. of brushwood and 1 foot of wire per 1 square foot of surface revetted.
12	„ work ...	2	1 sq. ft.	2		
13	Sandbag or sack ...	3	1 sq. ft.	2	—	Sandbags (already filled) in course of alternate headers and stretchers. 1 sack or 2 bags per 1 sq. ft.
14	Gabions, placing and filling	5	1 sq. ft.	1	1 shovel, 1 pick	Gabions 2 ft. wide by 2 ft. 9 in. high; area revetted 5½ sq. ft.; contents 8½ cub. ft. Earth to be excavated.

revetted

No.	Work	Task	Unit	No. of men	Tools	Remarks
15	Sods, building with...	6	1 sq. ft.	2	1 shovel or spade	Allow 5 sods each about 18 in. by 9 in. (say 1 sq. ft. each) by 4 in. thick, per 1 square foot of *surface revetted* 18 inches thick. Rate of cutting about 30 sods per hour by one man in 4 hours.
16	Sods, providing for 15	9	1 sq. ft.	3	3 sharp spades	
17	Gabions, band, making	20	1 gabion	2	—	Materials: 10 bands and clips, 10 pickets, weight 13 lbs. Filling 25 min. per gabion (see No. 14).
18	Gabions, brushwood, making	360	1 gabion	3	1 billhook, 2 knives / 1 mallet, 1 measure	Materials: 75 lbs. brushwood, for use and waste; finished weight about 50 lbs.
19	Hurdles, rough, making	60	1 hurdle	3	2 billhooks, 2 knives	Materials: 75 lbs. brushwood and 60 ft. of wire or yarn per hurdle, 6ft. by 2 ft. 9 in.
20	Hurdles, strong, making	450	1 hurdle	3	1 mallet, 1 pr. pliers	Weight of each complete, about 56 lbs.
21	Fascines, making ...	240	1 fascine	4	3 billhooks, 2 knives, 1 handsaw, 1 maul, 1 pr. pliers, 1 choker	Materials: 200 lbs. brushwood and 60 ft. of wire or hoop iron (40 ft.) per fascine, 18 ft. long by 9 in. diameter. Weight complete, about 140 lbs. Cradle for making requires 10 pickets, 6 ft. 6 in. by 3 in. diameter.
	CUTTING AND FELLING.					
22	Trees, felling ...	1	1 in. of diamr.	1	1 felling axe, or saw	Over 12 inches diameter allow time $= \dfrac{d^3}{144}$ where d = mean diameter in inches. If only hand axes are available allow twice the time as calculated by both these rules.
23	Woods, clearing of brushwood and small trees	2½	1 square yd.	20	10 billhooks, 4 felling axes, 4 hand axes, 2 saws, 1 grindstone, 2 whetstones	All hands felling at first; then a proportion detailed for collecting and removing according to purpose in view. Produce: about 5 lbs. brushwood per 1 square yd.
24	Hedges, felling stems	10	1 yard run	2	1 billhook or handaxe, 1 saw, 3 fathoms rope	Average stiff thorn up to 2 in. diameter. If necessary use rope to expose lower stems to the cutting tool.
25	Brick wall, notches in	10	1 notch	1	1 pick or crowbar	If possible obtain a mason's chisel and hammer. Walls up to 18 in. thick.
26	Brick walls, loopholes in	30	1 loophole	1		

TABLE OF TIME, MEN AND TOOLS.—*continued.*

No.	Nature of Work.	Minutes of one Man.	Per Unit of Task.	Suitable Unit Party.	Tools per Party.	Remarks and Notes.
	OBSTACLES.					
27	Abatis, and wired ...	120	1 yard run	20	As for item 23; also 2 mauls, 3 pr. pliers, 1 pickaxe, 1 shovel	strong row. The material must be close at hand. Allow 20 yards wire per run yard per row. The length of the branches is more important than their size. Wire each butt, securely to a separate stout picket driven at least 2 feet into the ground. Wire for density near the ground.
28	Wire entanglement	30	1 square yd.	3	1 billhook, 1 hand-saw, 1 maul, 1 pr. pliers, 1 pr. wire-cutters, 3 rag pads for gripping and straining wire. *In hard ground add:* 1 steel jumper, 1 sledge hammer	Materials : 1 stout post 5 to 9 feet long by 5 to 6 in. diam, per 4 square yards of obstacle. 1 stout picket 2 to 8 feet long by 5 in. diam. per yard run of finished obstacle, for side stays. 12 to 18 yards of wire per 1 square yard of finished obstacle. N.B.—A very formidable obstacle can be made with three stout posts, 1 stout picket and 160 yards wire per yard run complete. Barbed wire is most quickly handled and fixed if issued in lengths of about 10 feet, when issued in entanglements.

21. DEFENCE OF LOCALITIES, &c.

1. Localities of tactical importance may be commanding features of the ground, groups of substantial buildings and enclosures, or wooded knolls giving cover from view and a good field of fire to front and flanks.

2. Each locality should be capable of all-round defence, and each should be able to sweep with fire a large proportion of the ground lying between it and those on either side.

3. The principal defences will, as a rule, consist of fire trenches, hedges, and walls.

4. *Fire trenches* may be disposed in irregular lines or in groups with intervals, according to the character of the ground.

In selecting the sites for fire trenches, the following points require attention :—

    (*a*) Good field of fire. Most important within 400 yards of the trench. Range marks, if possible, to be added.

    (*b*) Concealment and invisibility. Obtained by adapting trenches to form of the ground, keeping parapets low, and by use of natural or artificial cover.

    (*c*) Parapet should be bullet-proof.

    (*d*) Head cover, which must be inconspicuous, should be provided, if possible.

    (*e*) Trenches should be traversed or recessed.

    (*f*) Cover for supports near at hand.

    (*g*) Trenches should have steep interior slope, be wide enough to allow men to pass, and drainage should be provided. (For types *see* Plates 11 and 12.)

5. *Walls* can be notched or loopholed. The latter give the best cover, but should not be closer than 3 feet from centre to centre. Dummy loopholes should be added. If firing over the tops of walls is to be employed they should be covered with sods, turf, &c.

6. *Hedges* may be used as screens, or revetments to support the earth of a parapet. They must be thick enough to prevent the earth showing through. Work should be concentrated at first only at the points to be occupied by each man.

7. *Overhead cover* to keep out splinters of shell, &c., should consist of 9 to 12 inches of earth or 3 inches of shingle supported on brushwood, boards, corrugated iron, &c.

8. *Protected look-outs* will be needed for commanders, &c. A type is shown on Plate 11. This is also suitable for a sentry group in the outpost line.

9. *Roads* of a temporary nature are usually required :—

    (*a*) In connection with a defensive position to enable troops or guns to be readily moved from one portion to another.

    (*b*) For movement across country devoid of suitable tracks.

Within a position, troops and messengers should be guided to their destination by signposts, by " blazing " trees or other means.

10. A roadway 10 feet wide (8 feet minimum) will take a single line of wagons* passing in one direction, or infantry in fours ; 12 feet is better for allowing horsemen to pass without difficulty : for each additional line of vehicles 8 feet should be added to the width of the road. A width of 6 feet is sufficient for infantry in file or pack animals moving in one direction.

Gaps in walls, hedges, &c., forming road boundaries should be made at least 15 feet wide if intended for wheeled traffic.

11. The gradient for a short distance, such as a ramp leading on to a bridge, may be one-third or even one-half for infantry and one-seventh for

---

* The width over all service vehicles varies from 6 feet (Telegraph Cable Cart, Mk. II) to 7 feet (Ambulance Wagon, Mk. VI), and 2 wheel tracks, each 1 foot wide, spaced at 5 feet apart between inside edges, will accommodate all service vehicles.

artillery, provided it is straight ; but for animals or wheeled traffic slopes steeper than one-tenth are inconvenient, and if an incline is a long one its slope should be at least one-twentieth.

Traction engines can draw their own weight up one-tenth, twice their weight up one-twentieth, three times their weight on the level or up slopes not exceeding one-thirty-third.

12. When a road has to be constructed, the centre line should be marked by pickets, or the margins by *spitlocking*, and some kind of pathway cleared. The more difficult portions *must* be dealt with first, and the whole road rendered passable by artillery before any portion is still further improved.

13. When ascending a hill by means of zig-zags the road should be made as level as possible at each angle, and half as wide again as in the straight portions. The road should be prolonged uphill about 12 yards beyond each turn to enable teams to pull straight until the vehicle reaches the level turn. Short zig-zags should be avoided, and no curves should be sharper than with a radius of 60 feet for traffic of all arms to meet and pass without producing a deadlock.

14. The best foundation for a temporary road over boggy ground is one or more layers of fascines or hurdles ; the top row must lie across the direction of the traffic, touching one another. When time is short or suitable material is not at hand, much can be done by throwing down brushwoods, heather, or even straw or grass laid across the road. It is quite useless to place stones or earth in small quantities upon a yielding foundation.

15. Where timber is available and heavy traffic is expected, a " corduroy " road may be made by felling trees, and laying them across the road at right angles to its direction, ribands being spiked to them at either end or the logs may be held together by interlacing with rope or wire.

The interstices between fascines, brushwood, logs, &c., may be filled with small stones and earth to make a better surface.

VILLAGES.

16. For the defence of a village, a definite garrison should be detailed under the command of a selected officer. The latter will be responsible for selecting the main and any interior lines of defence, for dividing the village into sub-sections, for allotting to each a proportion of the garrison, for arranging for a central hospital for wounded men, and for notifying the position of his headquarters. A general reserve should be retained to deliver local counter-attacks.

17. Each subordinate commander should consider the preparations for the defence of his sub-section in the following order :—

(a) Improvement of the field of fire.
(b) Provision of cover, much of which may be done concurrently with (a).
(c) Provision and improvement of communications.
(d) Provision of obstacles and barricades.
(e) Arrangements for extinguishing fires.
(f) Ammunition supply.
(g) Food and water.
(h) Removal of sick and wounded.
(j) Retrenchment.

18. At first the firing line should usually be placed in front of any buildings to prevent casualties from shells which burst against their walls.

POSTS.

19. For the defence of a post the following are points to remember :—

(a) Organization of inner and outer defences.
(b) Defenders should be quartered close to the positions they have to man.
(c) Arrangements for storage of ammunition, water and supplies.
(d) Provision of strong obstacles.
(e) Adequate cover with a clear field of fire.
(f) Provision of automatic alarms, if possible.
(g) Good communications, including telephones, telegraphs, and signalling.

PLATE XI.

COVER FOR SENTRY GROUP.

(Suitable for a Look-out Post).

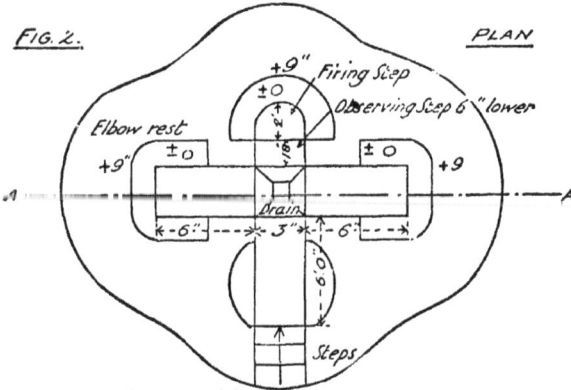

FIG. 2. PLAN

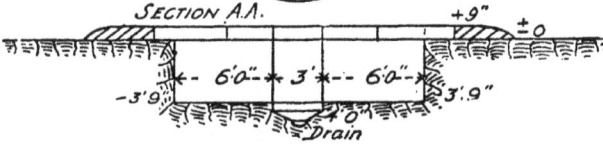

SECTION A.A.

COVER - LYING DOWN

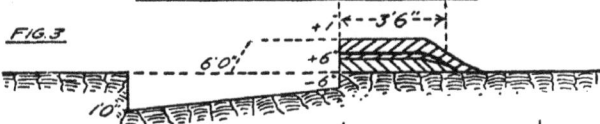

FIG.3

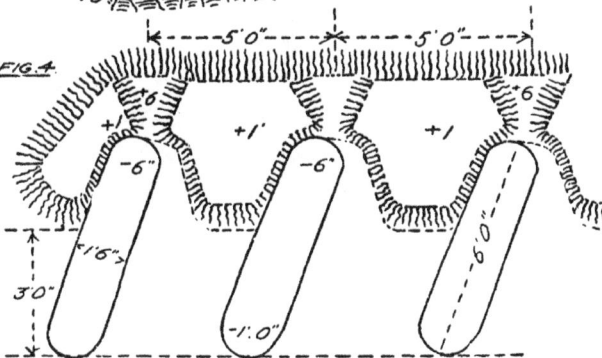

FIG.4

To face page 102.

FIRE TRENCHES.

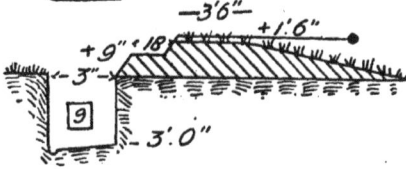

FIG. 1.

−3'6″ — +1'6″
+9″ +18″
−3″
9
−3'.0″

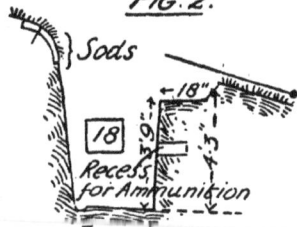

FIG. 2.

} Sods

18
Recess for Ammunition

18″

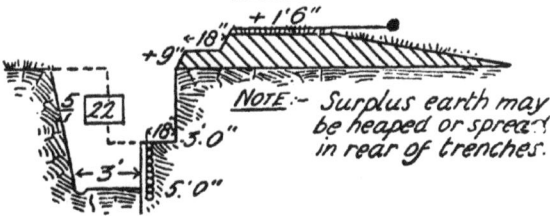

FIG. 3.

+1'6″
+9″ +18″
22
18″ 3.0″
3'
5'.0″
5'.0″

NOTE:— Surplus earth may be heaped or spread in rear of trenches.

HEDGES.

FIG. 4.

Natural Ditch in rear.

3'.0″

FIG. 5.

Natural Ditch in front.

5'6″
4'6″

COMMUNICATION TRENCH.

FIG. 6.

+2'6″   +2'6″
4'
16
3'   4'6″

BUILDINGS.

20. For the defence of a building the following points require attention :—

(a) Bullet-proof barricades to doors and windows. The means of exit, not necessarily on the ground floor, must be dealt with in a special way. It is easier to make loopholes in the barricades rather than to attempt to loophole the walls.

(b) Arrangements for ventilation, for the storage of ammunition, provisions and water, for a hospital and for latrines.

(c) Arrangements for extinguishing fires.

(d) Destruction of any outlying buildings which are not to be occupied, bearing in mind the importance of leaving no adjacent cover where an enemy might collect for assault.

21. If the building is large and strongly built, and it is intended to make an obstinate defence, arrangements must be made for interior defence by loopholing partition walls and upper floors made bullet-proof and strengthened if necessary to sustain the extra weight. Material with which to improvise additional cover or movable barricades to cover the retreat from one part of the building to the other, or from one building to another, must also be provided.

FIELD REDOUBTS.

22. Field redoubts are works entirely enclosed by defensible parapets which give all-round rifle fire, and may be of any command.

UNDER ORDINARY CONDITIONS REDOUBTS IN DEFENSIVE POSITIONS MUST NOT BE DESIGNED OR SITED IN SUCH A WAY THAT THEY CAN BE RECOGNIZED AS SUCH BY THE ENEMY. This will prevent their employment in the main zone of defence as a general rule.

Their principal use will be on the lines of communication, for isolated posts and sometimes as supporting points in rear of a defended position.

23. Rules for trenches apply to redoubts, but the following additional points are important :—

(a) Plan or trace of a redoubt depends on : (a) Fire effect required from it ; (b) Configuration of the ground ; (c) Proposed garrison.

(b) If possible interior not to be seen from ground which may be occupied by enemy. If the inside is exposed the garrison must burrow.

(c) Good splinter-proof cover.

(d) Good obstacles.

(e) No dead angles.

(f) Faces long enough to give an effective fire.

(g) Proportion of all defenders to size of work from 1 to 1½ men per yard of parapet.

(h) Overhead cover.

(j) Latrines and cooking places.

(k) Provide for water supply.

COVER FOR GUNS.

24. Plate 13 shows types of cover for guns.

WOODS.

25. The two attributes common to most woods are the obstruction they offer to the passage of troops, and the concealment they provide.

Special precautions are necessary for the defence of woods which run down from a position towards the enemy, since they make co-operation between the artillery and infantry of the defence almost impossible and afford the enemy a covered line of approach.

In the case of most woods the improvement of communications is one of the first considerations.

26. The front edge of a wood often has a boundary capable of being quickly made into a good fire position, but usually offers a good mark for artillery fire ; for this reason it may be desirable to place the firing line some 200 yards in advance, this being about the maximum distance short of the wood at which shrapnel should be burst, in order to be effective.

If by clearing the undergrowth a good field of fire can be obtained between the tree trunks, the firing line may, sometimes be placed with advantage 25 to 50 yards within the wood.

Where roads, rides or clearings exist in a wood, the rear edge may be organized as a second line of defence.

27. If defences in rear of a wood are more convenient than in front, the best arrangement will be to straighten and entangle the flanks and rear edge and take up an enfilading position some distance behind. Communications throughout the wood should be blocked.

22. OBSTACLES.

1. OBSTACLES ARE USED TO OBTAIN A DEFINITE CONTROL, BOTH AS REGARDS DIRECTION AND SPEED, OVER THE PROGRESS OF TROOPS ADVANCING TO THE ATTACK. THEIR CHIEF VALUE LIES IN THEIR POWER TO DEFLECT THE ATTACKING TROOPS INTO AREAS MOST FAVOURABLE FOR THEIR DESTRUCTION BY THE DEFENDERS. With this object in view they should be arranged : (a) to break up the unity of action and cohesion of the attacking troops, (b) to deflect the parties thus isolated into the best swept fields of fire, and (c) to arrest them under the close fire of the defenders. They are specially useful against night attacks.

2. They should fulfil the following conditions :—

(a) They should be under the close rifle of the defender, the outer edge not more than about 100 yards from the parapet. For small posts or redoubts they should be *quite close*, so that they may be effectively defended at night ; but, if they are much less than the distance given above, it will be possible to throw hand grenades into the work. They should be as wide as time and material will allow, should afford the enemy no cover, and should be sheltered from his artillery fire. Their actual position will generally be determined by placing them where they can be covered by the most effective fire of the defenders.

(b) They should be difficult to remove or surmount, and will be most effective if special appliances (not usually carried by troops) are required for their removal. Special attention should be paid to the security of their anchorages.

(c) They should, if possible, be so placed that their exact position and nature are unknown to the attacking force. With this object their sites may be sunk. Conspicuously placed obstacles may betray the existence of an otherwise well concealed position.

(d) They should be arranged so as not to impede counter-attacks.

(e) They should not be constructed without authority from the commander of the section of the defence.

(f) They need not be continuous, but may be constructed in sections. Occasional gaps in the line will often lead the attackers to crowd in towards them. Such passages may be provided with land mines and must be covered by gun and rifle fire. Roads passing through obstacles, and occasionally required for use by the defence, should be closed by portable obstacles, such as chevaux de frise, when not required for traffic.

3. The greatest length of obstacle which can be controlled by one man on a stormy and dark night is about 35 yards on either side. Where the total length of obstacle exceeds 70 yards, additional sentries, systematic patrolling, or efficient mechanical alarm signals will be necessary.

23. WORKING PARTIES AND THEIR TASKS.

1. With full-sized tools the average soldier should excavate in ordinary soil the following volumes in each hour :—

1st hour	30 cubic feet.
2nd ,, ...	25 ,,
3rd ,, ...	15 ,,
4th ,, and after, up to 8 hours	10 ,,

or 80 cubic feet in a 4-hour relief.

PLATE XIII.

Fig. 1.—GUN PIT FOR SHIELDED GUN.

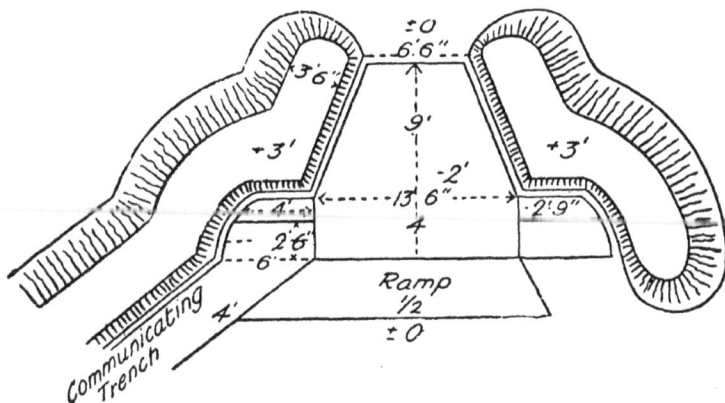

Fig. 2.—GUN EPAULMENT FOR SHIELDED GUN.

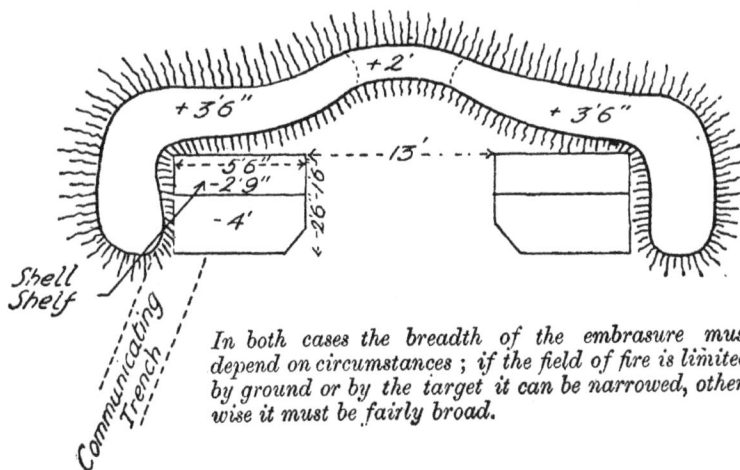

In both cases the breadth of the embrasure must
depend on circumstances ; if the field of fire is limited
by ground or by the target it can be narrowed, otherwise it must be fairly broad.

If the soil is very easy these rates may be increased, and *vice versa* ; and if 2 men are detailed to each set of tools these rates may be multiplied by ⅓.

These rates hold good for a maximum horizontal throw of 12 feet, combined with a lift out of a trench 4 feet deep.

2. The proportion of picks to shovels will be decided according to the nature of the soil. In ordinary soil the entrenching implement is almost equal to a pick. In moderately hard ground a good proportion of tools (excluding the entrenching implements) is 110 shovels, 55 picks with 60 helves, and 10 crowbars per 100 men, working continuous reliefs up to a total of 40 hours. This proportion gives sufficient spare to enable defective tools to be rejected.

3. IN THE CASE OF FIRE TRENCHES ALL QUESTIONS OF MECHANICAL SPACING AND DISTRIBUTION MUST GIVE WAY TO THE SELECTION, ON THE GROUND, OF THE BEST FIRING POINT FOR EACH AVAILABLE RIFLE.

4. For continuous trenchwork the normal distance apart at which men are spaced for work is two paces (5 feet).

5. The following form may be useful to facilitate *rapid commencement of work* and to ensure that *men and tools are employed in the most advantageous manner.*

The commander of the unit concerned (in this example a battalion) details his men and tools to the works in their respective order of importance, as shown in Cols. 1, 2, 3, 4 and 5. Should the tools with the unit not be sufficient, the commander would apply to his superior for the remainder.

The latter would then fill in Col. 6, showing whence the balance of tools required was to be obtained.

EXAMPLE OF WORKING PARTY TABLE.

WATLING RIDGE POSITION, No. 2 SECTION (13TH INFANTRY BRIGADE). 1ST SCOTS FUSILIERS.

1	2		3	4	5	6
Task. (1″ Map Sheet 384.)	Men.		Tools required.	Tools with unit.	Balance to complete.	Remarks.
	No.	From.				
1. East of HEXHAM COPSE at foot of slope (near rusty plough). Two 40-Rifle trenches, 18″ command, traversed, recessed and with head cover. Soil easy. Will probably take 7 hours.	80	C Co.	40 picks 80 shovels	40 80	... ...	
2. HEXHAM COPSE. Clear. Brushwood and small trees. About 8,000 sq. yards. Some brushwood required for trench above.	90	A Co.	10 felling axes 70 billhooks or handaxes	10 49	... 21	*1st Dublin Fusiliers.*
3. West of NORTHAM FARM at foot of slope (cleft stick and paper). Two 30-Rifle trenches, 12″ command. Soil very difficult. Probably take 8 hours.	60	B Co.	60 picks 60 shovels	60 60	... ...	
4. Communication trench from above trenches to east of NORTHAM FARM. 200 yards. Soil difficult. &c. &c.	120	D & E Cos.	120 picks 120 shovels	51 86	69 34	*Use grubbers. None available.* *20 only Brig. Res.*

24. KNOTS, CORDAGE, BLOCKS AND TACKLES.

Thumb

Figure of 8

1. To make a stop on a rope, or to prevent the end from unfraying, or to prevent its slipping through a block; the *thumb knot* or the *figure of* 8.

Reef   *Single Sheet Bend*   *Double Sheet Bend*

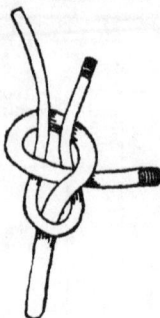

Hawser Bend   *Seizing*

2. To join two ropes together—
Same size (dry)...   ...   .   Reef.
Different sizes (dry) ...   .   Single Sheet Bend.
   ,,   ,,   (wet ropes) ...   ...   Double Sheet Bend.
   ,,   ,,   or large cables   ...   Hawser Bend.

Bowline

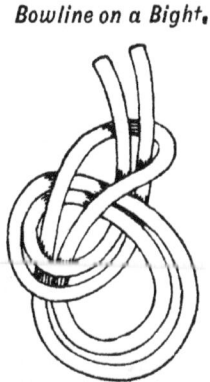

Bowline on a Bight.

3. To form a loop or *bight* on a rope which will not slip The *bowline* for a loop at the end of a rope, the *bowline* on a *bight* for a loop in the middle, with a double of the rope.

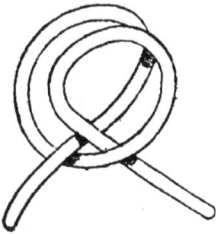

Clove Hitch

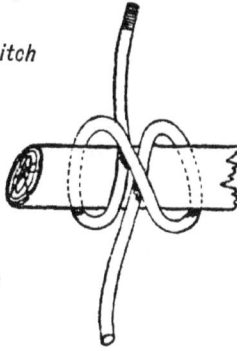

Timber Hitch

2 Half Hitches.   *Round Turn and 2 Half Hitches.*   *Fishermen's Bend.*

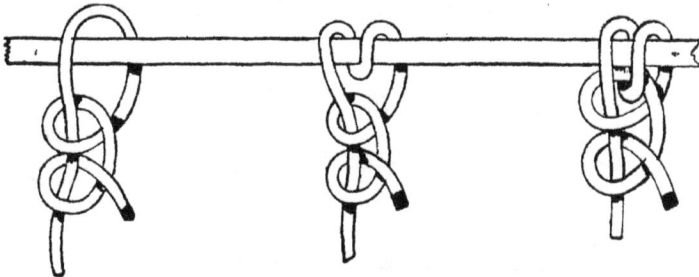

4. To secure the ends of ropes to spars or to other ropes.—2 Half Hitches, Clove Hitch, Timber Hitch, Round Turn and 2 Half Hitches.

Lever Hitch.

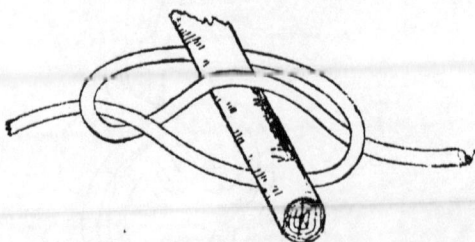

Man Harness-Hitch.

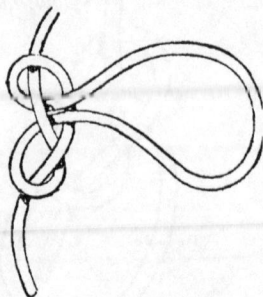

5. To fix a spar across a rope.—Lever Hitch.
6. To form a loop on a drag rope.—Man's Harness Hitch.

Draw Hitch

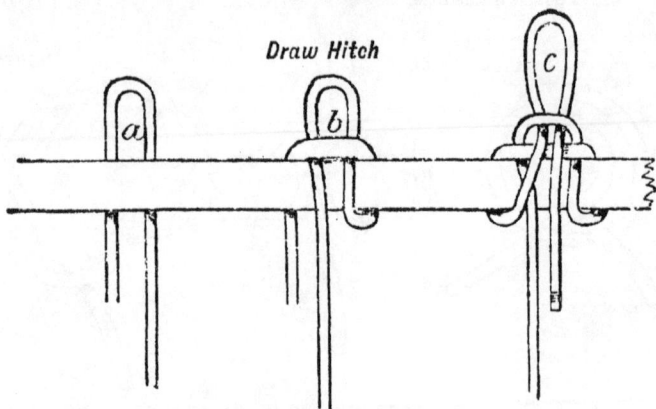

7. To secure a headrope, boat's painter, &c., to a post ring or rope, so that it can be quickly released.—Draw Hitch.

Stopper Hitch

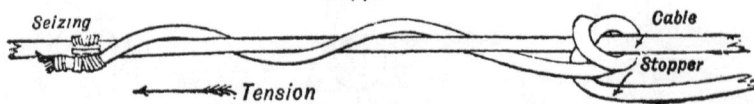

8. To transfer the strain on one rope to another.—Stopper Hitch.

Cat's Paw on Centre of Rope.

9. To fix a rope with a weight on it rapidly to a block—Cat's Paw or Blackwall Hitch.

CORDAGE, &c.

10. The size of a rope is denoted by its circumference in inches, and its length is given in fathoms. (A fathom is 6 feet.)

For field purposes, the safe working load for all cordage has been laid down as C^2 cwts., while for steel wire rope it may be taken as 9 C^2 cwts., where C is the circumference in inches. Steel wire rope may be taken as twice as strong as iron wire rope.

11. The strength of wire varies greatly ; as a very rough rule it may be taken that the breaking weight in pounds equals three times the weight per mile in pounds. Steel wire may be taken as about twice as strong.

12. The strength of a lashing round two objects may be taken as four-fifths of the number of times the lashing passes from one object to the other multiplied by the unit strength of the lashing, e.g., a square lashing with four turns has a holding power of $\frac{4}{5} \times 16 \times$ strength of lashing ; in the case of a hook lashed to a spar with four turns it is $\frac{4}{5} \times 8 \times$ strength of lashing.

When using wire in lashings multiply by three-fifths instead of four-fifths.

BLOCKS AND TACKLES.

13. Blocks are used for the purpose of changing the direction of ropes or of gaining power.

They are called single, double, treble, &c , according to the number of sheaves which they contain. The sheaves revolve on a pin, which should be kept well lubricated.

Snatch blocks are single blocks with an opening in one side of the shell, to admit a rope without passing its end through. This opening is closed by a hinged strap.

14. The rope with which tackles are *rove* is called a *fall*. To *overhaul* is to separate the blocks. To *round in* is to bring them closer together. When brought together the blocks are said to be *chock*.

In using tackle care must be taken to prevent it twisting.

15. In any system of two blocks, if P be the power required to raise a weight W, G the number of returns to the movable block, and N the total number of sheaves ; then

$$P = \frac{W}{G} + \left(\frac{N}{10} \times \frac{W}{G} \right).$$

25. BRIDGES AND BRIDGING EXPEDIENTS.

1. Tactical requirements will determine the locality for a military bridge, but the nature of the banks and approaches, the nature of the bed, width to be bridged, depth of water, strength of current, and the probability and extent of floods are important from a technical point of view. If a tidal river, the rise and fall of the tide should be ascertained.

2. THE APPROACHES AT BOTH ENDS OF A BRIDGE ARE A MATTER OF GREAT IMPORTANCE. EASY ACCESS AND A DIFFICULT EXIT ARE LIABLE TO CAUSE CROWDING AT THE ENTRANCE TO, AND ON, A BRIDGE, WHICH MAY LEAD TO ACCIDENTS AND DELAY.

BRIDGING EXPEDIENTS.

3. For tactical reasons it is often important to pass men, horses and artillery, across water at the earliest possible moment, and some expedient must precede work of a more deliberate nature.

A few of these bridging expedients are given below :—

(a) In shallow water, carts or wagons may be used to form the sub-structure for a bridge.

(b) Small gaps may be filled up with bundles of brushwood, channels being left for the passage of the water.

(c) Rafts or even piers for bridges may be made of waterproof material, such as tarpaulins, ground-sheets, &c., stuffed with hay, straw heather, ferns, &c.

A raft consisting of four 18 feet by 15 feet tarpaulins stuffed with hay will carry a load not exceeding 24 cwts. The best method of filling each tarpaulin is to make a light framework of poles 6 feet square by 2 feet 6 inches high, on the ground (a hole of similar dimensions will do almost as well). Then place two lashings about 24 feet long across the framework each way, and over these the tarpaulin, well soaked. Fill the tarpaulin with hay and trample it well down. The ends and sides of the tarpaulin are then folded over the hay, and the whole made into a compact bundle by securing the lashings across the top. (See Plate 14.)

The stores required are :—

Tarpaulins	4
Hay, &c. (tons)	1½
Planks	16
Spars (average 4″ diam.), four 16′, four 14′ and two 12′	10
Lashings, 1″ about 3 fms. long	40
„ 1½″ about 6 fms. long	16
Ropes, 2″, length according to width of river ..	2
Punting poles	2

Smaller rafts can similarly be made by stuffing ground-sheets with hay or straw ; 24 of these made into a raft will support a load of 1,800 lbs. It is essential for the sake of stability that, unless the buoyancy is much in excess of that actually required, the length of each pier of a raft should be twice the width of the platform of the raft. IF THE RAFT IS FORMED OF ONE PIER ONLY, THE PART OF THE PLATFORM LOADED SHOULD ONLY BE THE CENTRAL QUARTER.

(d) A rough boat can be made by covering the body of the Mark IX G.S. wagon with its tarpaulin cover. Any projecting points of the wagon must be covered with hay to protect the tarpaulin, and any holes in the wagon should be filled in the same way. The tarpaulin must be kept close to the wagon body by lashings. If sufficient lashings are available, one should be tied right round the wagon two-thirds of the way back from the front, while a second should be lashed round the wagon half way up its side, passing through the eyelet holes in the cover. Four to 6 men may be carried sitting down in this boat.

Rough boats may be made in a similar way by fastening tarpaulins over a brushwood framework.

BRIDGES.

4. Where better facilities for the passage of water or ravines are required some form of bridge will be needed.

The type of bridge will vary according to the materials available, the traffic expected, and the nature, breadth, depth, &c., of the span to be bridged ; but WHATEVER ARM OF THE SERVICE A BRIDGE IS CONSTRUCTED TO CARRY, IT SHOULD BE CAPABLE OF CARRYING THAT ARM WHEN CROWDED.

The most usual forms of bridges are trestle, cantilever and floating. Other methods sometimes employed are suspension, frame and crib work.

PLATE XIV.

RAFTS AND BRIDGES.

Fig. 1.—TARPAULIN RAFT.

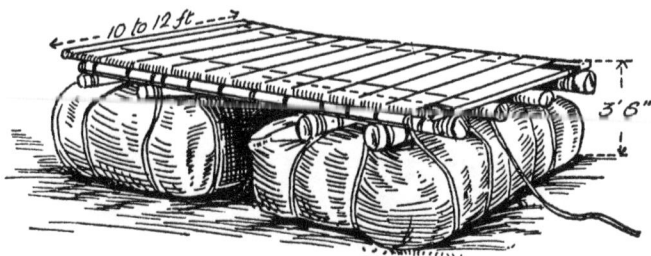

Fig. 2.—ROADWAY.

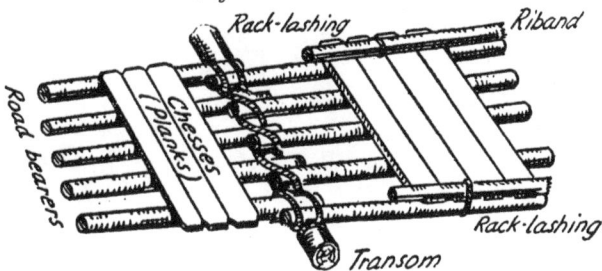

Fig. 3.

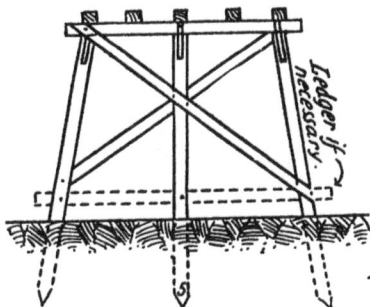

Fig. 4.—LASHED SPAR TRESTLE.

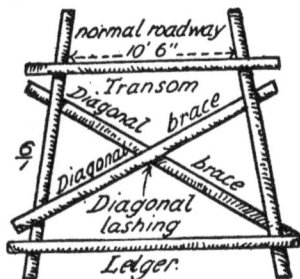

All junctions lashed with wire or rope, square lashings except where stated.

To face page 110.

PLATE XV.

Fig. 1.—LAUNCHING TRESTLES.

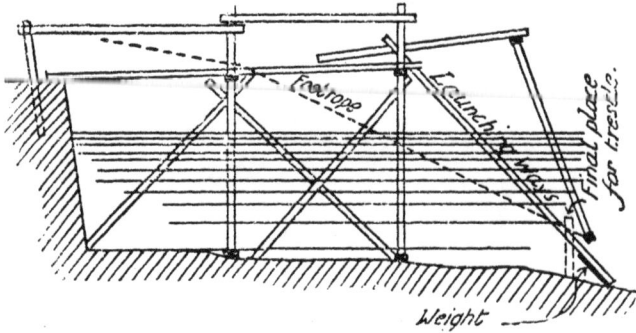

Fig. 2.—CANTILEVER BRIDGE.

Fig. 3.
CRIB PIER IN SHALLOW WATER.

Fig. 4.
FLYING BRIDGE.

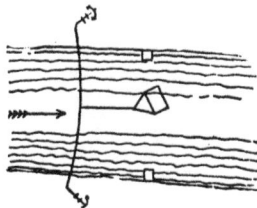

To follow Plate XIV.

5. A bridge that will carry infantry in fours crowded will carry field guns and 4·5-inch howitzers and most of the ordinary wagons that accompany an army in the field.

To prevent it being improperly used, a signboard should be placed at each end, stating the greatest permissible load, thus :—

"Bridge to carry infantry in fours."
"Bridge to carry infantry in file."
"Bridge to carry guns not heavier than 18-pr."
"Not for animals," &c.

6. The usual form of roadway is shown on Plate 14. The normal width of roadway is 9 feet between the ribands ; 8 feet will suffice for infantry in fours or cavalry in half sections ; 6 feet for infantry in file, cavalry in single file and field guns passed over by hand ; 1½ to 3 feet for infantry in single file. Types of trestles and bridges are shown on Plates 14 and 15. Planks 1½ to 2 inches thick are sufficient for ordinary traffic. Handrails 3 feet above the roadway should be provided.

BRIDGING MATERIAL CARRIED IN THE FIELD.

6a. A cavalry regiment carries air raft equipment for making a raft designed to carry any limbered vehicle with a cavalry division, including R.H.A. guns and R.E. tool carts. Its flotation is insufficient and its design is unsuitable for carrying loaded G.S. wagons or other 4-wheeled vehicles.

7. A field squadron carries 8 collapsible boats, each 18 feet 6 inches long, making 4 rafts. A field troop carries 2 collapsible boats, each 18 feet 6 inches long, making one raft. A field company carries 2 pontoons and 2 trestles, with superstructure, capable of constructing 75 feet of medium bridge.

8. A bridging train carries 42 pontoons and 42 bays of superstructure, capable of constructing 210 yards of medium bridge or 105 yards of heavy bridge, together with 16 trestles and 8 bays of superstructure, capable of constructing 40 yards of medium bridge or 20 yards of heavy bridge.

By placing the pontoons and trestles at half interval 125 yards of bridge, strong enough to carry mechanical transport, can be constructed from the material carried by the bridging train.

9. The following times are given as a guide in average conditions and with trained men. It is not, as a rule, the actual placing of the pontoons which takes the time, but the preparation of the approaches, and the distance pontoons and superstructure have to be carried.

    (a) Field company placing its pontoons and completing roadway. No allowance made for making ramps. Site without unusual difficulties. Includes unpacking pontoons—½-¾ hour.

    (b) As above, including the 2 trestles (this includes unpacking trestles and putting them together)—About 2 hours.

    (c) 50 *yards bridge.*—

        Ample labour assumed, sufficient for one party to make bridge and another to unload wagons. One trestle assumed at each end of bridge—2½-3 hours.

        If no trestles were required the time could probably be reduced to from 1-1½ hours.

    100 *yards bridge.*—

        Ample labour ; one trestle at each end—3½-4 hours.

        If no trestles were required—2¼-2½ hours.

    200 *yards bridge.*—

        Ample labour. All material of bridging train required, so 7 or 8 trestles will have to be put in. Time to make whole bridge will practically depend on the time taken to place the trestles—8-10 hours.

Night work will add from 50 to 100 per cent. to the above times.

WEIGHTS OF TROOPS, GUNS AND MATERIALS.

10. The maximum weights brought on a bridge by the passage of troops in marching order are :—

Infantry, in file, crowded at a check,	2½ cwts.			⎧ Per lineal foot of the
,, in fours	,,	,,	5 ,,	⎪ bridge irrespective of
Cavalry in single file	,,	,,	1¾ ,,	⎨ width of roadway,
,, in half-sections	,,	,,	3½ ,,	⎪ provided the forma-
				⎩ tion is preserved.

Armed men in a disorganized mass may weigh $1\frac{1}{4}$ cwts. per square foot of standing room.

11. The maximum weights brought on a bridge by guns of an army in the field are :—

13-pr. Q.F. gun, maximum concentrated weight on one bay, 13 cwts.
18-pr. Q.F. gun   do.   do.   24 ,,
4·5-in Howitzer   do.   do.   26 ,,
60-pr. B.L. gun   do.   do.   67 ,,

12. The weights brought on a bridge by certain animals are :—

Camels, loaded   ..   .. 15 cwts.
,,   ,,   weight on one leg ..   .. 10 ,,
Pack-bullocks ..   .. $5\frac{1}{2}$,,
,,   ,,   weight on one leg ..   ..   .. $3\frac{1}{2}$,,
Elephants, loaded, weight on one leg   ..   ..   .. 44 ,,

13. The weight of earth 1 inch thick may be taken as 10 lbs. per square foot covered ; and of soft timber 40 lbs. per cubic foot.

FORMULÆ FOR CALCULATING SIZE FOR ROADBEARERS, TRANSOMS AND CANTILEVERS.

14. Rough formulæ for calculating the sizes, necessary for roadbearers and transoms, &c., are given below. The formulæ include a factor of $1\frac{1}{2}$ for live load, in addition to a factor of safety of 3 ; they also allow for a normal weight of superstructure.

For unselected rectangular beams supported at both ends :—

$$W = \frac{bd^2}{L} \times K \quad . \quad . \quad . \quad . \quad . \quad . \quad (A)$$

For unselected round spars supported at both ends :—

$$W = \frac{6}{10} \times \frac{d^3}{L} \times K \quad . \quad . \quad . \quad . \quad (B)$$

The formulæ for strength of cantilevers are as follows :—
For unselected rectangular beams fixed at one end :—

$$W = \frac{1}{4} \times \frac{bd^2}{L} \times K \quad . \quad . \quad . \quad . \quad (C)$$

For unselected round spars fixed at one end :—

$$W = \frac{1}{4} \times \frac{6}{10} \times \frac{d^3}{L} \times K \quad . \quad . \quad . \quad (D)$$

In the above formulæ—

W = actual load on one beam in cwts. evenly distributed (without superstructure).
b = breadth of beam in inches.
d = depth of beam in inches.
$L = \begin{cases} \text{length of beam in feet between points of support for (A) and (B).} \\ \text{length of cantilever in feet from point of support for (C) and (D) ; or, if loaded at one point only (see below), length from point of support to position of load.} \end{cases}$
K = a variable quantity for different timbers.

For larch and cedar ..   .. $K = 1$
,,   Baltic fir ..   .. $K = \frac{4}{5}$
,,   American yellow pine ..   .. $K = \frac{3}{5}$
,,   beech and English oak ..   .. $K = \frac{1}{2}$

In the case of round spars b and d are identical, and their strength is only about six-tenths that of square beams of the same depth.

15. To use these formulæ for a *concentrated* weight, such as a gun, the total weight on the gun wheels must be multiplied by two to convert it to the equivalent *distributed* weight, when it can be substituted for W. When, as in the case of a transom, the load is applied at several points, it can be taken as distributed.

16. With several baulks under a roadway, the two outer carry only half as much of any weight as the inner ones.

17. Rectangular beams should always be used on edge, in order to obtain the maximum of rigidity and strength. In calculating the sizes of beams by the formulæ in 1 and 2 above, if b and d are unknown, d should be considered equal to $2b$.

A tapering spar, when supported at both ends and overloaded, will break in the centre.

18. Table Giving Sizes of Round Roadbearers and Transoms (supported at the ends only) for Various Loads and Spans (K = $\frac{1}{4}$).

Loads on Bridge.	Round Spars required.	Mean Diameter in Inches.					
Infantry in file..	3 Roadbearers each	6	$6\frac{1}{2}$	7	$7\frac{1}{2}$	$8\frac{1}{2}$	9
	Transoms .. ,,	$6\frac{1}{2}$	7	7	$7\frac{1}{2}$	8	8
Cavalry in single file	3 Roadbearers each	5	$5\frac{1}{2}$	$6\frac{1}{2}$	7	$7\frac{1}{2}$	8
	Transoms .. ,,	6	6	$6\frac{1}{2}$	7	7	$7\frac{1}{2}$
Infantry in fours	5 Roadbearers each	6	$6\frac{1}{2}$	7	$7\frac{1}{2}$	$8\frac{1}{2}$	9
	Transoms .. ,,	9	$9\frac{1}{2}$	10	$10\frac{1}{2}$	11	$11\frac{1}{2}$
Cavalry in half-sections	5 Roadbearers each	5	$5\frac{1}{2}$	$6\frac{1}{2}$	7	$7\frac{1}{2}$	8
	Transoms .. ,,	8	$8\frac{1}{2}$	9	$9\frac{1}{2}$	10	10
Q.F. 13-pr. gun, Marks I and II.	5 Roadbearers each	$5\frac{1}{2}$	6	6	$6\frac{1}{2}$	7	$7\frac{1}{2}$
	Transoms .. ,,	7	7	$7\frac{1}{2}$	$7\frac{1}{2}$	$7\frac{1}{2}$	$7\frac{1}{2}$
Q.F. 18-pr. gun, Marks I and II.	5 Roadbearers each	6	6	7	7	$7\frac{1}{2}$	$7\frac{1}{2}$
	Transoms .. ,,	$7\frac{1}{2}$	$7\frac{1}{2}$	8	8	8	8
5" Howitzer, Mark I.	5 Roadbearers each	6	$6\frac{1}{2}$	7	8	$8\frac{1}{2}$	9
	Transoms .. ,,	8	8	$8\frac{1}{2}$	$8\frac{1}{2}$	$8\frac{1}{2}$	$8\frac{1}{2}$
60-pr gun in travelling position	5 Roadbearers each	8	$8\frac{1}{2}$	9	9	$9\frac{1}{2}$	10
	Transoms .. ,,	10	10	10	10	$10\frac{1}{2}$	$10\frac{1}{2}$
4·7" gun on travelling carriage	5 Roadbearers each	$8\frac{1}{2}$	9	$9\frac{1}{2}$	10	$10\frac{1}{2}$	10
	Transoms .. ,,	11	11	11	11	11	11
	Spans in feet.. ..	10	12	14	16	18	20

Other timbers not affected by length of bay :—

Ledgers and handrails, mean diameter, 4-6 inches.
Braces and ribands, 3 inches at tip.

19. The depth (d) and breadth (b) of rectangular timber of equivalent strength to the round spars given in the above table can be found from the formula $ba^2 = \frac{6}{10} D^3$; where D is the mean diameter in inches given in the table. Some practical equivalents for ready reference are given below :—

D	b by d	D	b by d	D	b by d
3	2 by 3	6	3 by 6¾	9	5 by 9¾
3½	2 by 3¾	6½	3 by 7½	9½	5 by 10½
4	2 by 4½	7	3 by 8¼	10	5 by 11¼
4½	2 by 5¼	7½	3 by 9	10½	5 by 12
5	3 by 5¼	8	4 by 9	11	6 by 12
5½	3 by 6	8½	5 by 9	12	7 by 12

Size of Timber for Trestle Legs.

20. From the following table the size of timber required for trestle legs can be found. It allows for factor of safety and for factor for live load, so that the actual load applied should be taken :—

UNSUPPORTED HEIGHT IN FEET.

1 Cwt 3 Cwt 5 Cwt 10 Cwt 15 Cwt 1 Ton 30 Cwt 2 Tons 3 Tons 4 Tons 5 T

ABC, 16 TONS LIMIT SPARS ARE ANY TO FEET BY THEIR OWN WEIGHT WHEN LOADED

LIMIT OF DIRECT CRUSHING

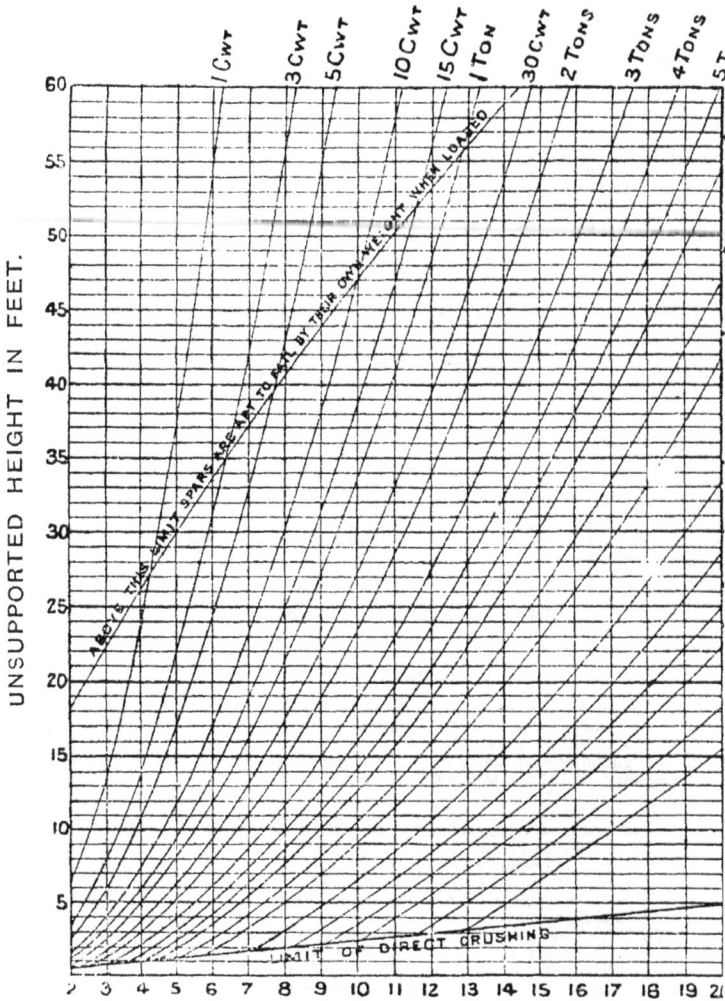

MEAN DIAMETER OF SPAR IN INCHES.

Baltic fir, " k " = $\frac{3}{4}$.

Safe crushing stress taken as 1,000 *lbs. per sq. inch.*

Formulæ for Calculating Buoyancy.

21. In using closed vessels such as casks for floating piers, the *safe* buoyancy for bridging purposes may be taken at nine-tenths the *actual* buoyancy.

When calculating the buoyancy required for a raft or pier for a floating bridge, it is necessary to work to the actual weight of the load to be carried, *plus that of the superstructure.* The superstructure of the actual roadway of a bridge of normal width to carry infantry in fours may be taken at 120 lbs. per foot run, up to 15 feet span.

22. The buoyancy of closed vessels can be determined with sufficient accuracy by the following methods :—

    (*a*) When the contents are known—

        Multiply the contents, in gallons, by 9, this will give the safe buoyancy in pounds.

    (*b*) For casks, when the contents are not known—

$$\text{Actual buoyancy} = 5C^2L - W \text{ lbs.}$$

$$\text{Safe buoyancy} = \tfrac{9}{10}\left\{ 5C^2L - W \right\} \text{lbs.}$$

Where C is the circumference of the cask, in FEET halfway between the bung and the extreme end ; L is the extreme length, exclusive of projections, along the curve, in FEET ; W is the weight of the cask in pounds.

23. The buoyancy of a log can be obtained by multiplying its cubic content by the difference between its weight per cubic foot and that of a cubic foot of water. One cubic foot of water = $6\tfrac{1}{4}$ gallons, and 1 gallon weighs 10 lbs.

As, however, timber absorbs a great deal of water, only five-sixths of the *actual* buoyancy thus found can be relied upon.

Thus, the *safe* buoyancy of a pine log of which the cubic content is 96 cubic feet would be :—

$$\tfrac{5}{6} \times 96 \times (62\tfrac{1}{2} - 40)$$
$$= 80 \times 22\tfrac{1}{2}$$
$$= 1,800 \text{ lbs.}$$

40 lbs. being the weight of a cubic foot of pine.

24. The contents in cubic feet of an unsquared log of timber can be found by the following rule :—

$$\frac{L}{4}(D^2 + Dl + d^2),$$

Where L = length of log in feet.

    D, d = diameter at ends in feet.

26. DEMOLITIONS.

1. The service explosives available for hasty demolitions in the field are guncotton and cordite. Other explosives may sometimes be obtained, the most likely being gunpowder and dynamite. Where a lifting effect is desired, gunpowder should be used ; but, when a cutting or shattering effect is necessary, one of the others (high explosives) is better.

Guncotton.

2. A charge of wet guncotton is detonated by means of the explosion of a dry primer in close contact with it.

3. The slabs and primers for field service are as follows :—

    (*a*) Slab.—Weight 15 oz. Dimensions, 6 inches × 3 inches × $1\tfrac{1}{2}$ inches, with one perforation for the primer. Each slab is in an hermetically sealed copper-tinned case.

    (*b*) Primer.—Weight 1 oz. Dimensions, 1·35 inches to 1·15 inches in diameter by 1·25 inches long, with one perforation for the detonator. The primer is conical in form.

4. A charge is connected up for detonation as follows :—

    The fuze (safety alone or safety with instantaneous) is cut to the required length. The end to be ignited is cut on a slant to expose as much of the composition as possible. The end to be inserted in the detonator is cut straight across. The straight cut end is then gently inserted into the open end of No. 8 detonator, from which the paper cap has been torn. This end of the detonator is then pinched (or with old-pattern detonator, slightly bent) to make it grip on the fuze and so prevent its being withdrawn.

The primer having been tested to receive a detonator is placed in close contact with one of the slabs of the charge, either in one of the holes or tied to a slab, and the small end of the detonator is gently inserted into it so as to fill the entire length of the hole. If the hole is too large, a piece of paper or grass must be wrapped round the detonator to make it fit tightly; if too small, it must be enlarged with a rectifier or piece of wood, *but not with the detonator*.

5. THE CHARGE MUST BE IN CLOSE CONTACT WITH THE OBJECT TO BE DEMOLISHED AND EACH SLAB MUST BE IN CONTACT WITH THOSE NEXT IT.

The charge must extend across the whole length of the object to be cut. One detonator is sufficient for a continuous guncotton charge.

6. The amount of guncotton (untamped) required for various charges can be calculated or obtained direct from the following table :—

Object attacked.	lbs.	Remarks.
Masonry arch—haunch or crown	$\frac{3}{4}BT^2$	Continuous charges.
Masonry wall—up to 2 ft. thick	2 per foot	Length of breech B not to be less than the height of the wall to be brought down.
Masonry wall—over 2 ft. thick	$\frac{1}{4}BT^2$	
Masonry pier	$\frac{3}{8}BT^2$	
Hard wood—stockade or single	$3BT^2$	In a single charge outside. For a round timber charge = $3T^3$. Where the timber is not round, T = smaller axis. } Soft wood half this.
Hard wood—auger hole ...	$\frac{3}{5}T^2$	
Stockade of earth between timber up to 3 ft. 6 ins. thick	4 per foot	}
Heavy rail stockade	7 per foot	} Single charge outside.
Fort gate	50	}
Breech loading guns	—	For 3-inch gun use 2 lbs. Double the charge for every inch increase in calibre.
First class rail	1	Charge fastened against the web near a chair (if used).
Iron or steel plate	$\frac{3}{4}Bt^2$	t is in INCHES.
Frontier tower, stone and mud	—	5 lbs. plus 1 lb. per foot of longer side if rectangular, or of diameter if circular. In one charge in centre of tower.
Steel wire cable	1	Up to 5 inches circumference; above 5 inches $\frac{C^2}{24}$, C being the circumference in inches.

Where B = length to be demolished in FEET.
T = thickness to be demolished in FEET.
t = thickness to be demolished in INCHES (in the case of steel or iron plate only).

Note.—The charge is in pounds ; if the charge is tamped, the amount can be halved. Masonry includes concrete, stone, or brickwork.

In the presence of the enemy, charges may be placed hurriedly, and so under unfavourable conditions, and should therefore be increased by 50 per cent.

For emergency purposes BT^2 is effective with all classes of masonry and $2Bt^2$ for all steelwork. A slab will cut its own thickness of steel plate.

CORDITE

7. For demolition purposes cordite is uncertain in its action and should only be used when no better explosive is available. The small sizes are the more reliable.

It is fired similarly to guncotton; a primer of guncotton or other high explosive must always be used.

No portion of a cordite charge should be more than 12 inches from a primer, since the rate of communicating detonation is slow.

8. Where good contact can be obtained, the power of cordite may be taken as equal to guncotton, otherwise a cordite charge should be increased by about 25 per cent.

GUNPOWDER.

9. Gunpowder charges must be tamped, and should be made up in as compact a form as possible. The powder should be placed in a well-tarred sandbag, or, failing that, in one sandbag inside a second one.

The service sandbag will hold about 40 lbs.

10. The amount of gunpowder (tamped), required for various charges, can be calculated from the following table:—

Object attacked.	lbs.	Remarks.
Masonry arch—haunch or crown	$\frac{3}{4}BT^2$	Total amount divided into charges and placed at intervals of about twice the thickness of the masonry. Fire simultaneously.
Masonry wall		
Wood stockade—hard wood ...	40 to 100	One charge. Soft wood half this.
Stockade of earth between timber up to 3 ft. 6 ins. thick	100 per 7 ft.	Charges twice the thickness of stockade apart.
Fort gate	200	One charge.
Tunnels	$\frac{1}{8}T^3$	Where T = total distance from the surface of the lining to the charge.

DYNAMITES.

11. Dynamites cannot be used after exposure to wet, which separates the nitro-glycerine and makes it dangerous.

Dynamites freeze at 40° F., and remain frozen at higher temperatures.

FROZEN DYNAMITES MUST NOT BE WARMED ON OR NEAR FIRES, STOVES, OVENS, OR STEAM-PIPES; NOR EXPOSED TO THE DIRECT RAYS OF A TROPICAL SUN.

They are usually obtained in 2-oz. cartridges, wrapped in parchment paper, in boxes of 5 and 50 lbs.

They can be detonated by fuze and No. 8 detonator, or by fuze and cap.

12. They are fired in a similar manner to guncotton, but no primer is required.

When a dynamite charge requires ramming, as in a bore hole, each cartridge must be gently squeezed into place with a wooden rammer, the fuzed one being the last.

FUZES.

13. The present pattern of safety fuze is known as "Safety No. 9."

It is coloured BLACK, and will burn under water.

For practical work the rate of burning can be taken at 4 feet per minute.

14. It is difficult to light safety fuze with a match or flame, the head of a match inserted in the fuze and lit by another match or rubbed by the prepared portion of a matchbox, is usually successful.

15. Instantaneous fuze is coloured ORANGE.

It burns at the rate of 30 yards a second, or practically instantaneously.

It can be distinguished in the dark from safety fuze by feeling the open crossed thread snaking round it.

16. Unless the safety of the firer or the depth of the tamping requires it, instantaneous fuze should not be used with safety fuze.

SPECIAL CASES.

17. *Masonry or brick bridges.*—Use guncotton. Attack pier where thinnest; if possible, cut groove; or else tie charge to a board and fix it against pier.

Thick piers, attack haunches. Dig trench to back of arch ring at each haunch and lay charge. If time is short, attack the crown.

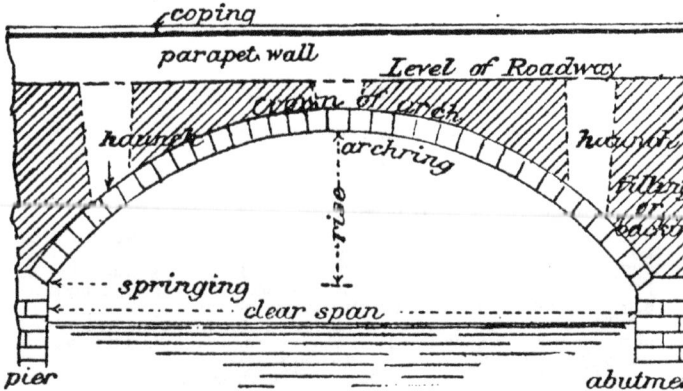

18. *Houses.*—(Weakly built), put charge in centre of each room or hearth of fireplaces, fire simultaneously. Mud huts up to 18 ft. square with walls 2 feet thick at bottom, 4 lbs. guncotton in one corner. Four-room cottage, 6 to 12 lbs.

19. *Towers.*—Place charge in hole 2 to 3 feet deep in centre of floor, tamp well. Charge in pounds equal inside diameter or side in feet plus 5.

20. *Fort gates.*—Guncotton, 50 lbs. charge on ground or hung on nail. Gunpowder, 200 lbs. tamped with sand bags.

21. *Iron or steel bridges.*—Use guncotton. Attack main girders near abutment. For hasty demolition of spans 20–80 ft. $C = \dfrac{L^2}{15D}$.

Where C = charge of guncotton in slabs (15-oz.) for one girder of single line of standard railway, L = length of girder in feet, D = total depth of girder in feet.

Where one girder has to bear the whole load of a line of railway, *e.g.*, two girders carrying a double line, or a centre girder carrying half of two single lines, the amount given by the formula should be doubled.

22. *Guns.*—Load with a shell, pack in charge, in contact with shell and sides of chamber. Connect up charge, add sods, earth, &c., to keep it in place and to tamp it. Close breech as far as possible. A shell is not absolutely necessary, but charge must be tamped.

DEMOLITIONS WITHOUT EXPLOSIVES.

23. *Railways.*—Sever or block main lines of rails; remove technical tools and personnel; destroy signals, points and crossings, and water supply.

Locomotives.—Take off injector, piston or safety valve.

Rolling stock.—Burn or remove springs. Trains may be run against each other, or a rail turned to block a line temporarily.

Telegraphs.—Cut down or break poles, cut up and twist wires.

Guns.—Close breech, then withdraw hand-lever about 1 inch, and with handspike or pick beat down lever until hinge-joint is distorted. A few shots fired at carrier would jam mechanism still more.

Arms.—The best way is to first break off the butts and then to destroy the barrels. For the latter the rifle barrels with parts of the wood still on them, should be well heated over fire in a trench after which they can be smashed up with heavy hammers. A party of five should be able to destroy 25 rifles in half an hour.

Ammunition to be destroyed should be placed in a deep pit and set on fire.

CHAPTER V.

27. TRANSPORT.

(*See* F.S.R., Part II, Chap. VIII.)

The transport of a force is divided into :—

(a) Transport on the Lines of Communication.
(b) Transport with Field Units.

2. Transport on the L. of C. comprises (a) Railway transport; (b) Road transport; (c) Inland water transport.

The traffic arrangements under all three heads are co-ordinated by the I.G.C., who is responsible for the punctual movements of the army's requirements between the base and rendezvous inclusive.

3. The administrative and executive control of *railway transport* is vested in the director of railway transport, who is responsible to the I.G.C. for the efficiency of everything connected with that service.

For the defence of a railway and of working parties on it the commander of the L. of C. defences is solely responsible.

4. *Road transport.*—The representative of the director of transport at the headquarters of the I.G.C. is responsible for all road transport on the L. of C.

It is divided into three classes :—

(a) Parks and columns, working between railheads and the field force, which form the connecting link between the railway and the ammunition columns and trains.

(b) Transport to supplement the railway. It works between the base and railheads or along such portion of the railway lines as may be decided on by the I.G.C. On good roads mechanical transport is specially suitable.

(c) Transport for local work at the base or at posts on the L. of C.

5. *Inland water transport.*—When inland waterways are used on a large scale, a separate director may be appointed, who will be directly responsible for this service to the I.G.C. In other circumstances, the organization of this service may be delegated to a representative of the director of transport.

6. Transport may be requisitioned similarly to ordinary stores (*see* Sec. 36) but separate requisition receipt notes should be issued.

7. *Transport with field units.*—The transport with field units is divided into two classes :—

(a) The transport of fighting units, which is again divided into first line transport and trains.

(b) The transport of administrative units, *i.e.*, field ambulances, cavalry field ambulances, which is not subdivided but marches with the unit as a whole.

8. The director of transport is responsible that all the available transport with field units is allotted in the manner best calculated to further the C.-in-C.'s intentions. He is also responsible that material is available for the punctual replacement of all deficiencies in transport other than the technical vehicles of artillery, engineer, and flying units.

The O.C. a Train supervises all transport in the formation to which he is attached.

The Regimental Transport officer is responsible to his C.O. for the efficiency of vehicles, animals and equipment of 1st line transport of his unit.

9. First line transport is an integral part of the war organization of a fighting unit, without which it cannot perform its tactical functions, and by which it must be accompanied in action and at all times.

First line transport includes the following vehicles and animals :—Gun carriages; ammunition wagons; pack animals, limbered or G.S. wagons or carts carrying ammunition, tools, machine guns, technical stores or medical equipment ; telephone wagons, water carts, and travelling kitchens or other vehicles for cooks, and in the case of cavalry and horse artillery units, for which no trains are provided, vehicles for the conveyance of baggage and stores.

10. Trains are allotted to fighting units (except cavalry and horse artillery) for the conveyance of the baggage, stores, and supplies necessary for their subsistence. They are not usually required for tactical purposes in action and should therefore, when battle is imminent, be kept well outside the area in which fighting is probable, so as to ensure freedom of movement to the troops, and to the vehicles required near the troops in action.

11. Commanders of units are responsible for the care and efficiency of the personnel, animals, vehicles and equipment of all the transport of their units. Indents to replace deficiencies will be forwarded direct to the representative of the director of transport at the headquarters of the division or other formation to which the unit belongs.

12. Each company of the Train is organized in two sections, viz., Baggage Section and Supply Section.

When fighting is imminent, the baggage and supply sections should usually march together.

In other circumstances the hour of movement for the baggage section will be regulated by the requirements of the troops, whose baggage should be available as soon as they have occupied their new quarters.

Any necessary orders for the movements of baggage sections will normally be issued by divisional headquarters unless Army Headquarters desire to control these movements as an exceptional measure. The responsibility of subordinate commanders in regard to baggage sections is limited to the period when the vehicles are in brigade areas.

13. For space occupied by transport on the march, *see* pp. 38–42.

For allotment of transport to units, *see* p. 122 *et seq.*

14. The light draught horse should draw a weight of about 1,200 lbs., and the heavy draught one of about 1,600 lbs. for approximately 20 miles per day ; walk about 3 miles an hour and trot at an average rate of 6 miles. He requires a space of 3′ 0″ × 9′ 0″ standing, and, at sea, a measurement space of 9 tons.

15. *Indian transport.*—Transport with field units is divided into 1st and 2nd line transport. 1st line transport consists of pack mules. 2nd line transport is carried on the most suitable transport available, generally camels. Water supply and men's great coats on summer scale or 1 blanket per man on winter scale are carried on mules to allow of their accompanying the 1st line when required. On winter scale the men carry their own great coats.

The 2nd line transport of a unit consists of mules, carts, bullocks, camels ponies, or coolies, in accordance with circumstances.

16. *Carriers.*—Carriers are organized into gangs of 20, 1 headman to each gang ; 4 gangs to a section ; 1 conductor to a section ; carriers numbered and registered, and given a disc with number.

17.—1st Line Transport.

	Two-horsed										Four-horsed									Six-horsed													Spare horses.	Pack animals.	Motor cars.	Motor cycles.	Bicycles.
	Carts, Maltese, one-horsed.	Carts, water.	Carts, Maltese.	Carts, forage, or limbered wagons.	Carts, S.A.A.	Wagons, limbered G.S. and wireless pack.	Wagons, light spring.	Carts, tool, R.E.	Wagons, ambulance.	Carts, cooks', or travelling kitchens.	Wagons, telephone.	Wagons, G.S., technical stores.	Wagons, cable.	Wagons, limbered G.S.	Wagons, air-line.	Wagons, reservoir gas.	Wagons, ambulance.	Wagons, cooks', or travelling kitchens.	Wagons, G.S. for baggage.	Gun carriages.	Carts, tool, R.E.	Wagons, ammunition.	Wagons, air-line.	Wagons, cable.	Wagons, G.S., technical stores.	Wagons, G.S., for ammunition.	Wagons for collapsible boats.	Wagons, trestle.	Wagons, pontoon.	Wagons, limbered wireless.	Wagons, ambulance.					
Headqrs. cavalry division ...		1																	1														1	116		
" division ...		1		1						1								1	1													1	15		7
" cav. bde. (with cav. div.)			1	1						1									1														1		7
" cav. bde. not allotted to a cav. div.																																	5		
" infantry brigade																																			7
", cav. div. A.S.C. ...		1	1	1						1		2a		5					1													2	1		8
Cav. regt., headqrs. and M.G. sec. ...						6								2					1													2			4
" squadron ...						6								11					1													6			20
" complete ...														2					4													2			6
Cav. sqdn. (div. cav.)														2																		2			8
Squadron Irish Horse ...		1	1							1									1																8
Headqrs. cav. div. or div. art.										1	1								2																3
H.A. battery (13-pr.) ...	1	1	1																2	6		12				20						22			3
" ammun'tion column		3	1																5	6		12				20						26			3
" brigade ...		1								1									12	12		36										70			12

battery with cav. bde. not allotted to a cav. div.
    amm. col.
F.A. battery (18-pr.) "
  " amm. col. "
  " brigade "
  " battery (4·5-in. howitzer) "
  " amm. col. "
  " brigade "
Heavy battery (60-pr.) "
  " ammunition column
Divisional ammunition column
Headqrs. divl. eng.
Field squadron
Field troop
Field company
Bridging train
Signal squadron A troop
  " " B "
  " " C "
  " " D "
  " " complete
Signal trp. with cav. bde. (cav. div.)
  " " cav. bde. not allotted to a cav. div.
Signal compy. with div. No. 1 sec.
  " " Nos. 2, 3 or 4 secs.
  " " complete
Headqrs. G.H.Q. Sig. coy.
Headqrs. A.H.Q. Sig. coy.
An air-line section
A cable section
A wireless section
Flying Cps. Hdqrs. and Kite Sec.
Aeroplane Squadron
Inf. batn., headqrs. and M.G. sqdn.
  " company
  " battalion complete

a G.S. for entrenching tools. *b* For cavalry divisional artillery headquarters. *c* 2 for divisional artillery headquarters. *d* 3 of these are 4-horsed. *e* With 8 horses each. *f* With 4 heavy draught horses each. *g* 6 have only 4 horses (heavy draught). *h* 24 horses with 4 double tool carts. *j* 12 horses for the 2 double tool carts. *k* G.S., R.E. *l* Includes motor lorries. *m* Motor lorries. *n* Kite (winch and store) wagons. *o* Travelling kitchens. Battalions which do not possess travelling kitchens will have one wagon, cooks', 2-horsed.

18.—Train Transport.

The transport shown below is mobilized by units, but on arrival in the area of concentration is handed over to the A.S.C. :—

Name of Unit.	Carts, Forage or Limbered Wagons. 2-horsed.	Wagons, G.S. 2-horsed.	Motor Lorries.
Hd. Qrs. of a Div.	1	2	...
Hd. Qrs. of an Inf. Bde.	1	1	...
Cav. Sqdn. (Div. Cav.) or Sqdn. Irish Horse	...	2	...
Hd. Qrs. Divl. Art.	1	1	...
F.A. Batt. (18-pr. or 4·5″ howr.)	...	2	...
F.A. Amm. Coln. (18-pr. or 4·5″ howr.)...	...	2	...
F.A. Bde. (18-pr. or 4·5″ howr.)	...	9	...
Heavy Batt. and Amm. Coln. (60-pr.) ...	...	2	...
Divl. Amm. Coln. Section	...	2	...
Divl. Amm. Coln. (complete)	...	9	...
Hd. Qrs. Divl. Eng.	2	...	...
Field Company	...	1	...
Bridging Train	...	3	...
Signal Company Divisional	1	...	...
Hd. Qrs. G.H.Q. Sig. Co.	...	2	...
Hd. Qrs. A.H.Q. Sig. Co.	...	1	...
Hd. Qrs. R.F.C. and Kite Squadron ...	...	...	1
Aeroplane Squadron	...	...	2
Infantry Battalion	...	4	...
Field Ambulance	...	1	...

10.—TRAINS AND FIELD AMBULANCES.
(After Concentration).

		6-horsed		2-horsed										Spare Horses	Motor Cars	Motor Cycles	Bicycles	Remarks
	Carts, Maltese (1-horsed)	Carts, Water	Carts, Maltese	Carts, Forage, or Limbered Wagons	Carts, Cook's	Wagons, Ambulance	Wagons, G.S., technical stores baggage, &c.	Wagons, G.S.	Wagons, Cook's	Wagons, Ambulance	Wagons, G.S.	Wagons, Ambulance					
Divisional Train																	
Hd. Qrs.a ...	1	4		12			9	108	8				29	4		30	
Hd. Qrs. Co. :—	1						16									2	
Hd. Qrs.a...		1		1			2	30	2				14	1		7	
Baggage Sec.				1													
Supply Sec.				4				24									
Other Cos. (3) :—																	
Hd. Qrs.a...		1		1			2	9	2				5	1		7	
Baggage Sec.				1													
Supply Sec.				1			3c	9	2							9	
Army Troops Train		1		1	1		3c	20	2			6	6	1		9	
Hd. Qrs.a ...							3d		1d			3	6				
Baggage Sec.		2		2			1d	4				10				2	
Supply Sec.		1		3			6	16				4				1	
Cav. Field Ambulance e						4	2					3				1	
Sec. A or B ...						2											
Field Ambulance e													6				
Sec. A																	
Sec. B or C ...													6				

Remarks:
a Mobilizes with A.S.C. Co. to which it belongs.
b For postal service.
c 1 for postal service.
d 4-horsed.
e Cavalry Field Ambulances and Field Ambulances may be composed of 3-horsed ambulance wagons and 7 motor ambulance cars instead of 10-horsed ambulance wagons.

20. To convert the above transport tables into any other form of transport, allow 700 lbs. load to be carried for every horse in draught. For example a battalion of infantry has in 2nd line regimental transport 16 horses in draught (excluding water-carts); this represents a load of 11,200 lbs. If it is required to carry this on camels, each camel carrying 320 lbs., we can easily reckon we shall want 35 camels, with such percentage of spare camels as circumstances seem to demand. In the same way by using the informa tion contained in Sec. 28 (4) the number of mules, bullocks, coolies, &c., can be calculated.

21. No blankets for men are included in the normal scale of war outfit, but 1 blanket per man will be carried when specially ordered. This will necessitate the following additions to regimental transport :—

Infantry Battalion.—2 G.S. wagons, with 2 heavy horses each.
Cavalry Field Ambulance.—2 forage carts or limbered wagons with 2 horses each.
Field Ambulance.—3 forage carts or limbered wagons with 2 horses each

22.—INDIA.
REGIMENTAL TRANSPORT (WINTER SCALE).
1st Line.

Details.	Without Tents.								With Tents.								Remarks.
	Pack mules.	Draught Mules.	Mule Carts.	Camels.	Bullocks.	Bullock Carts.	Tongas.	Personnel.	Pack Mules.	Draught Mules.	Mule Carts.	Camels.	Bullocks.	Bullock carts.	Tongas.	Personnel.	
British Cavalry Regiment	46							21	46							21	
„ Squadron	9							4	9							4	
Indian Cavalry Regiment (a)	46							40	46							40	(a) When mobilized with draught transport.
„ „ Squadron (b)	51							40	51							40	(b) When mobilized with pack transport.
„ „ Squadron (b)	9							8	10							8	
Battery Horse Artillery	10							8	6							8	
H.Q. F.A. Brigade	6							3	2							3	
Battery Field Artillery	2							1	6							1	
Battery Mountain Artil. (Brit.)	6							3								3	
Cav. Bde. Amm. Column	1	56	28					29	1	56	28					29	(c) Approximate only.
Divl. Amm. Column	4	458	229					231	4	458	229					231	
H.Q. Div. Artillery																	(d) Excluding ambulance riding animals.
H.Q. Div. Engineers																	
Field Troop, S. & M. (c)																	
Field Company, S. and M.	58							38	58							38	
British Infantry Battalion	80							24	80							24	
Indian Infantry Battalion	72							21	72							21	
Pioneer Battalion	114							25	114							25	
British Field Ambulance	9							3	9							3	
Brit. Cav. Field Ambulance (d)	9							3	9							3	
Indian Field Ambulance	9							3	9							3	
„ Cav. Field Ambulance (d)	9							3	9							3	

INDIA.—REGIMENTAL TRANSPORT (WINTER SCALE)—*continued.*
2nd Line.

Details.	Without Tents								With Tents								Remarks.
	Pack Mules.	Draught Mules.	Mule Carts.	Camels.	Bullocks.	Bullock Carts.	Tongas.	Personnel.	Pack Mules.	Draught Mules.	Mule Carts.	Camels.	Bullocks.	Bullock Carts.	Tongas.	Personnel.	
H.Q. of a Division	34	...	...	10	...	...	...	14	31	...	...	1?	...	...	...	18	
" Cavalry Brigade	...	6	3	...	...	...	...	3	...	8	4	...	...	...	...	4	
" Infantry Brigade	...	...	...	...	...	...	...	4	7	...	...	...	...	...	...	4	
British Cavalry Regiment	13	81	42	2	...	...	...	47	13	102	51	3	...	...	...	56	
" " Squadron	3	16	8	...	...	...	...	9	3	20	10	...	...	...	...	11	
Indian Cavalry Regiment (a)	18	81	42	...	...	...	...	51	18	94	47	...	...	...	...	56	
" " Squadron (i)	248	...	8	...	...	...	...	210	290	...	9	...	...	...	...	224	
" " Squadron (b)	4	16	...	...	...	...	...	10	4	18	...	...	...	...	...	11	
Battery Horse Artillery	50	26	13	...	...	...	...	48	59	32	16	33	...	...	...	51	
H.Q. F.A. Brigade	...	4	2	...	...	...	...	13	...	4	2	...	...	...	...	16	
Battery Field Artillery	...	24	12	...	...	...	...	2	...	30	15	...	...	...	...	2	
Battery Mountain Artil. (Brit.)	...	...	...	25	...	...	...	12	...	...	...	33	...	...	...	15	
Cav. Bde. Amm. Column	...	14	7	...	...	...	...	9	...	18	9	47	...	...	...	12	
Divl. Amm. Column	...	10	5	40	...	...	...	7	...	12	6	...	...	...	...	9	
H.Q. Divl. Artillery	...	4	2	...	...	...	...	19	...	4	2	...	...	...	...	23	
H.Q. Divl. Engineers	...	...	...	3	...	...	...	2	...	...	...	3	...	...	...	2	
Field Troop S. and M. (c)	12	12	6	...	...	...	...	1	12	12	6	...	...	...	...	1	
Field Company, S. and M.	55	...	...	16	...	...	...	6	...	...	...	22	...	...	...	6	
British Infantry Battalion	46	...	...	72	...	...	...	10	55	...	...	98	...	...	...	12	
Indian Infantry Battalion	71	...	...	65	...	...	...	43	46	...	...	85	...	...	...	52	
Pioneer Battalion	7	...	...	70	...	...	...	38	71	...	...	91	...	...	...	45	
British Field Ambulance	7	...	...	43	16	...	8	26	7	...	...	49	16	...	8	28	

Brit. Cav. Field Ambulance (d)	7	44	22	...	...	...	...	7	50	25	...	...	...	28
Indian Field Ambulance	7	...	...	...	40	16	...	8	7	...	...	45	16	...	8	27
,, Cav. Field Ambulance (d)	7	42	21	...	...	...	...	7	48	2,	...	...	...	27

TOTALS.

Cavalry Brigade, 1st and 2nd Line Transport	249	627	291	...	...	...	523	249	679	317	...	...	...	549
Infantry Brigade, 1st and 2nd Line Transport	448	...	...	269	...	...	248	448	...	...	356	...	...	278
Division, 1st and 2nd Line Transport	2,499	507	274	3,180	100	...	40	2,532	2,541	615	284	3,528	100	...	40	2,677

28. DETAILS OF VEHICLES AND STORES IN COMMON USE.

1.—VEHICLES.

	Weight Equipped Without Load. (cwts. qrs. lbs.)	Weight Equipped With Load. (cwts. qrs. lbs.)	Width Over All. (ft. ins.)	Length Exclusive of Shafts or Pole. (ft. ins.)	Height Over All. (ft. ins.)	Remarks.
13-pr. Q.F. gun and limber ...		32 3 24	6 3	17 5	4 8*	*Dial sight removed.
13-pr. Q.F. ammunition wagon and limber		30 2 23	6 3	13 8½	5 0	
8-pr. Q.F. gun and limber ...		40 1 21	6 3	19 0½	4 9*	
8-pr. Q.F. ammunition wagon and limber		36 2 26	6 3	13 9½	5 2	
1·5″ Q.F. howitzer and limber ...		41 3 0	6 3½	17 10	4 10†	†Dial sight removed and upper portion of shield "down."
1·5″ Q.F. ammunition wagon and limber		40 2 27	6 3½	15 5	4 11‡	‡Carriage. outriggers folded.
60-pr. gun and limber ...		108 1 7	{ 7 6 / §7 0 }	{ 23 6¶ }	5 8¶	§Limber folded. ¶Gun in travelling position.
60-pr. ammunition wagon and limber		48 0 12	6 0	13 9	5 8	‖All sights removed.
Cart, forage, Mark II ...	8 3 1	23 3 1	6 3	15 6 (with shafts)	{ 6 10 / 5 9 }	With hoops and cases in position. With hoops and cases removed.
C.G.S., Maltese, Mark V* ...	7 2 0	22 2 0	6 1	6 5	4 8	But may be slightly exceeded.
Cart, S.A.A., Mark II** ...	9 3 20	23 3 20	6 4	7 9	5 10	
Cart, tool, R.E., Mark I ...	10 1 20	25 3 20	6 0	6 9	5 11	
Cart, tool, R.E., Mark II ...	10 0 26	23 0 25	6 2½	6 9	4 10	
Cart, water tank, Mark II ...	9 1 7	19 3 11	6 1	6 10	4 10	
Cart, water tank, Mark II* ...	12 0 21	{ 23 1 3 / 23 2 8 }	{ 6 1 / 6 2 }	6 10	5 6	
Cart, water tank, Mark III ...	15 1 4	26 0 21	6 2	7 3	6 3	

													Remarks
Wagon, ambulance, Mark VI	23	3	18	37 / 43	3 / 1	20 / 4	7	0½	13	9	9 7 / 5 9		Hood folded. Roof lowered.
Wagon, ambulance, Sight Mark I													
With No. 159 wheels	17	1	16	29	1	22	6	3	12	6	7 / 1		With cover and hoops removed.
With No. 46 wheels	16	0	16	28	0	22	6	3	12	6	4 (body) 5 / 8 5		
Wag'n, cable …	18	1	11	32	0	11	6	2½	16	1	5 (limber) 5 / 7		
Wagon, G.S., Mark IX	17	2	5	47	2	5	6	2½	13	9	7		Without spare wheel fitted.
Wagon, G.S., Mark X	17	0	5	47	0	5	6	2½	13	6½	6 / 11		Without spare wheel fitted.
Wagon, G.S., Mark X*	17	0	7	47	0	7	6	4	13	6½	6 / 11		Without cover and hale hoops.
Wagon, light spring, R.E.…	10	1	27	21	0	0	6	2½	10	7	6 / 5		
Wagon, limbered, G.S.—													
With No. 198A wheels	11	2	9	31	2	9	6	4	13	9	4 / 8		May be slightly exceeded.
With No. 200 wheels	13	0	21	43	0	21	6	4	13	9	4 / 8		
Wagon, limbered, G.S., Mark I* for S.A.A. …	16	0	4	31	1	4	6	2½	13	0	5 (body) 5 / 8 0		
Wagon, limbered, telephone	13	2	0	17	0	0	6	4	14	2	5 (limber) 4 / 6 8		
Wagon, limbered { wagon } wireless telegraph { limber }	22 / 8	0 / 3	7 / 0	44	0	0*	6	3	16	0	5 (body) 6 (limber) 6 10 (coupled) 7 0		*Liable to alteration.
Wagon, pontoon, Mark V …	19	0	1	47	2	1	6	7	17	4	(uncoupled) 7 10		
SPECIAL FOR INDIA.													
Transport cart	5¾	0	0	13	0	0	…	…	…	…	…		
Pontoon wagon	30	0	0	50	0	0	…	…	…	…	…		
Ambulance tonga	11	0	0	…	…	…	…	…	…	…	…		
Dandy …	0	0	80				…	…	…	…	…		

NOTE.—(1) The totals given in the above table for guns and vehicles belonging to the artillery make no allowance for the weight of the detachments carried on them.

(2) The track of all military vehicles, except a pontoon wagon and Mark VI ambulance wagon, may be taken at 5' 2". That of a pontoon wagon is 5' 10", and of the ambulance wagon 6' 0".

2. MECHANICAL TRANSPORT (h).

Description.	Over all Measurements. Length.	Over all Measurements. Width.	Weight. (N.B.—For Engine and Lorries the weight includes fuel and water.)	Composition of Train.	Net useful Load.	Average Speed loaded (a).	Minimum Driver Personnel (b).	General Remarks re Fuel, Water, &c.
Traction Engines	15' 6" to 19'	4' to 8' 6"	12 to 16 tons	3 or 4 trucks	12 to 18 tons	3 miles per hour.	3	The coal consumption for traction engines per gross ton-mile is approximately 1·5 lbs., and for small tractors and steam lorries it is 2 lbs. Traction engines require to refill their water tanks every 10 to 12 miles. Light tractors and steam lorries every 15 to 20 miles. Internal-combustion-engined lorries can usually travel 50 to 100 miles without re-filling their fuel tanks, &c.
Light Tractors ...	13' 6" to 16' 6"	5' 6" to 6'	5 tons 10 cwt. to 7 tons	1 or 2 trucks or 3 trailers.	4 to 6 tons	4 miles per hour.	2	
Internal-combustion Tractor.	14' 6" to 16' 6"	6' 8"	6 tons 10 cwt.	1 or 2 trucks or 3 trailers.	4 to 6 tons	5 miles per hour.	2	
Steam Lorries (c)	20' to 22'	6' 6" to 7' 6"	5 tons to 6 tons 10 cwt.	1 trailer	3 to 5 tons	5 miles per hour.	2	
Internal-combustion - engined Lorries (d)	19' to 23'	6' 6" to 7' 0"	2 tons 10 cwt. to 4 tons	...	2 to 5 tons	7 to 10 miles per hour.	2	
Motor Omnibus...	19' to 23'	6' 6" to 7' 6"	3 to 4 tons	...	20 to 30 persons (g)	8 to 12 miles per hour.	2	
Motor Cars ...	10' to 15'	5' 6" to 6' 6"	15 cwt. to 1 ton 10 cwt.	...	2 to 5 persons (j)	15 to 20 miles per hour.	1	The average road spaces occupied by mechanical transport vehicles are given in Sec. 7.
Trucks ...	13' to 15' (S)	6' 6" to 7' 6"	1 ton 15 cwt. to 2 tons ·5 cwt.	...	4 to 6 tons	...	...	

Trailers (e) ...	12' to 14'	6'4" to 7'	17 cwt. to 1 ton	...	1½ to 2 tons	...	...	Five small tractors with trains, or 5 steam lorries with trailers are approximately the equivalent of 2 traction engines with the necessary trucks.
Water Tanks ...	11' to 12'	6' to 7'	1½ tons to 3 tons	...	350 to 480 gals.	...	...	
Travelling Vans...	11' to 17'	7' to 8'	1 to 2½ tons	...	...	...	...	

NOTES. (a) The speeds are based on those which the ordinary motor vehicles in commercial use may be expected to perform under military conditions when marching apart from other troops.

(b) Whenever mechanical transport is employed, arrangements must be made to have efficient artificers with the necessary tools to execute all repairs and adjustments required at the end of each day's work.

(c) When using a trailer 1½ to 2 tons additional can be drawn in it.

(d) It is not considered economical to utilise lorries with less than 30 cwt. carrying capacity for transport purposes.

(e) General Service wagons, fitted with drawbars, can be used as trailers.

(f) This does not include the drawbar, which is about 3' to 4' long, and can be easily detached.

(g) With rifles and equipment.

(h) 30-cwt. lorries are normally used with cavalry and army troops supply columns, 3-ton lorries with divisional supply columns.

A G.S. Wagon-load.

3. A G.S. wagon can carry any one of the following loads :—400 blankets;
300 felling axes ; 600 hand axes ; 290 picks ; 780 billhooks ; 200 kettles
(camp) ; 600 picketing pegs ; 240 large horse rugs ; 260 small horse rugs ;
640 G.S. shovels ; 350 R.L. spades ; 28 circular tents (single) : 20 circular
tents (double) ; 4 hospital marquees ; 1,800 ropes, picketing (4 feet 9 inches) ;
40 boxes S.A.A. (chargers), 1,000 rounds each, or 45 boxes S.A.A. (chargers),
840 rounds each ; 600 sheets, ground, in cases, or 900 loose ; 8 Soyer's
stoves.

Reduce above by one-sixth for distances of over 15 miles.

Ammunition 13-pr. Q.F.	..	144 rounds per wagon.
„ 18-pr. Q.F.	..	108 „ „ „
„ 4·5" Howitzer, Q.F.	..	66 „ „ „
„ 5" Howitzer, B.L.	..	46 „ „ „
„ 60-pr. B.L.	..	40 „ „ „
„ 6" Howitzer, B.L. {100-lb. shell	25 „ „ „
{122-lb. „	20 „ „ „

4. Other Loads.

Description.	Load.	Notes.
S. African ox-wagon	5,000 lb.	
S. African mule wagon ..	2,000 to 3,000 lb.	
Scotch cart, S. Africa ..	1,700 to 2,000 lb.	
Small carts	400 lb.	
Pack-animals—		
Mules and ponies	160 lb.	
Pack-horses	200 lb.	
Camels	320 to 400 lb.	
Bullocks	200 lb.	
Men	50 lb.	
Donkeys	100 lb.	
In India, authorized loads—		
Pack-mules and ponies ..	2 maunds	
Camels	5 maunds	Supplies for 1 Division for
Mule carts	10 maunds	1 day in India (exclusive
Bullock carts	10 to 12 maunds	of hay or bhoosa for
Pack-bullocks	2 maunds	animals)=1,600 maunds.
Donkeys	1½ maunds	
Coolie	⅓ maund	

A maund = 80 lbs. approximately.

5. The following loads should not as a rule be exceeded :—

Vehicle.	No. of horses.	Slow moving units.	Rapid moving units— i.e., Cav., M.I., R.H.A., Field Troop, R.E.
Forage cart	1	1,200 lb.	..
Forage cart	2	1,500 lb.	1,200 lb.
G.S. wagon	4	3,000 lb.	2,700 lb.
G.S. wagon	6	..	3,000 lb.

6. METHOD OF PACKING AND WEIGHT OF AMMUNITION.

Article.	How Packed.	Size of Package in Inches.			Weight.	
		width.	depth.	length.	lbs.	oz.
Ammunition—						
13-pr. Q.F. ..	Box (M. I) of 4 rounds ..	9·7	9·7	25·2	91	0
	Box (M. II)	9·8	9·8	26·3	89	12
18-pr. Q.F. ..	Box (M. I) of 4 rounds ..	10·5	10·4	26·3	118	0
	Box (M. II)	10·4	10·4	27·6	117	8
4·5″ Howr. ..	Box (M. I) of 2 rounds (shrapnel)	19·0	13·1	7·5	95	14
	Box (M. II)	17·6	14·8	7·5	97	13
	Box (M. I) (lyddite) ..	19·6	17·3	6·8	98	8½
5″ Howr. ..	120 cartridges in case M.L. whole	17	21·6	17·6	136	0
	2 shells in box projectile ..	22·4	13	7·9	119	0
60-pr. ..	12 cartridges in case M.L. whole	17	21·6	17·6	163	0
	1 shell in sling	17	21·6	17·6	62	3
·303	Box of 1,000 rounds ..	8·3	10·9	17	80	8
Mk. VII. ..	20 bandoliers of 50 rounds in chargers in box	8·3	10·9	17	75	0
(India) ..	Box of 1,120 rounds ..	8·3	10·9	17	93	10
Pistol ..	276 rounds in 23 bundles of 12 rounds each in box	6·5	4·6	8·6	16	8
(India) ..	Box of 276 rounds	6·5	4·6	8·6	17	4

7. WEIGHTS OF A FEW COMMON ARTICLES.

Articles.	Weight.		Remarks.
	lbs.	oz.	
Armourers' bag	8	14	
Binoculars (in case)	1	14	
Blanket, for man	4	8	
Butcher's Implements, in case.. ..	37	0	
Camp kettle (12 qts.)	8	8	
Farriers' Tools	14	6½	
Food—			
Day's ration for man	4	4	Includes small amount
Iron ration	2	8	of fuel.
Corn ration for horse	12	0	
Case preserved meat	70–75	0	Contains 60 rations.
Case biscuit	70–75	0	Contains 50 rations.
Bale patent forage	82	0	Contains 4 rations (including hay ration).
Mekometers (complete sets	6	7	
Rug, horse { large	8	8	
{ small	7	0	
Saddles, pack, complete	65	0	
Saddles, universal, complete	29	4	
Shoemakers , tool bag filled	26	0	
Signalling Equipment—			
Message cases with forms and manuals	2	4	
Small blue or white flags	0	6½	
Heliographs, 5″	8	4	
Stands, lamp or heliograph.. ..	4	13	
Prismatic compass in case	0	8	
Watch	0	4	

WEIGHTS OF A FEW COMMON ARTICLES—*continued.*

Articles.	Weight.	Remarks.
	lbs. oz.	
Stationery box, filled	56 0	
Stretcher	31 0	
Telescopes—		
Signalling and reconnaissance ..	3 2	
Signalling and reconnaissance (with stand)	3 15	
Field Artillery	5 0	
Field Artillery (with stand) ..	7 0	
Artificers' Tools—		
Cavalry Regiment .. }	lbs.	
Mounted Infantry Battalion }	140	
Horse or Field Artillery Brigade—		
Brigade Headquarters	270	
Battery (each)	235	
Ammunition Column ..	435	
Field Troop, R.E. ..	434	
Field Company, R.E.	1,582½	
Infantry Battalion	98½	
Army Service Corps Cos.—		
Wheelers	195	
Saddlers	13½	
Smiths and Farriers	140	
Cavalry Field Ambulance ..	67½	
Field Ambulance	88½	
	lbs. oz.	
Wallet, veterinary	7 3½	
Wire-cutter (in frog)	1 3½	
	INDIA.	
	lbs.	
Blanket stretcher	14	
Field stretcher	34	
Packhal (metal)	21	
Packhal (filled with 6½ galls.).. ..	100	
Yakdan 1 pair	38	

8. METHOD OF PACKING A FEW COMMON MILITARY ARTICLES, WITH THE SIZE OF THE PACKAGE.

Article.	How packed.	Size in Inches.
Blankets	Bales of 25 ..	18 ×21 ×32
Boots	Cases of 45 ..	38 ×21½ ×15
Braces	Cases of 500 ..	36 ×23½ ×17
Greatcoats (dismounted) ..	Bales of 25 ..	29 ×20 ×29
Dressings, field	Cases of 500 ..	30½ ×19½ ×16
Helmets	Cases of 20 ..	36 ×23½ ×17
Kettles, camp	Cradles of 5 ..	30 ×14 ×14
Puttees	Bales of 200 pairs	29 ×20 ×24
Service Dress—		
Jackets	Bales of 50 ..	30 ×20 ×23
Trousers	Bales of 50 ..	25 ×15 ×28
Sheets, ground	Cases of 60 ..	26 ×22 ×19
Shirts, flannel	Bales of 100 ..	26 ×20 ×24
Socks, worsted	Bales of 200 pairs	29 ×18 ×20
Towels	Bales of 200 ..	25 ×21 ×20

29. CONVOYS.

(*See* F.S.R., Part I, Sec. 157.)

COMMAND.

1. The senior combatant officer with a convoy will command both the transport and its escort. He will consult the senior transport officer on all matters which affect the welfare and convenience of the transport, will avoid all interference with his technical functions, and will give effect to his wishes unless, by so doing, the safety of the convoy would be endangered.

SYSTEM OF CONVOYS.

2. Horsed convoys may be worked on any of the three following systems :—

    (*a*) Through convoys.
    (*b*) Staging.
    (*c*) Meeting.

3. The through convoy system consists in the same animals and vehicles being employed from the start of the convoy until its arrival at its destination.
4. The staging system consists in the division of the road into stages, the same section of the transport working over the same ground, proceeding laden and returning empty.
5. The meeting system is that by which two sections, one laden and the other unladen, meet daily at a fixed point between two stages, when loads are transferred or vehicles exchanged, each section returning to its respective stage. (In this case it must be remembered that, to transfer loads, labour is required, and, to exchange vehicles, animals, harness, &c., must be similar.)
6. The through convoy system is generally adopted in front of the advanced depôt, and the staging or meeting systems on the lines of communication.

7. SHORT RULES FOR CONVOYS ON THE MARCH.

    (*a*) Do not load till necessary.
    (*b*) Keep strict march discipline, no straggling or opening out.
    (*c*) Pace of a column is the pace of the slowest animal, so they must lead.
    (*d*) If possible, do not put animals of different paces (*e.g.*, mules and camels) in the same convoy.
    (*e*) With pack animals each driver must lead his own animals (usually three). Long strings are prohibited.
    (*f*) No one but the driver to ride on a vehicle.
    (*g*) Keep some spare animals and vehicles in rear of the column.
    (*h*) Remove breakdowns from the roadway.
    (*j*) Do not make long halts unless animals can be outspanned and packs removed, but take advantage of every facility for watering.
    (*k*) Halt on the far side of a defile or obstacle.
    (*l*) Do not trot to make up lost ground.
    (*m*) When paths are narrow, certain sections of the path must be kept for certain definite hours for convoys moving in a given direction.
    (*n*) If attacked, a convoy should not be halted or parked except as a last resource. If the whole or part of a convoy is in danger of falling into the enemy's hands it should be destroyed or made unserviceable.
    (*o*) In laager leave space (5 yards) between wagons and line occupied by troops.
    (*p*) Cooking places and latrines outside laager; no fires near wagons.

30. TRANSPORT BY RAIL.

(See F.S.R., Part I, Secs. 34–39, and Part II, Secs. 59–64.)

1. GENERAL RULES.

(a) Interfere as little as possible with the railway management.
(b) Trucks and carriages must not be kept loaded up.
(c) Traffic should not be suspended except for very good reasons.
(d) No off-loading on the main line.
(e) No alteration once the time table is settled. But if unavoidable, an order in writing must be given to the railway staff.
(f) Troops must not occupy railway buildings or use the water supply without authority from a railway transport officer.
(g) Arrange rest camps near the station with their own water supply.
(h) Troops should never take tarpaulins, coal, wood, or other railway material.
(j) Provide a liberal allowance of sidings if a concentration is anticipated.

2. RULES FOR ENTRAINING.

(a) Send an officer ahead to ascertain facilities for entraining.
(b) Tell off parties to entrain horses, guns and wagons.
(c) Entrain baggage, horses, guns and wagons simultaneously before troops arrive, if possible.
(d) Detail men in charge of trucks containing horses or vehicles.
(e) Pack guns and wagons, fully equipped, and fasten securely to trucks. Occupy spare space with gear, kits, &c. Pontoon wagons may require an empty truck between every second truck.
(f) Guns or vehicles should be in the same trains as their teams, and horses as the men who ride or drive them.
(g) Inflammable stores should be at the end of a train, and risk of fire should be guarded against if in open trucks.

3. *Entrainment of horses.*—(a) On long journeys under peace conditions saddlery and harness may be removed at the discretion of the officer under whose authority the orders for the movement are issued, with a view to resting the horses, when this can be arranged without risk of the animals being separated from their equipment, or of causing delay in the service of trains.

Under active service conditions, horses will be entrained saddled or harnessed, unless orders to the contrary are issued. The authority competent to issue such orders will be the Army Council as regards movements in the United Kingdom, and elsewhere the Commander-in-Chief in the field or an Army Commander.

(b) At the entraining station, after stirrups have been crossed, bits removed, girths slackened, and traces secured, the horses will be led on to the platform in single file, the first horse to enter a truck being the quietest available.

(c) One method of entraining is to pass the horses alternately to right and left in the truck with their heads facing the loading platform, except the last two, which face the opposite way. Another method is to entrain them heads and tails alternately.

The closer horses are packed the quieter they travel. If there are not sufficient horses to fill a truck they should be closed up to one end and a sliding bar used to secure them.

(d) Horses' heads should be left free, whether the horses are harnessed or not. It is immaterial whether the horses' heads face the second line of rail.

(e) A man leading a horse into a truck should walk freely in with a loose head rope, as though leading it into a stall. He should not stare in the animal's face.

Much time may be lost by dealing timorously with a jibbing horse; two men should immediately clasp hands just above the animal's hocks and simply hustle it into the truck.

(f) If watering and feeding are to be carried out on the journey it is preferable that the horses face the platform, if this can be arranged, when entraining. To prevent delay at places where they are to be fed, nosebags should be filled *en route*. Hay or straw should be loaded up separately for fear of fire.

4. The time required to entrain ½ battalion infantry with regimental transport is about 45 minutes; for a squadron cavalry, about 40 minutes; and for ½ battery artillery, about 45 minutes.

The average speed of troop trains is from 15 to 20 miles per hour on narrow, 20 to 25 miles on broad gauge lines.

It may be necessary to entrain or detrain from the ground level by means of portable ramps. In the absence of ramps specially designed for the purpose, these can be improvised by means of rails and sleepers. It will take about three times as long to entrain a unit by means of portable ramps only.

5. RULES FOR DETRAINING.

(*a*) Ascertain arrangements for detraining and moving off before troops leave carriages.

(*b*) See to ramps for unloading; material for emergency ramps should be kept handy.

(*c*) Clear station and approaches as soon as possible.

(*d*) Riding horses to be led at once to the place of assembly, draught horses being taken to their vehicles, which are then taken to the place of assembly.

ROLLING STOCK CAPACITY FOR TROOP MOVEMENTS.

6. The railway train tables are based on the following data, which are the average figures for British rolling stock :—

    6 officers to each compartment.
    8 men to each compartment.
    7 horses or 6 heavy draught to each cattle truck.
    3 staff officers' chargers to each horse-box.
    1 four-wheeled vehicle, or 1 gun and limber, to each open truck, except
      60-pr. guns and limbers, which are allowed 2 trucks ; and pontoons,
      which are allowed 3 trucks to 2 pontoons.
    2 two-wheeled vehicles to each open truck.
    5 to 8 compartments to a coach.

7. Should it be necessary to put men in trucks, allow 5½ square feet to each man, but for journeys over 8 hours' duration 7 square feet per man should usually be allowed.

8. To reduce, as far as possible, the number of different train compositions, the composition required for a given train load is used without modification for a slightly smaller load, and the accommodation allowed does not therefore agree in all cases with the above figures.

These train loads may be considered normal for broad gauge railways in war. But the loads are, generally speaking, heavy, and though most of the railways in the United Kingdom could deal with them, it might be necessary, even in this country, to run some of the heavier loads in two portions over sections of lines where gradients are severe or on lines whose engines are light.

9. The numbers, as regards Home, are based on War Establishments for 1914, except Territorial Force which are based on War Establishments, Part II, 1911, and do not include details left at the base or first reinforcements. Divisional trains (horse transport) are included with units. Supply Columns (M.T.) are not shown, as it is assumed that these will generally move by road. When journeys exceed 8 hours, or when rolling stock is not scarce, only 75 per cent. of the numbers of personnel given below should be allotted to each compartment. Horses are allowed 7 feet 2 inches ; width saddled, 2 feet 6 inches, unsaddled or unharnessed, 2 feet 3 inches. If time permits, and the movement of troops is to continue over a long period on long journeys abroad, covered trucks can be fitted with the required ventilation, and with removable planks resting on wood chocks, which form an upper tier of sleeping berths. The compartments of passenger coaches can be similarly fitted. This may be necessary in climates where the men travel in open trucks, or hammocks may be slung. In passenger coaches on British railways, men will not be able to sleep with the accommodation allowed below. With 5 men to a compartment they can take it in turn to sleep 3 at a time.

10. Composition of Railway Trains.

Standard Compositions.

	A	B	C	D	E	F	G	H	K	L	M	N	O	P	Q	R	S	T	U	V
Compartments	17	21	15	14	18	17	6	6	10	29	20	8	10	8	9	16	11	30	16	18
Horse Boxes											5	3	5	4		6				8
Cattle Trucks	12	21	16	13	9	11	6	14	12	6	12	5	4	6	7	6	19	8	14	20
Vehicle Trucks	9	5	10	14	12	16	8	15	13	8	17	4	8	6	11	6	19	8	4	15
Brake Vans	2	2	2	2	2	2	2	2	2	2	2	2	2	2	2	2	2	2	2	2
Total Railway Vehicles	26	34	31	31	26	32	26	33	31	19	33	18	19	16	22	17	34	27	29	28

Special Compositions.

	Hd. Qrs. Cav. Division, Hd. Qrs. Cav. Divnl. Art. and Hd. Qrs. Cav. Divnl. A.S.C.	Hd. Qrs. Cav. Brigade and 1 Signal Troop, not allotted to a Cav. Division.	Hd. Qrs. Inf. Division and Hd. Qrs. Divnl. Artillery.	Hd. Qrs. Divnl. R.E., Hd. Qrs. and No. 1 Section Divnl. Signal Company.	Mtd. Brigade Hd. Qrs., and Hd. Qrs. and Machine Gun Section of a Yeomanry Regt. (T.F.)	Hd. Qrs. of a Division, and Hd. Qrs. Divnl. Artillery. (T.F.)	Hd. Qrs. of 3 Infantry Brigades. (T.F.)
Compartments	24	13	16	13	13	16	16
Horse Boxes	10	1	12	2	5	14	6
Cattle Trucks	9	11	7	10	10	6	5
Vehicle Trucks	5	6	6	12	5	4	6
Brake Vans	2	2	2	2	2	2	2
Total Railway Vehicles	50	22	30	28	24	29	23

11. RAILWAY TRAINS FOR 1 CAVALRY DIVISION.

Unit.	Train Load.	Number of Trains.	Composition. *See* para.10.
Headquarters of Division (less motor cars), Headquarters Cavalry Divisional Artillery and Headquarters Cavalry Divisional A.S.C.	..	1	Special
4 Cavalry Brigades (12 Cavalry Regiments) 4 Signal Troops	Headquarters of Brigade and 1 Signal Troop	4	N
	Headquarters of Regiment and Machine Gun Section	12	T
	1 Squadron of Cavalry ..	36	B
	Half Battery	8	C
Divisional Artillery— 2 Horse Artillery Brigades	Brigade Headquarters, and "C" Sub-section Ammunition Column	2	D
	"A" and "B" Sub-sections Ammunition Column	2	D
	Ammunition Column Headquarters and " F " Subsection	2	D
Divisional Engineers— 1 Field Squadron ..	Headquarters Bridging Detachment and 1 Troop	1	D
	3 Troops	1	T
Divisional Signal Service— 1 Signal Squadron ..	Headquarters, " A " and " B " Troops	1	D
	" C " and " D " Troops ..	1	A
Divisional Medical Units-- 4 Cavalry Field Ambulances	1 Cavalry Field Ambulance	4	F
	Total Railway Trains ..	75	

12. RAILWAY TRAINS FOR 1 INFANTRY DIVISION.

Unit.	Train Load.	Number of Trains.	Composition. *See* para. 10.
Headquarters of the Division and Headquarters Divisional Artillery	..	1	Special
3 Infantry Brigades ..	Brigade Headquarters and a Section Divisional Signal Company ..	3	O
	Headquarters of Battalion (less Major, Quartermaster - Serjeant, Transport Serjeant, Pioneers, Half Stretcher Bearers, 2 S.A.A. Carts, 1 Water Cart, 1 Tool Wagon, Spare Horses, Major's Batman and Horse, 3 R.A.M.C. personnel, and 2 Train Wagons), and 2 Companies of Infantry ..	12	G
	Remainder of Headquarters .. Machine Gun Section .. 2 Companies of Infantry ..	12	G
Divisional Mounted Troops— 1 Cavalry Squadron ..	1 Cavalry Squadron ..	1	B
Divisional Artillery— 3 Field Artillery Brigades	Brigade Headquarters, "B" Sub-section Ammunition Column and 1 Train Wagon	3	D
	"A" and "C" Sub-sections Ammunition Column	3	D
	"D" and "E" Sub-sections Ammunition Column and 1 Train Wagon	3	E
	Half Battery and 1 Train Wagon	18	D
1 Field Artillery (Howr.) Brigade	Headquarters "A" Sub-section Ammunition Column and 1 Train Wagon	1	D
	"B" and "C" Sub-sections Ammunition Column and 1 Train Wagon	1	D
	Half Battery	6	D
1 Heavy Artillery Battery and Ammunition Column	Half Battery and Half Ammunition Column	2	D
1 Divisional Ammunition Column	Headquarters and No. 4 Section (Heavy portion)	1	E
	Half Section (Nos. 1, 2 or 3)	6	H
	No. 4 Section (Howitzer portion)	1	D

RAILWAY TRAINS FOR 1 INFANTRY DIVISION—*continued*.

Unit.	Train Load.	Number of Trains.	Composition. See para.10.
Divisional Engineers— Headquarters, 2 Field Companies and Headquarters and No. 1 Section Divisional Signal Company	Headquarters Divisional Engineers and Headquarters and No. 1 Section Divisional Signal Company	1	Special
	1 Field Company	2	K
Divisional Transport and Supply Unit— Divisional Train (less Transport with Units)	Headquarters, Headquarters Company and No. 2 Company	1	K
	Nos. 3 and 4 Companies ..	1	E
Divisional Medical Units— 3 Field Ambulances ..	Half Field Ambulance ..	6	Q
	Total Railway Trains ..	85	

13. RAILWAY TRAINS FOR OTHER REGULAR UNITS.

Unit.	Train Load.	Number of Trains.	Composition. See para.10.
Headquarters of a Cavalry Brigade and 1 Signal Troop, not allotted to a Cavalry Division	...	1	Special
Headquarters of a General Headquarters Signal Co., and Headquarters of an Army Headquarters Signal Co. (less mechanical transport)	...	1	L
Air-Line Section (less 3-ton lorry) Cable Section	Two Sections ...	1	A
Wireless Section	Wireless Section ...	1	P
1 Bridging Train	One-fifth Train ...	5	M
Army Troops Train (less transport with units and motor car)	...	1	L (less 9 compartments)

15. RAILWAY TRAINS FOR A TERRITORIAL FORCE DIVISION.

Unit.	Train Load.	Number of Trains.	Composition. See para. 10.
Headquarters of Division and Headquarters of Divisional Artillery	..	1	Special
3 Infantry Brigades ..	{ 3 Brigade Headquarters ..	1	Special
	{ Half Infantry Battalion ..	24	G
Divisional Artillery— Headquarters and 3 R.F.A. Brigades	⎧ Brigade Headquarters and Half Battery	3	D
	⎨ Half Battery Artillery ..	15	A
	⎩ Half Ammunition Column	6	H
Field Artillery (Howr.) Brigade	⎧ Headquarters and Half Battery	1	D
	⎨ Three - quarter Battery Artillery	2	D
	⎩ Ammunition Column ..	1	K (less 18 compartments)
Heavy Artillery Battery and Ammunition Column	⎧ Three-quarter Battery Artillery	1	D
	⎨ Quarter Battery Artillery and Ammunition Column	1	E (plus 1 vehicle truck)
Divisional Engineers— 2 Field Companies ..	1 Field Company	2	K
1 Divisional Signal Company	Headquarters Divisional Engineers and 1 Signal Company	1	R
Yeomanry Regiment ..	Quarter Regiment	4	U
Divisional Transport and Supply Column (Excluding Mechanical Transport)	Quarter Transport and Supply Column	4	S (less 21 compartments)
3 Field Ambulances ..	1 Field Ambulance	3	S
	Total Railway Trains ..	70	

16. RAILWAY TRAINS FOR A MOUNTED BRIGADE (T.F.).

Unit.	Train Load.	Number of Trains.	Composition. *See para.* 10.
Mounted Brigade Headquarters 3 Yeomanry Regiments..	Mounted Brigade Headquarters and Headquarters and Machine Gun Section of 1 Yeomanry Regiment	1	Special
	Headquarters and Machine Gun Section of 2 Yeomanry Regiments	1	T
	Squadron Yeomanry ..	9	U
Horse Artillery Battery and Mounted Brigade Ammunition Column	Half Battery	2	A
	Ammunition Column ..	1	K (less 19 compartments)
Mounted Brigade Transport and Supply Column	T. & S. Column complete ..	1	V
Mounted Brigade Field Ambulance	1 Field Ambulance	1	V
	Total Railway Trains for a Mounted Brigade (T.F.)	16	

INDIA.

17. The following tables give the composition of troop and transport trains required for each unit on field service scale on a 5 feet 6 inch gauge line.

These tables are based on units of four-wheel vehicles, and lay down the description of rolling stock which will normally be supplied. Trains, with a few exceptions, are limited to 45 (four-wheeled) vehicles.

18. Rolling stock in India varies somewhat in carrying capacity on the different lines, but for purposes of calculating the stock required for troop movements during concentration, the following carrying capacities have been adopted for the broad gauge (5 feet 6 inches) and metre gauge (3 feet 3¾ inches) respectively :—

Vehicles (4-wheeled).	Load.	Capacity.		Notes.
		Broad gauge.	Metre gauge.	
1st class...	Lying down accommodation	8	6	
2nd class...	Seating accommodation ...	18	12	
1st & 2nd composite	Lying down accommodation, 1st class	4	3	
	Seating accommodation, 2nd class	9	8	

Vehicles (4-wheeled).	Load.	Capacity.		Notes.
		Broad gauge.	Metre gauge.	
3rd class...	Seating accommodation, rank and file	36	22	
,,	Seating accommodation, followers	60	30	
Covered goods wagons	Tons of average supplies ...	10–15	5–10	
,,	Tons of Ordnance supplies ...	15	5–10	
,,	Army Transport carts (dismantled)	20	12	
,,	Men and followers	25	16	If necessary.
,,	Transport camels	6	—	Must have smooth floors.
Horse wagons	Horses or Ordnance mules	8	6	These must have breast bars.
,,	Transport mules or riding ponies	10	8	Each wagon also carries two attendants, line gear, and grain and fodder for two days.
,,	Large bullocks	8	4	
,,	Small bullocks	10	6	
,,	Donkeys	12	8	
Open trucks	Riding camels	4	2	Must have smooth floors.
,,	Tongas	4	2	
,,	Men and followers	25	16	If necessary.
,,	Large country carts (dismantled)	6	—	12 to 16 small carts of the type used in Central India can go in a broad gauge truck.
,,	Small country carts (dismantled)	8	—	
,,	Pairs of gun or limber wheels	4	3	Must have end falling doors.
,,	G.S. or Pontoon wagons ...	1	1	
Horse boxes	Horses	6	4	

NOTE.—When bogies are supplied, 1 bogie = 2 four-wheeled vehicles.

19. For purposes of calculating the length of trains all 4-wheeled stock may be taken as measuring 28 feet over buffers.

20. In India the average speed, including posts, of a 45-vehicle troop train is 15 miles an hour on broad gauge railways over distances exceeding 500 miles.

21. The average train on metre gauge lines, with normal gradients, may be taken as 40 vehicles, including brakes.

On narrow gauge lines with normal gradients, 20 vehicles.

22. To ascertain the time required for massing an army in a given locality reckoning from the arrival of the first troop train :—

Divide the total number of troop trains necessary for the transport of a given force by the number of trains that can be run each day on the line or lines by which the force is to be despatched. The number of trains which can be run is usually limited by the capacities of the entraining and detraining stations.

23. Composition of Trains for Units on Broad Gauge Lines (45-Vehicle Load).

Units.	1st class.	2nd class.	Composites, 1st and 2nd class.	3rd class.	Wagons, covered goods	Horse boxes.	Horse wagons	Open trucks.	Brake vans.	Total.
Headquarters	Will usually proceed by ordinary trains, and will requisition for accommodation in the usual way.									
Cavalry :—										
British regiments :—										
Train A	1	...	1	5	3	4	29	...	2	45
,, B	1	...	1	5	3	2	31	...	2	45
Indian (Silladar) (mobilized with draught transport) :—										
Train A	...	...	1	4	3	2	23	2	2	37
,, B	...	...	1	4	3	1	24	...	2	35
,, C	...	...	1	4	3	1	23	...	2	34
Indian (Silladar) (mobilized with pack transport) :—										
Train A	...	...	1	5	3	2	30	...	2	43
,, B	...	...	1	5	3	2	30	1	2	44
,, C	...	...	1	5	3	1	30	1	...	43
Indian (Non-Silladar) :—										
Train A	...	...	1	4	3	2	21	...	2	33
,, B	...	...	1	4	3	1	21	1	2	33
,, C	...	...	1	4	3	1	21	1	2	33
Artillery :—										
Royal Horse Artillery Battery	...	...	1	4	1	2	28	11	...	47
Cavalry Brigade Ammunition Column (R.H.A. Section)	...	...	1	1	1	1	12	9	2	27
Royal Field Artillery Battery	...	...	1	4	2	2	22	11	2	44
Divisional Ammunition Col. (R.F.A. Section) :—										
Train A	...	...	1	2	1	1	20	16	2	43
,, B	...	...	1	2	1	1	21	14	2	42

23. COMPOSITION OF TRAINS FOR UNITS ON BROAD GAUGE LINES
(45-VEHICLE LOAD)—*continued.*

Units.	1st class.	2nd class.	Composites, 1st and 2nd class.	3rd class.	Wagons, covered goods.	Horse boxes.	Horse wagons.	Open trucks.	Brake vans.	Total.
Artillery—*continued***—**										
Royal Field Artillery Battery (Howitzer)	...	...	1	5	2	2	19	10	2	41
2 (Howitzer) Batteries with Ammunition Column :—										
Train A	...	...	1	5	2	2	20	12	2	44
,, B	...	...	1	5	2	2	20	12	2	44
,, C	...	...	1	2	1	1	26	12	2	45
British or Indian Mountain Batt. (including Mountain Artillery Section of Divnl. Ammunition Column)	...	...	1	8	5	1	22	...	2	39
Heavy Battery (30-pr. or 4-inch), partly Horsed, and its Ammunition Column	...	...	1	5	1	2	22	9	2	42
Engineers :—										
Field Company, Sappers and Miners	...	...	1	6	2	1	3	...	2	15
Railway Company, Sappers and Miners	...	...	1	6	5	...	1	...	2	15
Divisional Signal Company ...	...	...	1	6	1	2	7	...	2	19
Bridging Train ...	...	...	...	...	...	...	...	38	2	40
Engineer Field Park ...	...	...	1	1	7	1	...	...	...	10
Infantry :—										
British Battalion	2	...	2	24	2	2	2	...	2	36
Indian ,,	1	1	1	22	2	2	2	...	2	33
Pioneer ,,	1	1	1	22	3	2	5	...	2	37
Transport :—										
Cavalry Brigade Mule Corps :										
Train A	...	...	1	2	2	1	31	6	2	45
,, B	...	1	...	2	2	...	32	6	2	45
,, C	...	...	...	2	2	...	25	3	2	34

23. COMPOSITION OF TRAINS FOR UNITS ON BROAD GAUGE LINES
(45-VEHICLE LOAD)—*continued.*

Units.	\multicolumn{10}{c}{Number of vehicles required.}									
	1st class.	2nd class.	Composites, 1st and 2nd class.	3rd class.	Wagons, covered goods.	Horse boxes.	Horse wagons.	Open trucks.	Brake vans.	Total.
Transport – *continued* –										
Pack Mule Corps:—										
Train A	...	...	1	1	1	...	40	...	2	45
„ B	...	1	...	3	1	...	39	...	1	45
Camel Corps :—										
Train A	...	...	...	1	42	...	...	...	2	45
„ B	...	...	...	1	41	...	1	...	2	45
„ C	...	...	...	1	42	...	...	...	2	45
„ D	...	...	1	1	40	1	...	...	2	45
Hired Bullock Corps :—										
Train A	...	...	...	2	1	...	38	...	2	43
„ B	...	...	...	2	1	...	38	...	2	43
„ C	1	...	...	2	1	1	35	...	2	42
Half Troops of Army Transport or Siege Train Bullocks	...	...	...	1	...	...	6	...	...	7
Medical :—										
2 British and 3 Indian Field Ambulances	...	...	6	18	6	3	6	...	2	41
British General Hospital (100 beds)	...	...	2	1	2	...	...	...	...	5
British General Hospital (500 beds)	1	...	6	6	10	...	...	...	2	25
Indian General Hospital (100 beds)	...	...	1	1	2	...	...	...	...	4
Indian General Hospital (500 beds)	...	...	3	4	10	...	...	...	2	19

NOTE I.—Brake vans are calculated at the rate of 2 per train, this number being necessary for traffic reasons. Ordinarily a train is run at a maximum load of 45 vehicles, but limitations of load may make it necessary to despatch a unit in a number of trains of less than 45 vehicles.

NOTE II.—For further details as to the composition of trains *see* the Field Service Manuals of Units.

23A. Approximate Numbers of Vehicles Required for Units on Metre Gauge Lines (40-Vehicle Load).

Unit.	First Class.	Second Class.	Composite.	Third Class.	Wagon, covered goods.	Horse box.	Horse wagons.	Open trucks.	Brake vans.	Total.
Headquarters										
Cavalry—										
British Regiment	3	...	3	12	6	13	77	...	6	120
Indian Regiment (mobilized with pack transport)	...	...	5	22	10	6	118	4	10	175
Artillery—										
Battery, Royal Horse Artillery	...	...	2	4	5	2	38	14	4	69
Cavalry Brigade Ammunition Column (R.H.A. Section)	...	...	1	2	3	1	16	11	2	36
Battery, Royal Field Artillery	...	...	2	5	5	2	29	14	4	61
Divisional Ammunition Column (R.F.A. Section)	...	...	1	5	2	2	55	40	6	111
Battery, Royal Field Artillery (Howitzer)	...	...	2	7	5	1	26	12	4	57
Ammunition Column, Royal Field Artillery (Howitzer)	...	...	2	5	3	2	37	21	4	74
Mountain Battery, British or Indian	...	...	2	12	9	2	30	...	4	59
30-pr. or 4″ Heavy Battery Ammunition Column	...	...	2	7	4	2	36	15	4	70
Engineers—										
Field Company, Sappers and Miners	...	...	1	10	3	2	3	...	2	21
Railway Company, Sappers and Miners	...	...	1	10	6	1	1	...	2	21
Engineer Field Park	...	...	1	2	10	...	2	...	...	15
Infantry—										
British Battalion	4	...	1	40	4	2	3	...	4	58
Indian ,, ...	2	2	1	36	4	3	2	...	4	54
Pioneer ,, ...	2	2	1	37	4	2	6	...	4	58
Transport—										
Cavalry Brigade Mule Corps	...	...	1	8	8	1	109	25	8	160
Pack Mule Corps	...	...	1	3	6	1	97	...	6	114
Bullock Corps	...	...	1	...	6	1	212	...	12	232
One-half troop Army Transport Bullocks	...	...	...	1	2	...	8	...	2	13
Four-half troop Army Transport Bullocks	...	...	...	2	2	...	32	...	2	38
Medical—										
2 British Field Ambulances	...	...	3	16	3	2	3	...	2	29
3 Indian ,, ,,	...	1	3	20	4	3	5	...	2	38

Headquarters — Will usually proceed by ordinary trains and will requisition for accommodation in the usual way.

Note.—Brake vans are calculated at the rate of two per train, this number being necessary for traffic reasons. Ordinarily a train is run at a maximum load of 40 vehicles, but limitations of load may make it necessary to despatch a unit in a number of trains of less than 40 vehicles.

24. Average Times Required for Entraining Various Units.

One train load of the following :—	Minimum time required.		Normal time allowed on concentration.	
	Entraining.	Detraining and clearing platform.	En. training.	Detraining and clearing platform.
	Hrs.Mins.	Hrs.Mins.	Hrs.Mins.	Hrs.Mins.
Regiment British Cavalry	1 10	1 0	2 0	1 30
Regiment Indian Cavalry	1 10	1 0	2 0	1 00
Battery R.H.A.	0 40	0 30	1 30	1 0
Battery R.F.A.	0 40	0 30	1 30	1 0
Ammunition Column R.F.A.*—				
With end loading dock	1 15	0 50	2 0	1 30
With side loading dock	1 35	1 0	2 0	1 30
Mountain Battery, Brit. or Indian	0 25	0 35	1 9	1 0
Heavy Battery	1 30	1 30	2 0	1 30
Battalion British Infantry... ...	0 35	0 40	1 30	1 30
Battalion Indian Infantry	0 25	0 30	1 0	1 0
Battalion Pioneers	0 25	0 30	1 0	1 0
Mule Corps	1 15	1 10	2 0	2 0
Camel Corps	2 0	1 40	3 0	2 30

* A fatigue party of 25 men per train load is required in addition to establishment.

Notes.—1. Platforms are only necessary for wagons with animals. Each four-wheeler requires 28 feet of platform. Side loading platforms for entrainment of animals should be 3 feet 9 inches in height above rail, but lower platforms can be used when necessary.

2. If successive trains run at 2 hours interval, all trains receive ample time for loading and unloading except camel trains, which should run at 3 hours interval per platform.

3. Open stock is not desirable for camels, or necessary for carts A.T. Large riding camels, however, may require open stock. Carts, A.T., are taken to pieces for packing.

4. In marshalling a train all the vacuum brake stock should be placed next to the engine. If the train has to reverse *en route* the vacuum brake stock should be at either end, and the non-braked stock in the centre, and there should be a brake van at either end. If such a train is hauled by two engines they should be coupled tender to tender, when it will be necessary to turn them when the train reverses.

5. An engine can, without pressing it, work 70 miles a day for a short rush of traffic and 60 miles for a long period. Extra engines should be allowed for at the rate of one-seventh for washing out, and one-seventh for repairs. An engine's run is from 80 to 100 miles for slow trains and water should be available about every 30 miles. A safe allowance for water is 1,500 gallons per broad gauge engine, 800 per metre gauge and 400 per narrow gauge. Thirty minutes should be allowed at engine changing stations to allow of the train-examining staff doing their work, 7 minutes is necessary to water one engine and 10 minutes for two.

GAUGES.

25. Great Britain, France, Germany, Holland, Belgium, Denmark,
  Austria-Hungary, Italy, Switzerland, Sweden, Turkey,   ft. ins.
  Egypt,* Canada, U.S.A.   4   8¼
  Russia   5   0
  Ireland   5   3

' Also 3 feet 6 inch.

GAUGES—*continued*.

								ft.	ins.
Ceylon	..	..	..	..	..	..	..	5	6
Japan ..	..	..	..	..	..	..	..	3	6
Australia, N.S. Wales	..	..	..	..	.. 3 ft. 6 ins. and		4	8½
„ Victoria and South Australia	..		..	..	..		5	3
„ Queensland and W. Australia	..		..	..	..		3	6
New Zealand ..	..	..	..	..	..	..	..	3	6
Spain and Portugal ..	..	..	..	..	..		5	6
Asiatic Turkey	..	..	..		4 ft. 8½ ins. and		3	5½
India ..	..	..	..	..2 ft. 6 ins., 3 ft. 3¾ ins., and			5	6
S. Africa	..	..	..	..	..	..	..	3	6
Width of roadway required for a single line (4 ft. 8½ in. gauge)								12	0
„ „ „ double „				..	..	..	..	23	0

26. AMERICAN OR CANADIAN ROLLING STOCK.

Passenger car carries	..	..	..	50 men.
Horse car carries	..	..	..	16 horses unsaddled, or
				12 „ saddled.
Stock car carries	..	..	..	18 „ unsaddled.
30-ton freight box car carries		..	..	30 men.
Flat cars	..	..	..	..	2 guns with limbers.

27. RUSSIAN ROLLING STOCK.

Wagon, ordinary, carries ..   ..   ..   40 men or 8 horses.

28. SOUTH AFRICAN STOCK.

(On South African railways the length of trains for men is usually limited to about 8 to 10 vehicles, and 30 short trucks in a goods train.)

Passenger Stock.	Normal Accommodation.
First class	..	6 compartments. Sitting, 36. Lying, 24.
Second class	..	6½ compartments. Sitting, 52. Lying, 39.
Composite saloon	..⌈ First class. Sitting, 18. Lying, 12. ⌊ Second class. Sitting, 27. Lying, 21.
*Third class ..	..	7½ compartments. Sitting, 60. Lying, 15.

Other Stock.

Long bogies	..	60 to 80,000 lbs. ⌉ These are not suitable to
Short bogies	..	22,000 lbs. ⌋ accommodate men.
†Short sheep	..	22,500 lbs. or 8 horses, or 10 mules or 20 men.
Bogie cattle truck		40,009 lbs. or 16 horses, or 20 mules or 40 men.
Short cattle truck..		22,000 lbs. or 8 horses, or 10 mules or 20 men.
Horse boxes	..	Seldom available. Accommodate 2, 3 or 4 horses with proportion of attendants.

---

* For short coaches, calculate half this accommodation. This type is being eliminated. It is intended eventually to adopt the long coach as a standard type.
† Not procurable on Natal lines.

TYPES OF TEMPORARY RAILWAY PLATFORMS (made of Railway Material only).

Platform constructed of Sleepers only.

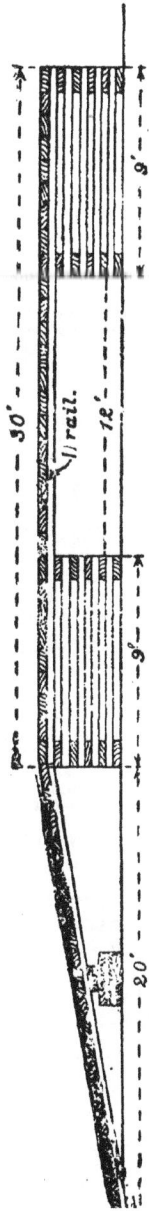

Double Platform constructed of Sleepers and Rails.

PLATFORMS.

Constructed of Railway Material only.

29. A platform constructed of sleepers, to be serviceable, must be very carefully made.

The chief points to be noted are :—

The site should be level if possible, the approaches good, and it must be remembered that space is required for ramps up to the platform.

A truck should be obtained and brought on the siding to the place where the platform is to be constructed.

To fix a longitudinal line for the front edge of the platform, drop a plumbob from the edge of the truck to the ground, and allow a space of 4 inches on a straight siding and 6 inches on a curved line.

To fix the height of the platform, measure the height of the floor of the truck above the level of the ground and deduct 3 inches.

Having ascertained this, calculate the number of sleepers in the cribs. If an even number the bottom sleepers should be laid longitudinally, and *vice versa*, so that the top layer of sleepers may always lie transversely.

When using rails, always spike the rails to the top sleepers of the cribs. If possible fasten a lath or batten along the top of the front edge of the platform by a nail to every sleeper to prevent any sleeper working forward and fouling a train.

Platforms for troop trains are only required for animals and vehicles. For animals the average length required is 100 yards. They should be 3 feet 6 inches to 4 feet above rail level, and 2 feet 3 inches from nearest rail.

30. In India, military platforms are ramped throughout to the rear, when possible, and the type of platform shown in the sketch would not be paved with sleepers ; rammed earth, possibly finished off with road metal, would be used.

31. Under favourable conditions, with the necessary material close to the site, the following may be taken as the time required for construction :—

Platform of sleepers only, single width, 100 yards long : 80 men, 4 hours, 800 sleepers.

Platform of sleepers and rails, single width, 100 yards long : 80 men, 4 hours, 500 sleepers, 30 30-feet rails.

For a double width platform, double the time and material, but the same number of men are required.

For each ramp add 35 sleepers, or 35 sleepers and 3 rails.

32. Temporary platform of sleepers filled in with earth. Sleeper revetment Section—

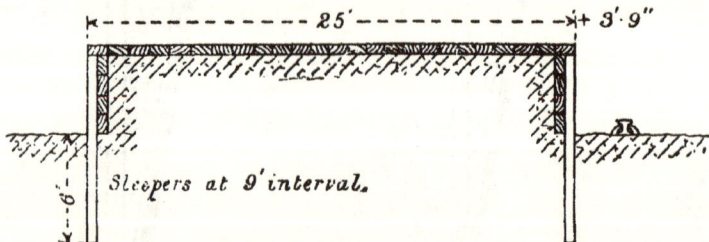

Sleepers at 9′ interval.

112 men, 8 hours, 124 feet length, 2 ballast trains used, 883 sleepers.

DEFINITIONS.

33. Terms requiring definition :—

Chairs—connect rails with sleepers.
Keys—connect rails with chairs (they are wedges).
Fishplates—plates connecting one rail with another.
Cross-over roads--to pass rolling stock from one line to another.
Points—rails fixed at one end and movable at the other, to lead a vehicle in either of two directions.
Crossings—gaps in rails by means of which a vehicle on one line of rails crosses another line of rails.
Through road—combination of crossings, enables one line of rails to cross another without means of communication between the two.
Sidings—allow rolling stock to remain out of danger while traffic is carried on on the main line.

31. TRANSPORT BY SEA.
(*See* F.S.R., Part II, Sec. 56.)

1. The control, provision and despatch of the sea transport of military forces is the duty of the naval authorities, who are responsible for their protection while at sea and for their oversea communications. The requirements of the C.-in-C. are notified to the Admiralty by the Q.M.G. to the Forces.

2. A director of sea transport, appointed by the Admiralty, controls the arrangements in connection with the provision of sea transport on their behalf.

3. The general division of duties between the navy and army is dealt with in Sec. 16.

4. Conveyance is provided by :—

Transports (ships wholly engaged for the Government service).
Freightships (ships in which conveyance is engaged for troops, but not wholly at the disposal of the Government).

TONNAGE TABLES.

5. Gross tonnage is the total cubic space below deck and the total cubic contents of closed spaces above deck.

Net tonnage is the gross tonnage minus all spaces not available for freight and after deducting accommodation for the crew and space occupied by engine rooms, coal bunkers, &c.

Freight tonnage is a measure of cubic capacity, a freight-ton being 40 cubic feet of cargo space.

6. In making calculations as to the tonnage required by a body of troops 4 tons per man and 12 tons per horse for ocean voyages, and 2 tons per man and 8 tons per horse for short voyages should be allowed. An ocean voyage in this connection means that troops are conveyed in transports fitted up in accordance with the Admiralty Transport Regulations. For short voyages no fittings for men would be provided and only the simplest fittings, consistent with security, for the horses.

7. As regards the tonnage required for guns, vehicles, &c., the stowage of such articles depends solely on clear floor space, and all height above that of the vehicles is lost tonnage. In some ships the holds may be only just deep enough to take the highest vehicles, while in others there may be 9 or 10 feet to spare, yet only the same number of vehicles can be stowed in each. No attempt is, therefore, made to give this information. The space required for the various vehicles in common use can be obtained from the table given in Sections 28 and 32 (10) and (11).

8. POINTS IN INSPECTING SHIPS.

(a) *Accommodation*.—Officers, W.O.'s and Staff Sjts., other ranks, sick, prison, state of hammocks and bedding, state of troop decks, places for kits and accoutrements, mess utensils, arm racks, magazines, baggage space, cooking galleys.

(b) *Water.*—Amount, quality, arrangements for issue.

(c) *Provisions.*—Good, sufficient.

(d) *Sanitary.*—Latrines, urinals.

(e) *Boats.*—Condition. Number. Life-saving apparatus.

(f) *Animals (for).*—Stalls, fittings, forage, places for saddlery, harness, &c., space for transport wagons, hoisting appliances.

9. POINTS IN FITTING OF TRANSPORTS.

(a) Be able to embark or disembark night or day.

(b) Derricks should be numerous and well fitted, with clear leads for whips and guys, and with rapid running winches to each hatch.

(c) Hatches should be free from obstruction.

(d) All hatches and decks to be worked during disembarkation should be well lighted.

(e) Numerous boat ropes, accommodation ladders, and rope ladders should be available for each gangway.

(f) Derricks should be capable of lifting 10 tons.

10. TROOPS ON BOARD SHIP—EMBARKING.

(a) Embark units complete on one ship, if possible.

(b) Remember to embark last what is wanted first on disembarking.

(c) Men must be told off to their messes. (Better if done in consultation with first officer of the ship.)

(d) Stow sea-kit bags over mess tables.

(e) Stow kit bags and waterproof bags in separate baggage room.

(f) Stow rifles (without slings), properly labelled, in the armoury, if there is one, and the ammunition in the magazine.

(g) Take over the bedding and utensils.

(h) Instruct men how to roll bedding and sling hammocks.

(i) Put ship's halters on horses and unsaddle and unharness.

(j) See to stowing of saddlery and harness. (Put together in sets and label.)

(k) See to safe stowing of vehicles.

(l) Leave 5 per cent. spare stalls, half on each side.

(m) Troops are generally told off into guard (detailed daily), swabbers, &c. Tell off troop deck serjeants, sanitary serjeant, police, stable guard, &c.

(n) Tell off troops to fire stations and boat stations, in consultation with ship's authorities.

(o) Acquaint troops with ship's orders, fire signals, &c.

11. BUGLE CALLS ON BOARD SHIP.

Standfast	Silence; Man overboard, everyone to remain still. Those below will remain there.
Continue	Carry on. (Continue your business.)
Retire	Everyone off upper deck but the guard.
4 G's	Sweepers.
4 G's and double	Swabbers.
Charge	Permission to smoke.
Lights out	Leave off smoking.
Fire alarm	Fire and collision. Troops fall in at their respective stations. All others remain quiet.
Commence firing	Heave round pumps.
Cease firing	Avast pumping.

12. SHIP'S SIGNALS.

(a) Ship's bell rung violently, strokes in quick succession .. Fire.

(b) Ship's bell rung quickly, followed by several short blasts on siren or whistle .. .. Collision.

At these signals all buglers will sound the necessary calls.

(c) For man overboard. At the cry of man overboard the steam whistle is sounded, several short blasts in quick succession. At this signal the bugler on duty will, if ordered by the officer of the watch, at once sound the "stand fast."

SLINGING HORSES ON TO A SHIP.*

13. Horses should be unsaddled and unharnessed; ship's halter undei head-collar, bridoon reins loose but knotted.

Do not let horse's head loose, fasten with double guy, one end being held ōii shore or in the boat, and one on the ship. Horses may fall backwards out of slings, but will never fall forward.

14. Five men required, one at head, one at each side, one at the breast, and one behind.

Pass one end of sling under belly, both ends being brought up to meet over back; one man passes his loop through the other loop, and it is received by the man on the other side, who hauls it through, hooking the tackle to it, both men holding the ends of the sling till taut. Men at the breast and behind then bring their ropes round and make them fast to grummets, and the man who holds the horse's head makes fast the guys to the ship's head-collar.

Fasten the breech band and the breast girth securely.

Blindfold timid or restive horses.

15. Two or three men must be at the hatchway and between the decks to guide the horse when being lowered.

Provide a mat or straw for the horse to alight on.

16. HORSES ON BOARD SHIP—POINTS TO BE ATTENDED TO.

(a) Sufficient and good water and forage.
(b) Fittings good, sound and up to date.
(c) Animals properly sheltered.
(d) Stores good and sufficient.
(e) Ventilation good, windsails and fans in good order.
(f) Feeding. Average ration, $\frac{1}{2}$ and $\frac{1}{3}$; at first few oats and much bran, subsequently increase oats. Full ration of hay all through.
(g) Clean ship frequently. Exercise on deck in fine weather. Cinders spread will give horses foothold.
(h) Put horses next to each other who are accustomed to each other.
(j) Hand rub horses' legs regularly.
(k) In rough weather, sacks filled with anything soft will often preserve horses from injury.

SLINGING CAMELS ON TO A SHIP.

17. Camels about to be slung should be provided with a head collar with rope attached (a rope fastened round the neck so as not to form a slip knot and then a loop taken round the jaw will answer equally well). This prevents the men from hanging on to the nose-rope to steady the animal when first taken off its feet—a practice which is likely to tear out the nose-bag and cause great suffering to the animal.

Camels should be made to kneel down under the crane. The man holding the nose-rope then blindfolds the animal; two other men stand, one on each forearm, to prevent its rising; others slip the sling under the belly. Vicious animals require to have their mouths secured, and forelegs tied with a rope passing over the neck from one leg to the other. If necessary, two men stand one on each hock, to render the animal powerless.

CAMELS ON BOARD SHIP—POINTS TO BE ATTENDED TO.

18. Large-sized camels should be accommodated in the lower hold, medium-sized camels on the upper deck, small camels between decks; those on upper

---

* If a ship is alongside a quay, horses can be more rapidly embarked by walking them on board by means of brows.

decks heads outwards, those between decks and in holds heads inwards; 8 feet 6 inches between decks is sufficient to enable camels to stand up.

19. On board, camels should be ranged side by side, round the sides of the ship and made to sit, with their forelegs tied. No animals should be stowed amidships.

The decks should be covered with at least 6 inches of sand, and there should be ¼ ton of sand per camel, in addition, for a voyage not exceeding 15 days.

20. Every camel should be fitted with harness, secured to rings or spars lashed on to the deck, to prevent the animals from shifting their positions.

In fine weather the leg ropes of a few at a time may be cast off and the animals allowed to rise ; and, if space allows, they should be exercised.

21. During the voyage great care should be paid to the bend of the knees, and hocks. The sand the animals lie upon works into these parts, and if they be kept sitting for long periods, it causes irritation and the formation of ulcers.

SLINGING GUNS AND VEHICLES.

22. For slinging guns and limbers, the following method has been found to work well.

Two 4-inch slings are used, one round each axletree, and a hook rope hooked into the trail eye. The bights of the sling placed on the tackle hook, to which the end of the hook rope is also made fast.

Limbers have their poles removed and are slung in the same way as guns, the hook rope in their case being made fast to the tackle hook from the trail hook.

23. G.S. wagons and pontoon wagons can be slung by four chain slings connected to a common link at one end and provided with hooks at the other, these four hooks are then secured to all four wheels of the vehicle.

Vehicles will, as a rule, be embarked loaded on their wheels, all loose articles being stowed within the wagons, the poles and shafts being removed before slinging. If the wheels are removed, special care must be taken that the linch pins and washers are put away. Those carriages first required on disembarkation should be stowed away last.

CHAPTER VI.

32. SMALL ARMS AND GUNS.

1. Rifle, Short, Magazine, Lee-Enfield Pattern 1903.

Weight, without bayonet, 8 lbs. 10½ ozs.
  „   with   „   9 lbs. 11 ozs.
Length, without „   3 ft. 8·5 ins.
  „   with   „   5 ft. 2 ins.

Mark VII ·303″ Ammunition.

Cartridge, weight 386 grains, 20 rounds (in chargers), 20 ozs.
Bullet, length 1·28 inches, weight 174 grains.
Charge, cordite M.D.T., 39 grains.
Muzzle velocity, 2,440 feet per second.

Mark VI ·303″ Ammunition.

Cartridge, length 3·05 inches, weight 415 grains, 20 rounds (in chargers) 22 ozs.
Bullet, envelope cupro-nickel, length 1·25 inches, diameter (at base), ·311 inch, weight 215 grains.
Charge, cordite, 31·5 grains.
Muzzle velocity, 2,060 feet per second.

2. Notes on the Use of the Rifle.

Dangerous space decreases as the range increases.
Extent of dangerous space depends on :—

  (a) Firer's position.
  (b) Height of object fired at.
  (c) Flatness of trajectory.
  (d) Conformation of ground.

The nearer the rifle is to the ground
The higher the object fired at
The flatter the trajectory..
The more nearly the slope of the ground conforms to the angle at which the bullet falls
  } the greater is the dangerous space.

3. The accuracy of the short magazine L.E. rifle is not appreciably affected by fixing the bayonet, but with the long L.E. or the L.M. rifle additional elevation is required when the bayonet is fixed.

4. More elevation is required :—
  When the weather is cold.
Less elevation is required :—
  (a) When the weather is hot.
  (b) High up above sea level.
  (c) Firing up or down hill.

5. Rifles are sighted for the following conditions :—
  Barometric pressure 30 inches (sea level).
  Thermometer, 60° Fahrenheit.
  Still air.
  A horizontal line of sight.

6. The following rule for correction in case of variations in barometric pressure is approximately correct :—
  For every inch the barometer rises or falls, add, or deduct, 1½ yards per 100 yards of range.

Thus a reduction of some 30 yards in 2,000 yards range would be required if the barometer stood at 29 inches.
The barometer falls about 1 inch for every 1,000 feet of altitude. Therefore, at an altitude of 5,000 feet it would, in normal conditions of weather, stand at 25 inches, and for 2,000 yards range the elevation required would be 1,850 yards only.
Every degree which the temperature rises or falls above and below 60° necessitates the subtraction or addition of about one-tenth of a yard for each 100 yards of range.

7. Ranges of objects are over-estimated :—
   When kneeling or lying.
   When both background and object are of a similar colour.
   On broken ground.
   When looking over a valley or undulating ground.
   In avenues, long streets, or ravines.
   When the object lies in the shade.
   When the object is viewed in mist or failing light.
   When the object is only partially seen.
   When heat is rising from the ground.

8. Ranges of objects are under-estimated :—
   When the sun is behind the observer.
   In bright light or clear atmosphere.
   When both background and object are of different colours.
   When the intervening ground is level or covered with snow.
   When looking over water or a deep chasm.
   When looking upwards or downwards.
   When the object is large.

9. Details Regarding Field Guns and Howitzers.

—	13-Pr. Q.F.	18-Pr. Q.F.	60-Pr. B.L.	4·5-in. Q.F.Howr.	5-in. B.L. Hewr.
Muzzle velocity... ...	1,675 f.s.	1,590 f.s.	2,080 f.s.	1,010 f.s.	782 f.s.
Calibre	3 ins.	3·3 ins.	5 ins.	4·5 ins.	5 ins.
Weight of projectile ...	12½ lb.	18½ lb.	60 lb.	35 lb.	50 lb.
No. of rounds in limber	24	24	2	12	16
No. of rounds in wagon	38	38	26	32	32
No. of rounds in wagon limber	38	38	12	16	16
*Maximum range ...	6,100 yds.	6,200 yds.	9,500 yds.	7,200 yds.	3,400 yds.

* For time shrapnel.

10. Details of Artillery and Machine Gun Equipment.

Guns.	Weights.		Width between points of axle-tree arms.	Calibre.	Length of Carriage Gun.	Length of Limber, poles exclusive.
	Gun and Carriage.	Gun, Carriage, and Limber.				
	cwt. qrs. lbs.	cwt. qrs. lbs.	ft. ins.	ins.	ft. ins.	ft. ins.
13-pr. Q.F.	19 3 24	32 3 24	6 3	3	12 2	5 3
18-pr. Q.F.	25 0 21	40 1 21	6 3	3·3	13 8	5 4½
5″ B.L. Howitzer ...	23 3 13 {	43 1 8a / 46 2 8b }	6 2	5	9 2¼	5 6
4·5″ Q.F. Howitzer	26 3 14	41 3 0	6 3½	4·5	12 3	5 7
60-pr. B.L.	91 3 7	108 1 7	6 6½	5	21 7	7 7
Maxim gun, (Inf.) Carriage Mk. III	9 3 20	...	6 0⅞	...	10 3	...
30-pr. B.L. gun, India	...	65 0 0	6 2	4	13 2	5 7½
4″ B.L. gun, India	55 0 0	67 7 10	...	4	12 4	...
5″ B.L. gun, ,,	73 0 0	85 7 10	6 7	5	14 3	5 8
10-pr. Mountain gun, India	7 3 9	...	...	2·75	7 9½	...

a Mark I Carriage and Mark II Limber.
b Mark I Carriage and Mark I Limber.

Gun.	Mounting Tripod.	Gun and Tripod.
Maxim ... ... { Mark II ... ... „ III ... ... „ IV		cwt. qrs. lbs. 1 0 25 1 0 18 1 0 17

11.—DETAILS OF AMMUNITION WAGONS.

Wagon.	Weights.			Length.	
	Without Limber.	With Limber.	Width overall.	Without Limber.	With Limber and Pole.
	cwt.qrs. lbs.	cwt.qrs. lbs.	ft. ins.	ft. ins.	ft. ins.
13-pr. Q.F. ... ... { a { b	17 0 10 16 2 10	32 3 23 32 1 23	} 6 3	8 4	22 6
18-pr. Q.F. ... ... { a { b	19 3 17 19 1 17	38 3 17 38 1 17	} 6 3	8 5	22 7
4·5″ Q.F. Howitzer { a { b	24 1 21 23 3 21	40 2 7 40 0 7	} 6 3½	9 10	24 3
5″ B.L. { Mark I ... Howitzer { Mark II ...	23 2 13 29 1 18½	46 1 8 48 3 13½	6 2 6 2	9 2 9 2	22 5 22 5
60-pr. B.L. ... ... { a { b	29 3 12 29 1 10	48 0 12 47 2 10	} 6 0	8 3	22 3

a With spare pole.
b Without spare pole.

12.—APPROXIMATE NUMBER OF ROUNDS PROVIDED IN THE FIELD PER GUN.

Description of Gun.	With Battery.	With Brigade Ammunition Column.	With Divisional Ammunition Column.	Total with Field Units.	With Ammunition Park.	Other reserve to be maintained on the lines of communication.	Total to be maintained in the Field.
13-pr. Q.F.	176	220*	...	396	150	454	1,000
18-pr. Q.F.	176	76	126	378	150	472	1,000
4·5″ Q.F. Howitzer ...	108	48	44	200	80	520	800
60-pr. B.L.	80	40†	60	180	70	250	500
6″ B.L. { 100-lb. shell	50	50	...	...	...	...	...
Howitzer { or { 122-lb. shell	40	40	...	...	...	...	...

* 76 rounds in ammunition wagons, and 144 rounds in G.S. wagons.
† Ammunition column with the battery.

(B 11925)   O

13. APPROXIMATE NUMBER OF ROUNDS PROVIDED IN THE FIELD FOR EACH MAN ARMED WITH THE RIFLE.

For each rifle of	With Unit.				Total with field units.	With ammunition Park.	Further supply of reserve ammunition on lines of communication.‡	Total to be maintained in the field.
	On the soldier.	In regimental reserve.	With brigade ammunition column.	With divisional ammunition column.				
Cavalry and Irish Horse	100	100	100	...	300	100	100	500
Divisional Cavalry ...	100	100	50§	50§	300	100	100	500
Artillery	50†	...	...	...	50	...	...	50
Engineers	50	50*	...	...	100	...	...	100
Infantry	120	100	80	50	350	100	100	550
Army Service Corps ...	20	...	...	...	20	...	...	20
Army Ordnance Corps	20	...	...	...	20	...	...	20

* For dismounted men only.
† Per man.
‡ This reserve will, if necessary, be increased to 300 rounds per rifle for cavalry regiments, mounted infantry and infantry battalions as soon as possible after the commencement of the campaign.
§ No special provision is made for carriage of this ammunition.

NOTES.—1. For the purpose of arriving approximately at the number of rounds to be carried in ammunition columns, the number of rifles in units is calculated at 500 for cavalry regiments and at 1,000 for infantry battalions ; other units are not considered.

2. The capacity, in rounds, of vehicles and animals allotted for small-arm ammunition is as follows :—S.A.A. cart, 16,000 ; Limbered G.S. wagon, 16,000 ; G.S. wagon, 40,000 ; Pack animal, 2,000 ; Lorry (3-ton), 80,000.

14. APPROXIMATE NUMBER OF ROUNDS (·303-INCH) PROVIDED IN THE FIELD FOR EACH MACHINE GUN.

For each machine gun of	With Units.		With brigade (gun) ammunition column.	With divisional ammunition column.	Total with field units.	With Ammunition Park.	On L. of C.	Total in the field.
	Service ammunition.	Regimental reserve.						
Cavalry	3,500	16,000	10,000	...	29,500	6,000	14,000	49,500
Infantry	3,500	8,000	5 000	5,000	21,500	6,000	14,000	41,500.

15. APPROXIMATE NUMBER OF ROUNDS PROVIDED IN THE FIELD FOR EACH PISTOL.

For each pistol a total of 36 rounds is carried in the field. viz., 12 rounds on the man, 12 rounds in regimental transport, and 12 rounds in the brigade (gun) ammunition column.

16   SCALE AND DISTRIBUTION OF AMMUNITION ON FIELD SERVICE IN INDIA.

(a) *Gun Ammunition.*

Distribution.	No. of Rounds per Gun*—					
	Horse Artillery.	Field Artillery.		Heavy Artillery.		Mountain Artillery.
	13-pr. Q.F.	18-pr. Q.F.	B.L. 5-inch Howitzer.	B.L. 30-pr.	B.L. 4-inch.	B.L. 10-pr.
With Battery	176	176	88†	110†	96†	137§
With Ammunition Column	260	272	74†	169†	168†	98‖
With Ordnance Field Park:—						
In Advanced Depôts, Intermediate Depôts, and Base Depôts	564	552	838†	221†	236†	765¶
Total	1,000	1,000	1,000	500	500	1,000

* A heavy battery consists of 4 pieces, all other batteries consist of 6 pieces.
† 70 per cent. shrapnel shell and 30 per cent. common lyddite shell.
§ Includes 4 star shell, 5 common shell, and 128 shrapnel shell.
‖ Includes 7 star shell, 7 common shell, and 84 shrapnel shell.
¶ Includes 22 star shell, 28 common shell, and 715 shrapnel shell.

(b.)—SMALL-ARM AND MACHINE GUN AMMUNITION.

Distribution.	Pistol.		Rifle.							Machine Gun.
	Artillery.	Other Arms.	British Cavalry.	Indian Cavalry.	British Infantry.	Indian Infantry.	Pioneers.	Mounted Infantry.	Sappers, and Miners.	
						No. of Rounds per—				
On the soldier	24	24	120	120	100	100	70	120	70*	...
With Gun or Battery ...	26	...								6,000
With troop or Section Reserve	...	...	84	76	91	99	99	78	53	6,000
With Regimental Reserve ...		26	96	104	109	101	131	102	77	4,480
With Ammunition Column ...			175	175	175	175	175	175	100	8,960
With Ordnance Field Park:— In Advanced Depôt, Intermediate Depôts, and Base Depôt	50	50	225	225	225	225	225	225	100	10,560
Total	100	100	700	700	700	700	700	700	400	30,000

NOTE.—The 120 rounds per rifle shown as carried by cavalrymen on the "soldier" will be distributed as follows:—

In the bandolier on the man ... ... 90 rounds
In the bandolier on the horse ... ... 30 rounds

Total ... ... 120 rounds

* 40 for those armed with carbines.

AMMUNITION SUPPLY OF A DIVISION.

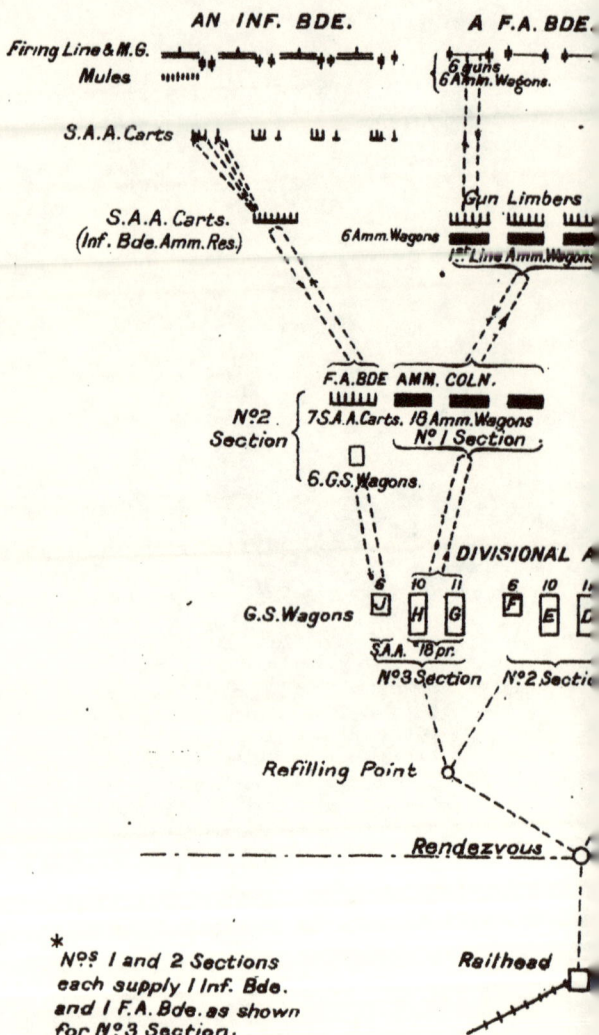

AN INF. BDE.

A F.A. BDE.

Firing Line & M.G.
Mules

6 guns
6 Amm. Wagons.

S.A.A. Carts

Gun Limbers

S.A.A. Carts.
(Inf. Bde. Amm. Res.)

6 Amm. Wagons

1st Line Amm. Wagons

F.A. BDE AMM. COLN.

Nº2
Section

7 S.A.A. Carts. 18 Amm. Wagons
Nº 1 Section

6. G.S. Wagons.

DIVISIONAL A

G.S. Wagons

6   10   11
J   H   G

6   10   1
F   E   D

S.A.A. 18 pr.
Nº 3 Section   Nº 2 Sectio

Refilling Point

Rendezvous

Railhead

*
Nºs 1 and 2 Sections
each supply 1 Inf. Bde.
and 1 F.A. Bde. as shown
for Nº 3 Section.

To face page 165.

6385, 63186.718.150,000. 4:17.

Plate 16.

A F.A.(HOWR)BDE.   **A HEAVY BATT.**

Gun Limbers

1st Line Amm.Wagons

4 Amm. Wagons

Gun Limbers

1st Line Amm.Wagons

F.A.(HOWR)BDE.AMM.COLN.

18 Amm. Wagons.

HEAVY BATT.
AMM. COLN.

4 Amm.Wagons.

LUMN

10   11

g   A

K   L   M

N

4·5" howr. 60 pr.

Section

No 4 Section.

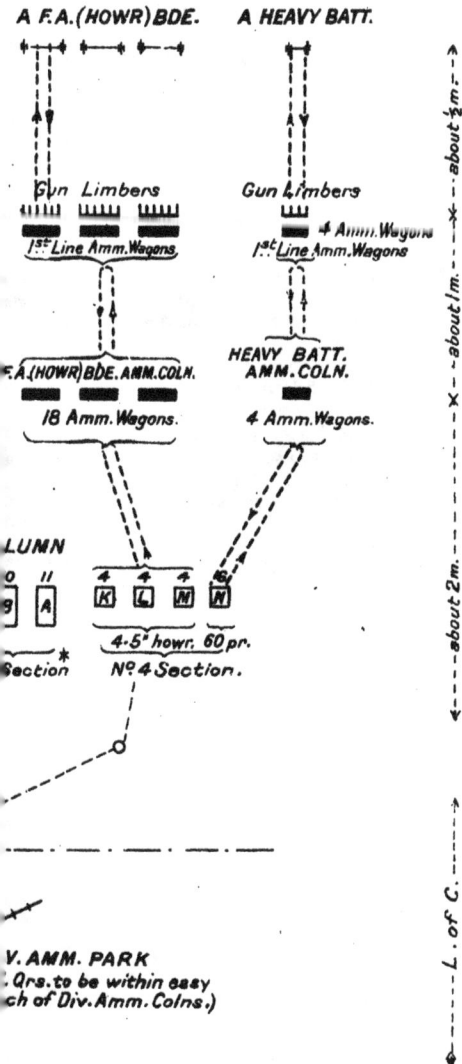

V. AMM. PARK
Qrs.to be within easy
ch of Div.Amm.Colns.)

about ½ m.

about 1 m.

about 2 m.

L. of C.

Malby & Sons. Lith.

A CAV. BDE.   A CAV.   A R.H.A. BDE.
BDE.

Firing Line & M.Guns.

6 Guns
6 Wagons

Limbered G.S. Wagons
1 per Squad, 2 per M:Gun

Limbered G.S. Wagons
(Bde. Amm. Res.)

Gun Limbers

6   6
1st Line Amm. Wagons.

R.H.A. Bde. Amm. Coln.
3 Limbered 6 Amm.
G.S. Wagons. Wagons.

4 G.S. Wag.ns   6 G.S. Wag.ns

No.2 Section   No.1 Section

Refilling Points

Rendezvous

Cav. Divl.
Amm. Park.   Rail

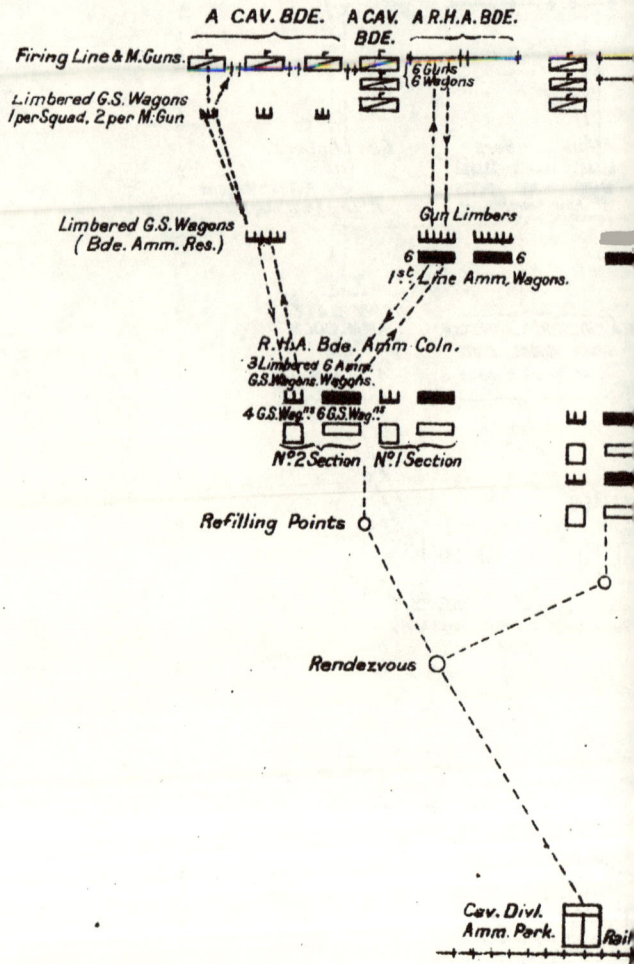

To follow Plate 16.

6365.

Plate 17.

A CAVALRY BDE. NOT ALLOTTED TO A CAV. DIVN.

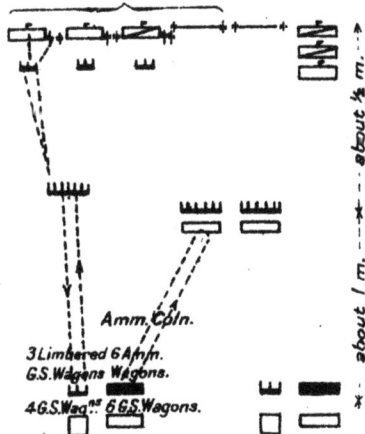

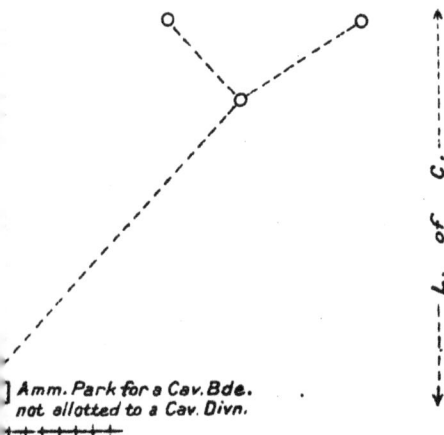

about ½ m.

about 1 m.

Amm. Coln.

3 Limbered 6 Amn.
G.S. Wagons Wagons.

4 G.S. Wag^{ns.} 6 G.S. Wagons.

L. of C.

] Amm. Park for a Cav. Bde.
not allotted to a Cav. Divn.

Malby & Sons. Lith

33. SUPPLY OF AMMUNITION IN THE FIELD.

(See F.S.R., Part I, Chap. XII, and Part II, Secs. 70–74.)

1. The work of replenishing ammunition is divided between :—

   (*a*) Units working under the I.G.C.
   (*b*) Units with divisions, cavalry division, or army troops.

2. The reserves of ammunition held by fighting troops are divided into three lines, as follows :—

   (*a*) Regimental reserves, carried on pack animals or in 1st line transport vehicles. Ammunition expended in the firing line is replaced from this source.
   (*b*) Artillery brigade ammunition columns, forming part of each artillery brigade. With the exception of howitzer brigade and heavy battery ammunition columns they carry both small-arm and gun ammunition. Regimental reserves are replenished from these columns.
   (*c*) Divisional ammunition columns, forming part of the divisional artillery. Brigade or heavy battery ammunition columns are replenished from these columns, except in the case of the cavalry division and army troops which receive their ammunition direct from the ammunition parks. Divisional ammunition columns are divided into headquarters and 4 sections, of which the first three contain only 18-pr. gun and S.A.A. ammunition, the fourth section 4·5-inch howitzers and 60-pr. ammunition.

An infantry brigade normally forms a reserve of ammunition by detaching from each battalion about a third of its regimental reserve under a selected officer, which forms a link between the regimental reserve and the artillery brigade ammunition column (*see* I.T. Sec. 166, 2).

3. The reserves of ammunition held on the lines of communication are divided between ammunition parks (M.T.) and ordnance depôts. Plates 16 and 17 illustrate the system of supply of ammunition of field units. A fundamental principle of this system is that troops in action should never have to go back to fetch ammunition. It is the business of the troops in rear to send it forward.

4. During an action ammunition parks are sent forward under the orders of the I.G.C. to rendezvous fixed by General (or Army Corps) Headquarters, beyond which points the responsibility of the I.G.C. ceases. From these rendezvous, sections or smaller portions of the parks are sent forward to refilling points (see para. 5 below), whence the replenishment of divisional ammunition columns is carried out. For cavalry divisions the ammunition parks carry the ammunition direct to the brigade ammunition columns, or to regiments, as may be most convenient.

5. When an action is imminent, sections of the divisional ammunition column will be ordered to form reserves of ammunition at convenient points, which will also be the refilling points for such sections (see para. 4 above). The position of these points will be fixed by divisional headquarters, and should usually be about two miles in rear of brigade ammunition columns.

6. The position of brigade ammunition columns during a battle are normally regulated by artillery brigade commanders, in accordance with the instructions of divisional artillery commanders, and should usually be about a mile in rear of the battery wagon lines.

7. The above principles apply equally to India though the details of ammunition supply differ to a certain extent.

The reserves held by fighting troops are divided into three lines, viz.—(*a*) Section reserves on pack mules, (*b*) Regimental reserves on camels or A.T. carts, (*c*) Divisional ammunition columns.

There is no unit working under the I.G.C. corresponding to the ammunition park, but convoys of ammunition are sent forward as necessary from the ordnance depôt at the advanced base to replenish divisional ammunition columns. A further approximation to the home system is under consideration in India.

34. RATIONS AND FUEL.

1. Detail of rations and fuel carried in the field with units, and in A.S.C. trains and supply columns

How carried normally.	Field Ration.			Iron Ration.	Remarks.
	Bread and Meat Ration.	Grocery Ration.	Vegetable Ration.		
	1¼ lbs. fresh or frozen, or 1 lb. (nominal) preserved a or salt meat. 1¼ lbs. bread b, or 1 lb. biscuit c or flour, 4 ozs. bacon d.	Tea, sugar, jam, salt, pepper, cheese and mustard (as detailed in Allowance Regulations).	2 ozs. dried.	1 lb. (nominal) preserved meat, 12 ozs. biscuit, ⅝ oz. tea, 2 ozs. sugar, ½ oz. salt, 3 ozs. cheese, 2 cubes (1 oz.) meat extract.	a Packed in wooden cases not exceeding 80 lbs. weight, containing 60 rations in nominal 1-lb. tins. b Carried in sacks. c Packed in wooden cases not exceeding 80 lbs. weight, containing 50 rations. d Packed in wooden cases containing 60 lbs. bacon, not exceeding 80 lbs. gross weight. e The day's bread and cheese ration issued the previous evening, less any portion consumed. In the case of arms other than infantry, this ration may be carried in the vehicle for cooks.
On the soldier ...	e	e	...	1 h	
	1	1	...	...	
In vehicles for cooks or travelling kitchens	f	f	1	...	

In A.S.C. trains or in supply columns	1	1	1	...
Total ...	2 g	2 g	2 g	1 h

f. The day's ration (except bread and cheese) issued the previous evening, less any portion consumed.

g Less any portion consumed of the ration carried on the soldier and in the vehicles for cooks.

h A second iron ration may be carried when so ordered by the C.-in-C.

NOTES.—1. No fuel will be carried normally, except for mechanically propelled vehicles and the wood of the ration boxes, which will be issued for kindling purposes, and be supplemented by fuel obtained locally.

2. Reserve Parks, each with a carrying capacity of 2 days' iron rations, will be available for use if required.

3. Fresh vegetables will be issued when available.

4. Lime juice, rum and tobacco to be issued as detailed in Allowance Regulations, but not carried normally in A.S.C. trains or in supply columns.

2. FORAGE.

How carried.	Corn ration. 12 lbs. (a)	Remarks.
On the horse	1b	a In the case of heavy draught horses the corn ration is 15 lbs.
In A.S.C. trains or In supply columns .. }	1	b The day's ration issued the previous evening, less any portion consumed.
Total ..	2c	c Less any portion consumed of the ration carried on the horse.

NOTES.

(1) The above scale of forage is applicable to a country where hay is available.

(2) Reserve parks, each with carrying capacity for 2 days' reserve grain, will be available for use if required.

RATIONS.

3. In case of active operations in the field, a special scale of rations, dependent on the climate and the circumstances of the expedition, will be fixed by the G.O.C., and reported to the War Office, but the following scale will, as far as possible, be adopted as a guide :—

     1¼ lbs. fresh or frozen meat, or 1 lb. (nominal) preserved meat or 1 lb. salt meat.
     1¼ lbs. bread, or 1 lb. biscuit, or 1 lb. flour.
     ¼ lb. bacon.
     3 ozs. cheese.
     ⅝ oz. tea.
     ¼ lb. jam.
     3 ozs. sugar.
     ½ oz. salt.
     $\frac{1}{36}$ oz. pepper.
     $\frac{1}{20}$ oz. mustard.
     ½ lb. fresh vegetables, or 2 ozs. dried vegetables.
     $\frac{1}{30}$ gal. limejuice ($\frac{1}{15}$ gill) on days ⎫
        when fresh vegetables are not ⎪ At the discretion of the general
        issued .. .. .. ⎬ officer commanding, on the
     $\frac{1}{64}$ gal. rum (½ gill) .. .. .. ⎪ recommendation of the
     Tobacco, not exceeding 2 ozs. per ⎪ medical officer.
        week, for those who smoke .. ⎭

TABLE OF EQUIVALENTS.

4. When it may be necessary or, in the opinion of the general officer commanding, expedient to depart from the scales before laid down, the following scale of equivalents will be followed :—

Oatmeal	4 ozs.	= 4 ozs. bread or biscuit.
Biscuit	1 lb.	= 1¼ lb. bread.
Rice	4 ozs.	= 4 ozs. bread or biscuit.
Chocolate	½ oz.	= ⅝ oz. tea.
Preserved meat ..	1 lb. (nominal)	= 1 ration fresh meat, 1¼ lb.
Porter	1 pint	= 1 ration spirit.
Dried fruit of any sort ..	4 ozs.	= 4 ozs. jam.
Bacon	4 ozs.	= 4 ozs. butter, lard or margarine, or ½ gill sweet oil.

MEAT AND VEGETABLE RATION.

5. This consists of ¾ lb. meat and ½ lb. vegetables, and 2 ozs. gravy, put up in a convenient sized tin ; gross weight, 1 lb. 10½ ozs.

EXAMPLES OF NATIVE RATIONS.

6. Aden camel drivers :—
Rice, 1½ lbs.
Dates, wet, 1 lb.
Ghi, 2 ozs.
Sugar, 2 ozs
Coffee, ½ oz.
Salt, ½ oz.
Onions, when procurable, 2 ozs. or Dal, 4 ozs.

7. South African natives :—
Mealies, in the form of flour or meal, 1½ lbs.
Fresh meat, 1½ lbs.
Salt, ½ oz.

FORAGE RATION.

8. The ordinary ration for animals in camp is :—

	Oats.	Hay.
	lbs.	lbs.
Horses (over 15 hands ½ inch)	12*	12†
Others ..	10	12
Mules (15 hands)	12	12
Small mules ..	6	12

* 15 lbs. for heavy draught horses.
† 16 lbs.   „   „   „

These rates may be varied on service by authority of G.O.C.

9. FORAGE EQUIVALENTS.

Barley   ..   ..   .. 1 lb. ⎫
Straw   ..   .. 2 lbs. ⎪
Bran   ..   .. 1½ lbs. ⎪
Malt   ..   .. ¾ lb. ⎬ All equivalent of each other.
Oatmeal ..   .. ¾ lb. ⎪
Hay   ..   .. 1½ lbs. ⎪
Oats   ..   .. 1 lb. ⎭
Compressed forage   ..   .. 18 lbs. = 10 lbs. oats and 12 lbs. hay.
    or
Forage cake   ..   ..   .. 20 lbs. = 12 lbs. oats and 12 lbs. hay.

10. Indian rates for animals are :—

	Oats, Barley or Gram.	Hay.	Salt.
	lbs.	lbs.	ozs.
Horses	8-10	20	1
M.I. ponies	6	20	¾
Ordnance mules	6	20	¾
1st class mules (baggage)	6	15	¾
R.A. bullocks	7	25	¾
Bullocks (transport)	6	20	
Camels	6	25	1½
Pack bullocks	4	14	¾
Donkeys	3-4	10-13	¼

RATIONS AND FORAGE IN INDIA.

11. In estimating transport for food supplies to be carried with troops, the approximate weight of rations, substitutes and extras (exclusive of emergency rations) may be taken at :—

British ration, biscuits, groceries and tinned meat .. 3½ lbs. per diem.
"   "   flour, groceries and dried vegetables,
    when meat is on hoof   ..   ..   ..   1¾ lbs. "   "
Indian ration ..   .. 2¼ lbs. "   "

Fuel, fresh meat, and such articles as will not be carried, such as fresh vegetables, have not been taken into account in this estimate.
In addition 3 lbs. of fuel may be carried per British and 1½ lbs. per Indian soldier.
Troops and followers will, as a rule, cut their own fuel in localities where this is practicable.
Of the meat ration, six-sevenths travels on the hoof.
Extras are issued on occasions.

12. The proportion of fighting men to followers in a division is :—

1 fighting man to ·44 followers and ·68 animals.
The average weight of daily grain ration for animals is :—

6½ lbs. per animal in a division   ..   ..⎫ Includes   all   transport
8 lbs.   "   "   cavalry brigade .. ⎭ animals.

13. Normal number of days' rations for men and grain for animals carried in the field in addition to the unconsumed portion of the current day's ration.

Detail.	British.				Indian.			Animals	
	Field ration.			Emergency rations.	Fighting men.		Fol- lowers.		
	Preserved meat and biscuits.	Meat on hoof and flour.	Groceries.		Field ration.	Emergency ration.	Field ration.	Horses or ponies.	Mules, camels, or bullocks.
One man or animal, days	...	...	...	1	...	1	1a	...	1
In unit transport, days	1	...	1	...	1	...	1	1	...
In supply column, days	1	1	2	b	2	b	2	2	2
In supply park, days	2	2	4	...	4	...	4	4	4
Totals ...	4	3	7	1	7	1	8	7	7

a As emergency ration.
b 50% reserve.

14.—ORDINARY DAILY RATIONS—INDIA.

Detail.	Bread. lbs.	Fresh Meat. lbs.	Bacon. ozs.	Potatoes. lbs.	Tea.	Sugar. ozs.	Salt. ozs.	Pepper. ozs.	Atta. lbs.	Dhall. ozs.	Ghi. ozs.	Chillies. ozs.	Turmeric. ozs.	Ginger. ozs.	Garlic. ozs.	Gur. ozs.	Fuel. lbs.
British troops	1	$1\frac{1}{4}$	3	$1\frac{1}{8}$	$1\frac{1}{3}$	$2\frac{1}{2}$	$\frac{1}{...}$	...	...	...	...	...	...	...	...	...	3
Indian troops and followers	...	...	...	...	...	...	...	$\frac{1}{16}$	$1\frac{1}{2}$	4	2	$\frac{1}{6}$	$\frac{1}{8}$	$\frac{1}{3}$	$\frac{1}{6}$	1	$1\frac{1}{2}$

LIVE STOCK.

Slaughter cattle furnish about 150 lbs. each of meat ready for cooking.
A sheep or goat furnishes about 25 lbs. of meat ready for cooking.

Scales of daily rations for animals on field service.

Detail.	Colonial Horses and O. B. Horses with British Mounted Corps.	Arabs and other small Horses [Horses of British Mounted Corps, Officers' Chargers, Non-Silladar Horses]	Infantry — Mounted Ponies.	Silladar — Horses.	Silladar — Ponies.	Other Horses and Ponies including Mess Transport Animals.	Ordnance — S. T. Bullocks.	Ordnance — Mules.	Battery Mountain Baggage Mules.	Transport — A. T. Bullocks.	Transport — Camels.	Transport — Mules.*
Gram or barley, and bran lbs.	10	8	6	8	4	5	7	6	6	6	6	$5\frac{3}{4}$
Bhoosa or lbs.	{ 20	20	20	18	13	10	20	16	15	14	16	14
Hay or dry grass lbs.	{			20	10	10	25	20	15	20	25	14
Salt ozs.	1	1	$\frac{3}{...}$	1	$\frac{1}{8}$	$\frac{3}{...}$	$\frac{1}{...}$	$\frac{2}{...}$	$\frac{2}{...}$	$\frac{2}{...}$	$1\frac{1}{2}$	$\frac{1}{2}$

* For purposes of calculation, transport mules may be taken as ½ first class and ½ second class. Consequently an average ration of 6½ lbs. gram or barley, and bran and 14 lbs. bhoosa or hay or dry grass is approximately correct.

35. NOTES ON SUPPLIES.

CATTLE.

1. Oxen should be between 2 and 5 years old.   Should yield 600 lbs. dead meat fit for issue.

Cows should be between 2 and 4 years old.   Should yield 400 lbs. dead meat fit for issue.

2. To estimate age of cattle :—

By the teeth.   Incisors (front of lower jaw) are complete at 3½ years. At two years the two centre ones are well up.   After incisors are complete, estimate must be made by amount of wear.   Gums recede with age.

3. To estimate weight.—

(a) Pass animals over weighbridge and then take 50 to 60 per cent. for dead meat.

Use this formula

$$\frac{L \text{ (in feet)} \times 10 \times G^2 \text{ (in feet)}}{3} = \text{weight in lbs.}$$

L = length from hollow on crop (forepart of shoulder-blade) to root of tail.

G = girth close behind the shoulder.

4. Cattle in health should have :—Eye bright, muzzle cool and moist, dung normal, coat glossy.   Should stretch on rising and should chew the cud.

SHEEP.

5. Ram is male sheep, wether is castrated male sheep, ewe is female after she has lambed.

Sheep out of health have :—Loose wool, dropping ears, arching back, legs drawn together under body, no fatty secretion under skin.

6. Sheep should yield 50 to 80 lbs. dead meat fit for issue and should not be more than 5 years old.   If it is possible to weigh a few, 50 to 60 per cent. of the average live weight may be taken as the amount of meat to be expected.

To estimate age of sheep :—

By the teeth.   Teeth come up about 6 months earlier than those of cattle.

7. Pigs should yield about 100 lbs. dead meat fit for issue.

Animals should be deprived of food 12 hours before being slaughtered.
Meat loses when hung 1¼ per cent. in 24 hours (in temperate climates).

      ,,   ,,   2   ,,   48   ,,   ,,   ,,
      ,,   ,,   2½   ,,   72   ,,   ,,   ,,

More would be lost in hot, dry climates.

BREAD.

8. Bread should be light, flaky and elastic ; not acid ; creamy white.
Crust should be brownish yellow and not burnt.
Biscuit should be light yellow, crisp, and not burnt.
Army biscuit weighs 2 ozs.
Flour should be pale cream white.
100 lbs. wheat produces 70 lbs. flour.
Flour is bought and sold by the sack of 280 lbs.
100 lbs. flour produces 130 lbs. bread.

FORAGE.

9. Forage includes all articles of food consumed by animals used for military purposes.

10. Hay should smell sweet and should not be damp or dusty.
An acre of grass gives 1 to 2 tons of hay.
In England a truss of hay, old, should weigh 56 lbs.
        ,,   ,,   new   ,,   60   ,,
A load of hay is 36 trusses.   A ton of hay is 40 trusses.

The weight of hay per cubic yard in the stack varies from 112 to 300 lbs., depending on the nature of the hay, its age, the size of the stack and the part of the stack taken. 200 lbs. is a fair average.

11. Straw should be long, stout, clean, sweet, dry; wheat straw best. Straw weighs 36 lbs. to truss. A load of straw is 36 trusses.

12. To estimate contents of stack of hay or straw :—

$$\text{Hay} \quad \frac{\text{height} \times \text{breadth} \times \text{length}}{11} = \text{tons of hay.}$$

$$\text{Straw} \quad \frac{\text{height} \times \text{breadth} \times \text{length}}{16} = \text{tons of straw.}$$

Dimensions in yards—
Height = distance from ground to eaves + half the distance from eaves to ridge.

Circular stack—

$$\frac{3\frac{1}{7} \times \text{radius}^2 \times \text{height}}{11} = \text{tons of hay.}$$

$$\frac{3\frac{1}{7} \times \text{radius}^2 \times \text{height}}{16} = \text{tons of straw.}$$

Height = distance from the ground to eaves + one-third the distance from eaves to apex.

As a rough guide in making calculations 9 men should cut from the stack, weigh and tie 15 trusses (840 lbs.) hay in an hour. Half an hour extra should be allowed for preparations, *e.g.*, unroofing the stack.

13. Oats should be free from dirt, sweet, thin husked, hard. Oats should weigh from 38 lbs. upwards to the bushel. Squeeze an oat—the kernel should leave the husk. An acre of oats yields 40 to 60 bushels and 1½ tons straw. Substitutes for oats are maize, barley, grain.

14. Acre of barley yields about 40 bushels (50 lbs. to bushel) (1 ton straw). Acre of wheat yields about 25 to 30 bushels (60 lbs. to bushel) (1½ tons straw).

15. Bran is composed of the two outer envelopes of the wheat grain, and should be dry, clean, sweet. Dry it is astringent, wet laxative.

16. Beans should be hard, dry, sweet, sound. Should be split before being given to animals. Weight, 60 lbs. to the bushel.

17. Peas should be dry, sound. Weight, 60 lbs. to the bushel.

18. Compressed forage is a mixture of hay and oats. Ration for horse 20 lbs. daily. Ton occupies 45 cubic feet. Bales weigh 40 lbs. net and 80 lbs. net.

19. Linseed should be clean, round, large, plump. It is the seed of the flax plant. Is soothing and laxative.

20. Green foods are rye grass, lucerne, sainfoin, clover.

Acre of potatoes yields about 8 tons.
,,   carrots   ,,   10 to 20 tons.
,,   cabbage   ,,   35 ,, 40 ,,

India.

21. In India (Western) the average yield per acre of certain crops is as follows :—

Grain	..	..	..	..	..	..	500–600 lbs.
Barley	..	..	..	..	..	..	1,500–1,800 lbs.
Wheat	..	..	..	..	..	..	600–650 lbs.
Potatoes	..	..	..	..	..	10,200 lbs.
Oats	..	..	..	..	..	..	1,800–2,200 lbs.
Carrots	..	..	..	..	..	25,000 lbs.
Hay	..	..	..	..	..	..	1,200 lbs

22. If bhoosa is in stacks (which are almost always circular across the border) the contents may be calculated by the following formula :—

Divide the square of average girth of the stack by 12 and then multiply the result by the perpendicular height. This will give the contents of the stack from eaves to the ground. For the conical top multiply the area at the eaves (*i.e.*, the square of the girth divided by 12) by one-third of the perpendicular height from the eaves to the ridge. The contents may be estimated at about 8 lbs. per cubic foot.

Bhoosa in bales weighs 19 to 25 lbs. per cubic foot.
A 1-maund bale of bhoosa measures 2′ × 1′ × 1′ 6″.
Hay and straw weigh 3½ to 4 lbs. per cubic foot .
23. When foraging across the Indian frontier look for foodstuffs as follows :—

Waziristan.—Buried beneath the floor of their huts.
Baluchistan.—Hidden in *karezes* and nullahs.
Tirah.—Behind the false walls in houses.
Swat, Bajaur and Buner.—In partitions and compartments built on to inside walls of houses.
Burma.—In granaries in the fields ; usually no concealment

36. SUPPLY ARRANGEMENTS.

(*See* F.S.R., Part II, Chap. VII.)

1. The director of supplies is responsible for the provision of food, forage, &c., for an army, and is assisted by the assistant directors of supplies. He receives instructions from the Q.M.G.'s branch of the staff.

2. When troops operating in a civilized theatre of war are not wholly subsisted in billets by the inhabitants, nor dependent upon supplies requisitioned either in advance or in their immediate neighbourhood, the means of supplying them will normally be effected by rail and fast-moving mechanical transport, delivering daily to Army Service Corps units, designated trains (the composition of which is shown hereafter), and thence to the troops.
Plates 18 and 19 illustrate the system to be adopted.

3. *Supply Depôts.*—Main supply depôts will be established at advanced bases or at convenient positions on the railway ; they will be filled up by rail, according to the stocks authorized from the oversea base or from supplies collected from the country.
Field bakeries and butcheries will be established at the advanced bases or at convenient points on the railway line other than the regulating station. It may be necessary to establish field butcheries in advance of the railway.

4. *Regulating Station.*—All supplies drawn from the L. of C. will be despatched by rail, in the charge of a railway supply detachment, as required, from these main supply depôts to a regulating station, where railway trains will be marshalled and thence despatched daily to railheads conveniently situated for the supply of the troops.

5. *Railheads.*—At the railheads the supplies are received by supply columns (mechanical transport), and conveyed to rendezvous, and refilling points selected so that by the time a supply column has returned to railhead the total distance covered will not have exceeded 90 miles.

6. On arrival at the rendezvous the supply columns* will be ordered by representatives of the headquarters concerned to proceed to refilling points situated in localities most suitable to the circumstances. When troops are marching, such localities may, as is most convenient, either be near the front of the areas from which the divisions, &c., moved the same morning, or at suitable localities in advance of these areas, and on or near the routes followed by the troops ; or, again, they may be in or near the areas where troops have

---

* In the case of cavalry formations which are not provided with trains, supply columns will deliver direct to the troops.

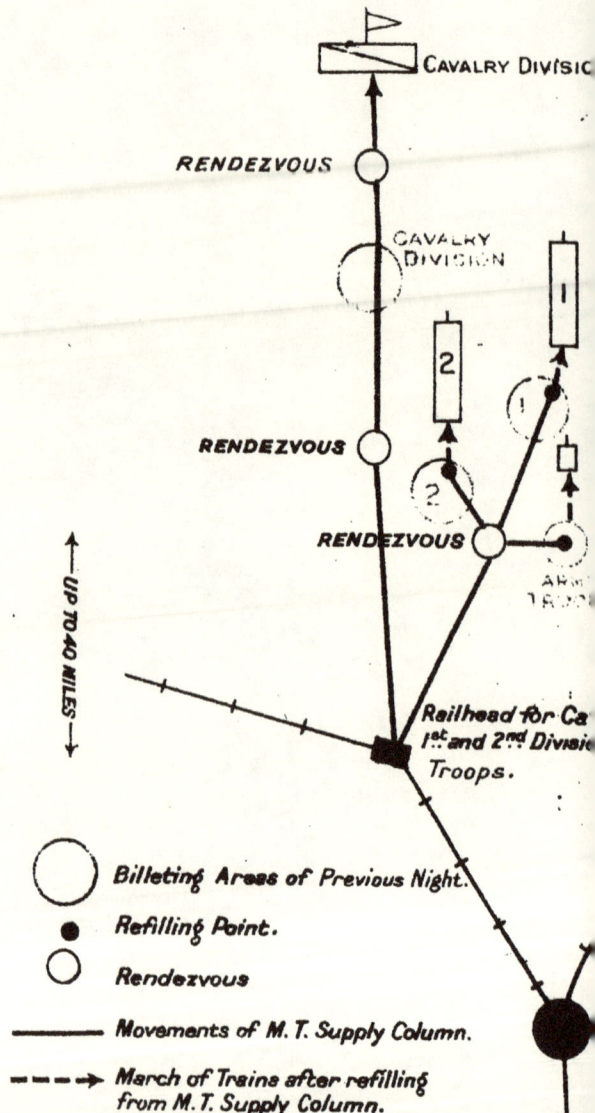

CAVALRY DIVISION

RENDEZVOUS

CAVALRY
DIVISION

2

1

RENDEZVOUS

2

RENDEZVOUS

ARMY
TROOPS

UP TO 40 MILES

Railhead for Ca
1st and 2nd Divisio
Troops.

Billeting Areas of Previous Night.

Refilling Point.

Rendezvous

—————— Movements of M. T. Supply Column.

‐ ‐ ‐ → March of Trains after refilling
from M. T. Supply Column.

NOTE. – This Diagram is not drawn to scale, nor does it
represent the tactical positions of fighting troops, but
merely indicates the system under which troops would
be supplied when marching.

To face page 174.

Plate 18.

ILLUSTRATING SUPPLY
SERVICE IN AN ARMY
OF 4 DIVISIONS,
I CAVALRY DIVISION,
AND OTHER ARMY TROOPS,
WHEN THE FORCE IS MARCHING.

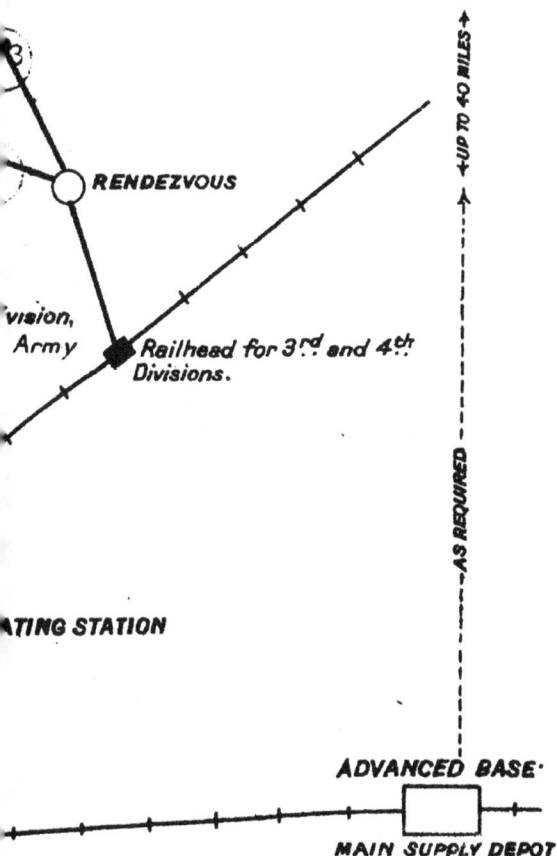

3

○ **RENDEZVOUS**

↑ *UP TO 40 MILES* →

vision,
Army

◆ *Railhead for 3rd and 4th Divisions.*

← *AS REQUIRED* →

ATING STATION

ADVANCED BASE

MAIN SUPPLY DEPOT

Malty & Sons, Lith.

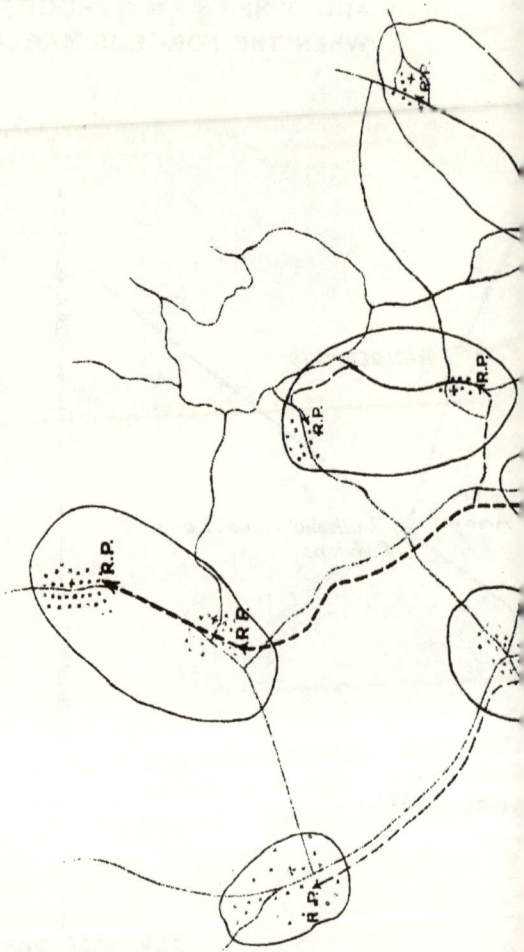

Plate 19.

ILLUSTRATING SUPPLY SERVICE FOR THREE DIVISIONS AND ARMY TROOPS, WHEN STATIONARY.

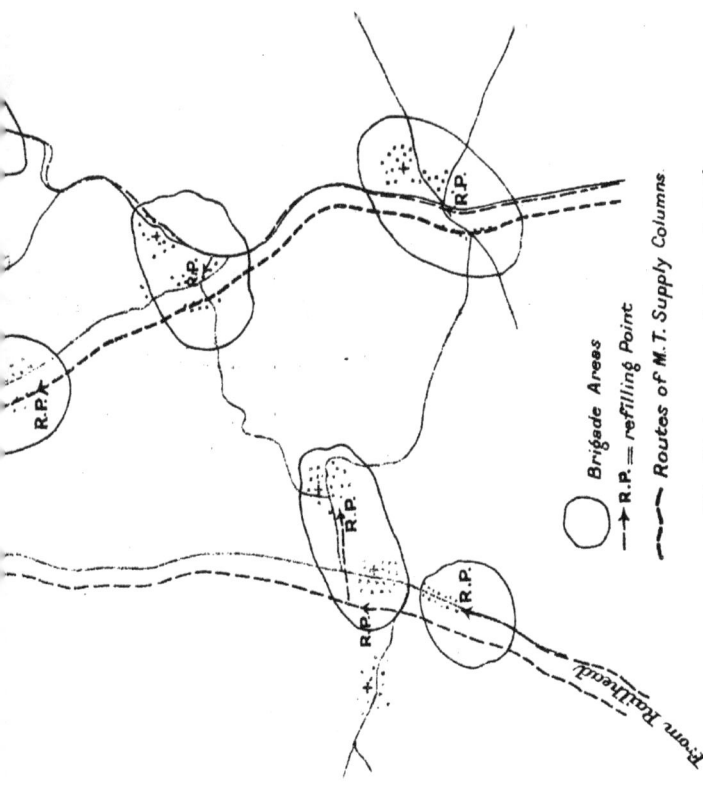

Brigade Areas
R.P. = refilling Point
Routes of M.T. Supply Columns.

This Diagram is not drawn to scale.

From Railhead.

To follow Plate 18.

6365. 6316c. 7/8. 150, COO. 4. 17.

Malby & Sons, Lith.

gone into quarters at the conclusion of the day's march. Here the supply columns will hand over their loads to the supply sections of the trains and return to the next day's railheads without delay.

When it is possible to do so, rendezvous may be fixed with advantage at the actual refilling points.

7. When troops are stationary, except during battle, it will usually be preferable to send the supply columns into brigade areas where the refilling points will be placed, thus obviating the necessity for transferring supplies from the columns to the trains and for working the horses of the trains.

8. During battle it may be necessary to send back the trains some distance to refill from the supply columns, in which case more than one refilling point will, if possible, be arranged for each division with the object of reducing to a minimum the movements of the supply sections.

9. *Reserve Parks (Horse).*—Horsed reserve parks, each capable of carrying 2 days' reserve (iron) rations and 2 days' grain for a division, plus one-sixth of the Cavalry Divisional and Army troops will be maintained for use in case of emergency.

HINTS ON THE SELECTION OF LOCALITIES AS REFILLING POINTS.

10. Wide open spaces having a hard level surface and solid foundations form ideal sites, but are rarely available. The transfer of loads must generally be carried out on the roadside.

In selecting a locality as a refilling point the following points should be borne in mind :—

- (*a*) Motor lorries in column occupy much less space than horsed wagons of equal total capacity, given that the vehicles are at suitable intervals for transferring loads from one to the other. Limitations of space therefore usually necessitate the supply column lorries being placed in position and the train wagons doing the shunting.
- (*b*) End-on loading, *i.e.*, tailboard to tailboard, is the only practical method.
- (*c*) Traffic along the line of lorries in position should be permitted in one direction only. The train wagons must therefore be so situated before refilling begins that they will never be required to reverse during the process.
- (*d*) When a force is advancing, both train and supply column usually approach the refilling point from the same direction, which will be the one that the train must keep to rejoin its units. To get into position for end-loading the supply column must be reversed before transfer of loads begins.
- (*e*) When a force is halted or retiring, train and supply column usually approach the refilling point from opposite directions. Their respective positions should be arranged according to the direction in which the train has to move after refilling.
- (*f*) Lead horses should be taken away to a station in advance of the refilling point before the supply column arrives, in order to reduce the space required for refilling as much as possible.

11. The following diagram illustrates the above principles, but must be modified to suit varying conditions :—

A B—Park for train.
C D—Actual refilling point.
M—Lorries in position.
W—Train wagons being filled.
x^x and y^x according to number of vehicles.

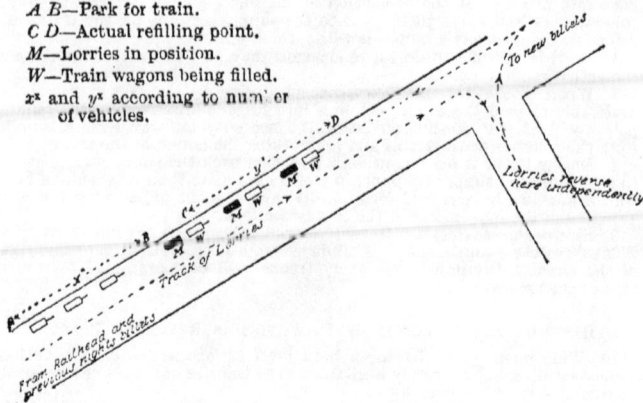

REQUISITIONS.

12. Requisitions can only be made for the needs of the army.
The quantity of food to be left in the possession of inhabitants must be decided by the commander ordering the requisition. The usual practice is to leave at least 3 days' supply of food for a household, and rather more than that at outlying farms or villages.
The details of the requisitioning service will be arranged under the direction of the Q.M.G. at the outbreak of hostilities.

13. As a general principle, only officers of the administrative service or department concerned detailed for the duty are authorized to requisition, but in cases of emergency, e.g., when troops are on patrol duty or where no officer of a service or department or duly appointed requisitioning officer is available, requisitions may be carried out by the commander, the circumstances being reported without delay to superior authority. Indiscriminate requisitioning and granting of requisition receipt notes are strictly forbidden

14. Authority to requisition will not be delegated to any but a commissioned officer, and requisitioning on the part of warrant officers, N.C.O.'s or men will be treated as plundering under the Army Act, unless the case is one of extreme urgency and no commissioned officer is present.
Requisitions will generally be made by a demand on A.F. F 780 (see below), which may be altered to suit local conditions.

15. Except when payment is made on the spot the requisitioning officer will give to each local civil authority a requisition receipt note on A.B. 361 (see below), for all goods or services rendered.
When payment is made on the spot no acknowledgment for the goods or services will be given by the requisitioning officer, but a receipt for the amount paid will be obtained.

16. When in exceptional circumstances requisitioning has to be carried out direct, i.e., without the agency of the civil authorities, it will not be necessary to present a demand; but, except when payment is made on the spot, a requisition receipt note will be given to the owners for goods or services rendered.

17. Requisition receipt notes will in all cases be made out in triplicate, but the original note only will be given to the civil authority (or owner in the exceptional circumstances when requisitioning has to be carried out direct).
The duplicate note will be sent direct to the Central Requisition Office by the representative of the administrative service or department concerned, or, if no representative is attached to the force, by the commander.

The *triplicate note* will be sent as soon as possible by the representative of the administrative service or department concerned to the officer in charge of the depôt from which supplies, &c., are next drawn.

18. The original requisition receipt note will in no circumstances show the rank, unit or force of the requisitioning officer, but this information will in all cases be inserted by that officer on the duplicate and triplicate of the note.

Unless special orders are issued to the contrary, face values will not be entered on requisition receipt notes. A requisition receipt note is merely a record of the transaction shown thereon. The quality of the articles should be indicated in each case by one of the words, " Good," " Average," " Indifferent."

19. If goods are taken for protection and not for the use of the troops a statement to that effect will be written by the requisitioning officer on the duplicate and triplicate of the requisition receipt note.

20. All authorities or persons to whom requisition receipt notes are given, will be directed to send them at the earliest possible date to the officer in command of the nearest British garrison. This officer will give an acknowledgment and will *at once* transmit the notes to the Central Requisition Office.

21. Should requisition receipt notes be presented for payment, such payment will on no account be made until the notes have been forwarded to the Central Requisition Office and the authority of that office to pay obtained.

Army Form F 780.

REQUISITION ON CIVIL AUTHORITIES.

As an Officer of the British Army, I, acting under powers conferred upon me, hereby direct the Local Authorities of

to supply for the

requirements of the troops, the following :—

to be ready at   on the

day of   precisely at   o'clock

under the direction of an official appointed by the local civil authorities for this duty, who will make delivery to the troops in accordance with instructions which will be addressed to him by me.

* The question of payment will be taken up on production of the requisition receipt notes which must be transmitted to the officer in command of the nearest British garrison.

In case of any disobedience on the part of the inhabitants in complying with the demands the local civil authorities will address the undersigned without loss of time in order that military force may be applied if necessary.

Place

Date

Signature of Officer

---

* Alter as necessary if payment is to be made on the spot.

Army Book 361.

REQUISITION RECEIPT NOTE.

(Not negotiable.)

No._____   Date_____

Requisition from (full name)_____

Address____ _____

Articles or Services requisitioned.	Quantity.	Quality (good, average, or indifferent).

Signature of Requisitioning Officer

CHAPTER VII.

37. PAY.

1. REGIMENTAL DAILY PAY.

(Not applicable to India.)

This table is for guidance only.

Rank.	R.H.A.		R.F.A.		R.G.A.		R.E.		Hld. Cav.		Cav.		Foot Gds.		Inf.		A.S.C.	
	s.	d.	s.	d.	s.	d.	s.	d.	s.	d.	s.	d.	s.	d.	s.	d.	s.	d.
Serjeant or Corporal-Major	6	0	5	10	5	10	6	0	5	10	5	4	5	2	5	0	5	6
Bandmaster	4	4		...	6	0	6	0	5	6	5	6	5	0	5	0		...
Quartermaster-Serjeant or Q'master-Corporal-Major	4	4	4	2	6	0	4	6	5	6	5	4	4	0	4	0	4	3
Squadron Serjeant-Major or Cpl.-Major, Colour-Serjeant, or Battery or Company Serjeant-Major			4	4	4	0	4	3	4	6	4	4	4	0	3	6	4	3
Farrier Quartermaster-Serjeant or Corporal	4	4	4	4			4	6	4	3	4	0		...			4	0
Squadron, Battery or Company Quartermaster-Serjeant	5	0	4	2		3 9	4	3	3	6	3	4					4	0
Corporal of Horse or Serjeant	3	4	3	2	3	2	3	3	3	0	2	8	2	6	2	4	2	7
Serjeant Trumpeter, drummer, bugler, or piper	3	4	3	2	3	2	3	4	3	2	2	8	2	6	2	4		
Corporal	3	4	2	6	2	6	3	3	3	2	2	2	2	9	1	8	2	0*
Shoeingsmith Corporal or Farrier Corporal	2	8	2	6	2	2	2	6	2	8	2	2					2	1
*Bombardier or 2nd Corporal	2	8	2	6	2	6	2	2	2	9	2	2					2	1
Paid Lance-Corporal or Acting Bombardier	2	5	1	7	2	3	2	6			1	6	1	4	1	3	1	9*
Trumpeter, drummer, bugler, or piper	2	0	1	2½	1	2½	1	7	1	11	1	4	1	2	1	1	1	5
Gunner, sapper, or private	2	4	1	2½	1	2½	1	2	1	9	1	2	1	1	1	0	1	2
Driver	1	3	1	2½	1	2½	1	2			1	1	1	1	1	0	1	1
Boy	0	8	0	8	1	0	1	0	0	8	0	8	0	8	0	8	0	8

* 2/6 and 2 2 Mech. Transport Cos.

NOTE.—In addition to the above, W.Os., N.C.Os. and men may receive—

(a) Messing allowance and clothing allowance at 3d. daily.

(b) Service pay varying from 4d. to 7d. daily. W.Os. and N.C.Os. are entitled to Class I; other men are granted it provided they fulfil certain conditions.

(c) Proficiency pay, varying from 3d. to 6d. daily. To be eligible for this, a soldier of whatever rank has to fulfil certain conditions laid down in the Royal Warrant. It is only issuable to cavalry, artillery, infantry, and School of Musketry.

(d) Engineer pay, i.e., additional pay issued to personnel of R.E. who cannot draw service pay concurrently.

(e) Corps pay, i.e., additional pay issuable to A.S.C., R.A.M.C., A.O.C., and A.V.C. under certain conditions.

2. Field allowances (all services)—   **s. d.**

Lieutenant-Col. and Major	..	..	..	..	..	4 0
Captain	..	..	..	..	..	3 0
Lieutenant and Second Lieutenant	..	..	..	..	2 6
Warrant Officer	..	..	..	..	..	1 0

PAY ARRANGEMENTS.

3. The pay accounts of soldiers on active service in the field will, as may be decided by the C. in-C. under instructions from the Government concerned, be compiled by the paymaster for regimental services at the base, or the paymaster at the station at which the records of their units are kept.

4. The accounts of men proceeding abroad on active service will be closed on the day preceding that of embarkation. From the date of embarkation, inclusive, issues of pay will be recorded in the acquittance roll and soldier's pay book and charged by the paymaster responsible for the compilation of the war pay accounts.

5. Funds required for all services will be drawn on imprest from the base cashier, or a field cashier, indents being made only for such amounts as are required for immediate use. Officers receiving imprests will be held responsible for all money so advanced to them until it has been satisfactorily accounted for.

6. No officer will be exempted from receiving an imprest of public money for the purpose of making a payment which cannot conveniently be made through another channel.

7. Officers holding imprests from a paymaster charged with the receipt of and accounting for public money, will usually account for the same on A.F. N 1531A, which will be rendered monthly, or as may be arranged, to the regimental or other paymaster. Informal accounts, if unavoidable owing to the conditions of active service, will, however, be accepted; but, in such case, the source and date of each receipt and particulars and date of each payment must be clearly shown.

8. The duty of making cash payments to the individual soldier will devolve upon company, &c., commanders. All such payments will at once be entered on the acquittance roll (A.F. N 1513) and in the soldier's pay book (A.B. 64). The acquittance roll will, immediately after payments have been made, be forwarded to the pay office at the base through the A.G.'s office at the base. A copy of the acquittance roll will be retained by the company, &c., commander concerned.

9. Issues of pay to the individual soldier will be based upon the net rate of pay shown in his pay book (A.B. 64), and will not be made more often than is necessary. If the pay book be lost a new book will be issued, but no cash issues will be made in respect of any period prior to the date on which the loss was reported by the soldier; pay ultimately found to be due for any such period will be issued on final settlement with the soldier.

10. Temporary additional emoluments claimed by a soldier will not be issued until a notification is received from the paymaster showing that the sum claimed has been placed to the credit in the soldier's pay account. All terminal claims, such as for gratuities or deferred pay, will be paid by the paymaster, and a company, &c., commander will not make cash advances in respect of them.

11. If a soldier dies either on active service or before he has handed in his pay book on the conclusion of a term of active service, any will contained in the book will be cut out and sent to the military authorities concerned with A.F. B 2090A. The book will then be sent to the paymaster compiling the man's account.

12. A company, &c., commander will take special care to ensure that the total expenditure charged in his accounts in respect of issues of pay to the individual soldier is in agreement with the amounts shown by him on the acquittance rolls forwarded to the regimental paymaster.

(INDIA.)

13. In India there are no field allowances. Certain officers, mostly medical officers, are allowed to draw horse allowance in the field if they are not entitled to it in peace. Rations are free to all except officers. The latter are supplied with rations on payment, and are required to credit Government with the value when drawing their pay.

14. Cash is drawn from treasury chest officers, attached to headquarters of divisions, armies and detached forces.

15. The accounts of Indian units are kept at their depôts, and of British units by the divisional disbursing officer of their divisions.

16. A soldier may obtain a cash advance from any officer having charge of public money in the field, the officer in charge of the accounts of the man's corps being informed.

38. CLOTHING.

1. The arrangements for the clothing and equipment of an army in the field are controlled by the director of ordnance services, under the instructions of the I.G.C.

2. Clothing is divided into—

(a) *Personal.*—Ankle boots and shoes, caps, drawers, canvas suits, service dress suits, puttees, sashes, cardigan waistcoats, trousers, tunics, leather gloves, foreign service helmets, gauntlets, cotton drawers.

    These become the property of the soldier and may be sold by permission of the O.C. the squadron, battery, or company (in peace only).

(b) *Public.*—Greatcoats, full dress head-dresses, knee boots, leather breeches, jack spurs, leggings, waterproof capes, purses and belts for Highland regiments.

    These must be returned to store, and are the property of the public.

(c) *Necessaries.*—Badges, blacking, laces, braces, brushes, button brasses, combs, forks, grease tins, worsted gloves, holdalls, hosetops, housewives, knives, razors, shirts, socks. sponges. spoons, spurs swan-neck, towels, vests.

    A free list of necessaries is supplied to each soldier on enlistment, and this has to be kept up afterwards at the soldier's expense, for which purpose an allowance is made to him (in peace only). On field service, necessaries are issued free to replace losses not caused by negligence.

(d) *Sea-kit.*—Clothes bags.

39. FIELD KITS.

(Not applicable to India.)
1. MOUNTED OFFICERS.

Detail.	No.	Approximate weight.		Remarks.
		lbs.	ozs.	
A.—CLOTHING WORN BY THE OFFICER.				
Boots, lace .. .. pair	1	2	11	
Braces .. .. .. ,,	1	0	4	
Cap, service dress, with badge	1	0	9	
Disc, identity, with cord ..	1	0	0½	
Leggings .. .. .. pair	1	0	13	
Socks .. .. .. ,,	1	0	4	
Suit, service dress (jacket and riding breeches)	1	4	13	
Spurs .. .. .. pair	1	0	12	
Underclothing .. .. suit	1	3	0	
Total (A)	..	13	2½	
B.—OTHER PERSONAL EFFECTS.				
Book { A.B. 155	1	1	0	
Field Service Pocket Book	1	0	6½	
Cap, comforter (in pocket of greatcoat)	1	0	3½	
Compass, magnetic, pocket (or prismatic, in case)	1	0	4	
Cutters, wire (in wallets) pairs	1	1	4	
Dressing, field (in skirt of jacket)	1	0	2	
Glasses (binoculars or telescope, or both, in one case)*	1	2	0	* Slung from left shoulder
Grease (or vaseline) in wallets tin	1	0	2	
Greatcoat†	1	7	1½	† Rolled, 26 inches long, behind saddle
Handkerchief	1	0	2	
Holdall (in wallets), containing knife, fork and spoon, hairbrush and comb, toothbrush, shaving brush and razor	1	1	3	
Knife, clasp, with ring and swivel	1	0	6	
Map	1	0	2	
Matches .. .. .. box	1	0	1	
Soap (in wallets) .. piece	1	0	3	
Socks (in wallets) .. pairs	1	0	4	
Towel (in wallets)	1	0	13	
Watch (in wrist strap)	1	0	4	
Whistle and lanyard	1	0	2½	
Total (B)	..	16	0	

MOUNTED OFFICERS—*continued*.

Detail.	No.	Approximate weight.		Remarks.
		lbs.	ozs.	
C.—ACCOUTREMENTS (SEALED PATTERN).				
Belt, " Sam Browne " (waist-belt, 2 shoulder belts, ammunition pouch and pistol-case, and sword frog)	1	2	0	
Haversack	1	0	11	
Mess tin*	1	1	9	* Fastened by off baggage strap to off side of saddle
Sword knot	1	0	1½	
Waterbottle (aluminium) and sling	1	0	1¼	
Total (C)	..	5	3½	
D.—ARMS.				
Pistol (no special pattern, but must carry Government ammunition)	1	2	3	On left side of S.B. belt
Sword	1	2	1½	} On near shoe case, edge to rear
Scabbard, leather	1	0	9½	
Total (D)	..	4	14	
E.—AMMUNITION.				
Cartridges, S.A. ball, pistol, Webley	12	0	9½	
F.—RATIONS AND WATER.				
Bread ration (unconsumed portion) say	..	0	12	
Cheese	..	0	3	
Biscuit	..	0	12	
Preserved meat nominal	..	1	0	
Iron ration { Tea ⅝ oz. / Sugar 2 oz. } in a tin / Salt ¼ oz.	..	0	6½	
Cheese	..	0	3	
Meat extract .. cubes	2	1	0	
Water .. .. .. pints	2½	2	13	
Total (F)	..	6	2½	

MOUNTED OFFICERS—*continued.*

Detail.	No.	lbs.	ozs.	Remarks.
G.—*SADDLERY, PICKETING GEAR, STABLE NECESSARIES, &c.				* In addition to this list, officers may, at their own discretion, provide a despatch or saddle-bag, sealed pattern. If an officer is allowed more than one horse, the saddlebag can be carried on the spare horse.
Bags, corn	1	0	6	
†Bag, nose, G.S., with 6 lbs. corn	1	7	0	
‡Brush, horse ..	1	0	10	
Pad, surcingle	1	0	10	† When empty, on the off shoe case fastened to the baggage strap. When oats are carried the strap of the nosebag must be fastened to the back arch of the saddle.
§Peg, picketing	1	1	3	
Ropes { §heel	1	0	11	
{ picketing	1	0	15	
‡Rubber, horse	1	0	10	‡ The method of carrying the horse brush and rubber is left to the discretion of the O.C., except that these articles are not to be carried in the nosebag.
‖Saddlery, complete, with bridle and head rope set	1	33	12	
Shoe cases, each with shoe and nails	2	3	4	
Total (G)	..	49	1	§ Heel ropes are allowed for use with restive horses on a scale of 25 per cent. An additional peg is issued with each heel rope. Pegs for heel ropes are only required in artillery and engineer units, and these are carried in transport vehicles.
TOTAL WEIGHT CARRIED ON THE HORSE.				
A.—Clothing	..	13	2½	
B.—Other personal effects ..	..	15	10	
C.—Accoutrements	..	5	3½	
D.—Arms	..	4	14	‖ Excludes weight of saddle blanket. Saddle blankets for officers' horses are carried in transport vehicles on the march.
E.—Ammunition	..	0	9½	
F.—Rations and water ..	..	6	2½	
G.—Saddlery, picketing gear, stable necessaries, &c.	..	49	1	
H.—Rider .. .. say	..	150	0	
Total on horse	..	245	1	Say 17½ st. about.

CARRIED IN TRAIN TRANSPORT.

The following list is drawn up as a general guide, and the articles in it may be varied, but the total weights (excluding articles in camp kettles) of 50 lbs. for a commanding officer and 35 lbs. for other officers must not be exceeded :—

CARRIED IN TRAIN TRANSPORT—*continued.*

Detail.	No.	Approximate weight.		Remarks.
		lbs.	ozs.	
A.F. B 122 (cover and pad), Field Conduct Book	1	..	11	⎫ Squadron, battery and
A.B. 6 (covers), A.F. N 1513 (pad). Acquittance Roll	1	..	15	⎬ company command- ⎭ ers only.
Boots, lace .. .. pair	1	2	11	*In Camp Kettle.*
Bucket, canvas	1	1	4	
Housewife	1	0	4	One camp kettle is al-
Lantern, collapsible, with talc sides	1	0	12	lowed for every 3 officers who pack into it, each :—
Leggings .. .. .. pair	1	0	13	Cup, enamelled .. 1
Portfolio, with writing materials	1	1	0	Plates, enamelled 2
Shoes, canvas .. .. pair	1	1	5	Pots { pepper .. 1
Socks .. .. .. „	1	0	4	{ salt .. 1
Suit, service dress	1	4	13	The weight of these
Towels	2	1	10	articles is not included
Underclothing .. .. suit	1	3	0	in the 50 or 35 lbs. al-
Valise, Wolseley (or other pattern)	1	11	3	lowed to each officer.
Total	..	28	15	

Note.—Officers may leave at the base a bullock trunk packed with 100 lbs. of personal baggage. This reserve baggage will be forwarded only when it may be deemed convenient to the service by the C.-in-C.

2. DISMOUNTED OFFICERS.

Detail.	No.	Approximate weight.		Remarks.
		lbs.	ozs.	
A.—CLOTHING WORN BY THE OFFICER.				* Officers of kilted regi-
*Boots, lace .. .. pair	1	2	11	ments wear in lieu :—
*Braces .. .. .. „	1	0	4	Apron,
Cap, service dress (or glengarry) with badge	1	0	9	Garters,
Disc, identity, with cord ..	1	0	0½	Hosetops,
Puttees .. .. .. pair	1	0	13	Kilt,
Socks .. .. .. „	1	0	4	Shoes,
*Suit, service dress	1	4	13	Spats,
Underclothing .. .. suit	1	3	0	which add about 1 lb.
Total (A)	..	12	6½	12 oz. to the weight of the clothing.

DISMOUNTED OFFICERS—*continued.*

Detail.	No.	lbs.	ozs.	Remarks.
B.—OTHER PERSONAL EFFECTS CARRIED BY THE OFFICER.				
Books { A.B. 153	1	0	10	
Field Service Pocket Book	1	0	6½	
Cap, comforter (in pocket of greatcoat)	1	0	3½	
Compass, magnetic, pocket (or prismatic, in case)	1	0	4	
Cutters, wire .. .. pair	1	1	4	
Dressing, field (in skirt of jacket)	1	0	2	
Glasses (binoculars or telescope, or both, in one case)	1	2	0	
Greatcoat	1	7	1½	
Handkerchief	1	0	2	
Knife, clasp, with ring and swivel	1	0	6	
Map	1	0	2	
Matches .. .. .. box	1	0	1	
Watch (in wrist strap) ..	1	0	4	
Whistle and lanyard	1	0	2½	
Total (B)	..	13	1	
C.—ACCOUTREMENTS (SEALED PATTERN).				
Belt, Sam Browne, complete (waistbelt, 2 shoulder belts, sword frog, ammunition pouch, pistol case)	1	2	0	
Carrier, greatcoat and coat straps	1	0	9	
Haversack	1	0	11	
Mess tin	1	1	9	
Sword knot	1	0	1½	
Waterbottle (aluminium) and sling	1	0	14	
Total (C)	..	5	12½	
D.—ARMS.				
Pistol (no special pattern, but must carry Government ammunition)	1	2	3	
Sword	1	2	1½	
Scabbard, leather	1	0	9½	
Total (D)	..	4	14	

DISMOUNTED OFFICERS—*continued*.

Detail.	No.	Approximate weight.		Remarks.
		lbs.	ozs.	
E.—AMMUNITION.				
Cartridges, S.A., ball, pistol, Webley rounds	12	0	9½	
F.—RATIONS AND WATER.				
Bread ration, unconsumed portion ; say	..	0	12	
Cheese	..	0	3	
Iron ration { Biscuit	..	0	12	
Preserved meat (nominal)	..	1	0	
Tea ½ oz. Sugar 2 oz. in tin Salt ½ oz.	..	..	6½	
Cheese	..	0	3	
Meat extract .. cubes	2	0	1	
Water .. .. .. pints	2¼	2	13	
Total (F)	..	6	2½	
TOTAL WEIGHT CARRIED ON THE PERSON.				
A.—Clothing	..	12	6½	
B.—Other personal effects	..	13	1	
C.—Accoutrements	..	5	12½	
D.—Arms	..	4	14	
E.—Ammunition	..	0	9½	
F.—Rations and water	..	6	2½	
Total carried	..	42	14	

CARRIED IN TRAIN TRANSPORT.

The following list is drawn up as a general guide, and the articles in it may be varied, but the total weights (excluding articles in camp kettles) of 50 lbs. for a commanding officer or 35 lbs. for other officers, must not be exceeded :—

CARRIED IN TRAIN TRANSPORT—*continued*.

Detail.	No.	Approximate weight.		Remarks.
		lbs.	ozs.	
A.F. B 122 (cover and pad). Field Conduct Book	1	0	11	⎫ Company commanders
A.B. 6 cover), A.F. N 1518 (pad). Acquittance Roll	1	0	15	⎬ only, ⎭
Boots, lace .. .. pair	1	2	11	*In Camp Kettle.*
Bucket, canvas	1	1	4	
Grease or vaseline) .. tin	1	0	2	One camp kettle is
Holdall, containing hair brush and comb, tooth brush, shaving brush and razor	1	1	0	allowed for every 3 officers, who will pack into it—each :—
Housewife	1	0	4	Cup, enamelled 1
Lantern, collapsible, with talc sides	1	0	12	Fork, table .. 1 Knife, table .. 1
Puttees .. .. .. pair	1	0	13	Plates, enamelled 2
Portfolio with writing materials	1	1	0	Pots ⎰ pepper 1
Shoes, canvas .. .. pair	1	1	5	⎱ salt .. 1
Soap .. .. .. piece	1	0	3	Spoon, table .. 1
Socks .. .. .. pairs	2	0	8	The weight of these
Suit, service dress	1	4	13	articles is not included in
Towels	2	1	10	the 50 or 35 lbs. allowed
Underclothing .. .. suit	1	3	0	to each officer.
Valise (Wolseley) or other pattern	1	11	3	
Total	..	30	8	

Note.—Officers may leave at the base a bullock trunk packed with 100 lbs. of personal baggage. This reserve baggage will be forwarded only when it may be deemed convenient to the service by the C.-in-C.

3. MOUNTED MEN.*

Detail.	No.	Approximate weight.		Remarks.
		lbs.	ozs.	
A.—CLOTHING, NECESSARIES, &c., WORN BY THE SOLDIER OR CARRIED ON THE HORSE.				
Boots, ankle .. .. pair	1	4	0	
Braces .. .. .. ”	1	0	4½	
Cap, service dress, with badge..	1	0	9	
Disc, identity, with cord ..	1	0	0½	
Drawers, cotton .. pair	1	0	15	

* This table applies primarily to cavalry. Certain alterations in arms, accoutrements and ammunition (prescribed in Equipment Regulations) are necessary in the case of mounted men of other arms.

MOUNTED MEN—*continued.*

Detail.	No.	Approximate weight. lbs.	ozs.	Remarks.
Dressing, field (in skirt of service dress jacket)	1	0	$2\frac{1}{2}$	
Greatcoat with metal titles (7 lbs. $8\frac{3}{4}$ ozs.) comforter cap (4 ozs.) and pair of socks ($4\frac{1}{4}$ ozs.) in pockets	1	8	1	* Troops wearing khaki drill sent on active service from a warm to a temperate climate will be supplied with service dress jackets as soon as available.
Jacket, service dress,* with metal titles	1	2	$5\frac{1}{2}$	
Knife, clasp, with marline spike, tin opener and lanyard	1	0	8	
Pay book (in right breast pocket of service dress jacket)	1	0	2	† In warm weather the cardigan may be carried in the folds of the greatcoat.
Pantaloons .. .. pair	1	2	$12\frac{1}{4}$	
Puttees .. .. .. ,,	1	0	13	
Shirt, flannel	1	1	2	
Socks, worsted .. .. pair	1	0	$4\frac{1}{4}$	
Spurs, jack .. .. ,,	1	0	13	‡ Warrant officers, staff-serjeants and serjeants have each a cavalry whistle and lanyard.
Waistcoat, cardigan†	1	1	7	
In haversack—				
Holdall ($3\frac{1}{4}$ ozs.), containing laces ($\frac{1}{4}$ oz.), toothbrush ($\frac{1}{2}$ oz.), razor and case (3 ozs.), shaving brush ($1\frac{1}{4}$ ozs.), comb ($\frac{1}{2}$ oz.) knife (3 ozs.), fork (3 ozs.), spoon ($2\frac{1}{2}$ ozs.)	1	1	$1\frac{1}{4}$	§ Rifles of drivers of G.S. limbered wagons will be carried in the clips provided on the wagon for that purpose. On vehicles not specially fitted the rifles will be carried on wagon footboards.
Housewife, fitted	1	0	$3\frac{1}{4}$	
Soap .. .. .. piece	1	0	3	
Towel, hand	1	0	9	
Total (A)‡	..	26	$3\frac{3}{4}$	The lance will form part of the war equipment of lancer regiments only. Lance flags will not be carried. Lances will be carried in rifle buckets when men dismount. Warrant officers, staff-serjeants and serjeants also carry the pistol, with lanyard, waist-belt, pistol case, ammunition pouch, and 12 rounds in lieu of rifles.
B.—ARMS.§				
Rifle, with oil bottle, pull-through and sling	1	8	$15\frac{3}{4}$	
Sword, scabbard and sword-knot‖	1	4	8	‖ Signallers will carry neither the sword nor lance.
Total (B)	..	13	$7\frac{3}{4}$	
C.—AMMUNITION.				
Cartridges, S.A., ball, ·303-inch¶ rounds	100	6	0	¶ Signallers will carry only 50 rounds.

MOUNTED MEN—*continued.*

Detail.	No.	lbs.	ozs.	Remarks.
D.—ACCOUTREMENTS.*				* Men carrying pistols
Bandolier, 90 rounds	1	1	13	or mekometers have a
Bottle, water, enamelled, with carrier and shoulder-strap	1	1	6	waist-belt, bandolier equipment, patt. '03.
Haversack	1	1	3	
Mess-tin and strap	1	1	6	
Total (D)	..	5	12	
E.—RATIONS AND WATER.				
Bread ration (unconsumed portion), say	..	0	12	
Cheese	..	0	3	
Iron ration { Biscuit	..	0	12	
Preserved meat ..	..	1	0	
Tea ½ oz. } Sugar 2 oz. } in a tin Salt ¼ oz. }	..	0	6½	
Cheese	..	0	3	
Meat extract cubes	2	0	1	
Water .. .. .. pints	2	2	8	
Total (E)	..	5	13½	
F.—SADDLERY, HORSE FURNITURE, STABLE NECESSARIES, AND OTHER ARTICLES CARRIED ON THE HORSE.				
Bags { corn	1	0	6	
nose, G.S., with 6 lbs. corn	1	7	0	
Brush, horse	1	0	10	
Pad, surcingle	1	0	10	† Heel-ropes are only
Peg, picketing†	1	1	4	issued to 25 per cent.
Ropes { heel†	1	0	11	for use with restive
picketing	1	1	1	horses. An additional
Rubber, horse	1	0	10	picketing peg is issued
Saddlery, with saddle blanket, head-rope and rifle-bucket set	1	31	0	with each heel-rope.
Shoes, horse; one fore, one hind (in shoe cases)	2	1	8	
Total (F)	..	44	12	
TOTAL WEIGHT CARRIED ON THE HORSE.				
A.—Clothing, necessaries, &c...	..	26	3¼	
B.—Arms	..	13	7¾	
C.—Ammunition	..	6	0	
D.—Accoutrements	..	5	12	
E.—Rations and water ..	..	5	13½	
F.—Saddlery, &c.	..	44	12	
G.—Rider .. .. (say)	..	150	0	
Total on horse	..	251	12	= 18 st. about.

NOTES.

1. A ground sheet (weight, 2 lbs. 8 ozs.) is carried in regimental transport for each warrant officer, N.C.O. and man.

2. When specially ordered, a blanket (4 lbs. 8 ozs.) will be carried, under the saddle or on limbers and ammunition wagons or on other wagons, for each man.

3. In the case of artillery picketing gear is carried in the wagons.

4. ARTICLES LEFT AT THE BASE BY MOUNTED MEN.
Warrant Officers, Non-Commissioned Officers and Men.

Kit bags containing the spare kit detailed below will be handed over to the O.C. base details to be taken to the oversea base with the base details, and will be left in charge of storemen at the General Base depôt to be forwarded only as may be deemed convenient to the service by the General Officer Commanding-in-Chief.

Articles.	No.	Remarks.
CLOTHING.		
Boots, ankle .. .. .. pair	1	
Drawers, cotton .. .. .. ,,	1	
Jacket, service dress (*a*)..	1	(*a*) Khaki drill frock and
Trousers, service dress (*a*) .. pair	1	trousers will be left at the base by troops wearing
NECESSARIES.		khaki drill clothing.
Brush, hair	1	
Shirt, flannel	1	
Socks, worsted .. .. .. pair	1	
Towel, hand	1	

The boots will be tied together, with the soles outwards, the regimental number of the man and the name of the unit to which he belongs being chalked or otherwise legibly marked on the soles. The boots will be placed in the mouth of the kit bag to admit of their being readily withdrawn, should it be necessary to forward them separately to the troops in the field.

5. DISMOUNTED MEN.*

Detail.	No.	Approximate weight.		Remarks.
		lbs.	ozs.	
A.—CLOTHING, &c., WORN BY THE SOLDIER.				* For kilted regiments substitute :—
				lbs. ozs.
*Boots, ankle .. .. pair	1	4	0	Apron, kilt .. 0 12½
*Braces .. .. ,,	1	0	4½	Gaiters, Highland .. 0 10½
Cap, service dress (or glengarry), with badge	1	0	9	Garters and rosettes .. 0 2
Disc, identity, with cord ..	1	0	0¼	Hosetops .. 0 4½
*Drawers, woollen .. pair	1	1	0½	Kilt 3 13
				Shoes, Highland 3 8

* This table applies primarily to infantry. Certain exceptions (prescribed in the Equipment Regulations) are necessary in the case of dismounted men of other arms. Range takers of infantry carrying the one-man instrument will be armed with pistols, and will carry neither rifles, bayonets, nor intrenching implements.

DISMOUNTED MEN—*continued*.

Detail.	No.	Approximate weight. lbs.	Approximate weight. ozs.	Remarks.
Jacket, service dress,* and metal titles, with field dressing	1	2	8	* Troops wearing khaki drill sent on active service from a warm to a temperate climate will be supplied with service dress jackets and trousers as soon as available.
Knife, clasp, with marline spike and tin opener	1	0	8	
Paybook (in right breast pocket of S.D. jacket)	1	0	2	
†Puttees .. .. .. pair	1	0	13	
Shirt	1	1	2	
Socks .. .. .. pair	1	0	4¼	In warm weather the cardigan may be carried in the pack.
Trousers, service dress† „	1	2	0½	
Waistcoat, cardigan	1	1	7	† See * note in Remarks column on previous page.
Total (A)	..	14	11	
B.—ARMS.				
Rifle, with oil bottle, pull-through, and sling	1	8	15¾	Drummers and buglers are unarmed. Men of the M.G. detachments will place their rifles in the limbered wagon when the M.G. is removed. Men leading pack animals will carry their rifles slung.
Bayonet and scabbard	1	1	8¾	N.C.Os. armed as staff-serjeants have no bayonet. Pipers wear dirks.
Total (B)	..	10	8½	
C.—AMMUNITION.				
Cartridges, S.A., ball, ·303-inch .. .. rounds	150	9	0	N.C.Os. equipped as staff-serjeants carry 25 rounds. Pioneers carry 80 rounds. Signallers „ 50 „ Drummers and buglers have no S.A.A. Pipers carry 12 rounds of pistol ammunition.
D.—TOOLS.				
Implement, intrenching, pattern, 1908 — head ..	1	1	5¾	Colour-serjeants, N.C.Os. armed as staff-serjeants, pipers and signallers carry no intrenching implements. (For signallers the implements are carried in tool wagons.)
Implement, intrenching, pattern, 1908 — helve ..	1	0	8¼	
Carriers for ditto — head ..	1	0	9½	
Carriers for ditto — helve ..	1	0	1¾	
Total (D)	..	2	9¼	
E.—ACCOUTREMENTS.				The armourer has a waist-belt and two 15-round cartridge pockets, bandolier equipment, pattern 1903; and a great-coat strap and mess-tin strap, valise equipment, pattern 1888.
Waterbottle, with carrier ..	1	1	6	
Web equipment, pattern 1908 :—				
Belt, waist	1	0	13	
Braces, with buckle	2	0	11	
Carriers, cartridge, 75 rounds — left ..	1	0	14½	
Carriers, cartridge, 75 rounds — right ..	1	0	14½	

DISMOUNTED MEN—*continued.*

Detail.	No.	Approximate weight. lbs.	ozs.	Remarks.
Frog	1	0	3	
Haversack (18¼ ozs.), with knife (3 ozs.), fork (3 ozs.), and spoon (2½ ozs.)	1	1	11	
Pack, with supporting straps (2)	1	1	11	
Total (E)	..	8	4¼	
F.—ARTICLES CARRIED IN THE PACK.				
Cap, comforter	1	0	4	Nos. 1 to 4 of M.G. section will have their packs carried for them on the march, in the G.S. limbered wagon for M.G.
Holdall (3¼ ozs.), containing laces (¼ oz.), toothbrush (½ oz.), razor and case (3 ozs.), shaving brush (1¼ oz.), and comb (1 oz.)	1	0	9¼	
Greatcoat, with metal titles ..	1	6	10½	
Housewife, fitted	1	0	3¼	
Mess-tin and cover	1	1	6½	
Socks, worsted .. .. pair	1	0	4¼	
Soap .. .. .. piece	1	0	3	
Towel, hand	1	0	9	
Total (F)	..	10	1¾	
G.—RATIONS AND WATER.				
Bread ration (unconsumed portion) .. .. .. say	..	0	12	
Cheese	..	0	3	
Iron ration: Biscuit	..	0	12	
Iron ration: Preserved meat (nominal)	..	1	0	
Iron ration: Tea ⅜ oz., Sugar 2 oz., Salt ½ oz. in a tin	..	0	6½	
Iron ration: Cheese	..	0	3	
Iron ration: Meat extract .. cubes	2	0	1	
Water .. .. .. pints	2	2	8	
Total (G)	..	5	13½	
TOTAL WEIGHT CARRIED.				
A.—Clothing worn	..	14	11	
B.—Arms	..	10	8½	
C.—Ammunition	..	9	0	
D.—Tools	..	2	9¼	
E.—Accoutrements	..	8	4¼	
F.—Articles in pack	..	10	1¾	
G.—Rations and water ..	..	5	13½	
*Total	..	61	0¼	

* This is the normal weight carried by a private. But exceptions occur in the case of N.C.Os. and certain other ranks (signallers, range takers, &c.)

MARCHING ORDER WITHOUT PACKS.

The above arrangements allow of the soldier having normally with him the whole of his equipment; but in certain circumstances the commander may decide to increase the amount of S.A.A. carried on the person, and to discard temporarily certain articles of equipment, *e.g.*, pack and contents.

	lbs.	ozs.
Marching order (as above)	60	11½
Deduct pack and contents (F)	11	11¾
	48	15½
Add 100 rounds S.A.A., in two 50-round cotton bandoliers	6	2
Total " fighting equipment " (without pack, but with 250 rounds S.A.A.)	55	1½

6. MOUNTED MEN OF INFANTRY.

The transport serjeant and regimental drivers are equipped, as are other infantrymen, with the following exceptions :—

(a) Bedford cord pantaloons are worn instead of service dress trousers; each man has a pair of jack spurs.
(b) Intrenching implements are not carried.
(c) Each driver has a whip and legging.

The following are carried on the horses of the transport serjeant and regimental drivers :—

Articles.	Transport Serjeant (on the horse).	Drivers.		Approximate weight of each.	
		Near horse.	Off horse.	lbs.	ozs.
Bags, nose, G.S., each with 6 lbs. corn	1	..	2	7	0
Brushes, horse	1	..	2	0	10
Harness .. .. sets	..	1	1	{ 73 / 75	0 / 0
Pads, surcingle (on surcingle under horse)	1	1	1	0	10
Pegs, picketing, with rope loops	1	1	1	1	3
Ropes, heel	1	1	1	1	1
Rubbers, horse	1	..	2	0	4
Saddlery, complete, with saddle blanket and head-rope.. .. .. set	1	..	..	29	4

Instructions for A.S.C. drivers will be found in A.S.C. Training, Part I.
Men leading pack animals are not clothed as drivers, but in the same manner as other privates.
Rifles of drivers of G.S. limbered wagons will be carried in the clips provided on the wagon for that purpose. On vehicles not specially fitted the rifles will be carried on wagon footboards.

NOTES.

Packs.—The packs of the transport serjeant and of the regimental drivers of 1st line transport vehicles may be carried on the vehicles. Those of drivers of spare horses and of pack animals will be on the man.

Saddle blanket.—Under the riding or pack saddle. Saddle blankets for officers' horses and horses with luggage saddles are carried in the vehicles on the march.

Heel ropes are allowed for use with restive horses on a scale of 25 per cent. An additional peg is issued with each heel rope.

Picketing gear (or any part of it) may, at the discretion of the commanding officer, be carried in the regimental transport vehicles. A proportion of mallets, heel peg (about 1 to 20 horses), will be carried on 1st line transport vehicles.

Nose bags.—When luggage saddle is worn on the off horse, one bag on each side of the luggage saddle is fastened to the near arch (or ring with O.P. saddle).

Carried in the wagon when luggage saddle is not worn.

Horse brush and rubber.—The method of carrying is left to the discretion of officers commanding, except that these articles are not to be in the nose bag.

7. ARTICLES LEFT AT THE BASE FOR EACH MAN.

Kit bags, containing the spare kit detailed below, will be handed over to the O.C. base details to be taken to the oversea base with the base details, and will be left in charge of company storemen at the Infantry Base Depot, to be forwarded only as may be deemed convenient to the service by the C.-in-C.

Articles.	No.	Remarks.
Clothing.		(a) Shoes, Highland, for kilted regiments, but cyclists of kilted regiments will not leave a spare pair of boots or shoes at the base.
Boots, ankle (a) .. .. pair	1	
Drawers (b) .. .. .. ,,	1	
Jacket, service dress (c)	1	
Shoes, canvas (if in possession).. pair	1	
Trousers, service dress (d) .. ,,	1	(b) Not for kilted men.
		(c) Not for serving soldiers of Foot Guards, and Highland Light Infantry and kilted regiments.
Necessaries.		
Brush, hair	1	
Hosetops (e) .. .. .. pair	1	
Shirt, flannel	1	(d) Not for serving soldiers of Foot Guards and kilted regiments.
Socks, worsted .. .. .. pair	1	
Towel, hand	1	(e) Men of kilted regiments only, cyclists excepted.

The boots (or Highland shoes) will be tied together, with the soles outwards, the regimental number of the man and the name and number of the battalion being chalked or otherwise legibly marked on the soles. The boots (or shoes) will be placed in the mouth of the kit bag to admit of them being readily withdrawn, should it be necessary to forward them separately to the troops in the field.

6. SCALES OF FREE ISSUES OF FIELD SERVICE CLOTHING FOR BRITISH TROOPS, INDIAN TROOPS AND FOLLOWERS.

Item No.	Articles of Clothing. The Summer scale is issued between 1st April and 1st October; the Winter scale between 1st October and 1st April.	British Troops.		Departmental Officers with hon. rank and W.Os. of the ordnance and subordinate medical depts, S. & T. corps, military works services, and miscellaneous unattached list. *b*		N.C.Os. of the ordnance and subordinate army veterinary departments, S. & T. corps, military works services, and miscellaneous unattached list. *g*		Native Troops.		Public followers and regimental private followers (paid by the unit) who are permitted to be taken on service under the F.S. Manuals. *h*		Telegraph department. Summer and Winter. of field service clothing, corps, see F S Manual.	Postal department. Summer and Winter. Europeans as for British troops, natives as for native troops. As for public followers.	Clerks and agents and men of this class, and subordinates of the civil departments below the status of an officer. Summer and Winter. Europeans and Eurasians as for British troops, others as for native troops, *m*. As for public followers.
		Summer.	Winter.	Summer.	Winter.	Summer.	Winter.	Summer.	Winter.	Summer.	Winter.			
		3	4	5	6	7	8	9	10	11	12	13	14	15
1	Back pads ... No.	1a	1a	1a	1a	1a	1a	...	...	...	...			
2	Belts, leather ,,	1	1	1	1	1	1	1	...	1	1			
3	Blankets, barrack ,,	...	2	...	2	...	2	...	2	...	2			
4	Blouses, khaki ,,	1	...	1	...	1	...	1	...	1	...			1
5	,, country ,,	...	...	...	...	...	...	...	...	...	...			
6	Boots, ammunition ,,	1c	1c	1	1	...	...	1k	1k	1i	1i			
7	,, ,, country made ,,	...	...	...	...	1j	1j	1k	1k	1 0	1 0			1 0
8	Caps, Balaclava (comforters in case of Sikhs) ,,	...	1c	...	...	...	...	...	...	...	...			
9	Coats, warm ,,	1	1	1	1	...	1j	1k	1	1	1			
10	,, ,, followers ,,	1a	1n	1a	1n	...	...	...	*q*	...	...			

		Telegraphs. Postmasters, inspectors, sub-postmasters and clerks.	Clerks, writers, munshis, interpreters, treasurers, agents, store-keepers, chowdries, assistants of the veterinary and stationery departments, sub-surveyors, khalasis and political orderlies. m Others.			Other establishments.	
				For free issues and renewals supplied by the S. and T.		Renewals only, as follows:—	
11	Coats, waterproof, with hoods ,,	...	...	...	...	...	...
12	Haversacks ,,	...	...	...	...	...	...
13	Jerseys ,,	...	...	...	...	...	...
14	Mittens Pairs	...	...	...	...	...	...
15	Pyjamas, warm No.	1	1	1	1	1	1
16	Pagris ,,	1e	1	f	f	f	...
17	Putties Pairs	1	1	1	1	1p	1
18	Sheets, waterproof No.	...	...	...	...	1p	...
19	Shoes, country-made Pairs	2l	2	2l	2	k	1
20	Socks, worsted ,,	1a	1a	1a	1a	k	1
21	Sun spectacles ,,	1a	1a	1a	1a	2	...
22	Sunshades, khaki, for helmets No.	1a	1a	1a	1a	...	...
23	Water-bottles, zinc ,,	...	...	...	...	...	1

a When considered necessary.   *b* One pair of khaki cord pantaloons will be issued to each man of the military works services which will be renewed as required.   *c* First issue to cavalry only.   Renewals to all.

d 50 per regiment and 10 per battery in Sikkim or Burma only.

e First issue to horse and field artillery and mounted men of heavy batteries only.   Renewals to all.

f Compensation in lieu of first issues will be paid.

g N.C.Os. of army and command headquarters attached to army or divisional headquarters are entitled to a water-bottle when proceeding on service.   These articles will be replaced when renewal is ordered.

h Officers commanding and all concerned are responsible that followers not entitled to a free issue of clothing are duly provided with it, either by payment indent or by payment indent on S. and T. corps.

i Not to be issued to permanent followers who have these articles in possession.

j As renewals only.   *k* Renewals only.   *l* As renewals only.

m European and Indian clerks, agents and store-keepers, hospital storekeepers, who are not required to keep up boots or shoes as part of their equipment in peace time, should be provided with a pair of boots as a first issue at a cost to the State not exceeding 5 rupees per pair.

All clerks and agents of the S. and T. corps and native clerks accompanying inspecting veterinary officers, or ordnance field parks, are entitled to a zinc water-bottle and haversack each when proceeding on field service.   European and Eurasian clerks of the S. and T. corps and medical department are entitled to two pairs of socks, and all clerks and agents of the S. and T. corps, ordnance, medical and veterinary services to one pair of putties each when proceeding on field service.   Each transport veterinary duffadar is entitled to a water-bottle when proceeding on service.   Renewals of all the above articles will be made as required.

n Not for mounted units who take cloaks or great coats on service instead.   *o* For camel sillidars only.

p Renewals only.   *q* 23 per Indian mountain battery, half squadron, or company.

9. FIELD ALLOWANCES OF BAGGAGE AND TENTAGE.

Rank or Description.	Baggage.		Tentage.
	Summer.	Winter.	
British Officers (a).	lbs.	lbs.	lbs.
General Officers Commanding	70	70	160
Officers with headquarters and Officers			
Commanding Units	70	70	40
Cavalry and Artillery	55	60	40
All others	60	60	40
British Troops.			
Cavalry—			
Warrant Officers	25	30	40
N.C.Os. and men	23¼	28¼	10
Artillery (ex-mountain batteries)—			
Warrant Officers	35	40	40
N.C.Os. and men	25 (b)	30	10
Infantry and Mountain Batteries—			
Warrant Officers	30	30	40
N.C.Os. and men	25¾	25¾	10
Indian Troops (c).			
Cavalry—			
N.C.Os. and men	19½	24	8
Artillery (ex-mountain batteries)—			
N.C.Os. and men	20 (d)	25 (d)	8
Infantry, Mountain Batteries and Suppers			
and Miners—			
N.C.Os. and men	24¼	24¾	8
Followers—			
Public and private (e)	13½	13½	5

(a) Not provided by Government.
(b) 15 lbs. of which is carried on horse or battery vehicles.
(c) Tentage for all Indian officers, 40 lbs., except cavalry, 2 to a 45-lb. tent.   Baggage, 10 lbs. more than for N.C.Os. and men.
(d) 10 lbs. (5 lbs. for bullock drivers) of which is carried on horse or battery vehicles.
(e) Officers provide their private servants with shelter.

40. MEDICAL SERVICE.

1. The director of medical services is responsible for the medical and sanitary services of an army in the field.   He receives his instructions through the A.G.'s branch of the staff.

2. With each division is an assistant director of medical services and a deputy assistant director of medical services.

3. The mobile medical units in the field are :—
The Field Ambulance and the Cavalry Field Ambulance.   (See Chap. 1.)
Motor Ambulance Convoys (40 to 50 cars).

4. The remaining medical units are :—

Clearing hospitals	..	..	..	200 sick.
Stationary ,,	..	..	..	200 beds.
General ,,	..	..	..	520 ,,
Convalescent depôts	..	..	..	500 or 1,000 convalescents.
Ambulance trains	..	..	..	396 lying down cases.
Hospital ships ..	..	..	..	220 beds.

SANITATION.

5. The field sanitation of units is under regimental control.

The unit provides 1 N.C.O. and men, according to the strength of the unit, for sanitary duties (see F.S. Manual for the various arms). These men supervise the cookhouses, ablution places, latrines, &c., and act as sanitary police.

The R.A.M.C. provide a N.C.O. and men, as laid down in W.E., for water duties. These men receive special instruction in their duties, and will be concerned with the purification of water ; they may, if circumstances permit, be employed on duties in connection with disinfection and with the care of the sick. They have charge of the water carts and of any apparatus or chemicals that may be issued for sterilization of water.

6. On a L. of C. a sanitary squad is provided for each permanent post or railhead, and two for each advanced base.

For each base a sanitary section is provided.

7. A sanitary committee, consisting of a senior combatant officer as president and two or three selected medical experts, military or civil, as members, may be formed under special circumstances, their function being to assist general officers and the medical service in their efforts to maintain the health of the army.

DISPOSAL OF CASUALTIES.

8. A wounded man is generally first attended to by the M.O. with his unit and (unless able to walk) is carried back by the regimental stretcher-bearers to the regimental aid post, if one has been formed, and is removed thence by the bearers to the nearest field ambulance to the advanced dressing station or direct to the main dressing station of the ambulance.

From the field ambulance he is transferred by means of motor ambulance convoys through a clearing hospital to a stationary or general hospital on the L. of C., when, if no further treatment is required, he is transferred to a convalescent depôt.

If the journey is by rail, he is ordinarily conveyed by an ambulance train. If sent to England he proceeds in a hospital ship, thence he is transferred to a military hospital. Should he require no further active treatment, although still unfit for duty, he is transferred to a convalescent depôt ; from this he may proceed on sick furlough or be discharged to duty.

MEDICAL NOTES.

9. Normal pulse	..	..	..	..	..	72 per minute.
,, respiration	..	..	..	..	..	15 to 18 per minute.
,, temperature	..	..	..	..	..	98·4° Fahr.

FIRST FIELD DRESSING.

10. Every officer and man carries on the field a dressing which is placed in the pocket of the right side of the skirt of the frock. It consists of a packet of khaki cotton cloth containing in a linen cover two dressings, each composed of 2½ yards of bandages, some gauze and a safety pin. Simple instructions as to the method of using it are printed on the outer and inner cover .

TREATMENT OF CASES OF EMERGENCY.

11. *Bleeding—*

Bleeding may be either external or internal, and may be arterial, venous, or capillary.

(a) Arterial bleeding. The blood is of a bright red colour, and at first escapes in spurts.

Treatment.—Expose the wound, apply the gauze of the first field dressing, and first try pressure on the bleeding point with the fingers over this protection ; if this fails compress the artery against the bone close to the wound but between it and the heart. Pressure should be maintained until some more permanent means can be employed (such as an improvized tourniquet, *see* p. 190), or medical assistance procured.

Absolute rest is essential. If the bleeding is from a limb, raise it.

(*b*) Venous bleeding.—The blood is of a dark colour; it flows or oozes out, but there is no appearance of pulsation.

Treatment.—Lay the patient down, remove any constriction which may be round the limb, elevate the limb, and apply a pad and firm bandage.

(*c*) Capillary bleeding.—The blood oozes from the entire surface, not from any one point.

Treatment.—Bathe the part with cold water, or preferably with hot, of a temperature of 140° to 160° Fahr., or rather hotter than the hand can comfortably bear, and apply a pad and bandage firmly over the wound.

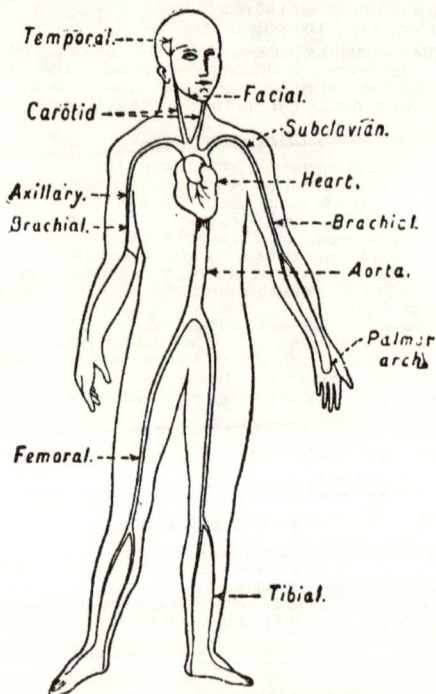

FIG. 1.—General Plan of Main Arteries.

12. The following table shows the situation of the main arteries and their treatment when wounded :—

Position (*see* Fig. 1).	Name of Artery.	Treatment.
Head	Temporal and facial	Apply first field dressing over the wound and bandage tightly.
Arm-pit	Axillary	(1) Compress subclavian downwards and backwards behind the middle of the collar-bone.
Arm (on inner side in line with the seam of the coat)	Brachial	Compress the artery by hand (*see* Fig. 2).
Palm of the hand	Palmar arch	*Very difficult to treat.*—Place a roll of bandage, or a firm pad, in the hand, close the fingers over the pad and bandage firmly, bend up the arm from the elbow and, if necessary, apply pressure to the brachial artery. as in Fig. 2.
Thigh	Femoral	Pressure in the groin by fingers or tourniquet (*see* Fig. 3).

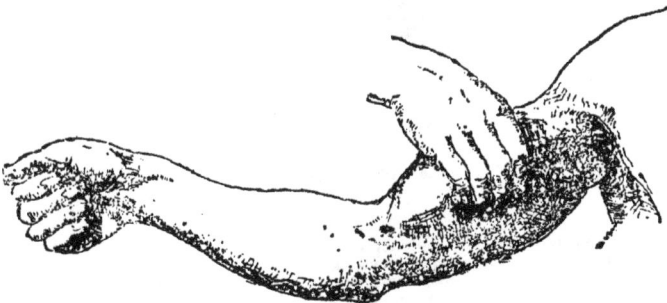

FIG. 2 —Digital Compression of the Brachial Artery (Best Method).

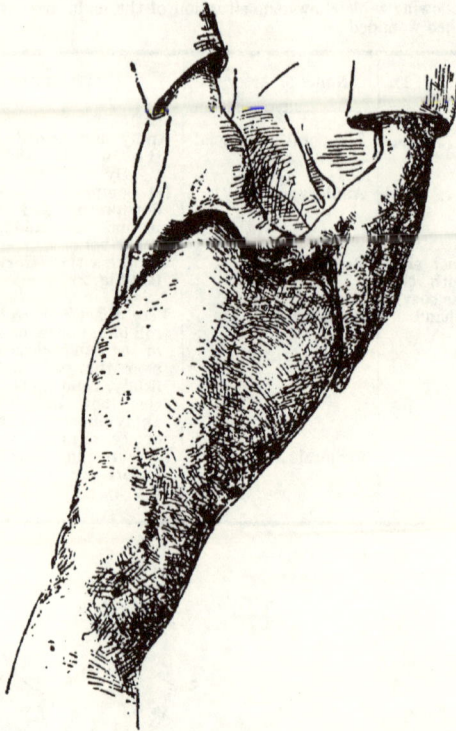

FIG. 3.—Digital Compression of the Femoral Artery.

13. An improvized tourniquet may be made as follows :—Take a handkerchief, a smooth, rounded stone, and a stick, wrap up the stone in the
centre of the handkerchief, tie a knot over it and place the stone over the
artery, pass the ends of the handkerchief round the limb and tie them securely,
leaving sufficient space for the stick to be admitted ; pass the stick then
between the handkerchief and the skin, and carefully twist it until by tighten-
ing the handkerchief the stone is pressed upon the artery with sufficient force
to arrest the flow of blood. A pad should be placed between the stick and
the skin to prevent the latter being bruised, and the end of the stick must be
secured with a bandage to prevent the tourniquet untwisting.

Many other substitutes for the above may be adopted.

The tourniquet should be applied no tighter than is absolutely necessary
to stop the arterial bleeding, and should only be used as a last resource. A
medical officer should be sent for as soon as possible.

14. Internal bleeding.—The symptoms of internal hæmorrhage are pros-
tration and weakness. The surface of the body is cold and the face pale,
the lips lose their colour. The pulse is weak or imperceptible ; there is sighing
respiration and a cold clammy sweat.

Treatment—

    (a) Keep the patient absolutely quiet.

    (b) Do not give stimulants.

15. *Drowning.—Restoration by Schäfer's method—*

    If breathing has ceased, immediately on removal from the water, place the patient face downwards on the ground, with the arms drawn forward and the face turned to the side.

    Then, without stopping to remove or loosen clothing, commence artificial respiration. To effect artificial respiration, put yourself astride, or on one side of the patient's body, in a kneeling or squatting position, facing his head. Placing your hands flat on the small of his back, with the thumbs parallel and nearly touching, and the fingers spread out over the lowest ribs, lean forward with the arms straight and steadily allow the weight of your body to fall on the wrists, and so produce a firm, downward pressure, which must not be violent, on the loins and the lower part of the back. This part of the operation should occupy the time necessary to count—slowly— *one, two, three.* By this means the air (and water, if there be any) is driven out of the patient's lungs. Water and slime from the air passages may also run out.

    Immediately after making the downward pressure, swing backwards so as to relax the pressure and allow air to enter the lungs. Do not lift the hands from the patient's body. This part of the operation should occupy the time necessary to count—slowly—*one, two.* Repeat this forward and backward movement (pressure and relaxation of pressure) 12 or 15 time a minute, without any marked pause between the movements.

    Whilst the operator is carrying out artificial respiration, others may' if there be opportunity, busy themselves with applying hot flannels' hot bottles, &c., between the thighs and to the armpits and feet, or promote circulation by friction, but no attempt should be made to remove wet clothing, or give restoratives by the mouth, till natural breathing has recommenced.

    When this has taken place, allow the patient to lie on the right side and apply friction over the surface of the body by using handkerchiefs, flannels, &c., rubbing legs, arms and body, all towards the heart, and continue after the patient has been wrapped in blankets or dry clothing. As soon as possible after complete recovery of respiration, remove patient to nearest shelter. On restoration, and if power of swallowing has returned, small quantities of warm coffee, tea, milk, wine, &c., may be given. Encourage patient to sleep, but watch carefully for some time and allow free circulation of air around patient.

Note.—Artificial respiration must also be resorted to in case of suffocation by charcoal fumes or coal gas, mining accidents, hanging, lightning stroke. and severe electric shock.

16. *Snake bite or poisoned wound :—*

    Apply a ligature or tourniquet above the bite, *i.e.*, between it and the heart.

    Make ½-inch deep cruciform incision with a clean knife and rub in crystals or solution of permanganate of potash.

    Give stimulants such as brandy, salvolatile, or hot black coffee.

    If breathing is bad artificial respiration should be tried.

17. *Stings of venomous insects :—*

Apply solution of ammonia, or bi-carbonate of soda if available.

18. *Burns and scalds :—*

Apply oil, vaseline, or boracic powder. Cover from air ; quickly cut
clothes off ; never pull them off.

19. *Shock, loss of consciousness and fits :—*
   Shock :—

   Put to bed and cover with warm blankets or rugs if possible.
   Give hot drinks and stimulants if conscious.

   Loss of consciousness :—

   Send for medical aid at once.
   Lay patient on his back.
   Loosen all tight clothing round the body.
   Give no food or drink unless under medical **direction.**
   Allow plenty of fresh air to the patient.

   Fainting :—

   Lay patient on his back, with the head low.
   Loosen clothing.
   Allow plenty of fresh air.

   Fits :—

   Lay patient on his back, with the head slightly raised.
   Loosen the clothes about the neck and chest and prevent him from
      biting his tongue by placing the handle of a toothbrush, or
      similar article, as a gag, between his teeth.
   Employ sufficient restraint only to prevent him injuring himself.
   Do not give stimulants.

20. *Sunstroke or heatstroke :—*

Place patient at once in shade or cool place.
Allow plenty of fresh air.
Raise head and remove clothing from neck and upper part of body.
Douche head, neck and spine, or whole body, with cold water.
Do not give stimulants.

21. *Frost bite :—*

Rub affected part with snow or cold water. Avoid taking the patient
   into a warm room until the part has been thoroughly, but very
   gradually, thawed. Do not apply heat in any form.

22. *Sprains :—*

Bandage firmly as soon as possible after the accident, keep the bandage
   wetted with some evaporating lotion ; raise and rest the injured part.

23. *Wounds :—*

Do not attempt to clean up the wound on the field.
Stop the bleeding and apply a dressing.
In applying the field dressing care should be taken to place it directly on
   the wound without in any way touching with the fingers either
   the wound or the surface of the dressing which comes in contact
   with the wound.
This may be done by taking hold of the dressing by pinching it up at
   the back, turning it inside out, and applying the fresh surface
   direct to the wound.

24. *Fractures :—*

Splints are required for the treatment of broken limbs. They are made
of any unyielding substance, such as wood, bark, bundles of twigs,
wire, rifles, bayonets, swords, &c. They should be padded with
some soft material. They are bound to the limb with bandages,
tapes, &c. Cases of suspected fracture should not be moved without first applying a splint.

25. *Poisoning :—*

Send at once for medical assistance. Look for the source of the poison.
Try to lessen the poisonous effects by giving the proper remedy, called
an antidote. The labels of bottles containing poisons frequently
have the antidotes printed on them.

Poisons are divided into :—

(a) Corrosive.
(b) Irritant.
(c) Systematic. (Constitutional.)

Symptoms.—(a) Great pain, immediately after poison has been swallowed,
in mouth and throat. which look as if scalded. Lips stained and blistered.
Shock, difficulty of breathing, and breath smells sour.
(b) Pain at first is not very marked. There is a sensation of burning,
and vomiting sets in accompanied by pain in the stomach and collapse.
(c) No sign of burning, redness or pain. May be giddiness, dimness of
sight, drowsiness, difficulty of breathing, delirium, cramps and convulsions.
Give emetics, for example, mustard or salt, a tablespoonful to a tumbler
of water in (b) and (c), but *not* in (a). An emetic promptly given may save
patient's life.
In (a) give scrapings from whitewashed walls or ceilings, mixed with
water.
In (c) after emetic, if the patient is drowsy, walk him about and give him
hot coffee ; if breathing fails, resort to artificial respiration.

41. REMOUNT SERVICE.

1. The director of remounts is responsible for the provision, training and
distribution of all animals and for the administration of remount personnel.
He receives instructions through the Q.M.G.'s branch of the staff.

2. Each unit will furnish :—

(a) On landing, a return to the D.A.D.R. at base port showing number
of horses, cobs and mules landed.
(b) Animal a/c (A.F. A 2004). The numbers landed will form the first
entry of the monthly account to be rendered at the end of each
month.

3. To replace casualties in field units indents will normally be sent by
commanders to the commander of the nearest remount depôt of the division
or formation to which the unit belongs. A duplicate will be rendered to
divisional headquarters.

4. All riding, draught or pack animals, taken in action, brought in by
deserters, or otherwise obtained, will, if serviceable, and after being certified
by a veterinary officer as free from contagious disease, be handed over to
the nearest unit requiring them, the commander of which will report the
transaction to the O.C. the nearest remount depôt, who will take them on
the strength of his depôt and strike them off as issued to the unit or units
concerned. If practicable, a receipt showing descriptive numbers, &c., will be
obtained by the person handing them over. If unserviceable they will be
destroyed.

42. VETERINARY SERVICE.

1. The veterinary service in war is under a director of veterinary services, who receives instructions from the Q.M.G.'s branch of the staff. He is assisted by a deputy director and represented in divisions by assistant directors.

2. The veterinary service is organized with the view of securing the efficiency of the animals of the forces in the field :—

(a) By preventing the introduction and spread of contagious disease.

(b) By reducing wastage amongst animals by means of prompt application of first aid.

(c) By relieving the field army of the care of sick and inefficient animals.

To carry out the duties specified in (a) and (b) veterinary officers are detailed for duty with the various portions of the field army. To these officers is confided the veterinary supervision and care of animals, and it is their duty to bring to the notice of commanders any measure necessary for the health and condition of the animals under their professional care.

3. Veterinary hospitals are established on the L. of C., to which sick and injured animals are sent for treatment. When fit for duty they are transfered to the nearest remount depôt for disposal.

4. All animals, including slaughter cattle, before being utilized by troops, will be examined by a veterinary officer as to freedom from disease.

5. Cold shoeing will be invariably adopted in the field. No charge will be made for shoeing public animals.

VETERINARY HINTS FOR COMMON AILMENTS AND INJURIES WHEN VETERINARY ADVICE IS NOT AVAILABLE.

Ailment or Injury.	Symptoms, Treatment, &c.
6. Ringworm　..　　..	Symptoms. Hair falls out in circular patches. Treatment. Clip affected parts and burn clippings. Wash animal all over with some disinfectant (*i.e.*, cresol, 1 part to 80 of water). Apply tincture of iodine, if available, paraffin or soft soap to spots. Disinfect harness, &c.
7. Mange　..　　..　　..	Symptoms. Marked skin irritation. Horse bites and rubs himself against any available object. Hair comes off in patches and skin becomes thickened and corrugated. Prevention of spread. Obtain veterinary aid without delay. Very contagious. Isolate affected and suspicious cases with their equipment. Men looking after them should not go amongst healthy animals, as they may carry infection in their clothing. Thoroughly disinfect all stables, utensils, harness, &c. Discontinue clothing. Picket in open. Change standings. Treatment. Clip, burn clippings, dress all over with a mixture of paraffin 1 pint, soap 1 lb. and water 1 gallon. Regular exercise and dress immediately on return every third day. If horses urgently required make up troop of affected animals to work by themselves. Contagious to man; suspect any rash.

VETERINARY HINTS—*continued.*

Ailment or Injury.	Symptoms, Treatment, &c.
8. Ticks	Treatment. Pull out, taking care not to leave head in the skin ; or touch with paraffin, turpentine or carbolic acid.
9. Sprain tendons, &c.	Treatment. Rest. Apply cotton wool and linen bandage and stand in cold water ; or apply layer of soft clay. Renew when dry.
10. Heel rope galls	Prevention. Keep head rope short. Treatment. Grease when marching. On return to camp wash with soap and warm water, thoroughly dry and apply dry bran poultice.
11. Cracked heels and mud fever	Prevention. Do not wash legs when muddy but leave until dry and then brush dirt out. Treatment. Cleanse and dry (if greasy, apply dry bran poultice), dust on boric acid or powdered starch.
12. Thrush	Treatment. Clean frog, dress cleft with boric acid and then plug with piece of tow. If severe, poultice or soak foot before applying dressing. Stand on driest ground available. Shoe with tips.
13. Dirty sheath	Treatment. Draw out penis and wash it and sheath with soap and warm water or dirt will accumulate and maggots may appear.
14. Bullet wounds	Treatment. Observe cleanliness in the treatment of all wounds. Dust with boric acid and cover with clean pad of lint, wool or tow and bandage, which must not be applied tightly unless to stop bleeding.
15. Broken knees	Treatment. Do not poultice. Clean with cold water and treat as for 10.
16. Cuts and tears	Treatment. As for 10 and 11.
17. Bit injuries	Treatment. Work in snaffle or with bridle over nose ; improvize martingale if necessary. Rinse mouth with clean water after feeding.
18. Girth galls	Treatment. If simply a swelling, lightly smooth over the swollen surface with the hand in the direction of the hair, as if to smooth it out, for 15 minutes at a time. If skin is chafed treat as for wounds. To work horse, strap girth back, tying it under the belly to surcingle, which should be placed over fans of saddle. When healed, place piece of sheep-skin under girth.

Ailment or Injury.	Symptoms, Treatment, &c.
19. Sore backs and saddle galls	Prevention. Careful supervision and fitting of saddlery. Treatment. If swelling only, treat as at 14 or bathe with cold salt water. If skin chafed, treat as for wounds. Keep saddle off back until healed.
20. Sore withers	Treatment. Keep arch of saddle well clear of withers. If swelling only, bathe with cold salt water. If skin broken, treat as for wounds.
21. Coughs and colds ..	Any animal with a nasal discharge should be isolated and veterinary aid obtained as soon as possible. Treatment. Steam head and apply liniment, or mustard mixed as for the table, to throat from ear to ear, and leave on for 15 minutes. Give soft food. Keep body warm with rugs and bandages and give plenty of fresh air.
22. Fever	Symptoms. Horse off feed, dull temperature over 100° F. Treatment. Isolate and apply for veterinary aid. Give soft food, and green stuff when available. Keep water always by and change frequently. If procurable, give a handful of Epsom salts in each bucket of water. Keep body warm with rugs and bandages and give plenty of fresh air.
23. Exhaustion after hard work	Treatment. Give pint of warm beer, or half tumbler of rum or whiskey in a pint of water. Rug up and bandage. Rest and light exercise. Feed with bran mashes, steamed oats, boiled linseed, oatmeal, gruel, &c., it available, in small quantities and often.
24. Colic	Symptoms. Horse looks round at his sides, tries to lie down and roll, stamps with hind legs and kicks at belly. Treatment. Walk about, give chloral hydrate ball, if available, or 2 ozs. turpentine well shaken up, either with a pint of linseed oil or eggs and milk. If not relieved in an hour repeat the dose and give in addition an aloes ball. In the absence of drugs give half tumbler of rum or whiskey in a pint of warm water, or 1½ pints of warm beer with a teaspoonful of ginger mixed in it. Hand-rub belly and give frequent enemas of soapy water. A large bottle with the bottom knocked out makes a useful enema funnel.

VETERINARY HINTS—*continued*.

Ailment or Injury.	Symptoms, Treatment, &c.
25. Sand colic	Prevention. Feed off blankets, &c. Clean food. Treatment. Give chloral hydrate balls and linseed oil.
26. Constipation	Treatment. Soft food and green also, if available, regular work and frequent enemas.
27. Diarrhœa	Treatment. Dry bran. Keep body warm with rugs and bandages.
28. Strangles	Symptoms. Swelling at the back of or under the jaw. May be some difficulty in swallowing. Treatment. Isolate and obtain veterinary aid. Rest, soft food, rug up and bandage, plenty of fresh air and foment swelling. When swelling bursts treat as for wounds.
29. Glanders	Symptoms. Thick, gluey discharge from one or both nostrils, ulcers on the membrane, inside nostrils, glands between lower jaws enlarged, hard, and appear to be fixed to bone. Treatment. Very contagious. Rigid isolation of affected cases, in-contacts and whole unit, if possible. On suspicion immediately obtain veterinary aid. Very contagious to man.
30. Farcy	Symptoms. Skin form of glanders. Appears as a string of running sores, usually on inside of hind legs, occasionally neck and face. No tendency to heal. Treatment. As for glanders.
31. Epizootic Lymphangitis	Symptoms. Sores similar to and in similar situations to farcy. They have a greater tendency to heal. Usually originates from a wound, from which point cord-like swellings appear, and on the course of which these sores form. Treatment. Very contagious. Proceed as for farcy.

32. To make :—
  (a) Bran mash.—Put 2 double handfuls of bran in a bucket and pour on as much boiling water as the bran will soak up. Cover bucket with rug and leave till cool enough to eat.
    Teaspoonful of salt improves.
  (b) Steamed oats.—Substitute oats for bran and proceed as above.
    Gruel.—Cook oatmeal as for porridge and thin down with water, or may mix oatmeal with water straight away.
33. To shoot a horse.—Lift up forelock and place it under brow band. Place muzzle of revolver almost touching the skin where the lowest hairs of the forelock grow.

CHAPTER VIII.

43. OFFICE WORK AND PRIVATE CORRESPONDENCE.

GENERAL RULES.

1. Office work in the field is to be restricted to what is absolutely indispensable ; no office work will be transacted with a unit on service in the field that can possibly be dealt with at a stationary office.

2. Equipment accounts will not be kept by units.

3. Papers, except those required for reference, will be sent to the A.G.'s office at the base or destroyed. Those which it is necessary to keep with the unit will be marked " K," those for the record office " R."

4. War diaries and documents, which contain anything of a nature likely to prove useful when the history of the campaign is written, will, when no longer required, be sent to the A.G.'s office at the base.

5. A *state* is a report whereby a commander is kept informed of the fighting condition of his command. Punctuality in rendering it is usually more important than extreme accuracy.

A *return* is a document for statistical purposes, or to show the condition of the forces more accurately than is possible in a state. Accuracy in their compilation is essential.

A return (A.F. B 213) will be furnished weekly, on Sunday, by a commander of a unit or detachment to the A.G.'s office at the base for all persons and animals rationed by him the previous day.

6. An officer in whose custody are secret or confidential books, &c., is responsible for taking precautions to prevent them falling into the hands of the enemy.

7. Letters in the field should be drawn up in minute form. The same rules should be applied to them as have been given in Sections 12–13 for orders and messages.

A.G.'S OFFICE AT THE BASE.

8. A portion of the A.G.'s branch of the staff of general headquarters will be located at the base or other convenient place under a D.A.G.

9. This officer receives instructions from and corresponds directly with the A.G.'s branch of the staff at general headquarters in regard to all duties with which he is charged, except those of local discipline and interior economy. He also communicates directly with the I.G.C. on matters in regard to which the interests of each are affected. He is responsible for :—

    (a) Notification to the military authorities concerned of the prospective or immediate requirements of the army in the field as regards personnel.

    (b) Compilation of returns as regards personnel.

    (c) Verification and communication to the military authorities concerned of casualties in the field.

    (d) Notification to the military authorities concerned of requirements in the way of officers for improvized cadres or appointments.

    (e) Personal services, postings, transfers ; promotion of N.C.Os. above the rank of serjeant ; provisional promotion of officers.

    (f) Registration of prisoners of war and the custody of personal effects of the enemy's dead ; supply to the War Office of the necessary information required by The Hague and Geneva Conventions.

    (g) Opinions and remarks on all cases which may be referred regarding military, martial, and international law ; discipline, confidential reports, resignations and retirements ; custody of courts-martial documents.

    (h) Custody and transmission of war diaries and other documents of an historical nature ; and custody of regimental documents.

WAR DIARIES.

10. War diaries are confidential documents. Their object is :—
  (a) To furnish an accurate record of the operations from which the history of the war can subsequently be prepared.
  (b) To collect information for future reference with a view to effecting improvements in the organization, education, training, equipment and administration of the army for war.

11. A diary will be kept in duplicate by :—
  Each branch of the staff at general headquarters and at the headquarters of an army, and of all subordinate commands, including garrisons and posts, except intelligence sections of the general staff.
  Commanders of permanent and provisional units, detachments from a unit, and base depôts, and the officer i/c A.G.'s office at the base.
  Directors and heads of administrative services and departments, and their representatives and officers holding special and personal appointments, from the first day of mobilization or creation of the particular command or appointment.
  The original copy will be forwarded on the last day of each month, unless otherwise ordered, direct to the officer i/c of the A.G.'s office • . the base for transmission to the military authorities concerned.

12. In so far as they apply to each case the following points should be recorded :—
  (a) All important orders, despatches, instructions, reports and telegrams issued and received, and decisions taken.
  (b) Daily situation, i.e., arrival at, departure from, or halt at a place ; all movements and dispositions on the march, in camp, bivouac, or billets.
  (c) All important matters relating to the duties of the staff under their respective headings.
  (d) All important matters relating to the administrative services and departments under their respective headings.
  (e) Detailed account of all operations, noting connection with other units in the neighbourhood, formations adopted, ranges at which fire was opened, &c. The hour at which important occurrences took place should be entered with exactitude. The state of the weather, condition of the roads and ground, and general description of the locality should be recorded.
  (f) Changes in establishment or strength. As regards casualties, the names and ranks of officers, and the number of other ranks and followers, and animals should be noted.
  (g) Nature and description of field works constructed or quarters occupied.
  (h) Meteorological notes.
  (i) Summary of information received and of all matters of importance, military or political, which may occur from day to day.
  (k) In what respect organizations and regulations have stood the test of war.

13. In all diaries writing will be on one side of the page only.

14. References to appendices, such as orders, reports, telegrams, sketches, statements of evidence of spies and other persons, tabular statements, &c., will be made in the last column.

CIPHERS.

15. A cipher system for use in the field should conform to the following conditions :—
  (a) It must be comparatively secure, i.e., it should necessitate considerable trouble to decipher without a knowledge of the key word.
  (b) It must not require written notes for its use.
  (c) The keyword must be easy to remember, easy to spell, and should contain as many different letters as possible.
  (d) The keyword must be necessary, even when the system is known.
  (e) The method of enciphering and deciphering must be simple.

16. The following instructions should be observed in enciphering or deciphering messages :—

    (a) No cipher message should ever contain paragraphs partly in clear and partly in cipher.

    (b) Ciphers or deciphers should never be written on the same sheet of paper as the original message.

    (c) Every cipher message should be checked before despatch.

    (d) References to cipher messages should be avoided in ordinary correspondence.

    (e) Cipher messages should be arranged in groups of five letters.

    (f) Enciphering and deciphering should be done in a mechanical manner, i.e., no attempt to guess should be made.

    (g) All papers used in the process of enciphering or deciphering must be destroyed. If records are necessary a paraphrase should be made, unless the exact wording of a particular sentence appears to be specially important. Such records should be marked with the letter " P."

17. The sliding alphabet and Playfair ciphers are simple and comparatively secure. They belong to what are known as substitution ciphers.

The Sliding Alphabet Cipher. (Plate 20.)

18. In order to use the cipher each correspondent requires a fixed and sliding alphabet. The sliding alphabet contains the alphabet twice over, so that, whatever the position of the sliding alphabet, there will always be some letter of this alphabet under each letter of the fixed alphabet.

An easily-remembered keyword is chosen, and the letters of the text written out in as many columns as there are letters in the keyword. For instance, if the keyword agreed upon were " Thames," and that the message to be sent were " Great activity in arsenal here," the letters would be written out in six columns, thus* :—

```
G   R   E   A   T   A
C   T   I   V   I   T
Y   I   N   A   R   S
E   N   A   L   H   E
R   E
```

Next, the first letter of the keyword, " T," in the sliding alphabet is brought under the A of the fixed alphabet, and the first column of letters is enciphered, each letter being looked up in the sliding alphabet and represented in cipher by the letter standing immediately above it in the fixed alphabet. The second letter of the keyword is then brought under the A of the fixed alphabet, and the second column of letters is similarly enciphered, and the same procedure followed with the remaining columns of letters. Each column of letters is thus enciphered by a different alphabet, and the number of alphabets used corresponds to the number of different letters in the key word.

19. The above columns would be represented in cipher thus :—

```
N   K   E   O   P   I
J   M   I   J   E   B
F   B   N   O   N   A
L   G   A   Z   D   M
Y   X
```

and the cryptogram, arranged in groups of five letters, would read as follows :—

    NKEOP   IJMIJ   EBFBN   ONALG   AZDMY   X

---

* With practice in the use of this cipher, it will be unnecessary to actually write out the letters of the message in columns, as it will suffice to tick off the letters in groups of six, thus, Great a [ctivit [y in ars [enal he [re. Writing the letters in columns is recommended, however, for beginners, as it does not take long and reduces the possibility of mistakes.

PLATE XX.

SLIDING ALPHABET CIPHER.

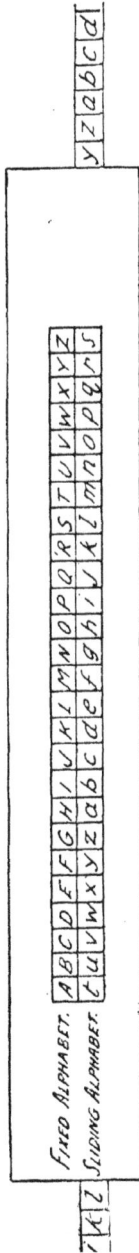

FIXED ALPHABET. | A B C D E F G H I J K L M N O P Q R S T U V W X Y Z

SLIDING ALPHABET. | t u v w x y z a b c d e f g h i j k l m n o p q r s

20. The above cipher may be **varied** as follows :—

The letters of the text form the key letters, each letter being enciphered by using the letter immediately before or after it. For instance, if the preceding letter is to be taken as the key letter, and the words " Great activity " are to be enciphered, the 1st letter, " g " remains the same in cipher, the 2nd letter " r " is enciphered by using the 1st letter " g " as the key letter, the 3rd letter " e " by the aid of the 2nd letter " r," and so on.

21. In order to decipher the cryptogram the receiver writes the letters out in the same number of columns as there are letters in the keyword, and then, by reversing the process employed when enciphering, finds the true letters represented by the letters of each column successively.

Playfair Cipher.

22. According to this system the letters of the text are enciphered in pairs, and one letter of a pair is represented in cipher by the same letter only when the other letter of the pair remains the same. This fact greatly increases the difficulty of solution, and messages so enciphered, if not actually insoluble, would as a rule cause sufficient delay to prevent the enemy from deriving advantage from the solution.

Example.

Keyword—" Soldier."

S	O	L	D	I
E	R	A	B	C
F	G	H	K	M
N	P	Q	T	U
V	W	X	Y	Z

23. The method of using the Playfair system is as follows :—

Construct a square, containing 25 spaces,* and inscribe first the letters of the keyword, omitting repetitions, and then the remaining letters of the alphabet, J being counted as I.

There are other ways of inscribing the letters of the alphabet in the table in order to avoid the constant occurrence of the less frequently used letters in the last line of the table. For instance, the last 5 letters may be written along a diagonal, or all the letters may be written in alternate squares, or in every third square, until the alphabet is completed.

24. To encipher the message the letters are taken in pairs, and equivalents are found for each pair of letters. A pair of letters must occur—

(a) In the same vertical column.
(b) In the same horizontal line.
(c) At opposite angles of some rectangle.

---

* By using K for both K and Q a rectangle of 24 spaces can be employed instead of a square of 25, and this variation is often introduced in French cipher systems, in which language K seldom occurs.

In the first case each letter is represented in cipher by that which stands below it, and the bottom letter by the top one of the same column, *e.g.*, F V would be represented by N S.

In the second case each letter would be represented by the letter on its right and in the same line, and the letter on the extreme right by that on the extreme left, *e.g.*, R C would be represented by A E.

In the third case the two letters are represented by those on the other diagonal of the rectangle, each by that which is in the same horizontal line, *e.g.*, S G would be represented by O F.

If, on dividing the letters of the text into pairs, a pair is found to be composed of a double letter, a dummy letter such as Q, X, Y or Z, which is not likely to mislead the receiver of the message, should be introduced, care being taken that the dummy letter employed is constantly varied.

If the message contains an uneven number of letters a dummy letter, should be added to complete a pair.

Example.—If the message—" Enemy attacked at noon and were repulsed "—were to be enciphered with keyword " Soldier " (*vide* preceding table), the letters would be divided into pairs as follows :—

> EN—EM—YA—TY—TA—CK—ED—AT—
> NO—ON—AN—DW—ER—ER—EP—UL—
> SE—DE—ND—SX.

The pairs of letters would then be enciphered thus :

> FV—CF—XB—YD—QB—BM—BS—BQ—PS—SP—
> EQ—OY—RA—RA—RN—QI—EF—SB—TS—LV.

The cryptogram, when grouped for transmission by telegraph or signalling would be—

> FVCFX—BYDQB—BMBSB—QPSSP—EQOYR—ARARN—
> QIEFS—BTSLV.

25. In order to decipher the cryptogram, the receiver divides it into pairs, and from this table finds the equivalents for each pair ; taking the letters next above each when they are in the same vertical column, those next on the left when they are in the same horizontal column, or those at the opposite angles of the rectangle.

26. In the solution of a cryptogram a knowledge of the comparative recurrence of the letters of the alphabet is very important. The frequency of recurrence is practically constant for all messages, &c., of 10,000 letters or over. The following table is applicable to military cryptograms for the solution of which the ordinary table of frequency requires modification :—

Letter.	English.	German.	French.	Italian.	Portu-guese. (*†)	Spanish.
A	7·7	5·2	8·0	11·7	14·0	13·4
B	1·5	1·8	0·5	0·6	0·6	1·6
C	2·9	3·1	3·3	4·5	3·4	4·0
Ch						0·2
D	4·1	5·1	4·0	*3·1	4·0	4·9
E	12·5	17·3	19·7	12·6	14·2	13·3
F	2·2	2·1	0·9	1·0	1·2	0·8
G	1·8	4·2	0·7	1·7	1·0	1·3
H	5·9	4·1	0·6	0·6	1·0	0·5
I	6·7	8·1	6·5	11·4	5·9	6·6
J	0·5	0·1	0·3	†		0·4
K	0·8	1·0		**	0·5	
L	4·7	2·8	4·9	7·2	3·2	4·9
Ll						0·5
M	2·0	2·0	3·1	3·0	4·6	2·8

Letter.	English.	German.	French.	Italian.	Portu- guese. ('†)	Spanish.
N	6·4	12·0	7·9	6·6	4·8	7·0
ñ	..	..	..	..	..	0·2
O	7·8	2·8	5·7	9·3	11·0	8·8
P	2·3	0·8	3·2	3·0	2·8	2·7
Q	0·1	††	1·2	0·3	1·6	1·0
R	6·7	6·9	7·4	6·4	6·4	6·5
Rr	..	..	..	..	..	0·4
S	6·0	‖5·7	6·6	4·9	8·8	7·6
T	8·0	0·0	6·5	*6·0	4·3	4·3
U	2·9	5·1	6·2	2·9	4·6	4·0
V	1·0	0·9	2·1	2·0	1·5	1·0
W	1·7	1·5	††	..	..	..
X	0·3	††	0·3	**	0·1	0·1
Y	2·4	††	0·2	**	0·06	0·8
Z	0·2	1·4	0·1	1·2	0·4	0·4

NOTE.—To avoid confusion, the Spanish compound letters are suppressed.

*† Permanent diagraphs not considered.

* "t" and "d" are interchangeable; therefore the individual percentages assigned will vary more or less.

† Substitute for double "i" at beginning, middle and end of word. Is an auxiliary only.

†† Occasional.

** "k" equals "c" or "ch"; "x" equals "s" or "ss," and "y" equals "i."

‖ "ss" ("sz") treated as two characters.

PRIVATE POSTAL CORRESPONDENCE.

27. Private postal correspondence of officers, soldiers, foreign attachés, and civilians employed by or accompanying the army is permitted by means of—

(a) Printed post cards (A.F. A 2042, see Appendix VII).
(b) Ordinary post cards.
(c) Letters (registered or unregistered).
(d) Urgent letters, enclosed in special envelopes.
(e) Parcels, including photographs and sketches, or private diaries.

All such correspondence must be posted in boxes or offices controlled by the army postal service.

28. Correspondence carried out under para. 1 (b), (c) and (e) is liable to serious delay in transmission owing to the necessity for censorship. All ranks should therefore in their own interests preferably carry on correspondence by means of the printed post cards.

29. Urgent letters may be sent in circumstances when immediate action is required in respect of some family or financial matter, and are not subject to delay, or to censorship, except as mentioned below. Such letters will be confined strictly to the business in question, and will, before despatch, be submitted to the C.O. (or officer in charge) of the sender, who, if he approves of their contents, will place them in the special envelopes (A.F. A 2043) provided for the purpose, which will be closed in his presence and counter-signed by him, no reference being made either to rank or unit.

30. In no circumstances is specific reference to be made on post cards, in letters, on matter posted in parcels, or in private diaries sent from the theatre of operations, to the place from which they are written or despatched; to plans of future operations, whether rumoured, surmised, or known; to organization, numbers and movements of troops; to the armament of troops or fortresses; to defensive works; to the moral or physical condition of the

troops; to casualties previous to the publication of official lists; to the service of maintenance; or in case the writer is one of the garrison of a besieged fortress, to the effects of hostile fire.

Criticism of operations is forbidden, as are statements calculated to bring the army or individuals into disrepute.

All correspondence must be in " clear." The rank and unit of the writer will not be added to his signature.

44. DISCIPLINE.

POWERS OF A COMMANDING OFFICER.

1. A commanding officer may, subject to the soldier's right to elect, previous to the award, to be tried by district court-martial, inflict the following summary punishments on a private soldier :—

    (a) Detention not exceeding 28 days, except that in cases of absence without leave not exceeding 7 days, detention can only be awarded up to 7 days, but if the absence exceeds 7 days the award of detention may be extended to the same number of days as the days of absence, not exceeding 28 days in the whole.

    (b) Field punishment not exceeding 28 days.

    (c) Forfeiture of all ordinary pay under Section 46 (2) (d) of the Army Act for a period commencing on the date of award and not exceeding 28 days.

    (d) In the case of drunkenness a fine not exceeding 10s.

    (e) Any deduction from ordinary pay allowed to be made by a commanding officer under Section 138 (4) and (6) of the Army Act.

A commanding officer may also inflict the following minor punishments, the offender having no right to elect trial by court-martial :—

    (f) Confinement to camp or barracks, not exceeding 14 days.

    (g) Extra guards or piquets; as punishment for minor offences or irregularities when on, or parading for, those duties.

    (h) Reprimand or severe reprimand.

    (i) Admonition.

(h) and (i) are applicable to N.C.Os., and (f), (g) and (i) to private soldiers.

INDIA.

2. As regards British troops, the powers of reduction and powers of a commanding officer (vide p. 205), and the detail as to courts-martial (vide p. 206), apply to those troops; but, in addition, a N.C.O. may be reduced to any lower grade or to the ranks by the C.-in-C. in India, the G.O.C. 1st, 2nd, 3rd, &c., and Burma Divisions, the Kohat, Derajat and Aden Brigades, and the O.C. the Bannu Brigade.

3. As regards native troops, a N.C.O. may be summarily reduced by the C.-in-C. in India, by the commander of an army, division or brigade or (on active service) by the O.C. the forces in the field.

POWERS OF A COMMANDING OFFICER OF NATIVE TROOPS.

4. Imprisonment (rigorous or simple) up to 28 days (a C.O. under field rank is restricted to 7 days).

Extra guards and piquets.

Confinement to lines up to 28 days.

Deprivation of acting rank, &c.

Forfeiture of one rate of g.s. or g.c. pay.

Reprimand or severe reprimand (W.Os. and N.C.Os. only).

Fine up to 7 days' pay a month (non-combatants, except W.Os.).

Stoppages as authorized by I.A. A. 50 (f).

N.B.—Imprisonment and confinement to lines are only awardable to persons below the rank of N.C.O. " Rigorous " imprisonment is equivalent to imprisonment with H.L

45. COURTS-MARTIAL.

1. COURTS-MARTIAL UNDER THE ARMY ACT.

Name of Court-Martial.	No. of Members, Minimum.	Service of Members, Minimum.	President, Rank of.	Powers, Maximum.	Convening Authority.
General ...	U.K., India, Malta, and Gibraltar 9, elsewhere 5	3 years	F.O. (Colonel, if possible.)	Death, and all less punishments	H.M., or G.O.C. by warrant.
District	4	2 years	F.O., but if a F.O. is not available a Captain may sit	2 years I.H.L. Reduction of N.C.O. Discharge	G.O.C. or other officer having a warrant to convene a D.C.M.
Regimental ...	3	1 year	Captain	42 days' detention	G.O.C. or C.O.
Field General ...	3*	...	Same as for a D.C.M.	Same as G.C.M. (unless less than 3 members)	O.C. Det. on service where G.C.M. not possible, or no superior authority.

* Except that, if 3 officers are not available, the court may consist of 2 officers.

NOTE.—Officers can only be tried by G.C.M. or F.G.C.M.

N.C.Os. above rank of corporal are not to be tried by any court inferior to a D.C.M., except when a D.C.M. or higher court cannot, having due regard to the public service, be assembled.

Any court-martial may award field punishment for any offence committed on active service and may, in addition to or without further punishment, sentence an offender to forfeiture of pay for a period not exceeding 3 months commencing on the day of sentence.

2. COURTS-MARTIAL UNDER THE INDIAN ARMY ACT (NATIVE FORCES ONLY).

Name of Court-Martial.	Number of Members.	Description of Members.	Maximum Powers.	Convening Authority.
General	7, or 5 if convening order states that 7 are not available.	All B.Os. or all N.Os., but not mixed. Accused may claim trial by B.Os. No restrictions as to rank of president or service of members.	Death.	C.-in-C. in India or officer empowered by warrant of C.-in-C. in India.
District	3.	Ditto.	2 years' rigorous imprisonment.	Officer empowered to convene a G.C.M. or officer holding D.C.M. warrant from him.
Summary	C.O. *alone* constitutes the Court, but it must be attended by 2 other officers.		*If held by C.O. a "corps"*—1 year's rigorous imprisonment. *If held by C.O. a detachment*—6 months' rigorous imprisonment.	No convening officer—power is inherent in C.O.
Summary General	3.	B.Os., N.Os. or mixed. Accused cannot claim trial by B.Os. No restrictions as to rank of president or service of members.	Death.	(*a*) Officer empowered by Governor-General in Council or C.-in-C. (*b*) O.C. forces in the field or officer empowered by him. (*c*) O.C. detached portion of H.M. Forces on active service when G.C.M. not possible.

Officers can only be tried by G.C.M. or S.G.C.M.
W.Os. cannot be tried by S.C.M.
Corporal punishment up to 30 lashes can be awarded, on active service, to any offender under rank of W.O. for any offence, by any court-martial competent to try him. It is inflicted with the regulation cat on the bare back.

3. FORMS OF CHARGES FOR COURTS-MARTIAL WHICH MAY OCCUR ON ACTIVE SERVICE ARE SHOWN BELOW.

Commencement of Charge Sheet.

The accused [*number, rank, name, battalion, regiment*], a soldier [officer] of the regular forces,

or,

The accused [*rank, name*], an officer of the regular forces on the active list on half-pay,

or,

The accused [*rank, name*] retired pay [*or* pensioner, *or* reservist], employed on military service under the orders of an officer of the regular forces,

or,

The accused [*rank, name*], an officer of the reserve of officers ordered on duty (or service),

or,

The accused [*rank, name, corps (if any)*], an officer of the special reserve of officers,

or,

The accused [*rank, name, corps*], an officer of the Territorial Force,

or,

The accused [*number, rank, name, battalion, regiment*], a soldier of the Territorial Force out for training [*or otherwise subject to military law*],

or,

The accused [*rank, name, regiment*], an officer of the Militia [*or* an officer of the Yeomanry commissioned since the 16th day of August, 1901],

or,

The accused [*rank, name*], an officer of the   volunteer battalion of the   regiment [*or* an officer of the yeomanry commissioned before the 17th day of August, 1901], whose corps is on actual military service [*or who is otherwise subject to military law*],

or,

The accused [*rank, name, corps*] an officer [a soldier], of a colonial force raised by order of His Majesty, and serving under the orders of an officer of the regular forces,

or,

The accused [*name*], being a person subject to military law as an officer [under the provisions of Section 175 (7) [*or* (8)] of the Army Act],

or,

The accused [*number, rank, name*], a militiaman [*or* yeoman] of the battalion   regiment, out for training [*or* embodied] [*or otherwise subject to military law*],

or,

The accused [*number, rank, name, corps*], of the   volunteer force of the United Kingdom, attached to the regular forces [*or otherwise subject to military law*],

or,

The accused [*name*], a follower [sutler] of His Majesty's forces, being subject to military law as a soldier [under the provisions of Section 176 (9) [*or* (10)] of the Army Act],

is charged with—

Where the offence has been committed by a person while subject to military law, and he has ceased to be so subject at the time when he is charged (in accordance with the provisions of Section 158 of the Army Act); as, for example, if a soldier has been transferred to the reserve, or discharged, or if the training period of a militiaman or yeoman has expired, the commencement of the charge will run as follows :—

The accused [*name*] is charged with having, while being [*number, rank*] of the   battalion,   regiment [a soldier of the regular forces] [*or otherwise subject to military law*], committed the following offence [offences], namely,

or,

The accused [*name*] is charged with having, while being [*number, rank*] of the   battalion,   regiment, a militiaman [*or yeoman*] out for training [*or otherwise subject to military law*], committed the following offence [offences], namely,

(CHARGES.)

Sec. 4 (1).   1. Shamefully delivering up a garrison,   in that he   on the   (date), when in command of the troops at (place), without due necessity, delivered up the garrison of that place to the enemy. Maximum punishment—Death.

Sec. 4 (2).   2. *Shamefully casting away his arms in the presence of the enemy. Maximum punishment—Death.*

Sec. 4 (7).   3. *Misbehaving before the enemy in such a manner as to show cowardice. Maximum punishment—Death.*

Sec. 5 (1).   4. *When on active service, without orders from his superior officer, leaving the ranks on pretence of taking wounded men to the rear. Maximum punishment—Penal Servitude.*

Sec. 5 (2).   5. *When on active service wilfully destroying property without orders from his superior officer. Maximum punishment—Penal Servitude.*

Sec. 6 (1a).   6. *When on active service leaving his commanding officer to go in search of plunder. Maximum punishment—Death.*

Sec. 6 (1c).   7. *When on active service forcing a safeguard. Maximum punishment—Death.*

Sec. 6 (1d).   8. *When on active service forcing a soldier when acting as sentinel. Maximum punishment—Death.*

Sec. 6 (1f).   9. *When on active service doing violence to a person bringing provisions to the forces. Maximum punishment—Death.*

Sec. 6 (1f).   10. The accused, A.B., sutler, being subject to military law as a soldier by reason of accompanying His Majesty's troops on active service, is charged with—
When on active service committing an offence against the person of a resident in the country in which he was serving. (Soldiers also can be tried under this section.) Maximum punishment—Death.

Sec. 6 (1*g*).   11. *When on active service breaking into a house in search of plunder. Maximum punishment—Death.*

Sec. 6 (1*h*).   12. *When on active service by discharging firearms intentionally occasioning false alarms on the march. Maximum punishment—Death.*
Note.—If there is a doubt as to whether the discharge of the rifle was intentional, a charge similar to No. 14 can be added as an alternative in the same charge sheet.

Sec. 6 (1*k*).   13. *When a soldier acting as sentinel on active service sleeping on his post. Maximum punishment—Death.*

Sec. 6 (2*a*).   14. *By discharging firearms negligently occasioning false alarms in camp. Maximum punishment—Cashiering or Imprisonment.*

Sec. 7 (1).   15. *The accused, No.   , Serjeant   , Battalion,   Regi-
First charge ment, a soldier of the Regular forces, is charged with—
Sec. 7 (2*b*).   *Causing a mutiny in forces belonging to His Majesty's Regular forces. Maxi-
Second mum punishment—Death.
charge.   Endeavouring to persuade persons in His Majesty's Regular forces to join in a mutiny. Maximum punishment—Death.*

(Joint Trial.)

Sec. 7 (3*a*).   16. *The accused persons, No.   , Private,   ,   Battalion,
Regiment, and No.   , Private   ,   Battalion,
Regiment, soldiers of the Regular forces, are charged with—
†Joining in a mutiny in forces belonging to His Majesty's Regular forces. Maximum punishment—Death.*

Sec. 7 (4).   17. *The accused, Bombardier   Royal
Artillery, a soldier of the Regular forces, is charged with—
After coming to the knowledge of an intended mutiny in forces belonging to His Majesty's Regular forces, failing to inform without delay his commanding officer of the same. Maximum punishment—Death.*

Sec. 8 (1).   18. *The accused, No.   , Private   ,   Battalion,
Regiment, a soldier of the Regular forces, is charged with—
Striking his superior officer, being in the execution of his office. Maximum punishment—Death.*

Sec. 8 (2*a*).   19. *When on active service offering violence to his superior officer. Maximum punishment—Penal Servitude.*

Sec. 8 (2*b*)   20. *When on active service using threatening language to his superior officer. Maximum punishment—Penal Servitude.*

Sec. 9 (1).   21. *Disobeying in such a manner as to show a wilful defiance of authority, a lawful command given personally by his superior officer, in the execution of his office. Maximum punishment—Death.*

* Equally applicable in peace and war.
† Equally applicable in the case of a single person.

Sec. 9 (2).   22. *When on active service, disobeying a lawful command given by his superior officer.* *Maximum punishment—Penal Servitude.*

Sec. 10 (1).   23. *The accused, Captain,   ,   Battalion,   Regiment, an officer of the Regular forces, is charged with—
When concerned in a quarrel, refusing to obey an officer who ordered him into arrest. *Maximum punishment—Cashiering.*

Sec. 10 (2).   24. *The accused, No.   , Corporal   ,   Dragoons, a soldier of the Regular forces, is charged with—
Striking a person in whose custody he was placed. *Maximum punishment— Imprisonment.* (Officer cashiering.)

Sec. 12 (1a).   25. The accused, No.   , Private   , ,   Battalion, Regiment, a soldier of the Regular forces, is charged with—
When on active service, deserting His Majesty's service.—Maximum punishment—Death.

Sec. 12 (1a).   26. *When on active service, attempting to desert His Majesty's service. Maximum punishment—Death.*

Note.—In the two preceding charges, if the soldier was under orders for active service, the charge will be the same, with the substitution of " under orders for active service " for " on active service."

Sec. 12 (1a).   27. *When under orders for active service, deserting His Majesty's service. Maximum punishment—Death.*

Sec. 13.   28. *Fraudulent enlistment. Maximum punishment—First offence, Imprisonment; second or subsequent offence, Penal Servitude.*

Sec. 14 (1).   29. *Assisting a person subject to military law to desert His Majesty's service. Maximum punishment—Imprisonment.*

Sec. 16.   30. *The accused, Lieutenant   ,   Regiment, an officer of the Regular forces, is charged with—
Behaving in a scandalous manner unbecoming the character of an officer and a gentleman. Punishment—Cashiering.

Sec. 17.   31. *The accused, Captain   ,   Battalion,   Regiment, an officer of the Regular forces, is charged with—
When charged with the care of public money, embezzling the same. Maximum punishment—Penal Servitude.
Note.—The particulars should state the acts which are alleged to have been committed by the accused and to amount to embezzlement.

Sec. 17.   32. *The accused, Quartermaster   , Royal Army Medical Corps, an officer of the Regular forces, is charged with—
When charged with the care of public goods, fraudulently misapplying the same. Maximum punishment—Penal Servitude.

----

* Equally applicable in peace and war.

Sec. 18 (2*a*).   33. *Wilfully maiming himself with intent thereby to render himsel unfit for service. Maximum punishment—Imprisonment.*

Sec. 19.   34. The accused, No.   , Private   , Battalion,
Regiment, a soldier of the Regular forces, is charged with—
*When on active service, drunkenness. Maximum punishment—Imprison-
ment. (Officer cashiering.)*
Note.—If a soldier was on special duty, *e.g.*, **parade** or piquet, that special
duty should be stated, or if he were on the line **of** march the fact should
likewise be stated.

Sec. 21.   35. *When on active service, committing the offence of murder. Maximum
punishment—Death.*

Each charge continues as in the following example (*see* No. 19 above):—,
" in that he, at   , on   "
and then follow the particulars, for instance, " struck with his fist in the face
Serjeant X, who was at the time in command of an escort taking accused
persons to the guard room." (*See also* above, first charge.)

Note.—In order to enable a court-martial to award field punishment it is
essential to allege " when on active service."

4. FIELD PUNISHMENT.

Two sorts—No. 1 and No. 2.

No. 1.—The offender may, unless the court-martial or C.O. otherwise
directs—
    (*a*) Be kept in irons.
    (*b*) Be attached by straps, irons or ropes for not more than 2 hours in
        1 day to a fixed object. Must not be attached for more than 3 out
        of 4 consecutive days or for more than 21 days in all.
    (*c*) Be made to labour as if he were undergoing imprisonment with hard
        labour.

No. 2. Same as No. 1, except he may not be treated as above in (*b*).
Field punishment is to be carried out regimentally when the unit is actually
on the move; when the unit is halted it is carried out under a P.M., or an
assistant P.M.
When the unit is on the move an offender sentenced to field punishment
No. 1 is exempt from the operation of (*b*), but all offenders sentenced to
field punishment are to march with their units, carry their arms and accoutrements, perform all their military duties as well as extra fatigue duties, and
be treated as defaulters.
Field punishment for a period not exceeding 3 months may be awarded
by a court-martial for any offence committed on active service. It may
also under the same conditions be awarded by a C.O. to a soldier not being
a N.C.O. for a period not exceeding 28 days.

5. FORMS OF CHARGES FOR COURTS-MARTIAL UNDER THE I.A.A. WHICH
MAY OCCUR ON ACTIVE SERVICE ARE SHOWN BELOW.

(Many of these are equally Applicable in Peace.)

Commencement of Charge Sheet.

The accused (*number*), *rank*, *name*, *corps*, is charged with—

or,

The accused (*name*), being a person subject to Indian military law under
the provisions of Section 2 (1) (*c*) of the Indian Army Act, is charged with—

or,

The accused (*name*) being a person subject to Indian Military Law as an officer (*or warrant officer, or non-commissioned officer*), under the provisions of Section 2 (1) (*c*) and Section 3 (1) of the Indian Army Act, is charged with—

Statement of Offence and Particulars.

Sec. 25 (*b*).   1. In presence of an enemy shamefully casting away his arms, in that he at   , on   , when on outlying piquet and attacked by the enemy, shamefully cast away his rifle, left his piquet and ran away.   Maximum punishment—Death.

Sec. 25 (*b*).   2. *In presence of an enemy misbehaving in such manner as to show cowardice. Maximum punishment—Death.*

Sec. 25 (*c*).   3. *Communicating intelligence to the enemy. Maximum punishment—Death.*

Sec. 25 (*f*).   4. *In time of war intentionally occasioning a false alarm in camp. Maximum punishment—Death.*

Sec. 25 (*g*).   5. *When a sentry in time of war sleeping upon his post. Maximum punishment—Death.*

Sec. 25 (*h*).   6. *In time of action leaving his commanding officer to go in search of plunder. Maximum punishment—Death.*

Sec. 25 (*i*).   7. *In time of war quitting his guard without leave.   Maximum punishment—Death.*

Note.—For " guard " any of the words " piquet," " party " or " patrol " may be substituted.

Sec. 25 (*j*).   8. *In time of war using criminal force to a person bringing provisions to the camp of His Majesty's forces. Maximum punishment—Death.*

Sec. 25 (*j*).   9. *In time of war forcing a safeguard. Maximum punishment—Death.*

Sec. 26 (*a*).   10. *Forcing a sentry. Maximum punishment—14 years R.I.*

Sec. 26 (*c*).   11. *When on guard plundering property placed under charge of his guard. Maximum punishment—14 years R.I.*

Sec. 27 (*a*).   12. *Joining in a mutiny. Maximum punishment—Death.*

Sec. 27 (*d*).   13. *Using criminal force to his superior officer, knowing him to be such. Maximum punishment—Death.*

Sec. 27 (*d*).   14. *Attempting to use criminal force to his superior officer, knowing him to be such. Maximum punishment—Death.*

Sec. 27 (*d*).   15. *Committing an assault on his superior officer, knowing him to be such. Maximum punishment—Death.*

Note.—An assault is a gesture or preparation intended to cause, or known to be likely to cause, an apprehension that the person making it is about to use criminal force.

Sec. 27 (*e*).   16. *Disobeying the lawful command of his superior officer. Maximum punishment—Death.*

Sec. 28 (*a*).   17. *Being grossly insubordinate to his superior officer in the execution of his office. Maximum punishment—14 years R.I.*

Sec. 28 (*b*).   18. *Refusing to assist in the making of a military work in the field. Maximum punishment—14 years R.I.*

Sec. 28 (*c*).   19. *Impeding a provost-marshal. Maximum punishment—14 years R.I.*

Sec. 29   20. *Deserting the service. Maximum punishment—Death.*

Sec. 29,   21. *Attempting to desert the service. Maximum punishment—Death.*

Sec. 30.

22. *Absenting himself without leave. Maximum punishment—14 years R.I.*

Sec. 31 (*a*).

23. *Dishonestly misappropriating military stores, the property of Government, entrusted to him. Maximum punishment—14 years R.I.*

Sec. 31 (*d*).

24. *Committing theft in respect of the property of Government. Maximum punishment—14 years R.I.*

Sec. 31 (*d*).

25. *Committing theft in respect of the property of a person subject to military law. Maximum punishment—14 years R.I.*

Sec. 32.

26. *Intoxication. Maximum punishment—14 years R.I.*

Note.—If the accused was on duty this circumstance and the nature of the duty, should be stated in the particulars of the charge.

Sec. 33.

27. *Negligently suffering to escape an enemy placed under his charge. Maximum punishment—Death.*

Sec. 39 (*i*).

28. *An act prejudicial to good order and military discipline. Maximum punishment—14 years R.I.*

Sec. 41.

29. *In a place beyond British India committing a civil offence, that is to say (here specify the offence). Maximum punishment—as in I.A.A., Section 41.*

Sec. 42.

30. *Committing murder against a person subject to military law. Punishment—Death or transportation for life.*

Note.—One or other of these punishments is obligatory on a conviction for murder. Nothing less can be awarded.

46. PROVOST-MARSHAL AND MILITARY POLICE.

1. The provost-marshal, under instructions from the A.G., will generally supervise the police duties of the army in the field, and will ensure that the military police are distributed to the best advantage. A.P.Ms. receive their instructions from an officer of the A.G.'s branch of the staff of the force to which they are attached. Each detachment of M.P. is under the immediate orders of the A.P.M. of the division, &c., to which it is attached.

2. The military police are responsible for arresting all persons found without passes, plundering, making unlawful requisitions, or committing offences of any kind ; for collecting stragglers and conducting them to the nearest troops, and for guarding against spies.

3. In case of emergency they may call on any troops to assist them by supplying guards, sentries, or patrols, as may be necessary.
All persons belonging to, or employed by, the army are required to give them every assistance.

4. In India, on active service, the provost-marshal can punish corporally, then and there, any person below the rank of N.C.O. who, in his view, or that of any of his assistants, commits any breach of good order and military discipline. Punishment not to exceed 30 lashes (or such lower amount as O.C. troops may determine) and to be inflicted with the regulation cat.

47. INTERNATIONAL LAW.

SUMMARY OF THE GENEVA CONVENTIONS, DECLARATION OF ST. PETERS-
BURG AND THE HAGUE CONVENTION.

1. SUMMARY OF THE GENEVA CONVENTION OF 22ND AUGUST, 1864.
(This is still in force between such of the parties as signed it but who have
not likewise ratified the Convention of 1906.)

(1) Military ambulances and military hospitals must be protected and
respected, provided there are any sick and wounded therein, and are not
held by a military force (Article I).   The material of a military hospital
is liable to capture, but that of an ambulance is not (Article IV).

(2) The personnel of military ambulances and military hospitals, com-
prising the staff for superintendence, medical service, administration, transport of wounded, as well as chaplains, are not liable to capture while actually
employed in them and so long as there remain any wounded to bring in and
succour (Article II).

(3) The personnel mentioned in the preceding Article are at liberty to
continue their duties or to withdraw in order to rejoin the corps to which
they belong if their ambulance or hospital is captured.   When they cease
their duties they must be delivered to their outposts (Article III).   They are
only entitled to carry away articles which are their own private property
(Article IV).

(4) Inhabitants who assist wounded must be left free; if they shelter
and take care of wounded in their houses they must be exempted from
billeting and part of war contributions.   They must be informed of these
privileges by the generals of the belligerents.

(5) Sick and wounded soldiers must be cared for regardless of their
nationality.   Wounded may be restored after an action by mutual consent.
Wounded prisoners who are recognized after their wounds are healed to be
incapable of further service must be sent back to their country; others may
be sent back if they pledge themselves not to bear arms again in the war
then being waged (Article VI).

(6) Convoys of evacuation with the personnel in charge of them must not
be captured.

(7) The distinctive flag for hospitals, ambulance and convoys of evacuation is the Red Cross on a white ground.   The national flag (of the belligerent) must be flown with it.   The personnel may wear an arm badge with
the same device.   This badge can only be issued by the military authorities.
(It should have a number and an official stamp.)

(8) Commanders-in-Chief must arrange for the execution of details of
the Convention in accordance with the instructions of their Governments
and in conformity with the general principles of the Convention.

Note.—Voluntary aid societies of belligerents and neutrals are not referred
to in the Convention and therefore have no rights under it.   The medical
assistance they supply must, therefore, be incorporated into the army medical
services namely, the military ambulances and military hospitals with which
the Convention alone deals.

The Convention is somewhat narrow in its terms, but it should always
be interpreted liberally.

The Convention has been acceded to by all the civilized Powers except
one or two of the South American Republics.

The French text of the Conventions is the authoritative one, and should
be referred to in all cases of dispute.

2. SUMMARY OF THE GENEVA CONVENTION OF 6TH JULY, 1906.
(This Convention has now been ratified by all the more important nations
except France.)

I.—The Wounded and Sick.

(1) *Officers, soldiers and other persons officially attached to armies must
be taken care of when wounded or sick without distinction of nationality;

---

* The paragraphs are numbered to correspond with the Articles of the
Convention.

but if a belligerent is compelled to abandon them he must, as far as military exigencies permit, leave some medical staff, with material, to take care of them.

(2) Wounded and sick, if captured, are prisoners of war; but belligerents are free to exchange or restore them, or to hand them over to a neutral State, with its consent for internment.

(3) After an action, the occupant of the field must have search made for the wounded, and protect wounded and dead from pillage and maltreatment. The dead must be carefully examined before burial or cremation.

(4) Each belligerent must send, as early as possible, to the enemy the military identification marks or tokens found on the dead, and nominal rolls of wounded or sick prisoners, also information as to any subsequent casualties among the prisoners. Articles of personal use, valuables, letters, &c., found on the battlefield, or belonging to wounded or sick who die in hospital, must be collected and forwarded to the authorities of the country for transmission to their relatives.

(5) Inhabitants may be appealed to to assist, under direction in collecting and caring for the wounded and sick. Those who respond may be granted special protection and certain immunities. (This Article is not obligatory and does not prevent the requisition of any labour that is necessary.)

II.—Medical Units and Establishments.

(6) Mobile military units and the fixed establishments of the medical service must be respected and protected.

(7) They lose this privilege if made use of to commit acts harmful to the enemy.

(8) The following are not reckoned harmful :—(a) That personnel is armed and uses arms for defence of themselves or of sick and wounded; (b) That in default of armed orderlies the unit or establishment is guarded by a piquet or sentries furnished with an authority in due form; (c) That the weapons and ammunition of the wounded are found in the medical formation.

III.—Personnel.

(9) Personnel engaged exclusively in collection, transport and treatment of wounded and sick, in the administration of medical formations, the guard mentioned in (8) (b) and all military chaplains must be respected and protected; they must not be treated as prisoners of war.

(10) Personnel of voluntary aid societies duly recognized and authorized by their Government, who are employed in military medical formations and are subject to military law, have the privileges mentioned in (9).

(11) A recognized society of a neutral country, before it can assist a belligerent with its personnel and units, must first obtain the consent of its own Government and the authorization of the belligerent, who, before making use of it, must notify his adversary.

(12) Persons designated in (9), (10) and (11), if they fall into enemy's hands, must continue their duties under his direction; when no longer indispensable they must be sent back to their army or their country; but at such times and by such route as their captors may think fit. They must be allowed to take with them their private instruments, arms, horses and effects.

(13) Persons mentioned in (9), while in the hands of enemy, must be given the same pay and allowances as persons of similar rank in his army.

IV.—Material.

(14) Mobile medical units (i.e., those which are intended to accompany an army into the field, e.g., field ambulances, hospital trains, hospital barges, &c.), retain their material, including teams, irrespectively of the means of transport and drivers employed. The material must be returned as laid down in (12) for the personnel, and so far as possible at the same time. If necessary, however, the material may be used for treatment of wounded and sick.

(15) In contradistinction the buildings and material of fixed establishments can be captured, but must be used for the wounded and sick as long as necessary; in cases, however, of urgent military necessity, the patients may be removed provided arrangements are made for them elsewhere.

(B 11925) T

(16) The property of the societies mentioned in (10) and (11) is considered private property, liable to requisition, but not to confiscation (*see*, however, (14) for mobile units).

V.—*Convoys of Evacuation.*

(17) Convoys of evacuation must be treated as mobile units in (14), except (*a*) an intercepted convoy may be broken up in case of necessity, provided the wounded and sick are taken charge of ; (*b*) if this is done the military personnel detailed for transport or guard, and furnished with authority in due form, must be sent back as in (12). Boats and railway trains specially fitted up for evacuations, as well as army medical material used for fitting up ordinary vehicles, trains and boats, must be restored as in (14). Military vehicles not belonging to the medical service may be captured with their teams. Any civilian personnel and transport requisitioned are subject to further requisition, but cannot be confiscated.

VI.—*Distinctive Emblem.*

(18) The Red Cross, on a white ground, is the sign and distinctive emblem of the army medical service.
(19) It will be shown on the flags, armlets and all material of the medical service, with permission of the military authorities.
(20) The personnel protected under (9), except the guard, (10) and (11), must wear the armlet, stamped by the military authorities, fixed to the left arm. Persons attached to the army medical service who have no military uniform must be provided with an identity certificate.
(21) The Red Cross flag must not be hoisted except over military medical formations, and then only with consent of the military authorities. It must be accompanied by the national flag of the belligerent, except when the formation is in the hands of the enemy.
(22) The units of neutral countries mentioned in (11) are included under (21).
(23) The Red Cross must not at any time be used except to protect the formations, personnel and material mentioned in the Convention.
(24) The Convention is only of force between signatories.
(25) Commanders-in-Chief must arrange the details for carrying out the Convention, as well as cases not provided for in the general spirit of the Convention.
(26) Troops must be instructed in, and civil population informed of, the provisions of the Convention.

3. Declaration of St. Petersburg, 1868.

The Contracting Parties bound themselves not to employ in war any projectile of a weight below 400 grammes (14 ozs.) which is either explosive or charged with fulminating or inflammable substances.
Signatory Powers :—Austria-Hungary, Belgium, Brazil, Denmark, France, Germany, Great Britain, Greece, Italy, Netherlands, Norway, Persia, Portugal, Russia, Sweden, Switzerland, Turkey.

4. Summary of the Regulations Respecting the Laws and Customs of War on Land.

Final Act of the Second Peace Conference Held at The Hague in 1907.

(This Convention has been ratified or acceded to by the States enumerated on page 221, with the exception of China.)
These Regulations are intended as General Rules of Conduct, so far as military necessities permit ; they have not the force of an International Convention.
The paragraphs are numbered to correspond with the Articles of the Regulations.

Section I.—Belligerents.

I.—*The Status of Belligerents.*

(1) Laws, rights and duties of war apply not only to the army but also to militia and volunteer corps, provided they—

(a) Are commanded by a person responsible for his subordinates.
(b) Have a fixed distinctive sign recognizable at a distance.
(c) Carry arms openly.
(d) Conduct operations in accordance with the laws and customs of war.

(2) Inhabitants of a territory not under occupation, who, on the enemy's approach, spontaneously take up arms without having time to organize in accordance with (1), will be regarded as belligerents if they carry arms openly and respect the laws and customs of war.

(3) Both combatants and non-combatants of an army have the right to be treated as prisoners of war.

II.—*Prisoners of War.*

(4) Prisoners of war belong to the Government, not to individuals ; they must be humanely treated ; they retain their personal belongings except arms, horses and military papers.

(5) They may be interned in any locality within fixed limits, but can only be confined as an indispensable measure of safety.

(6) The State may employ the labour of prisoners of war. other than officers, according to their rank and capacity, and prisoners may be authorized to work for the public service, private persons, or on their own account, but the tasks must have nothing to do with military operations. They must be paid for their work ; if it is done for the State at the rates paid to soldiers ; otherwise at rates settled in agreement with the military authorities. Pay must be used to improve their position ; the balance, after deducting cost of maintenance, will be paid on release.

(7) They must be given the same food, quarters and clothing as the captor's troops.

(8) They are subject to the military laws, &c., of the captor. Escaped prisoners who are retaken before rejoining their own army or before leaving the territory occupied by their captors are liable to punishment, but not otherwise.

(9) They must declare, if questioned, their true names and rank on pain of loss of privileges of their class.

(10) They may be released on parole if the laws of their country authorize it ; they are bound on honour to observe their parole, and their Government must not require or accept service incompatible with it.

(11) They cannot be made to accept parole, nor can they demand it.

(12) Those liberated on parole, who are re-captured in arms, forfeit their rights to be treated as prisoners of war and can be tried for the offence.

(13) Civilian followers, including contractors and correspondents, in possesion of a certificate from their military authorities, have the right to be treated as prisoners of war, if captured and detained.

(14) A bureau is to be formed in each belligerent State to collect and furnish information with regard to prisoners of war. It will also receive, collect and transmit to those concerned, all objects of personal use, valuables, letters, &c., found on battlefields or left by prisoners who die.

(15) Relief societies for prisoners, if legally constituted for charitable purposes, will, within bounds of military requirements, be given facilities. Their delegates, if furnished with a personal permit and on giving a written engagement to comply with all regulations, may be admitted to internment and halting places of repatriated prisoners.

(16) The Information Bureau has the privilege of free postage. Gifts, letters, &c., for prisoners, are to be admitted free of postage duty and carriage on Government railways.

(17) Officers taken prisoners will receive the same rate of pay as officers of corresponding rank in the country where they are detained ; the amount is refunded by their own Government.

(18) Prisoners are to be allowed religious freedom and to attend church, provided they comply with regulations for order and police issued by the military authorities.

(19) Wills of prisoners, death certificates and burials will be dealt with as in case of soldiers of the captor, due regard being paid to grade and rank.
(20) Prisoners are to be repatriated as soon as possible after peace.

III.—*Sick and Wounded.*

(21) Obligations are governed by the Geneva Convention.

SECTION II.—HOSTILITIES.

I.—*Means of Injuring the Enemy.*

(22) The right to adopt means of injuring the enemy is not unlimited.
(23) It is forbidden (a) to employ poison or poisoned arms ; (b) to kill or wound treacherously ; (c) to kill or wound an enemy who has surrendered ; (d) to declare no quarter will be given ; (e) to employ arms, &c., of a nature to cause unnecessary suffering ; (f) to make improper use of a flag of truce, national flag, the enemy's military insignia and uniform, and the Red Cross badge and flag ; (g) to destroy or seize enemy's property, unless imperatively demanded by the necessities of war ; (h) to declare abolished, suspended, or inadmissible, the right of subjects of enemy to institute legal proceedings ; also to compel subjects of the enemy to take part against their own country.
(24) Ruses of war and necessary methods for obtaining information are allowed.
(25) Attack or bombardment of undefended localities is forbidden.
(26) Notice of bombardment, except in case of assault, must, if possible, be given.
(27) In sieges and bombardments, buildings devoted to religion, art, science and charity, historic monuments, permanent and temporary hospitals, provided they are not at the same time used for military purposes, must be spared as far as possible. Such places should be marked by a visible sign and notified to the enemy beforehand.*
(28) Pillage of a captured town or place is prohibited.

II.—*Spies.*

(29) An individual can only be considered a spy if, acting clandestinely, or on false pretences, he obtains or seeks to obtain information in the zone of operations of a belligerent, with the intention of communicating it to the hostile party. Soldiers not in disguise, soldiers or civilians carrying despatches openly, and *balloonists* with despatches or maintaining communication between parts of an army or territory, are not spies.
(30) A spy taken in the act cannot be punished without trial.
(31) A spy who has rejoined his army, but is subsequently captured, incurs no responsibility for previous acts of espionage.

III.—*Flags of Truce.*

(32) A bearer of a flag of truce must be properly authorized and must carry a white flag. He and the trumpeter or drummer, flag-bearer and interpreter are inviolable.
(33) A commander is not obliged to receive a flag of truce. He may take all steps necessary to prevent the envoy getting information and detain him temporarily in case of abuse of his privileges.
(34) The envoy loses his inviolability if it is proved, beyond a doubt, that he has provoked or committed treachery.

IV.—*Capitulations.*

(35) Capitulations must be in accordance with rules of military honour and must be scrupulously observed.

---

* At present no special sign is laid down for universal use.

V.—*Armistices.*

(36) Armistices are mutual agreements for the suspension of hostilities. If duration is not fixed operations can be resumed at any time, provided the warning mentioned in the terms is given.

(37) They may be local or general. The former suspends hostilities only in a fixed zone, the latter the entire military operations of the belligerent States.

(38) They must be notified officially, and in good time, to authorities and troops. Hostilities are suspended after notification or at a fixed time.

(39) It should be precisely laid down in them what communication may be held in the theatre of war between the belligerents and the civil population and between the peoples of the belligerent States.

(40) Serious violation of an armistice gives the other party the right to denounce it and even, in case of urgency, to recommence hostilities immediately.

(41) Violations by individuals only confer right to demand punishment and indemnity.

SECTION III.—MILITARY AUTHORITY OVER HOSTILE TERRITORY.

(42) Territory is occupied when actually under the authority of the hostile army ; such authority must be established and operative.

(43) The occupant must as far as possible insure public order and safety, and respect, unless absolutely prevented, the laws of the country.

(44) *Compulsion of population of occupied territory to furnish information about the other belligerent's army or means of defence is prohibited.

(45) Pressure on population to take oath of allegiance is prohibited.

(46) Family honours, rights, religion, lives and liberty and private property, must be respected. The last must not be confiscated.

(47) Pillage is expressly prohibited.

(48) Taxes, &c., if collected, should be, as far as possible, in accordance with rules and assessment in force ; the occupant must then defray expenses of administration.

(49) If other money taxes are levied they can only be used for military necessities or the administration of the territory in question.

(50) No general penalty can be inflicted on the population for acts of individuals for which it is not collectively responsible.

(51) No contribution can be collected except on the written order of a general in command. Contributions should be made in accordance with the rules for the assessment of taxes in force at the time. Receipts must be given.

(52) Requisitions can only be demanded for military needs ; they must be proportionate to resources of the country and not involve the inhabitants taking part in military operations against their own country. They can only be demanded on the authority of the commander in the occupied locality. Contributions in kind must be paid for or receipts given.

(53) The occupant can only take possession of State property, including cash, which may be used for military operations. Property of companies and private persons, such as railways, telegraphs, ships, arms and war material may be used, but must be restored at peace and indemnities paid.

(54) Submarine cables connecting an occupied territory with a neutral territory are not to be seized or destroyed except when absolutely necessary, and must be restored and indemnities paid at the conclusion of peace.

(55) The captor is only the administrator, and has only the right to use public buildings, real property, forests and agricultural works belonging to the hostile State. He must not sell or dispose of them.

(56) The property of local authorities, of religious, charitable and educational institutions, of institutions of art and science, even when State property, must be treated as private property. Seizure, destruction or intentional damage to them or to historical monuments is prohibited.

---

*Reserved by Germany, Austria-Hungary, Japan, Montenegro and Russia.

THE RIGHTS AND DUTIES OF NEUTRAL POWERS AND PERSONS IN WAR

I.

RIGHTS AND DUTIES OF NEUTRAL POWERS.

(1) The territory of neutral Powers is inviolable.

(2) Belligerents are forbidden to move troops or convoys across neutral territory.

(3) Belligerents are forbidden to erect on neutral territory means of communication with forces on land or sea ; or to use any installation established by them for purely military purposes on neutral territory before the war and not previously opened for public messages.

(4) Corps of combatants must not be formed, nor recruiting agencies opened, on neutral territory.

(5) A neutral Power must not allow (2), (3), (4) to occur on its territory.

(6) Responsibility of a neutral Power is not involved by persons crossing the frontier individually to offer their services to one of the belligerents.

(7) A neutral Power is not bound to prevent the export or transit of arms, munitions of war, or anything of use to an army or fleet.

(8) A neutral Power is not bound to forbid or restrict the use on behalf of belligerents of telegraph or telephone cables or wireless telegraphy apparatus belonging to it or to companies or to private individuals.

(9) A neutral Power must apply restrictions in (7) and (8) impartially to the belligerents ; and is responsible that companies or private owners observe this obligation.

(10) The resistance of attempts to violate its neutrality offered by a neutral Power cannot be regarded as a hostile act.

II.

INTERNMENT OF BELLIGERENTS AND CARE OF THE WOUNDED IN NEUTRAL TERRITORY.

(11) Belligerent troops which enter a neutral State must be interned, as far as possible, at a distance from the theatre of war, in camps, fortresses, or other localities.   The neutral State decides whether officers may be admitted to remain in its territory on parole.

(12) The neutral Power shall, failing a special agreement, supply the interned with food, clothing and relief, the expense being refunded at the end of the war.

(13) The neutral Power receiving escaped prisoners of war shall leave them at liberty ; if it allows them to remain in its territory it may assign them a place of residence.   This also applies to prisoners of war brought by troops taking refuge in neutral territory.

(14) The neutral Power may permit wounded or sick to pass through its territory, provided the trains bringing them carry neither combatants nor war material ; it must take due measures of precaution.   Any sick and wounded prisoners brought into the neutral State, also any sick and wounded who are left instead of being passed through, must be detained, so as to insure their not again becoming belligerents.

(15) The Geneva Convention applies to sick and wounded interned in neutral territory.

III.

NEUTRAL PERSONS.

†(16) Subjects or citizens of a State which is not taking part in the war are deemed neutrals.

†(17) A neutral cannot claim the benefit of his neutrality if he commits hostile acts against a belligerent, or if he commits acts in favour of a belligerent ; in such a case he must not be more severely treated than a subject or citizen of the other belligerent State.

†(18) The furnishing of supplies, or making loans, provided that the persons so doing neither lives in the territory of the other party nor in the

---

* This Convention has been ratified or acceded to by the same States as those mentioned on page 222, with the exception of Great Britain.

† Reserved by Great Britain.

territory occupied by it, and that the supplies do not come from such territory, or services rendered in matters of police or civil administration, must not be considered as acts committed in favour of one belligerent within the meaning of (17).

IV.

RAILWAY MATERIAL.

(19) Except when absolutely necessary a belligerent must not requisition or use railway material coming from the territory of neutral Powers, whether the property of the said Powers, companies, or private persons, and when used it must be returned as soon as possible to the country of origin.

Likewise, a neutral Power may retain and utilize to a corresponding extent railway material coming from the territory of the belligerent Power.

On either side compensation will be paid.

BOMBARDMENT BY NAVAL FORCES.

(Under the reservations shown in the footnotes this Convention was signed by the Powers enumerated on p. 234.)

I.

BOMBARDMENT OF UNDEFENDED PORTS, TOWNS, VILLAGES, DWELLINGS OR BUILDINGS.

*(1) The bombardment by naval forces of undefended ports, towns, villages, dwellings, or buildings is forbidden : a place may not be bombarded solely on the ground that automatic submarine contact mines are anchored off the harbour.

(2) Military works, military or naval establishments, depôts of arms or war material, workshops or plant which could be utilized by the hostile fleet, or army, and ships of war in the harbour are not included in this prohibition. The commander of a naval force may destroy them with artillery after a summons followed by a reasonable interval, if all other means are impossible, and when the local authorities have not themselves destroyed them within the time fixed, and no responsibility is then incurred by the commander for any unavoidable damage. If for military reasons immediate action is necessary, the prohibition to bombard the undefended town holds good, and the commander will take all due measures in order that the town may suffer as little harm as possible.

(3) After due notice the bombardment of undefended ports, towns, &c., may be commenced, if the local authorities, on a formal summons being made to them, decline to comply with requisitions for provisions or supplies necessary for the naval force in question. Such requisitions will be proportional to the resources of the place and will be demanded in the name of the commander of the said naval force. When not paid for in ready money receipts will be given.

(4) The bombardment of undefended ports, &c., on account of failure to pay money contributions is forbidden.

II.

GENERAL PROVISIONS.

(5) In bombardments by naval forces the commander will take all necessary steps to spare buildings dedicated to public worship, art, science, or charitable purposes, historic monuments, hospitals and places where the sick or wounded are collected, provided that they are not used at that time for military purposes. Such buildings will be indicated by large stiff rectangular panels divided diagonally into two painted triangular portions, the upper portion black, the lower portion white.

(6) Unless military exigencies render it impossible the commander of a naval attacking force will warn the authorities before commencing the bombardment.

---

* The latter clause of this Article was reserved by France, Great Britain, Germany and Japan.

The following Powers have ratified or acceded to this Convention :—

Austria-Hungary.	Mexico.
Belgium.	Netherlands.
Bolivia.	Nicaragua.
China.	Norway.
Cuba.	Panama.
Denmark.	Portugal.
France.	Rumania.
Germany.	Russia.
Great Britain.	Salvador.
Guatemala.	Siam.
Hayti.	Sweden.
Japan.	Switzerland.
Luxemburg.	United States.

Three declarations :—
1. Prohibits until the conclusion of the next Peace Conference the discharge of projectiles and explosives from balloons or by other new methods of a similar nature.
2. Renounces the use of projectiles, sole object of which is the diffusion of asphyxiating or harmful gases.
3. Renounces the use of bullets which expand or flatten easily in the human body.

1 has been ratified or acceded to by Belgium, Bolivia, China, Great Britain, Hayti. Luxemburg, Netherlands, Nicaragua, Norway, Panama, Portugal, Salvador and the United States.

The representatives of France, Germany, Italy, Japan, Russia and Spain did not sign the Declaration, nor have they since acceded to it.

2 and 3 have been signed by practically all the Powers.

CHAPTER IX.

48. THE ARMY IN INDIA.

1. The Governor General in Council is the supreme head of the Army in India, and under him the business of the Army is managed by the Army Department of the Government of India.

2. The Commander-in-Chief in India is the Member of Council in charge of the Army Department. The organization of Army Administration is shown on the following diagrams :—

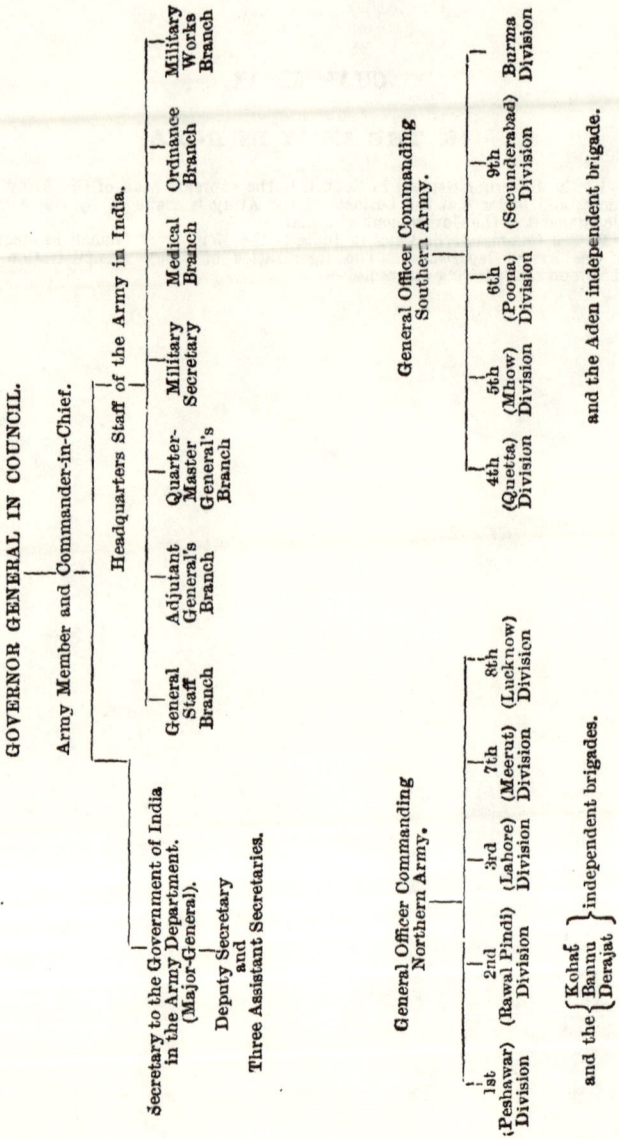

GOVERNOR GENERAL IN COUNCIL.

Army Member and Commander-in-Chief.

Headquarters Staff of the Army in India.

General Staff Branch — Adjutant General's Branch — Quarter-Master General's Branch — Military Secretary — Medical Branch — Ordnance Branch — Military Works Branch

Secretary to the Government of India in the Army Department. (Major-General).
Deputy Secretary and Three Assistant Secretaries.

General Officer Commanding Northern Army.

1st (Peshawar) Division — 2nd (Rawal Pindi) Division — 3rd (Lahore) Division — 7th (Meerut) Division — 8th (Lucknow) Division — and the { Kohat, Bannu, Derajat } independent brigades.

General Officer Commanding Southern Army.

4th (Quetta) Division — 5th (Mhow) Division — 6th (Poona) Division — 9th (Secunderabad) Division — Burma Division — and the Aden independent brigade.

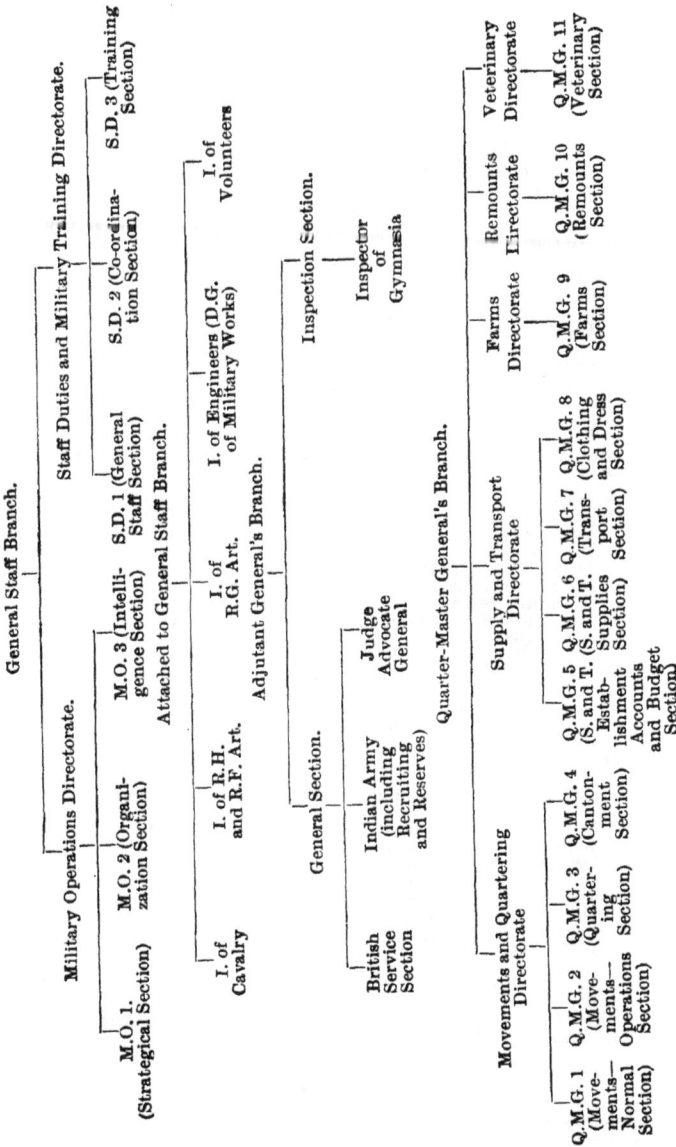

General Staff Branch.

- Military Operations Directorate.
- Staff Duties and Military Training Directorate.
  - S.D. 3 (Training Section)
  - S.D. 2 (Co-ordination Section)
  - S.D. 1 (General Staff Section)
- M.O. 3 (Intelligence Section)
- M.O. 2 (Organization Section)
- M.O. 1. (Strategical Section)
- I. of Cavalry
- I. of R.H. and R.F. Art.
- I. of R.G. Art.

Attached to General Staff Branch.

- I. of Engineers (D.G. of Military Works)
- I. of Volunteers
- Inspection Section.
- Inspector of Gymnasia

Adjutant General's Branch.

- General Section.
- British Service Section
- Indian Army (including Recruiting and Reserves)
- Judge Advocate General

Quarter-Master General's Branch.

- Movements and Quartering Directorate
  - Q.M.G. 1 (Movements—Normal Section)
  - Q.M.G. 2 (Movements—Operations Section)
  - Q.M.G. 3 (Quartering Section)
  - Q.M.G. 4 (Cantonment Section)
- Supply and Transport Directorate
  - Q.M.G. 5 (S. and T. Establishment Accounts and Budget Section)
  - Q.M.G. 6 (S. and T. Supplies Section)
  - Q.M.G. 7 (Transport Section)
  - Q.M.G. 8 (Clothing and Dress Section)
- Farms Directorate
  - Q.M.G. 9 (Farms Section)
- Remounts Directorate
  - Q.M.G. 10 (Remounts Section)
- Veterinary Directorate
  - Q.M.G. 11 (Veterinary Section)

3. The Army in India consists of :—

	British.	Native.
Cavalry regiments	9	39½
Infantry battalions	52	138†
R.H.A. batteries	11	—
R.F.A. batteries	45	—
Mountain batteries	8	12
Heavy batteries	6	—
Companies, R.G.A.	21	1*
„ R.E.	1	—
Field companies, sappers and miners	—	19‡

War establishments in India are given in Chapter I.

4. Men are enlisted in the Indian army for "General Service." The period of engagement is for 3 years, which may be extended to 32 years.

5. Transport in India consists of "Organized" and "Unorganized" transport. The former is maintained by Government in peace time and is formed into :—

Cavalry Brigade Mule Corps.
„ „ „ Cadres.
Pack Mule Corps.
„ „ Cadres.
Camel Corps.
Half Troops, Army Transport bullocks.
„ „ Siege Train bullocks.

The "Unorganized" transport consists of registered mules, ponies, camels, and bullocks, which would, on mobilization, be utilized for expanding the cadres of organized transport, forming additional corps and making good wastage.

6. There are the following Auxiliary Forces :—

	British.	Indian.
Volunteers	36,000§	—
Military Police	—	21,000‖
Border Military Police Militia and Levies	—	14,000‖
Imperial Service Troops (furnished by the Native States)	—	22,500

7. The Indian Army Reserve is in process of expansion, and will eventually consist of 50,000 men.

8. The Indian Army is divided into :—54 "Class" regiments and battalions, which are composed of entirely one class of men, e.g., Gurkhas, Sikhs or Dogras, &c.; and 123 "Class Company or Squadron" regiments and battalions. These consist of men of several classes or races, but squadrons and companies are generally of one class. Thus a "Class Company" battalion may contain 2 companies of Pathans, 2 of Punjabi Muhammadans and 4 of Sikhs.

Army Bearer Corps .. .. 11 Companies and a reserve.

Equipment is maintained for the under-mentioned numbers of medical units :—

British Field Ambulances	24
Indian Field Ambulances	41
British Clearing Hospitals	3
Indian Clearing Hospitals	12
British Stationary Hospitals	40
Indian Stationary Hospitals	0
British General Hospitals (500 beds)	4
Indian General Hospitals (500 beds)	8
Advanced Depôts of Medical Stores	7
Veterinary Field Sections	24
Base Depôts of Veterinary Stores	3

The men of the Indian Army may be divided into two main categories—Muhammadans and Hindus.

---

* Frontier Garrison Artillery.
† Of these, 5 are employed in China and the Colonies.
‡ There are, in addition, 2 railway companies, 1 fortress company, 4 divisional signal companies, 1 wireless signal unit, 1 field troop, and 3 depôt companies.
§ Efficients.   ‖ Including British officers.

The chief Muhammadan classes that are enlisted are the North-West Frontier Pathans (sub-divided into classes, such as Afridis, Orakzais, Khattaks, Usufzais, Mohmands, Waziris, &c.); Baluchis, Hazaras and Punjabi Muhammadans. Under the general term Hindu are included Sikhs, Gurkhas, Dogras, Jats, Mahrattas, Brahmans, Garhwalis and Punjabi and Hindustani Hindus.

The above are distributed in the army as follows :—

Muhammadans ..	..	..	74 Squadrons.	335	Companies.
Hindus ..	..	..	81 ,,	730	,,
Mixed ..	..	..	—	39	,,

Percentage throughout the whole army is :—

Muhammadans ..	..	..	..	..	..	..	35·3
Hindus ..	..	..	..	..	..	..	63·3
Christians	..	..	..	..	..	..	1·23
Jews ..	..	..	..	..	..	..	0·02
Others ..	..	..	..	..	..	..	0·15

Languages :—

Punjabi is spoken by	..	..	Punjabis, Sikhs, Dogras.
Pushtu ,,	,,	..	..	Frontier tribes (Afridis, Waziris, &c.).
Hindi ,,	,,	..	..	Rajputs, Jats.
Mahrathi ,,	,,	..	..	Mahrattas.
Parvatiya ,,	,,	..	..	Gurkhas.

Hindustani (the language of the camp) is the official language of the army, and is understood by all.

49. THE MILITARY FORCES OF THE OVERSEA DOMINIONS, CROWN COLONIES AND PROTECTORATES OTHER THAN INDIA.

1. A summary of the forces maintained in the British Dominions over the Seas other than in India is given in the following table ; the nature of these forces and an outline of their organization are also indicated.

2. At the Imperial Conference of 1909 it was unanimously agreed that the organization of all the forces of the Empire should be assimilated as far as possible. It is reasonable to hope, therefore, that any units which may be despatched by Oversea Dominions, to co-operate in an Imperial undertaking, will not differ greatly in establishment and organization from similar units of the Regular Army.

3.—LAND FORCES OF BRITISH DOMINIONS, COLONIES AND PROTECTORATES OTHER THAN IN INDIA.

Name of Dominion, Colony, or Protectorate.	Nature of Force.	Term of Engagement.	Arms and Armament (exclusive of that of Fixed Defences).	Organization.
Canada...	Permanent Militia	Years. 3	4·7″ Q.F., 18-pr. Q.F., 13-pr. Q.F., 12-pr. B.L., 60-prs. and howitzers, M.L.R. and Ross rifles, and Maxims.	Units of all arms and departments. The permanent force and active militia together comprise— 33 regiments and 2 independent squadrons, cavalry and mounted rifles. 2 batteries horse artillery. 31 ,, field artillery. 10 brigades (31 batts.) field artillery. 4 regiments (20 cos.) garrison artillery. 2 regiments (5 batts.) heavy artillery. Permanent corps } engineers. 5 field cos. 3 field troops 1 wireless detachment 1 section field telegraph company attached to each field company. Corps of Guides. 95 regiments and 6 independent companies of infantry. 13 signal sections. 15 companies and 7 detachments Army Service Corps. 7 cavalry field ambulances. 14 field ambulances. 2 general hospitals. Other departmental troops. Organized as 7 mounted brigades, 10 brigades field artillery, and 23 infantry brigades and army troops.
	Active Militia	... 3	As above	

Royal N.W. Mounted Police	5	M.L.M. and Winchester carbines, Colt revolvers, Maxims and Nordenfeldts.	A Militia Council, presided over by the Minister of Militia and Defence, administers the forces. Eastern Canada is sub-divided into six divisional areas, in each of which a division of all arms is organized, together with a cavalry brigades. Western Canada is divided into three military districts. Organized into 12 divisions and administered by a Controller at Ottawa.
All males between the ages of 18		and 60 are liable for service	in time of emergency.
Australia			
Administrative and Instructional Staff (permanent)	...	...	A separate organization to which admission by examination is open to all ranks and all branches of the Commonwealth forces; organized for command, administrative and instructional purposes.
Permanent Force ...	5	18-pr. Q.F.	3 field batteries, 1 district establishment and 13 companies of garrison artillery, S.M.M. companies and electric detachments engineers, and nucleus of departmental services.
Militia	3	4·7″ Q.F., 18-pr. Q.F., howitzers, and M.L.E. rifles, Maxims and other machine guns.	The forces are organized as— (i) *Field Force*—(Militia) organized in brigades, both mounted and infantry, with establishments similar to the British Army. (ii) *Garrison Troops*—(Permanent and Militia). The above are distributed among the 6 District Commands, which correspond nearly in area with the 6 States of the Commonwealth.

LAND FORCES OF BRITISH DOMINIONS, COLONIES AND PROTECTORATES OTHER THAN INDIA—*continued*.

Name of Dominion, Colony, or Protectorate.	Nature of Force.	Term of Engagement.	Arms and Armament (exclusive of that of Fixed Defences).	Organization.
Australia—*cont.*	Militia—*cont.*	Years.		The *Militia*, under the Universal Training Law, is providing additional units each year. For 1913-14 the numbers are:— 28 regiments Light Horse. 22 batteries F.A. 13 companies Garrison Artillery. 6½ field companies, engineers. 6 signal troops, engineers. 5 signal companies and 3 brigade sections, engineers. 8 fortress companies, engineers. 50 battalions of infantry and 2 extra territorial units. An Intelligence Corps. 20 companies, A.S.C. 20 field ambulances. 2 companies and 2 half-companies Army Medical Corps, Army Veterinary Corps. The *Volunteers* now include only an Automobile Corps and an Army Nursing Service.
	Reserve and Rifle Clubs	...	L.E. and M.E. rifles	The *Reserve* consists of—Members of rifle clubs who have taken the required oath, and of persons who, having served in the active forces, are enrolled as members of the reserve. The forces are under a Minister of Defence, advised by a Council of Defence, but they are administered by a Military Board of which the Minister is president.

All male inhabitants between the ages of 18 and 60 are liable to be called out for service in time of war. Men between the ages of 18 and 26 years are, under a recently passed Act, obliged to train in the Militia.

	Men	Guns	Organization
New Zealand... Permanent Force...	8	18-pr. Q.F. guns, 4·5″ Q.F. howitzers, and M.L.E. rifles.	*Permanent—* Staff Corps. Permanent staff. Field and garrison artillery (for instructional purposes).
Territorial Force ...	7		*Territorial Force—* 12 regiments mounted rifles. 8 batteries field artillery. 1 mountain battery. 9 companies garrison artillery. 4 field companies engineers. 4 mounted signal companies. 4 infantry signal companies. 2 railway battalions. 4 cavalry field ambulances. 4 field ambulances. 16 battalions of infantry. 2½ battalions coast defence troops. Departmental corps. The forces are commanded and administered by a commandant. The Dominion is divided into 4 military districts, the troops in each district comprising a mixed brigade and garrison troops. The volunteer force was recently converted into a Territorial Force under an amendment to the Defence Act which introduced compulsory service in the Militia.

All males between the ages of 17 and 55 are liable for service. Men between the ages 18 and 25 years are obliged to undergo training, and to belong to the reserve from 25 to 30 years of age.

LAND FORCES OF BRITISH DOMINIONS, COLONIES AND PROTECTORATES OTHER THAN INDIA—continued.

Name of Dominion, Colony, or Protectorate.	Nature of Force.	Term of Engagement. (Years.)	Arms and Armament (exclusive of that of Fixed Defences).	Organization.
Union of South Africa	Permanent Force	5	13-pr. Q.F., 2·75″ Q.F., howitzers and small arms	Administrative and instructional staff. 5 regiments S.A. Mounted Riflemen. 5 batteries field artillery (attached to S.A.M.R.).
	Coast Garrison Force	4	...	Cape Garrison Artillery. Durban Garrison Artillery. Cape Coast Defence Corps. Durban Coast Defence Corps.
	Active Citizen Force	4	Artillery—13-pr. Q.F. and 15-pr. B.L.	9 regiments mounted rifles (to be increased to 16 regiments and 6 independent squadrons). 4 regiments dismounted rifles (to be increased to 11 regiments and 6 independent squadrons). 3 batteries field artillery. 3 brigades (12 battalions) infantry. Aviation Corps. 4 mounted brigade trains } in course of formation. 3 dismounted ,, ,, 3 infantry ,, ,, 2 mounted brigade field ambulances (to be increased to 7). 2 field ambulances (in course of formation).
	Reserves and Rifle Associations	...	...	The defence forces are administered by a Council of Defence, of which the Minister of Defence is President.

Part IV.—UNION OF SOUTH AFRICA.

	Force	Armament	No.	Organization
Newfoundland	Constabulary ...	L.E. rifles	...	Civil organization.
Bahamas	Police (West Indians) ...	M.L.E. rifles	6	Civil organization.
Barbados	Volunteers (West Indians) ...	M.L.E. and M.I.L.M. rifles,	3	3 companies infantry and 1 company mounted infantry.
	Police (West Indians) ...	M.E. carbines, Maxim M.E. rifles and carbines, M.I.L.M. rifles	1	A civil organization comprising mounted and foot detachments and harbour police.
Bermuda	Militia and Volunteers	... ...	6 and 3	Maintained by Imperial Government.
British Guiana	Militia (Europeans and Natives)	L.E. rifles and M.E. carbines, and 9-pr. guns	3	1 artillery company (Europeans) and 1 infantry company (West Indians).
	Volunteers (Europeans and Creoles)	L.E. rifles	...	2 companies infantry.
	Police (West Indians) ...			
British Honduras	Volunteers (Europeans and West Indians)	M.E. rifles and carbines and Maxim	3	6 divisions and mounted detachment (European staff).
	Police (West Indians)	M.E. carbines and Maxims	3	2 sections mounted infantry.
		Snider carbines ...	1	2 companies infantry.
				Civil organization.
British North Borneo	Constabulary (Sikhs, Mohammedans and Malays)	7-pr. R.M.L. guns, M.E. and M.H. rifles, M.E. carbines and Maxims	5	Organized in two divisions. (i) military police; (ii) district police.
Ceylon ...	Volunteers (Europeans and natives)	M.I.L.E. rifles and M.E. carbines and Maxims	...	2 companies garrison artillery. 2 squadrons mounted rifles. 1 company engineers, 15 companies light infantry. 8 companies and motor cycle section Planters' Rifle Corps. 2 companies medical corps. The force is administered by a commandant of volunteers; training is supervised by the officer commanding the troops in Ceylon.
	Reserves (Europeans and natives)	M.I.L.E. rifles and M.E. carbines	...	Civil organization.
	Police (Europeans and natives)	M.H. carbines.	...	
Cyprus ...	Police (Turks and Greeks)	M.E. carbines.	5	

Part V.—NEWFOUNDLAND CROWN COLONIES AND PROTECTORATES OTHER THAN AFRICAN.

(B 11925)   U 2

LAND FORCES OF BRITISH DOMINIONS, COLONIES AND PROTECTORATES OTHER THAN INDIA—*continued.*

Name of Dominion, Colony, or Protectorate.	Nature of Force.	Term of Engagement. (Years.)	Arms and Armament (exclusive of that of Fixed Defences).	Organization.
Falkland Islands	Volunteers (British)	...	M.L.E. rifles and Maxim ...	1 company infantry.
Fanning Islands	Volunteer Reserve	...	L.E. rifles.	
Fiji	Constabulary (Fijians)	3	M.E. rifles and Maxim ...	Semi-military force.
	Rifle Clubs (Europeans)	...	M.L.E. rifles and Maxim ...	Can be called out for service.
Gilbert and Ellice Islands	Police (natives)	...	M.E. and Enfield carbines	
Hong-Kong	Volunteers (Europeans)	...	M.L.E. rifles, 10-pr. guns, howitzers and Maxims	1 section and 3 M.G. sections, scouts coy. 1 battery a-tillery. 1 company engineers. 1 machine-gun company.
	Volunteer Reserve (Europeans)	...	M.L.E. rifles ...	Civil organization. Members available in time of war.
	Police (mostly Sikhs and Mussulmans)	5	M.L.E. carbines ...	Civil organization.
Jamaica	Militia (West Indians)	3	M.E. carbines ...	1 company artillery.
	Rifle Corps ...	...	L.E. rifles.	
	Constabulary	5	M.E. carbines ...	Civil organization.
Leeward Islands	Volunteers (Europeans and natives)	...	L.E. rifles ...	Small detachments in each island.
Malta	Police (West Indians)	3	L.E. rifles.	Civil organization.
	Royal Malta Artillery	...	British regular troops maintained by Imperial Government	
	Militia	5	Engineers and 2 battalions infantry maintained by Imperial Government	

Part V.—NEWFOUNDLAND, CROWN COLONIES AND PROTECTORATES OTHER THAN AFRICAN—*cont.*

Malay States— Fed. Malay States	Permanent (Malay States Guides)	5	Maintained for F.M.S. for protection of their own territories M.E. rifles.	1 company artillery and 7 companies infantry.
Solomon Ilds.	Police (natives)	...		
Straits Settlements	Volunteers (Europeans) Rifle Club (Europeans)...	2	M.I.E. rifles	5 companies infantry and M.G. detachment.
	Volunteers (Europeans and Asiatics)	2	M.L.E. rifles. M.L.E. rifles and Maxims	1 company artillery. 1 company engineers. 5 companies infantry. 1 Maxim gun company 1 Medical Company.
Trinidad ...	Police (Europeans, Sikhs and Malays)	3 to 6	M.E. rifles, M.E. and Snider carbines	Semi-military organization.
	Volunteers (Europeans and West Indians)	3	M.E. rifles and carbines and Maxims	4 troops light horse. 5 companies of infantry.
	Constabulary (West Indians)	3	M.E. rifles	Organized as a military body and includes mounted, artillery and machine gun detachments.
Windward Islands	Volunteers (Europeans and West Indians)	3	M.L.E. rifles and L.E. carbines	2 sections mounted infantry in St. Lucia, Grenada, & St. Vincent. 2 companies infantry 1 Maxim gun section Volunteer reserve in St. Lucia.
	Police (West Indians) ...	2	M.E. and M.L.E. rifles	Liable for service.
	Rifle Clubs	...	M.L.E. rifles	Civil organization.
EAST AFRICA.				
East Africa Protectorate	King's African Rifles* ...	3	M.E. and M.L.E. rifles, and ·303 Maxims	1st Bn. K.A.R., 3 cos. infantry (Africans). 3rd Bn. K.A.R., 5 companies infantry, 1 company camelry (Africans).
	Volunteer Res. (British)	...	M.L.E. rifles and Colt guns	Liable for service.
	Police (Africans)... ...	3	M.E. and M.H. rifles ...	Civil organisation, but liable for service.

* The King's African Rifles furnish 2 companies, drawn either from the 1st or 3rd Battalion for service in Zanzibar.

Part VI.—AFRICAN COLONIES AND PROTECTORATES.

LAND FORCES OF BRITISH DOMINIONS, COLONIES AND PROTECTORATES OTHER THAN INDIA—*continued.*

Part VI.—AFRICAN COLONIES AND PROTECTORATES.—*cont.*

Name of Dominion, Colony, or Protectorate.	Nature of Force.	Term of Engagement. Years.	Arms and Armament (exclusive of that of Fixed Defences).	Organization.
EAST AFRICA—*cont.*				
Nyasaland	King's African Rifles	6	M.E. rifles and ·303 Maxims	½ battalion of infantry (3 companies Africans).
	Volunteer Reserve	...	M.L.E. rifles	Liable for service.
	Police	...	M.E. rifles	Civil organization.
Somaliland	Indian contingent (Sikhs)	...	M.L.E. rifles and Maxims	2 companies infantry.
	Camel Constabulary (Africans)	...	M.E. carbines	Liable for service.
	Police (Africans)	...	M.E. carbines	Civil organization.
Uganda	King's African Rifles	3	M.E. rifles and ·303 Maxims	1 battalion of infantry (7 companies Africans).
	Volunteer Reserve (British)	...	M.L.E. rifles	Liable for service.
	Police (Africans)	3	M.H. rifles	Liable for service.
SOUTH AFRICA.				
Basutoland	Police (Europeans and natives)	...	M.H. carbines and ·303 Maxims	Under Resident Commissioner.
Bechuanaland	Police (Europeans and natives)	2	L.E. and M.H. rifles and ·303 Maxims	Under Resident Commissioner.

Northern Rhodesia	Police (natives)	3	M.E. rifles, ·303 and ·450 Maxims	Civil organization, but liable for service.
	Rifle Association (British)	...	...	...
Southern Rhodesia	Volunteers (Europeans)...	1	M.L.E. rifles	2 divisions of infantry and mounted troops.
	B.S.A. Police (Europeans and natives)	3	M.E. rifles, 7-pr. R.M.L. and 75 m.m. Q.F. guns, ·303 and ·450 Maxims, Colt, Gatling and Nordenfeldt machine guns	Military organization. 9 troops.
	Rifle Clubs (Europeans)...	...	M.L.E. rifles.	
Swaziland	Police (Europeans and natives)...	...	M.L.E. and M.H. rifles ...	Civil organization.
WEST AFRICA.				
Gambia ...	West African Frontier Force (natives)	6	M.L.E. rifles and ·303 Maxim	1 company infantry.
	Police (natives)	5	M.E. carbines and 7-pr. R.M.L. guns	Military organization.
Gold Coast ...	West African Frontier Force	6	M.L.E. rifles, M.E. carbines, 2·95 Q.F. and 7-pr. guns and ·303 Maxims	Organized as a regiment— 1 battery artillery, 1 battalion infantry of 8 companies.
	Reserves	...	M.E. carbines.	
	Volunteers (Europeans and natives)	...	M.L.E. rifles, M.E. carbines, and ·303 Maxims	8 companies of infantry, 2 gun sections and 1 machine gun section, and 1 ambulance section.
	NorthernTerritories Constabulary (natives)	6	M.E. carbines, 7-pr. R.M.L. and ·303 Maxim guns	Semi-military organization.
	Police (natives)	...	M.E. and M.H. carbines ...	Civil organization, but liable for service.

AFRICAN COLONIES AND PROTECTORATES—cont.

LAND FORCES OF BRITISH DOMINIONS, COLONIES AND PROTECTORATES OTHER THAN INDIA—*continued.*

Name of Dominion, Colony, or Protectorate.	Nature of Force.	Term of Engagement.	Arms and Armament (exclusive of that of Fixed Defences).	Organization.
AFRICAN COLONIES AND PROTECTORATES—*cont.*				
WEST AFRICA—*cont.*		Years.		
Nigeria... ...	West African Frontier Force (natives)	6	2·9-5″ Q.F., ·303 Maxims and M.L.E. rifles	Organized as a regiment— 2 batteries artillery. 1 battalion mounted infantry. 4 battalions infantry.
	Reserves	...	Ditto	
	Volunteers (Europeans and natives)	...	M.E. rifles and ·303 Maxims	3 companies infantry.
	Police (Africans)...	6	M.E. carbines	Liable for service.
Sierra Leone ...	West African Frontier Force (natives)	6	M.L.E. rifles and ·303 Maxims M.M. and M.E. carbines.	Organized as an infantry battalion of 6 companies.
	Reserves	...		

50. FOREIGN ARMIES.

1. NORMAL WAR ORGANIZATION OF THE FIGHTING TROOPS.

Country	War Strength	Cavalry Division — Squadrons	Machine Guns	Field Guns	Army Corps — Squadrons	Battalions	Machine Guns	Field Guns	Division — Squadrons	Battalions	Machine Guns	Field Guns	Cavalry Units	Artillery Units	Infantry Units
Argentina …	5 Divisions 2 Cav. Divs. (Peace strength = 23,500 Trained men = 210,000)	16 or 24	12	36	16	24	48	82	8	12	24	41	Bde. =2 Regts. =8 Sqns. =1,875 Sabres	Regt. =2 Groups =4 Batts. =16 Guns	Bde. =2 Regts. =6 Bns. =24 Cos. =6,632 Rifles
Austria - Hungary	16 Army Corps (49 Divisions) 10 Cav. Divs. and 5 Cav. Bdes.	24	16 [1]	12	6 to 9	36 to 50	72 to 100	168 [2]	2 or 3	12 to 16	24 to 32	48 [2]	Div. =2 Bdes. =4 Regts. =24 Sqns. =3,600 Sabres	Regt =2 Divs. =4 or 6 Batts.[3] =24 or 36 Guns	Div. =2 Bdes. =4 Regts. =12 or 16 Bns. =48 or 64 Cos. =12,000 or 16,000 Rifles
Belgium …	6 Divisions [4] 1 Cav. Div.	30		12	…	…	…	…	4	18	18	48 [5]	Bde. =2 Regts. =10 Sqns. =1,500 Sabres	Group =3 Batts. =12 Guns	Regts. [6] =3 Bns. =12 Cos. =About 3,000 Rifles

FOREIGN ARMIES—continued.

NORMAL WAR ORGANIZATION OF THE FIGHTING TROOPS—continued.

Country	War Strength	Cavalry Division			Army Corps				Division				Cavalry Units	Artillery Units	Infantry Units
		Squadrons	Machine Guns	Field Guns	Squadrons	Battalions	Machine Guns	Field Guns	Squadrons	Battalions	Machine Guns	Field Guns			
Bulgaria ...	9 Divisions 1 Cav. Div.	16	16	N	...	...	...	...	2	16	16	36	Div. =2 Bdes. =4 Regts. =16 Sqns. =2,500 Sabres	Regt. =3 Bdes. =9 Batts. =36 Guns	Bde. =2 Regts. =8 Bns. =32 Cos. =8,000 Rifles
Chile ...	4 Divisions 4 Cav. Regiments (Peace Strength =18,800)	...	...	...	...	...	...	...	4	12	24	32	Regt. =4 Sqns. =600 Sabres	Bde. =2 Regts. =4 Groups =8 Batts. =32 Guns	Bde. =2 Regts. =6 Bns. =24 Cos. =6,000 Rifles
China ...	...	...	...	...	...	...	...	...	3	12	21	54 7	Regt. =3 Sqns. =672 Sabres	Regt. =3 Bns. =9 Batts. =54 Guns	Bde. =2 Regts. =6 Bns. =24 Cos. =6,048 Rifles
Denmark ...	3 Divisions and 1 Independent Brigade	...	...	...	...	...	...	...	3 or 6	10	...	16 or 32	Regt. =3 Sqns. =300 Sabres	Regt. =4 Batts. =16 Guns	Regt. =3 Bns. =12 Cos. =1,040 Rifles

Country	Organization	I	II	III	IV	V	VI	VII	VIII	IX	X	Cavalry	Artillery	Infantry
France[3] (exclusive of Reserve and Territorial Formations)	20 Army Corps[9] in France and 1 in Algeria, 10 Cavalry Divisions[10] as well as Cavalry attached to Army Corps	42	8 to 12	8 to 12	6 to 18	24 to 36	48 to 72	120 [12]			36	Bde. = 2 or 3 Regts. = 8 or 12 Sqns. = 1,280 or 1,920 Sabres	Regt. for Army Corps = 4 Groupes (bdes.) of 3 Batts. each Regt. for Inf. Div. = 3 Groupes of 3 Batts. each 1 Batty. = 4 Guns	Bde. = 2 Regts. = 6 Bns.[13] = 24 Cos. = 6,000 Rifles
Germany	25 Active Corps, 30 Reserve Cps.[11] (Cav. Dns.), about 60–70 Landwehr Bdes.	24	6	12	8	25 24[14]		160	4	12 12 or 13 24	72	Bde. = 2 Regts. = 8 Sqns. = 1,200 Sabres	Bde. = 2 Regts. = 4 Abteilungen = 12 Batts. = 72 Guns	Bde. = 2 Regts. = 6 Bns. = 24 Cos. = 6,000 Rifles
Greece	4 Divisions, 1 Cav. Bde.									9 ...	24	Bde. = 2 Regts. = 10 Sqns. = 1,500 Sabres	Regt.[15] = 6 Batts. = 24 Guns	Div. = 3 Regts. = 9 Bns. = 27 Cos. = 3,300 Rifles
Holland	4 Divisions, 1 Cav. Bde.								1 or 4[16]	15 8	36	Bde. = 4 Regts. (less 1 Sqn. each) = 12 Sqns. = 1,650 Sabres	Regt.[15] = 2 Afdeelingen = 6 Batts. = 36 Guns	Regt. = 4 Bns. = 16 Cos. = 4,000 Rifles
Italy	12 Army Corps, 3 Cav. Divs. of 2 Bdes., 17 other Cav. Regts.	20	8	8	5	40 to 42		126		12 24	30	Cav. Div. = 2 Bdes. = 4 Regts. = 10 Sqns. = 1,800 Sabres	Regt. = 2 Groups = 5 or 6 Batts. = 30–36 Guns	Bde. = 2 Regts. = 6 Bns. = 24 Cos. = 6,000 Rifles
Japan	19 Divs., 4 Cav. Bdes., 3 F.A. Bdes., 2 Heavy Art. Bdes., 6 Horse Art. Batts. and Reserve Divs.								3	12 24	36	Bde. = 2 Regts. = 8 Squs. = 960 Sabres	Regt. = 2 Bns. = 6 Batts. = 36 Guns	Bde. = 2 Regts. = 6 Bns. = 24 Cos. = 4,800 Rifles

FOREIGN ARMIES—continued.
NORMAL WAR ORGANIZATION OF THE FIGHTING TROOPS—continued.

Country.	War Strength.	Cavalry Division. Squadrons.	Machine Guns.	Field Guns.	Army Corps. Squadrons.	Battalions.	Machine Guns.	Field Guns.	Division. Squadrons.	Battalions.	Machine Guns.	Field Guns.	Cavalry Units.	Artillery Units.	Infantry Units.
Norway ...	6 Field Bdes.	...	...	...	...	...	...	...	Field Bde. 16	9	4	20 or 16	Regt. = 4 or 6 Sqns. = 400 or 600 Sabres and 4 or 8 machine guns	Regt. = 2 Bns. = 9 Batts. = 36 Guns	Bde. = 2 or 3 Regts. Regt, = 3 Bns. = 12 Cos. = 2,400 Rifles
Portugal ...	...	...	...	...	...	...	...	...	...	...	...	...	Reorganization in progress.		
Rumania ...	5 Army Corps (10 Divs. and 5 Reserve Divs.) 2 Cav. Divs.[17]	16	8	12	8	26	52	120	19	13	26	48	Div. = 2 Bdes. = 4 or 6 Regts. = 16 or 24 Sqns. = 1,400 or 2,100 Sabres.	Regt. = 2 Divs. = 6 Batts. = 24 Guns	Div. 2 Bdes. = 4 Regts. = 12 Bns. = 48 Cos. = 12,000 Rfls. and a Jager Bn.
Russia ...	Active Army in European Russia and the Caucasus.	24	8	12	...	32	64	108[a]	Inf. Div. 16,32	...		48	Div. = 2 Bdes. = 4 Regts. = 24 Sqns. (or Sotnias)	F.A. Bde. = 2 Divs. = 6 Batts. = 43 Guns (or Horse or Howitzer)	Div. = 2 Bdes. = 4 Regts. = 16 Bns. = 64 Cos.

			Infantry	Cavalry	Artillery (Horse / Mountain)	
	32 Army Corps 23 Cav. Divs,	16 ... 8		=14,140 Rfls.	=3,466 Sabres	*Horse Mountain* Div. =2 Batts. =12 Guns *Heavy.* Div. =3 Batts. =12 Guns *Mountain.* Batt. =8 Guns
Servia ...	5 Divs. 1 Cav. Div.	16 ... 3 16 ... 36 8		Div. =4 Regts. =16 Bns. =64 Cos. =16,500 Rfls.	Div. =4 Regts. =16 Sqns. =2,000 Sabres	Regt. =9 Batts. =36 Guns
Switzerland ...	6 Divs. 4 Cav. Bdes.	2 18 12 48		Div. =3 Bdes. =6 Regts. =18 Bns. =72 Cos. =10,800 Rfls.	Bde. =2 Regts. =6 Sqns. =950 Sabres	Regt. =2 Groupes =6 Batts. =24 Guns
Turkey ...	38 Composite Army Corps 20 Redif Divs. 14 Cav. Bdes.	10 12 ... 24 to 36 86 to 158 36 to 48 10 to 15 23 to 33		Div. =3 Regts. =10 Bns. =30 Cos. =8,000 Rifles	Bde. =2 or 3 Regts. =10 or 15 Sqns. =1,400 to 2,000 Sabres =12 Mach. Guns =8 Horse Guns	Regt. =2 or 3 Bns. each of 3 four-gun Batts. =24 or 36 guns
United States ...	18 Divisions 2 Cav. Divs. (Peace strength= 85,000. War strength to be made up by enlistment.)	27 54 24 3 27 54 48		Div. =3 Bdes. =9 Regts. =27 Bns. =14,220 Rfls.	Div. =2 Bdes. =9 Regts. =27 Sqns. =11,430 Sabres.	Bde. =2 Regts. =4 Bns. =12 Batts. =48 Guns.

[1] Machine guns are in course of provision: to each cavalry and Jäger battalion one section of 2 guns; to each infantry battalion one section of 2 guns.

[2] An Army Corps has at present 3 regiments of 6 batteries (guns), one regiment of 4 batteries (field howitzers), one division (12 guns) heavy howitzers and one regiment—2 batteries (gun) and 2 batteries (howitzers) of Landwehr Artillery. This is being increased by one regiment of 4 batteries (howitzer) and 4 batteries (gun) and 2 batteries (howitzer) of Landwehr Artillery.

[3] Normal establishment 4 batteries, but would probably be raised to 6 in war.

[4] The 3rd and 4th divisions each have an additional Mixed Brigade.

[5] It is intended to add 24 more guns (howitzers) per division; the 2nd and 6th divisions at present have 60 field guns.

[6] Brigades are Mixed Brigades, each consisting of two infantry regiments and one group field artillery.

[7] Field and mountain.

[8] In each case the first number given is the normal.

[9] Each Army Corps has normally 1 regiment of light cavalry, 4 squadrons and a depôt squadron (in peace) (6 squadrons on mobilization of which 2 form divisional squadrons). The 6th Corps d'Armée may have 2 or even 3 regiments of cavalry which will be organized as a brigade.

[10] Each cavalry division has a groupe cycliste of 350 men. Each cavalry division will eventually have 3 groupes horse artillery = 12 guns, but at present have only 2 groupes.

[11] Plus 12 guns in the Ammunition Column. If is also possible that the number of guns may be brought up to 144 guns per Army Corps on mobilization.

[12] Some Army Corps have in addition a brigade of howitzers.

[13] Rifle Bns. (Chasseurs à Pied) have 6 Cos. each of 175 rifles=1,050 rifles per Bn.

[14] To be increased later to 48.

[15] One regiment has 8 batteries.

[16] Normally 1 squadron, 4 squadrons only when the cavalry brigade is not formed.

[17] There are either 2 or 3 Bdes. of Cavalry in a Cav. Div.

[18] Excluding reserve divisions.

[19] As allotted by Corps Commanders.

[20] Corps provided with heavy artillery have 120 guns.

2. RIFLES.

Country.	Name of Rifle.	Calibre. Inches.	Loading System.	Shape* of Bullet.	Sighted up to— Yards.
Austria ...	Mannlicher ...	·315	Clip, 5 cart. ...	S	2,460
Belgium ...	Mauser	·301	Charger, 5 cart.	R	2,297
Bulgaria ...	Mannlicher ...	·315	Clip, 5 cart. ...	S	2,120
Denmark ...	Krag-Jorgensen	·315	Charger, 5 cart.	S	2,078
France ...	Lebel	·315	Tube fore end, 8 cart.	S	2,187
Germany ...	Mauser	·311	Charger, 5 cart,	S	2,187
Greece ...	Mannlicher-Schönauer	·254	...	R	2,600
Holland ...	Mannlicher ...	·256	Clip, 5 cart. ...	S	2,187
Italy	,, ...	·256	,, 6 ,, ...	S	2,187
Japan... ...	Year 38 (1905) ...	·256	Charger, 5 cart.	S	2,187
Norway ...	Krag-Jorgensen	·256	,, 5 ,,	S	2,400
Rumania ...	Mannlicher ...	·256	Clip, 5 cart. ...	R	2,187
Russia ...	3 Line	·3	Charger, 5 cart.	S	2,100
Servia ...	Mauser	·276	,, 5 ,,	R	2,187
Spain	,, ...	·276	,, 5 ,,	S	2,187
Sweden ...	,, ...	·256	,, 5 ,,	S	2,187
Switzerland...	Schmidt-Rubin ...	·295	,, 6 ,,	S	2,187
Turkey ...	Mauser	·301	,, 5 ,,	S	2,187
United States	Springfield ...	·3	,, 5 ,,	S	2,000

*S—Pointed.   R—Roundnose.

3. MACHINE GUNS.

Country.	Pattern.	Calibre.	Mounting.	Transport.	Sighted to—
Austria ...	Schwarzlose	·315	Tripod carriage ...	Pack	
Belgium ...	Hotchkiss ...	·301	Carriage with removable tripod	Limber	
Bulgaria ...	Maxim ...	·315	Tripod mounting	Pack	
Denmark ...	Madsen ...	·315	Portable	On saddle	
France ...	Hotchkiss ...	·315	Wheeled carriage	Pack	
	Puteaux ...	·315	Tripod	Pack	
Germany ...	Maxim ...	·311	Sleigh	M.G. wagon	
Holland ...	Schwarzlose	·311	...	Limber and pack	
Italy ...	Perino ...	·256	Tripod carriage ...	Pack	
Japan ...	Hotchkiss ...	·256	,, ...	,,	2188yds
Norway ...	,, ...	·256			
	Madsen ...	·256	...	On saddle	
Rumania ...	Maxim ...	·256	M.G. sleigh ...	M.G. wagon	
Russia ...	,, ...	·300	Wheeled carriage and tripod	Pack	2084yds
	Madsen ...	·300	Portable	On saddle	
Servia ...	Maxim ...	·276			
Spain ...	,, ...	·276		Pack saddle	
	Hotchkiss ...	·276			
Sweden ...	,, ...	·256			
	Madsen ...	·256	Portable	On saddle	
Switzerland	Maxim ...	·295	Tripod and Reff carriage	Pack and man's back	
	Madsen ...	...	Portable	On saddle	
Turkey ...	Maxim ...	·301	...	Wheeled carriage	
	Hotchkiss ...	·300			
United States	Maxim ...	·300	Tripod	Pack	
	Hotchkiss ...	·300	Portable	On saddle	

4. APPROXIMATE RANGES OF FOREIGN GUNS IN YARDS.

Country.	H.A.	F.A.	Fd. Howr.	Heavy.	Limit of Forward Effect of Shrapnel from Point of Burst in Yards.
France	9,000	9,000	6,233	7,000	330
Austria	6,800	6,800	6,600	...	260
Denmark	None	6,600	None	None	...
Italy	6,000	6,000	...	...	260
Germany—* Extreme range— Time fuse ...	5,500	5,500	6,150	10 cm. gun 9,400 15 cm. gun 9,020	275
Maximum elev. ...	8,800	8,800	7,700	15 cm. How. 6,650 21 cm. Mtr. 8,800 10 cm. gun 12,000 15 cm. gun 11,000	...
Holland	6,600	6,600	None	None	...
Russia	6,000	6,000	7,000	9,500	290
Norway	None	6,562	...	...	...
Krupp (2·95) ...	...	6,600	...	...	...
Sweden	7,650	7,650	...	...	...
United States ...	7,500	7,500	6″, 7,000	4·7″, 7,600	340
Switzerland— Extreme range— Time fuze ...	...	6,100	Mountain Gun.		
Extreme range— Per fuze ...	...	7,000	4,800	...	...
Japan...	8,195	9,295	6,441	10,334	340

* Germany is also in possession of 28 cm., 32 cm. and 42 cm. howitzers, and some 52 cm. howitzers are reported to be under construction.

5. PROPORTION OF GUNS AND SWORDS TO INFANTRY.

Foreign Army Corps.	Proportion of—	
	Guns to 1,000 Inf.	Sabres to 1,000 Inf.
Austria	3·25	76
France a	4·8	65·5
Germany...	6·4	48
Italy	3·4	32
Japan (Division)	4·1	40
Russia	4·4	120
United States	3·3	86
Switzerland	2·2	60

a For an Army Corps of 25 infantry battalions.

51. WEIGHTS, MEASURES, MONEYS, Etc.

1. The following tables contain information regarding English and foreign weights and measures, and the coinage of foreign countries, &c. :—

ENGLISH WEIGHTS AND MEASURES.

2. *Linear Measure.*

	In.	Ft.	Yds.	Pls.	Ch.	Fs.
Foot	12	1				
Yard	36	3	1			
Rod, pole, or perch ...	198	16½	5½	1		
Chain...	792	66	22	4	1	
Furlong	7,920	660	220	40	10	1
Mile	63,360	5,280	1,760	320	80	8

3. *Particular Measures of Length.*

A fathom = 6 feet.
A cable's length = ⅒ nautical mile = 202·7 yards.
A degree of latitude varies from 68·7 statute miles at the Equator to 69·41 at the Pole.
The following is the length in geographical miles of 1 degree of longitude at various latitudes :—At the Equator, 69·176 ; at 15° N. or S., 66·832 ; at 30° N. or S., 59·96 ; at 45° N. or S., 48·992 ; at 60° N. or S., 34·676.
A league = 3 miles.
A nautical mile or geographical mile = 2,026⅔ yards.
A half-penny is one inch in diameter.
An ordinary gentleman's visiting card measures 3″ × 1½″.

4. *Square Measure.*

	In.	Ft.	Yds.	Pls.	Ch.	R.
Square foot	144	1				
Square yard	1,296	9	1			
Rod, pole, or perch ...	39,204	272½	30¼	1		
Square chain	627,264	4,356	484	16	1	
Rood	1,568,160	10,890	1,210	40	2½	1
Acre	6,272,640	43,560	4,840	160	10	4

A square mile contains 640 acres = 2,560 roods = 6,400 chains = 102,400 rods, poles, or perches = 3,097,600 square yards.

N.B.—The term square feet must not be confounded with feet square. A piece of cloth said to measure 6 square feet consists of 6 squares of a foot each, but a piece said to measure 6 feet square would be 6 feet along each side, and comprise 36 squares of a foot each.

5. *Cubic Measure.*

1,728 cubic inches ...	...	...	...	...	1 cubic foot.
27 „ feet ...	...	...	...	...	1 „ yard.
42 „ „ timber ...	...	...	...	...	1 shipping ton.
108 „ „ ...	...	...	...	...	1 stack of wood.
128 „ „ ...	...	...	...	...	1 cord of wood.

6. *Liquid Measure.*

	Gals.	Qts.	Pts.
4 gills	...	...	1
Quart	...	1	2
Gallon	1	4	8
Firkin	9	36	72
Kilderkin	18	72	144
Barrel	36	144	288
Hogshead of ale	54	216	432
Puncheon	72	288	576
Butt of ale	108	432	864

7. *Dry Measure.*

4 gills	1 pint.
2 pints	1 quart.
4 quarts	1 gallon.
2 gallons	1 peck.
4 pecks	1 bushel.
8 bushels (2 sacks)	1 quarter.
36 ,, ...	1 chaldron.

MEASURES OF WEIGHT.

8. *Avoirdupois Weight.*

$27\frac{1}{3}$ grains	= 1 drachm	= 27·34375 grains.
16 drachms	= 1 ounce	= 437·5 ,,
16 ounces	= 1 pound	= 7,000 ,,
14 pounds	= 1 stone.	
28 ,, ...	= 1 quarter (qr.).	
4 quarters	= 1 hundredweight (cwt.).	
20 cwt.	= 1 ton.	

This weight is used in almost all commercial transactions and common dealings.

9. *Troy Weight.*

24 grains	= 1 pennyweight.
20 pennyweights	= 1 ounce.
12 ounces	= 1 lb.

10. *Apothecaries Weight.*

20 grains	= 1 scruple.
3 scruples	= 1 drachm (drm.).
8 drachms	= 1 oz.

11. *Apothecaries Fluid Measure.*

60 minims (drops)	= 1 fluid drachm.
8 drachms	= 1 oz.
20 ounces	= 1 pint.

Useful weights and measures :—1 sovereign = 2 drams ; 1 half-crown, $3\frac{1}{2}$ drs ; 1 florin, 3 drs.; 1 shilling, $1\frac{1}{2}$ drs. ; 1 threepenny piece, $\frac{4}{5}$ dr. ; 1 tablespoonful holds 1 oz. ; 1 dessert spoon, $\frac{1}{2}$ oz.; 1 teaspoon, $\frac{1}{4}$ oz. These measures are used for veterinary medicine.

12. *Particular Weights.*

A firkin of butter	= 56 lbs.
,, soft soap...	= 64 ,,
A barrel of raisins	= 112 ,,
,, (or pack) of soft soap...	= 256 ,,
A sack—Potatoes, 168 lbs.; coals, 224 lbs.; flour, 280 lbs.	
A muid of whole mealies	= 196 ,,
,, crushed mealies	= 200 ,,
Bag of coffee	= 1¼ to 1½ cwt.
,, rice (East India)	= about 1½ cwt.
Bale of coffee (Mocha)	= 2 to 2½ cwt.
Barrel of beef	= 200 lbs.
,, butter	= 224 ,,
,, gunpowder	= 100 ,,
,, tar	= 26¼ gallons.
Bushel of coal...	= 80 lbs.
Cask of rice (American)	= 6 cwts.
Chaldron of coal	= 36 bushels.
Chest of tea (Congou)	= about 84 lbs.
Gross	= 12 doz.
Hogshead of sugar	= 13 to 16 cwts.
Loaf, quartern	= 4 lbs.
Tierce of coffee	= 5 to 7 cwts.
,, sugar	= 7 to 9 ,,
Tub of butter	= 84 lbs.

13. *Hay and Straw.*

Truss of straw	= 36 lbs.
,, old hay	= 56 ,,
,, new hay	= 60 ,,

Load, 36 trusses=straw, 11 cwts. 2 qrs. 8 lbs.; old hay, 18 cwts.; new hay, 19 cwts. 1 qr. 4 lbs.

14. *Weight of Coal, Wood, &c.*

Anthracite, per cubic yard solid	= 2,160 lbs.
Bituminous ,, ,, ...	= 2,025 ,,
Cannel ,, ,, ...	= 1,400 ,,
Coal, stored in the usual way, solid ...	= 2,160 ,,
A cubic foot fresh water	weighs 62½ lbs.
,, salt ,, ...	,, 63¾ ,,
,, ash	,, 49 ,,
,, beech	,, 43 ,,
,, birch	,, 49 ,,
,, cork	,, 15 ,,
,, elm	, 36 ,,
,, pine	,, 41 ,,
,, oak	,, 59 ,,
,, clay	,, 125 ,,
,, loose earth	,, 95 ,,
A cubic yard compressed hay	about 225 lbs.
,, hay in stack	,, ,, 126 ,,
,, compressed straw	,, ,, 145 ,,
,, straw in stack	,, ,, 90 ,,
,, of grain	,, ,, 20 bushels.

FOREIGN WEIGHTS AND MEASURES.

15. *The Metric System used in—*

Argentine Republic, Austria-Hungary, Belgium, Bolivia, Brazil, Bulgaria, Chili, Colombia, Costa Rica, Ecuador, France, Germany, Greece, Hayti, Italy, Netherlands, Norway, Portugal, Rumania, San Domingo, Servia, Spain, Switzerland, Sweden, Turkey, United States (partially), Venezuela.

16. *Linear Measure.*

	Inches.	Yards.
Millimetre	·039	·001
Centimetre (= 10 millimetres)	·394	·011
Decimetre (= 10 centimetres)	3·937	·109
Metre (= 10 decimetres)	39·37	1·094
Kilometre (= 1,000 metres)	39,370·79	1,093·633

NOTE.—1 kilometre is approximately ⅝ mile.

17. *Square Measure.*

	Sq. yards.	Acre.
Centiare	1·196	...
Are (100 square metres)	119·803	·025
Hectare...	11,960·333	2·471

18. *Measures of Weight.*

	Oz. avoir.	Lbs.
Gramme	·032	·002
Kilogramme	35·26	2·204

19. *Measures of Capacity.*

	Pints.	Gallons.
Litre	1·759	·22
Hectolitre	175·976	21·997

To convert yards to metres multiply by ·914.
,, miles to kilometres multiply by 1·609.
,, acres to hectares multiply by ·405.
,, lbs. avoir. to kilogrammes multiply by ·454.
,, gallons to litres multiply by 4·54.

20.—OTHER FOREIGN WEIGHTS AND MEASURES.

Country.	Measures of Length.	Measures of Weight.	Measures of Capacity.
Burmah ...	1 Pulgat = 1 inch 1 Toung = 22 inches 1 Tain = 1069·44 yards 1 Dain = 2·430 miles	1 Moo = 31·5 Tr. gr. 1 Tikal = 252 ,, 1 Viss = 3·6 lb. av.	1 Salay = 1 pint 1 Sak = 1 gallon 1 Saik = 1 peck 1 Teng = 1 bushel
China...	1 Ts'un = 1·41 inches 1 Ch'ih = 14·1 ,, 1 Chang = 141 ,, 1 Li = ⅓ mile (app.)	1 Tael = 1·333 oz. av. 1 Chin = 1·333 lb. av. 1 Picul = 133·3 ,,	1 Ho = 2 pints 1 Shêng = 20 ,, (app.)
Denmark ...	1 Fod = 1·029 feet 1 Favn = 6·178 ,, 1 Rode = 12·556 ,, 1 Mil = 4·680 miles	1 Pfund = 1·10 lbs. 1 Centner = 110·23 lb. av.	1 Flaske = 1·2743 pints 1 Viertel = 1·699 gallons 1 Tonde = 28·885 ,, 1 Skeppe = ·4778 bushels 1 Tönde = 3·823 ,,
Egypt ...	1 Kirat = 1·125 inches 1 Kadam = 1 foot 1 Pik = 22·83 inches 1 Kassaba = 11·6 feet	1 Rottolo = ·9804 lb. av. 1 Cantar = 98·046 ,,	1 Ardeb (Alexand-ia) = 7·4457 bushels
India ...	1 Ungul = ·75 inches 1 Guz = 1 yard 1 Koss = 2000 yards	1 Chittak = 2 oz. av. 1 Seer (16 Chittak) = 2·204 lb. av. 1 Maund = 82·287 ,,	1 Seer = 1·760 pints
Japan...	1 Sun = 1·1931 inches 1 Shaku = 11·931 ,, 1 Jo = 3·314 yards 1 Ri = 2·44 miles	1 Fun = 5·797 Tr. gr. 1 Momme = 57·97 ,,	1 Gŏ = ·3176 pints 1 Shŏ = 3·176 ,, 1 To = 3·703 gallons 1 Kok = 4·962 bushels

OTHER FOREIGN WEIGHTS AND MEASURES —continued.

Country.	Measures of Length.	Measures of Weight.	Measures of Capacity.
Malta... ...	1 Piede = 11·166 inches 1 Canna = 2·283 yards	1 Libbra (12 Oncia) = 4886 Tr. gr. 1 Rotolo = 1·745 lb. av.	1 pint = ·8331 pint 1 Salma = 7·9672 bushels
Persia... ...	1 Zar = 40·95 inches 1 Farsakh = 3·87 miles (app.)	1 Seer = 1138 Tr. gr. 1 Rafal = 1·014 lb. av. 1 Maun = 6·49 ,,	1 Collothun = 1·809 gallons
Russia ...	1 Arshin = 28 inches 1 Sajen = 7 feet 1 Verst (500 Sajen) = 1166·6 yards	1 Zolotnik = 64·84 Tr. gr. 1 Funt = ·9028 lb. av. 1 Pood = 36·113 ,, or 40 funt	1 Garnets = 2·88 imp. quarts 1 Chetverik = 5·77 gallons 1 Osmina = 2·88 bushels 1 Chetvest = 5·77 ,,
Siam ...	1 Niw = ·83 inches 1 Kn'p = 10 ,, 1 Sen = 44·4 yards 1 Roeneng = 2·525 miles	1 Tael = 936·25 Tr. gr. 1 Chang = 2·675 lb. av.	1 Thang = 3·75 gallons 1 Cgaw = 375 ,,
Turkey ...	1 Arshin = 26·75 inches The metric system is mostly employed. Roads and railways are marked in "kilometro."	1 Oke (400 Drams) = 2·835 lb. av. 1 Kantar = 124·36 ,, 100 Kills = 78 Okes = 220·46 lbs.	1 Kileh = 1 bushel (app.)
United States ...	Weight, length and surface measures as in England ; the metric system is also permitted.		1 Pint (dry) = ·9694 pint 1 Gallon = ·9694 gallon 1 Bushel = ·9694 bushel 1 Pint (spirit) = ·8331 pint 1 ,, (beer) = 1·017 pints

CURRENCY OF BRITISH DOMINIONS AND COLONIES.

21. IMPERIAL sterling coins are the sole legal metallic currency in the
following :—

Union of South Africa and South Africa generally.	Gibraltar.
	New Zealand.
Falkland Islands. Fiji.	St. Helena.

In the following, special coins are current in addition to the Imperial
series :—

Australian Commonwealth.—Special florins, shillings, sixpences and three-
pences in silver, and pence and halfpence in bronze, of the same weights
and composition as Imperial coins of these denominations, but of
special designs.

British Guiana and certain W. Indian Islands.—A special groat or fourpence.

Guernsey.—Eight doubles (= one penny), four, two and one double.

Jamaica.—Nickel-bronze pence, halfpence and farthings.

Jersey.—Special pence, halfpence and farthings.

Malta.—One-third of a farthing.

Nigeria, North and South.—One penny (nickel-bronze), and one-tenth
penny (aluminium and nickel bronze), all perforated.

22. Dominions and Colonies Possessing Special Currencies.

Colony.	Monetary Unit (Standard Coin).	Value. In English Currency.	Value. Pieces to the Pound.	Gold Coins.	Silver and other Subsidiary Coins.
		s. d.			
British Honduras	Gold dollar ... ... Silver dollar	4 1⅓ 1 9*	4·867 11·43*	British and United States	Silver—50, 25, 10 and 5 cents. Nickel—5 cents. Bronze—cents.
British North Borneo	Mexican dollar ...	1 9*	11·43*	... ...	Nickel—5, 2½ and 1 cent. Bronze—1 and ½ cent.
Canada ...	Silver dollar on gold basis	4 1⅓	4·867	British and United States 10 and 5 dollars	Silver—1 dollar, 50, 25, 10 and 5 cents. Bronze—cents.
Ceylon... ...	Indian rupee, fixed rating	1 4	15	British gold	Silver—50, 25 and 10 cents. Nickel—5 cents. Copper—5, 1, ½ and ¼ cent.
Cyprus ...	Piastre...	0 1⅓	180	British gold	Silver—18, 9, 4 and 3 piastres. Bronze—1, ½ and ¼ piastre.
East Africa ...	Indian rupee, fixed rating	1 4	15	... ...	Silver—50 and 25 cents. Nickel (perforated)—10, 5, 1 and ½ cent. Aluminium (perforated)—1 and ½ cent.
Hong Kong (and Labuan)	Dollar, Mexican or British	1 9*	11·43*	... ...	Silver—50, 20, 10 and 5 cents. Bronze—1 and $\frac{1}{10}$ cent.
India	Rupee (fixed rating) = 16 annas = 64 pice	1 4	15	British gold	Silver—½, ¼ and ⅛ rupee. Nickel (serrated)—$\frac{1}{16}$ rupee (anna). Copper—2, 1, ½ and ⅓ pice or pie.
Mauritius (and Seychelles)	Indian rupee (fixed rating)	1 4	15	... ...	Silver—20 and 10 cents. Bronze—5, 2 and 1 cents.
Newfoundland	Dollar on gold basis...	4 2	4·8	... ...	Silver—50, 20, 10 and 5 cents. Bronze—cents.
Straits Settlements	S.S. dollar at fixed rating	2 4	8·57	British gold	Silver—1 dollar, 50, 20, 10 and 5 cents Bronze—1, ½ and ¼ cent.
Uganda ...	Same	as East	Africa.		

* Variable with the price of silver—now about 2s. 1d. per ounce.

23. INDIAN MONEYS.

| 3 pies = 1 pice. | 16 annas = 1 rupee = 16*d*. |
| 4 pice = 1 anna. | 15 rupees = £1. |

24. FOREIGN MONEYS.

Country.	Monetary Unit.	Standard Coin.		
		Denomination.	Value.	
			In English Currency.	Pieces to the Pound.
			s. d.	
Argentine Republic	Nominal, Gold Peso	Peso fuerte of	3 11½	5·04
	Actual, Paper ,,	100 centavos	1 9 abt.	11·4 abt.
Austria-Hungary	Krone of 100 heller or filler	Krone	0 10	24
Belgium ...	Franc	Franc	0 9·513	25·22
Bolivia ...	Nom., Gold Boliviano	Boliviano of	4 0	5
	Actual, Silver ,,	100 centavos	2 0 abt.	10
Brazil ...	Nom., Gold Milreis...	...	2 3	8·9
	Actual ,, ,, ...	Paper milreis...	1 3 abt.	15·8 abt.
Bulgaria ...	Lev	Lev of 100 stotinki	0 9·513	25·22
Chile ...	Nominal Gold Peso (Piastre) of 100 centavos	...	1 6	13·33
	Actual, Paper Peso...	Paper peso ...	0 7 to 1 0	34 to 20
China ...	Silver Yuan or dollar (new law) of 100 cents	Yuan	2 0 abt.	10 abt.
Colombia ...	Nom., Gold Peso fort of 100 centavos	Gold peso ...	4 11½	4·03
	Actual, Paper Peso...	...	0 0¾	480 to 16
Denmark ...	Gold Krone of 100 öre	Krone	1 1½	18·15
Ecuador ...	Silver Sucré (piastre fort) of 100 centavos	Sucré	2 0	10
France ...	Franc of 100 centimes	Franc	0 9·513	25·22
German Empire	Gold Reichsmark of 100 pfennige	Mark	0 11·7483	20·428
Greece ...	Drachma of 100 lepta	Drachma ...	0 9·513	25·22
	Actual, Paper Drach.	...	0 9	26·6
Holland ...	Gold Florin or Gulden of 100 cents	Florin or gulden	1 7·824	12·106
Italy ...	Lira of 100 centesimi	Lira	0 9·513	25·22
Japan ...	Gold Yen of 100 sen	Gold Yen ...	2 0½	9·76
Mexico ...	Nom., Gold Dollar ...	Silver of 100 centavos	2 0½	9·76
	Actual, Silver ,,			
Norway ...	Gold Krone of 100 öre	Gold Krone ...	1 1½	18·15
Ottoman Empire	Turkish gold £ of 100 piastres	Gold piastre ...	0 2·165	111
	Pound (lira)	...	18 0	1·1
Egypt ...	£E of 100 piastres ...	£E	20 3¾	·99
		Piastre... ...	0 2¼ abt.	98 abt.

FOREIGN MONEYS—*continued.*

Country.	Monetary Unit.	Standard Coin.		
		Denomination.	Value.	
			In English Currency.	Pieces to the Pound
			s. d.	
Persia ...	Silver Kran of 20 shahis or 1,000 dinaro	Gold toman ...	7 1	2·82
		Silver kran ...	0 4·8	50
Peru ...	Libra (pound) of 10 soles or 100 dineres (1,000 centavos)	Libra	20 0	1
Portugal ...	Nom., Gold Milreis...	Gold milreis ...	4 5¼	4·5
	Actual, Paper ,, ...	Paper ,, ...	4 1½	5·2 to 4·5
Rumania ...	Gold Leo or franc of 100 bani	Gold leo ...	0 9·513	25·22
Russia ...	Gold Rouble of 100 kopecks	Rouble... ...	2 1⅓	9·458
Servia ...	Dinar of 100 paras ...	Dinar (gold basis)	0 9·513	25·22
Siam ...	Tical of 100 satangs (centimes)	Tical	1 6½ abt.	13 abt.
Spain ...	Nom., Silver Peseta	Silver peseta ...	0 9·513	25·22
	Actual, Paper ,,	Paper ,, ...	0 9	26·6
Sweden ...	Gold Krona of 100 öre	Gold krona ...	1 1½	18·15
Switzerland	Franc of 100 centimes or rappen	Franc (10 batzen)	0 9·513	25·22
United States	Gold Dollar of 10 dimes or 100 cents	Gold dollar ...	4 1·32	4·867
Uruguay ...	Nom., Gold Peso ...	Peso of 100 centesimos	4 3	4·7
	Actual, Silver Peso...		4 2 abt.	4·8 abt.
Venezuela ...	Gold Bolivar of 100 centavos	Bolivar... ...	0 9½ abt.	25 abt.

52. THERMOMETER.

Fahrenheit.	Réaumur.	Centigrade.
0	− 14·2	− 17·8
14	− 8	− 10
32	0	0
50	8	10
68	16	20
86	24	30

To convert Centigrade or Réaumur degrees into Fahrenheit use formulæ as follows :—

$$F = \frac{9\,C}{5} + 32$$

$$F = \frac{9\,R}{4} + 32$$

$$F = C + R + 32$$

$$\frac{F - 32}{9} = \frac{C}{5} = \frac{R}{4}$$

APPENDIX I.

POINTS OF THE COMPASS.

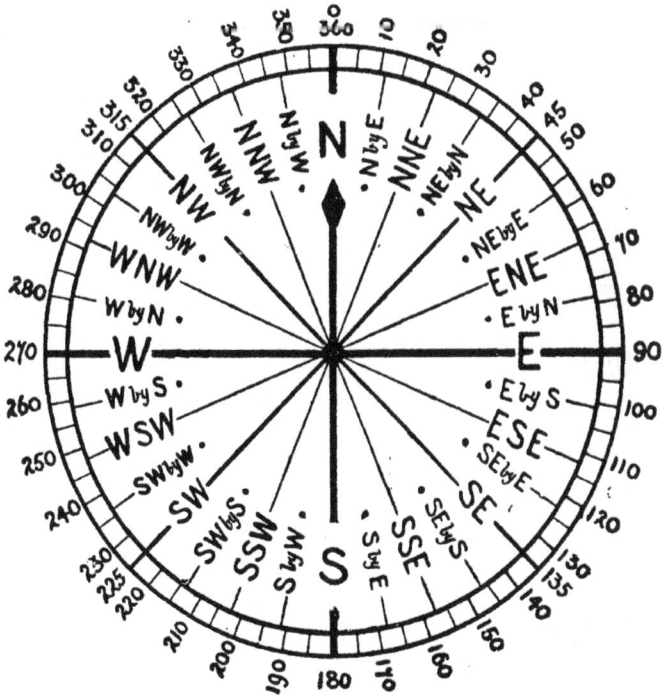

APPENDIX II.

MAGNETIC VARIATION, 1914.

UNITED KINGDOM.

London	...	...	...	15 ° W.
Dublin	...	...	...	19 ° ,,
Glasgow	...	...	...	18½° ,,
Galway	...	...	...	20 ° ,,

BRITISH DOMINIONS AND COLONIES.

Canada.

Halifax	...	...	...	22 ° W.
Quebec	...	...	...	19 ° ,,
Montreal	...	...	...	15 ° ,,
Winnipeg	...	...	...	11 ° E.
Esquimalt	...	...	...	25 ° ,,

Australia.

Sydney	..	...	...	9½° E.
Melbourne	...	...	...	8 ° ,,
Adelaide	...	...	...	5½° ,,
Brisbane	...	...	...	9½° ,,
Hobart	...	...	...	10 ° ,,
Perth ...	...	...	...	4 ° W.

New Zea'and.

Wellington	...	...	...	16½° E.

South Africa.

Cape Town	...	...	...	27½° W.
Durban	...	...	...	21½° ,,
Bloemfontein	...	...	...	22½° ,,
Pretoria	...	...	...	20½° ,,
Walfisch Bay	...	...	...	23 ° ,,
Victoria Falls	...	...	...	17 ° ,,
Gibraltar	...	...	...	14½° ,,

EUROPE (CONTINENT OF).

Paris	...	...	...	13½° W.
Bordeaux	...	...	...	14 ° ,,
Berlin ...	...	...	...	8 ° ,,
Brussels	...	...	...	13 ° ,,
Lisbon	...	...	...	16 ° ,,
Genoa ...	...	...	...	10 ° ,,
Athens	...	...	...	4½° ,,

Sudan and Egypt.

Cairo ...	...	...	...	2½° W.
Khartoum	...	...	...	4 ° ,,

Tropical Africa.

West Coast :—

Bathurst (Gambia) ...	...	18 ° W.
Freetown (Sierra Leone)	...	18½° ,,
Accra (Gold Coast) ...	...	15 ° ,,
Lagos (S. Nigeria) ...	...	14 ° ,,
Coomassie	...	...	15 ° ,,
Zungeru (N. Nigeria)	...	11 ° ,,

East Coast :—

Mombasa (E. Africa)	...	4½° W.
Lake Victoria	..	6½° ,,
Berbera (Somaliland)	...	1½° ,,

Jamaica.

Kingston	...	...	...	1½° E.

Indian Empire.

Bombay	...	...	...	¾° E.
Calcutta	...	...	...	1 ° ,,
Karachi	...	...	...	2 ° ,,
Peshawar	...	...	...	3½° ,,
Dehra Dun ...	...	...	2½° ,,
Mandalay	...	...	...	½° ,,

APPENDIX III.

The dates of the full moon (to the nearest night) for the years 1914–16 are shown below. By adding 15 to these dates the approximate date of the new moon can be obtained.

Month.	1914.	1915.	1916.
January	11	$\left\{ \begin{matrix} 1 \\ 30 \end{matrix} \right\}$	19
February	10	...	18
March	11	$\left\{ \begin{matrix} 1 \\ 30 \end{matrix} \right\}$	19
April	10	29	18
May	9	28	17
June...	7	26	15
July	7	26	15
August	5	24	13
September...	4	22	11
October	3	22	11
November	2	21	10
December	2	21	9

APPEN

The following table gives the time of sunrise and sunset on certain dates
for intermediate dates and latitudes

SUN'S RISING AND SETTING.

Latitude.	60° N.		50° N.		40° N.		30° N.		20° N.	
	rises.	sets.	rises.	sets.	rises.	sets.	rises.	sets.	rises.	sets.
	h. m.	h. m.	h. m.	h. m.	h. m.	h. m.	h. m.	h. m.	h. m.	h. m.
January 1	9 7	2 59	8 1	4 5	7 23	4 43	6 57	5 9	6 30	5 00
,, 16	8 52	3 28	7 56	4 24	7 22	4 58	6 59	5 21	6 40	5 49
February 1	8 20	4 8	7 37	4 51	7 11	5 17	6 53	5 35	6 38	5 50
,, 16	7 40	4 48	7 11	5 17	6 54	5 34	6 40	5 48	6 30	5 58
March 1 ...	7 3	5 22	6 47	5 39	6 36	5 49	6 28	5 57	6 22	6 4
,, 16 ...	6 19	5 59	6 15	6 3	6 13	6 5	6 11	6 7	6 10	6 8
April 1 ...	5 30	6 38	5 40	6 28	5 47	6 21	5 52	6 16	5 56	6 12
,, 16 ...	4 45	7 15	5 8	6 52	5 23	6 37	5 34	6 26	5 43	6 17
May 1 ...	4 2	7 52	4 39	7 15	5 2	6 52	5 19	6 35	5 32	6 22
,, 16 ...	3 24	8 28	4 15	7 37	4 46	7 6	5 8	6 44	5 25	6 27
June 1 ...	2 54	9 2	3 59	7 57	4 36	7 20	5 1	6 55	5 21	6 35
,, 16 ...	2 40	9 20	3 52	8 8	4 32	7 28	5 0	7 0	5 21	6 39
July 1 ...	2 44	9 22	3 56	8 10	4 35	7 31	5 3	7 3	5 25	6 41
,, 16 ...	3 7	9 4	4 10	8 2	4 46	7 26	5 10	7 1	5 30	6 41
August 1...	3 42	8 30	4 30	7 42	4 59	7 13	5 20	6 52	5 36	6 36
,, 16...	4 18	7 50	4 52	7 16	5 13	6 55	5 28	6 40	5 41	6 27
Sept. 1 ...	4 55	7 5	5 15	6 45	5 28	6 32	5 38	6 22	5 45	6 15
,, 16 ...	5 31	6 19	5 37	6 13	5 42	6 8	5 46	6 4	5 48	6 2
October 1	6 6	5 37	6 0	5 40	5 57	5 43	5 55	5 45	5 52	5 48
,, 16	6 43	4 49	6 24	5 8	6 13	5 19	6 4	5 28	5 56	5 36
Nov. 1 ...	7 23	4 5	6 51	4 37	6 30	4 58	6 15	5 13	6 3	5 25
,, 16 ...	8 2	3 28	7 16	4 14	6 48	4 42	6 27	5 3	6 11	5 19
Dec. 1 ...	8 37	3 1	7 38	4 0	7 4	4 34	6 39	4 59	6 20	5 18
,, 16 ...	9 2	2 49	7 54	3 57	7 17	4 34	6 51	5 1	6 29	5 22

DIX IV.

in each month of the year for latitudes between 60° N. and 40° S.; the times can be easily interpolated :—

MEAN LOCAL TIMES.

10° N.		Equator.		10° S.		20° S.		30° S.		40° S.	
rises.	sets.	rises.	sets.	rises.	sets.	rises.	sets.	rises.	sets.	rises.	sets.
h. m.	h. m.	h. m.	h. m	h m.	h. m.	h. m.	h. m.	h. m.	h. m.	h. m.	h. m.
6 18	5 48	6 1	6 5	5 44	6 22	5 25	6 41	5 4	7 2	4 36	7 30
6 23	5 57	6 8	6 12	5 52	6 28	5 35	6 45	5 16	7 4	4 52	7 28
6 24	6 4	6 12	6 16	5 58	6 29	5 45	6 43	5 30	6 58	5 11	7 17
6 21	6 7	6 12	6 16	6 2	6 26	5 53	6 35	5 42	6 46	5 28	7 0
6 16	6 9	6 10	6 14	6 5	6 20	5 59	6 26	5 52	6 33	5 44	6 42
6 8	6 10	6 7	6 11	6 5	6 13	6 4	6 14	6 2	6 16	6 0	6 18
5 59	6 9	6 2	6 6	6 5	6 3	6 8	6 0	6 12	5 56	6 16	5 52
5 51	6 9	5 58	6 2	6 5	5 55	6 12	5 48	6 21	5 39	6 31	5 29
5 44	6 10	5 55	5 59	6 6	5 48	6 17	5 37	6 30	5 24	6 46	5 8
5 40	6 12	5 54	5 58	6 8	5 44	6 22	5 30	6 39	5 13	7 0	4 52
5 39	6 17	5 55	6 0	6 12	5 44	6 29	5 26	6 49	5 6	7 14	4 42
5 41	6 19	5 58	6 2	6 15	5 45	6 34	5 26	6 55	5 5	7 22	4 38
5 44	6 22	6 1	6 5	6 18	5 48	6 36	5 30	6 58	5 8	7 24	4 42
5 47	6 24	6 4	6 8	6 19	5 52	6 36	5 35	6 56	5 16	7 20	4 52
5 51	6 21	6 4	6 8	6 17	5 55	6 31	5 41	6 47	5 25	7 8	5 4
5 52	6 16	6 2	6 6	6 12	5 56	6 23	5 45	6 35	5 33	6 49	5 19
5 51	6 9	5 58	6 2	6 4	5 56	6 10	5 50	6 17	5 43	6 26	5 34
5 51	5 59	5 53	5 57	5 55	5 55	5 57	5 53	6 0	5 50	6 2	5 48
5 50	5 50	5 48	5 52	5 46	5 54	5 43	5 57	5 41	5 59	5 37	6 3
5 50	5 42	5 44	5 48	5 37	5 55	5 31	6 1	5 23	6 9	5 14	6 18
5 52	5 36	5 42	5 46	5 32	5 56	5 21	6 7	5 8	6 20	4 52	6 36
5 56	5 34	5 43	5 47	5 29	6 1	5 14	6 16	4 58	6 32	4 37	6 53
6 3	5 35	5 47	5 51	5 30	6 8	5 13	6 25	4 53	6 45	4 28	7 10
6 11	5 41	5 54	5 58	5 37	6 15	5 17	6 34	4 56	6 56	4 28	7 24

APPENDIX V.

LIST OF AUTHORITIES TO WHOM INDENTS SHOULD BE ADDRESSED BY
UNITS REQUIRING FOOD, STORES, &C.

Requirements.	Where to Apply.	
	If on L. of C.	If with Field Troops.
Ammunition	Nearest Ordnance Depôt	O.C. Amm. Column.
Arms	,, ,, ,,	D.A.D.O.S.
Camp Equipment ...	,, ,, ,,	,,
*Clothing...	,, ,, ,,	,,
Disinfectants	Nearest Supply Depôt ...	Senior Supply Officer.
Equipment	A.O.D.	D.A.D.O.S.
Explosives	,, ...	,,
Forage	Nearest Supply Depôt ...	Senior Supply Officer.
Fuel	,, ,, ,,	,,
Harness	A.O.D.	D.A.D.O.S. ,,
Horses or Mules... ...	Nearest Remount Depôt	D. of Rmts. or his representative.
Light (Candles, Oil) ...	Nearest Supply Depôt ...	Senior Supply Officer.
Medical Comforts ...	,, ,, ,,	,,
Medical Stores	Nearest Hospital... ...	A.D.M.S.
Men	A.G.'s staff	A.G.'s Staff.
Money	Nearest Pay Office ...	Field Paymaster.
Necessaries	A.O.D.	Ordnance Officer.
†Oil (for lighting) ...	Nearest Supply Depôt ...	Senior Supply Officer.
Oil (for lubricating) ...	A.O.D.	D.A.D.O.S.
Ordnance Stores ...	,, ...	,,
Picketing Gear	,, ...	,,
Rations	Nearest Supply Depôt ...	Senior Supply Officer.
Saddlery	A.O.D.	D.A.D.O.S.
Signalling Gear (except Oil)	,, ...	,,
Stationery	,, ...	,,
Soap	,, ...	,, (if no Ordnance Officer available, Senior Supply Officer).
Tools	,, ...	Ordnance Officer.
Transport...	Nearest Transport Depôt	Senior Transport Officer
Veterinary Stores ...	A.V.D.	Veterinary Officer i/c of Unit, or nearest Veterinary Officer.

* In India Supply Depôt.
† Includes oil and wick for signalling.

APPENDIX VI.

Army Form F 789.

1. BILLETING DEMAND ON CIVIL AUTHORITIES.

As an Officer of the British Army, I, acting under powers conferred upon me, hereby direct the Local Authorities of
to supply billets for :—

Officers.			Warrant Officers.	Staff-Serjeants and Serjeants.	Rank and File.	Horses, &c.	Subsistence required. (Insert number of meals per day, number of days, &c. If no subsistence is required insert the word " none.")
Generals.	Field Officers.	Captains and Lieutenants.					

* In the event of subsistence being demanded and provided the question of payment therefore will be taken up on production of the requisition receipt notes, which must be transmitted to the officer in command of the nearest British garrison.

In case of any disobedience on the part of the inhabitants in complying with the demands, the local civil authorities will address the undersigned without loss of time in order that military force may be applied if necessary.

Place
Date
Signature of Officer

---

* Alter as necessary if payment is to be made on the spot.

2. BILLETING ORDER ON INHABITANTS.

(Issued by the mayor, magistrate, chief police officer, or other local authority.)

Number of the Billeting Demand................

1) Quarters for—
        Generals,
        Field Officers,
        Captains and Lieutenants,
        Warrant Officers,
        Staff-Serjeants and Serjeants,
        Rank and File,
        Horses, &c.,
are to be provided,* together with subsistence as follows :—

by ....(Name)...at No............
....Street.

Place and date

Signature of the Head of the Community.

---

* Strike out if no subsistence is to be provided.

APPENDIX VII.

(Referred to in Section 43.)

Army Form A 2042.

Nothing is to be written on this side except the dates and the signature of the sender.

Sentences not required may be erased.

If anything else is added the postcard will be destroyed.

I am quite well.

I have been admitted into hospital.

Sick   { and am going on well.

Wounded { and hope to be discharged soon.

I am being sent down to the base.

I have received your { letter, dated ....
  telegram, dated ....
  parcel, dated ....

Letter follows at first opportunity.

I have received no letter from you { lately.
  for a long time.

Signature

Date

APPENDIX VIII.

AERONAUTICAL TERMS AND THEIR MEANING.

DEFINITIONS.

1. Aeroplane ... ... A flying machine heavier than air.

Aviator ... ... The pilot or driver of an aeroplane.

Biplane ... ... An aeroplane with two sets of main planes one above the other.

Engine bearers ... Supports for the engine.

Fuselage ... ... The outrigger or framework connecting the main planes with the tail-piece or with the elevator.

Monoplane ... ... An aeroplane with one set of main planes.

Nacelle ... ... The car of a balloon or dirigible. An enclosed shelter for the pilot of a biplane.

Staggered planes ... A biplane or triplane in which the upper planes are set in advance of the lower.

Tail-plane or Empennage ... ... Supporting surfaces composing the tail.

Tractor machine ... An aeroplane having its propeller in front.

Triplane ... ... An aeroplane with three sets of main planes one above the other.

Under-carriage or landing chassis ... Wheels, skids, wires and struts under the body.

COMMON EXPRESSIONS.

2. A machine " rising " is said to be " climbing."

A machine descending without the engine running is said to be " gliding " or " volplane."

A machine descending too steeply is said to be " diving " or " vol pique."

A machine descending too flat and so losing flying speed is said to be " doing a pancake."

A machine " banking " describes the angle taken up by the planes when turning.

BALLOON TERMS.

3 Rigid... ... A term applied to a dirigible balloon whose envelope is provided with a stiff framework to keep it in shape.

Semi rigid ... A term applied to a dirigible balloon which maintains its shape partly by the assistance of a suitable framework.

INDEX.

A

	PAGE
Abatis	100
Abbreviated addresses	66
Abbreviations	v
Acreage for crops	172, 173
Addresses abbreviated	66
Administrative commandants, duties of	31
,, services, distribution of duties among	28
Advanced guards	70
Aeronautical terms	277
A.G.'s office at the base	210
Aircraft	75
Alarm posts	45
Allowances, field	180
Ambulance wagons, size of	131
Ambulances, field, war establishment of...	1
Ammunition, carts, S.A., weight and load	139
,, columns, divisional, war establishment of	9
,, packing of, and weights	135
,, scale and distribution of, in India	162
,, supply of	165
,, wagon, weight and load	130, 161
,, weight of	135
Animals, captured, disposal of	205
,, care of, and veterinary hints	35
,, for slaughter	206
,, indents for	200, 275
,, loads of	134
,, rations for	168
,, returns of	205
,, shoeing of	206
,, space occupied by, on march	38
,, ,, ,, in camps	46
Armies, foreign, details regarding...	251
Armistices	231
Arms, details regarding	159
,, of foreign armies	251
Army, Indian, details regarding	235
,, in the field, organization of staff duties... ...	25
Arteries, bleeding from	201
Articles of kit left at base	191, 195
,, ,, weight of	135
Artillery equipment, details regarding	160
,, fire	90
,, ,, range of...	91
,, units, detail of	8, 9
Attack, night	58
,, orders for	58
Attraction, local magnetic, of compass	270

B

Baggage allowed on service, officers'	198
Base, articles left at	191, 195
Bearings, true and magnetic	85
Belligerents, status of	227
,, internment of...	232

PAGE

Billeting 43
  ,, demands 275
  ,, order 275
  ,, reconnaissance 73
Billets, accommodation in 43
Biscuit 172
Bivouac shelters, types of 47
Bivouacs and camps 44
  ,, sanitation of 51
  ,, size of 44
  ,, ,, in India 44
Blankets, carriage of 195
  ,, weight of 195
Bleeding, how to stop... 199
Blocks and tackles 109
Boats, details of... 82
Bombardment by naval forces 233
  ,, general provisions 233
  ,, of undefended posts, etc. 233
Bran mash, how to make 209
  ,, ration of 169
Bread, details regarding 173
  ,, ration of... 168
Bridges 72, 109
  ,, destruction of... ... ... 116, 118, 119
  ,, maximum weights on 111
Bridging expedients 109
  ,, material carried in the field 111
  ,, train, establishment of 9
Brigade, cavalry, establishment of 3
  ,, infantry, establishment of 7, 17
Broken limbs 205
Brushwood, cutting 105
Bugle calls on board ship 156
Buildings, destruction of 119
  ,, use of, in defence 103
Bullet, height of, above sight 89
  ,, penetration of 89
Bullock-cart, load of 134
Bullocks, age of... 172
  ,, ration for 169
Buoyancy 116
Burns, treatment of 204
Bushel, weight of 173

C

Cable lines 64
Camels, care of 36, 157
  ,, load of 134
  ,, ration for 171
  ,, slinging on to a ship 157
Camp cooking 49
  ,, equipment, where obtained... 274
  ,, kettles, weight of 135
  ,, spaces 44
Camps and bivouacs 44
  ,, distribution of troops in 44
  ,, in mountain warfare... 44
  ,, sanitation of 51
  ,, selection of sites for 44
  ,, size of 44
  ,, ,, in India 44

PAGE

Cantilever bridge, formula for 112
Capitulations 230
Carriages, gun, details regarding 160
    ,,   railway, capacity of 139
Carriers 121
Cartridges, weight of 135, 159
Carts, weights and sizes of 130
Casualties, disposal of... 199
Cattle, transport, care of 36
    ,,   weight of 172
Cavalry brigade, establishment of... ... ... 3, 11-13
    ,,   division, establishment of... 2
    ,,   field ambulance, establishment of 2, 9, 11
    ,,   supply column, establishment of 12
    ,,   train, establishment of 2, 8
Charges, court-martial, forms of 219
    ,,   for demolitions 116
Ciphers 211
Circular tent 46
Civil authorities, requisition on 177
Clothing 191, 196
Codes, signalling 66
Coffee, ration of 168
Colic in horses 208, 209
Colonial forces, details regarding 239
Column of route, troops in 33
Command, naval words of 81
    ,,   system of, in the field 24
Commanding officer, powers of 216
Compass, how to find position with 86
    ,,   ,,   ,,   without 87
    ,,   night marching by 86
    ,,   points of 289
    ,,   service 86
    ,,   variation of 289
Contributions 231
Conventional signs 85
Convoys 137, 228
Cooking, hints on 49
Cordage, strength and size of 109
Cordite for demolition purposes 117
Correspondence... ... ... 210, 215
Cossack posts 78
Courts-martial 217, 219, 223
Cover, overhead 101
    ,,   provision of 102
Crops, acreage for 173
Currencies 266, 267
Cutting and felling 99

D.

Defence of localities and materials for 101
    ,,   ,,   posts, villages, outposts 102
Defences, lines of communication... 29
Defensive position, points in selecting 38, 101
Definitions viii
    ,,   of railway terms... 155
Demolitions with explosives 116
    ,,   without explosives 119
Departments, distribution of duties among 28

PAGE

Depth for fords... 34
Detached posts 78
Despatch riding 63
Detonators 116
Detraining 139
Diaries, war 211
Director of sea transport, duties of 32
Directors of services, duties of 28
Discipline 216
Disinfection 51
Distinguishing flags and lamps ... ... Plate 21
Division, cavalry, establishment of 2
  ,,   (composed of mixed brigades) establishment of ... 14
  ,,   establishment of 6, 14
Divisional ammunition column, establishment of 6
  ,,   supply column, establishment of 14
  ,,   train, establishment of 9
Drowned, half, to restore 203
Dust, indicating movements by 71
Dynamite, use of 118

E.

Earthworks for fieldworks 97
Elevation when firing 159
Embarkation, notes for 156
Engineering, field 88
Engines, traction, loads of, &c. 132
Entanglements, wire 100
Entraining 138
  ,,   times required, British 138, 151
  ,,   ,,   ,,   Indian 151
Entrenching 97
Equipment, artillery 160
  ,,   camp, indents for 274
  ,,   machine gun 160
  ,,   telephone 62
Equivalents, ration and forage 168, 169
Escorts for convoys 137
Establishments, war, Expeditionary Force 1
  ,,   ,,   India... 20–23
Explosives carried in the field 92
  ,,   use of 116

F.

Fainting, treatment of 204
Farcy in horses 209
Fascines 99
Feeding of horses 35
Feet, sore, treatment of 35
Felling trees 99
Fever in horses 208
Field air-line 64
  ,,   cable 64
  ,,   company, R.E., war establishment of 9
  ,,   ,,   ,,   bridging material carried by 111
  ,,   ,,   ,,   watering 53
  ,,   dressing, first 199
  ,,   engineering 88
  ,,   intelligence 69

PAGE

Field kits... 182
  ,, returns and states 210
  ,, troop, R.E., bridging material carried by 111
  ,, ,, ,, establishment of 9
  ,, ,, ,, watering... 53
  ,, works 89, 97-100
Filters 53
Fits, method of treating 204
Flags, distinguishing ... ... Plate 21
  ,, of truce 230
  ,, water supply 53
Floating bridges 109
Flour 172
Followers, camp 34
Food, indents for 274
Forage equivalents 169
  ,, indents for 274
  ,, Indian rates 169, 173
  ,, notes regarding 168, 172
  ,, ration of 169
Fords 34
Foreign armies, details regarding 251
  ,, arms, range of 257
Fort gates, destruction of 119
Fractures, treatment of 205
Freightships 155
Frostbite, treatment of 204
Fuel 166
Fuzes 118

G.

Gabions 98
Galls in horses 207, 208
Gauges, railway... 151
Geneva conventions 226
Glanders in horses 209
Gruel, how to make, for horses 209
Guards, advanced 75
  ,, rear and flank 75
Gun carriages, weight of 160
Guncotton, amount carried in the field 116
  ,, detonation of, and charges 116
Gunpowder 118
Guns, cover for 103
  ,, destruction of 119
  ,, details regarding 160
  ,, foreign 257
  ,, slinging 158
  ,, supply of ammunition for 161

H.

Hague, Convention of The 226
Halts 34
Harness, care of... 48
Headcover 101
Heatstroke, treatment of 204
Heavy battery, establishment of 9
Hedges, use of 101
Horses at sea 157
  ,, care of, and veterinary hints 35, 47

PAGE

Horses, coupling 49
,, draught, capabilities of 121
,, feeding 36, 48
,, how to shoot 209
,, in camp or bivouac 48
,, linking 49
,, method of securing 49
,, on board ship 157
,, picketing of 48
,, provision of 205
,, rations for 169
,, remedies for ailments of 206
,, slinging of 157
,, transport of, by rail 138
,, watering of 35
Hospitals, ... 199
Houses and huts, destruction of 119
Howitzer battery, establishment of 8
Howitzers, details of 160

I.

Ice, carrying powers of 73
I G.C., duties of 30
Incinerators 52
Indents, to whom addressed 274
India, allowance of baggage and tentage 198
,, issue of clothing 196
Indian ammunition supply 163
,, army 235
,, camps 44
,, languages 237
,, loads 134
,, money 267
,, railway stock 146
,, rations, men and animals 169, 170, 171
,, religions... 239
,, tents 47
,, transport 121, 127
,, weights and measures 259, 263
Infantry, arms of 159
,, brigade, establishment of 7, 17, 18
,, foreign, proportion of guns and swords to 258
Information, acquisition of 70
,, signs affording 71
Inhabitants, treatment of 229
Intelligence 70
Intercommunication 59, 63
,, equipment 60
,, personnel 60
,, service of 59
International law 226
Intervals in camp 44
Iron ration 166

K.

Kettles, camp, allowance of, for officers 185
,, ,, cooking capacity of 49
,, ,, weight of 135

		PAGE
Kitchens, camp	... ...	49
Kits, articles left at base	... ...	191, 195
,, carried in train transport	... ...	184, 187
,, dismounted men	... ...	191
,, mounted men	... ...	188, 194
,, officers'	... ...	182, 185
Knots	... ...	106

L.

Lamps, distinguishing	... ...	Plate 21
Land forces of British dominions	... ...	239
Languages of native troops	... ...	239
Lashings	... ...	110
Latrines	... ...	51
Law, international	... ...	226
Laws and customs of war on land	... ...	228
Limbered G.S. wagon, size and weight of	... ...	161
Limbs, broken	... ...	205
Lines of communication, defences, duties of commanders	... ...	29
,, ,, ,, organization and distribution of	29
,, ,, organization and distribution of duties on	29
Live stock, weight of, &c.	... ...	172
Loads, animals'	... ...	134
,, on bridges	... ...	111
,, vehicles	... ...	130
Localities, defence of	... ...	101
Locomotives, destruction of	... ...	119
Look-outs protected	... ...	101
Loss of consciousness, treatment for	... ...	204
Lymphangitis	... ...	209

M.

Machine guns equipment, details regarding	... ...	160
,, ,, foreign armies	... ...	257
,, ,, supply of ammunition for	... ...	162
Magnetic bearings	... ...	85
,, variation, 1914	... ...	270
,, ,,	... ...	85
Mange in horses	... ...	203
Map, enlarging	... ...	85
,, setting a	... ...	85
Maps, reading	... ...	84
,, scales of English and foreign	... ...	84
March discipline	... ...	33
,, formations	... ...	33
Marches by night, general rules	... ...	35
,, distances on	... ...	33
,, orders for	... ...	33
Marching in frost and snow	... ...	34
,, rate of	... ...	33
Marquee hospital, size and weight of	... ...	46
Materials, &c., for defence of localities	... ...	101
Measures, English and foreign	... ...	259
Meat, ration of	... ...	168
Mechanical transport	... ...	132
Medical arrangements in the field	... ...	198
,, comforts, indents for	... ...	274
,, notes	... ...	199

PAGE

Medical service 198
,, stores, indents for 274
,, units, accommodation of, and establishments 227
Messages, censorship of 65
,, general rules for preparation and despatch 66
,, precedence of 65
,, press... 65
Military landing officer, duties of 31
,, police ,, ... 225
Money, English and foreign 265
Moon, full, date of 271
Morse code 67
Motors and motor lorries, loads of, &c. 132
Mules, indents for 205
,, loads of 134
,, rations for 169

N.

Natives, rations for 169, 170
Naval terms 80, 81
,, words of command 81
Navy, communication with... 69
Necessaries 181
Neutral Powers, rights and duties of 232
Night attacks 58
,, operations, orders for... 58
North, to find 86

O.

Oats 209
Obstacles... 104
Office work, etc. 210
Officers' kit 182, 185
Official letters 210
Operating tent, size and weight of 46
Order of march... ... ... 33, 57
Orders arrangement of 55
,, for attack 58
,, movements by rail 59
,, night advances 58
,, ,, attacks 58
,, general rules regarding preparation of... 55
,, operation 56
,, routine... 58
,, standing 56
Outposts 76
,, defence of 76
Oversea forces 239
,, operations 79
,, ,, special terms in use 80
Oxen, care of 86

P.

Pack animals, loads of 134
Packing of military articles... 136
Parking vehicles 45

PAGE

Parties, working 104
Patrols, hints for commanders of 74
    ,,   reconnoitring, strength of 78
    ,,   standing, strength of 78
Pay arrangements 180
    ,,   ,,   India 181
    ,, regimental daily 179
Pendant, naval and military 69
Penetration of bullet 90
Pickaxe, weight of 92
Pickaxes, number carried ... ... ' 92
Picketing gear, indents for 274
    ,,   horses 48
Piquets 77, 78
Pistol, ammunition, supply of 162
Pitching tents, circular 47
Platforms, temporary, railway 154
Poisons, treatment of persons affected by 205
Police, military 225
Pontoons 110, 111
Positions, reconnaissance of 75
    ,,   requirements of defensive 88, 89
Postal service 215
Post card, private 276
Posts, defence of 102
Powder, gun, explosion of, and charges 118
Primers 117
Prisoners of war 70, 229
Proof cover 89
Proportion of guns and swords in foreign armies 258
Protected look-outs 101
Protection 76
Provost-Marshal, duties of 225
Pulse, rate of 199
Punishment, field 223
Punishments 220
Pumps, lift and force 54
Purification of water 53

Q.

Quarters 43

R.

Rafts 110
Rails, destruction of 117
Railway transport, India 146
Railways, definitions of terms used 155
    ,,   destruction of 119
    ,,   gauges of 151
    ,,   movements of troops by 133
    ,,   ,,   ,,   orders for 138
    ,,   platforms, construction of 154
    ,,   reconnaissance of 73
    ,,   rolling stock on, capacity of 130
Range of guns, foreign 258
    ,,   rifles 257
Ranges, definition of 91
Rate of marching 33

PAGE

Rations 166, 168
  ,,   emergency   170
  ,,   in India, field service, scale of   170
  ,,   indents for   274
  ,,   native 169, 170
  ,,   table of equivalents...   168
Rear guards   76
Recipes, cooking   50
Reconnaissance   70
  ,,   billeting   73
  ,,   methods of   70
  ,,   of various places, &c. 70, 72, 75
  ,,   railway   78
  ,,   reports   71
  ,,   river   73
  ,,   road   71
  ,,   strategical   70
  ,,   tactical   70
Redoubts, field   103
Refilling points   175
Refuse, disposal of   52
Regiment, cavalry, establishment of 8, 10
Reliefs   78
Religions, native troops   239
Remount service   205
Remounts, indents for   205
Reports, preparation and despatch of   55
  ,,   reconnaissance   71
Representative fraction   84
  ,,   fractions, table of scales and   84
Requisition receipt note   178
Requisitions 176, 274
Returns, field   210
Revetments   98
Rifle, details regarding   159
  ,,   ,,   ,,   fire   89
  ,,   ,,   ,,   foreign   257
Rifles, supply of ammunition for   162
Ringworm in horses   206
Rivers, current of   73
  ,,   reconnaissance of   73
Roadbearers, calculation of size for 113, 114
Road spaces   96
Roads, construction of   101
  ,,   gradients of, for traffic   101
  ,,   reconnaissance of   71
Rolling stock, capacity of   139
  ,,   destruction of   119
Ropes   106

S.

S.A.A., carts, size and weight of   130
  ,,   supply of   165
St. Petersburg, declaration of   226
Saddlery, care of   49
Salt, ration of   168
Sanitary considerations for camps...   51
Sanitation   199
Scales   84
  ,,   table of military   84

	PAGE
Scalds	204
Sea transport	155
Selection of sites for camps	44
,, ,, ,, trenches	101
Semaphore code	69
Sentries, duties of	78
Sheep	172
Shelters, types of	47
Ships, bugle calls on	156
,, duties on board	155
,, tonnage of	155
Ship's signals	156
Shock, treatment for	204
Shovel, size of	92
Sidings	155
Signal messages	64–67
,, service, administration of, in war	64
,, traffic	64
,, service, war establishments	9, 10
Signalling codes	67
,, equipment, weight of	135
Signals, prefixes	65
,, ship	156
,, special	68
Signs affording information	70
,, conventional	85
Sites of camps, selection of	44
Sketching field, hints for	84
Slaughtering places	52
Slinging camels on board ship	157
,, guns and vehicles on board ship	158
,, horses on board ship	157
Slopes, measurement of	85
Small arms and guns, details of	159
Snake bite, treatment of	204
Sore feet	35
Space and time, calculations for	36
Spade, size of	92
Spars, strength of	113
Spies	230
Spitlocking	102
Sprains, treatment of	204, 207
Spring wagons, light, size and weight of	131
Stacks, contents of, to find	173
Staff, division of responsibility in respect of duties in war	25
,, general organization and functions of	25
Standing patrols	78
Starting points	34
States, field	210
Stings, treatment of	204
Stockades	117
Stores, in common use, details of	130
,, medical	274
,, ordnance, indents for	274
Strangles in horses	209
Strength of ropes	109
Stretcher, weight of	136
Substitutes for rations, scale of	168
Suffocation	203
Sun's rising and setting	272
Sunstroke	204
Supplies, how carried in field	170
,, notes on	72, 172

PAGE

Supply organization of 174
,, system of 174

T.

Table of guncotton charges 118
,, round roadbearers and transoms for various loads 113
,, time, men and tools for various field works 97
Tables, road space 38
Tackles 106
Tea, ration of 168
Telegraph, destruction of 119
,, rates of laying 64
Telephone equipment 63
Temperature, normal... 198
Tents, d'abri 47
,, Indian 46
,, pitching of, circular 46
,, space, weight and accommodation 47
Tentage 193
Terms, naval 80
Territory, hostile 231
Thermometers, scales of 268
Thrush, treatment of, in horses 207
Ticks, in horses... 207
Timber, buoyancy of 116
,, cubic contents of 116
Time and space... 36
,, men and tools, table of 97
Tonnage, definitions of 155
,, tables (sea) 155
Tools and explosives carried on person and in 1st line transport ... 92
,, size and weight of 92
Tourniquets 202
Tows, detail of 83
Traffic through the outposts 76
Train transport 124
Trains, railway, tables of, for units 140, 147
Transoms, calculation of size for 113, 114
Transport, ambulances 125
,, carriers 121
,, indents for 274
,, India 121, 127
,, inland, water 120
,, mechanical 132
,, officer, naval 155
,, organization of 120
,, railway 138
,, sea 155
,, train 124
,, 1st line, regimental, table of 122
,, 2nd ,, ,, ,, ... 128
,, vehicles, weights and loads of 130
,, with field units 120
Transports, fitting of 156
,, inspection of 155
Trenches, fire 101
Trenches, latrine 51
Trestles 114
Trestle legs, size of timber for 114
Troughs, watering 53
Truce, flag of 230

V.

	PAGE
Variation of compass	269-70
Vedettes	78
Vegetable ration	168
Vehicles, noises caused by, to silence	35
„ on board ship	158
„ parking	44
„ transport, details of	130
Velocity of river, how to find	73
Veterinary hints	206
„ organization	206
„ service	206
„ stores, indents for	274
Villages, use of, in defence	102
Visual signalling	64

W.

	PAGE
Wagons, ammunition, size and weight of	161
„ G.S., loads of	134
„ size and weight of	130
Walls, use of	101
War diaries	211
„ establishments (home)...	1
„ „ India	11, 20-23
Warfare, mountain, camps in	44
Watch, use of, in field sketching	87
Water, purification of...	53
„ supply of	52
„ weight of	53
Watercarts, size and weight of	130
Watering arrangements	51
„ places, rules regarding	35
Weights and measures, English and foreign	259
„ of articles	135
„ of troops, guns and materials on bridges ...	111
„ raising	109
Wire entanglements	100
Wireless stations	64
„ messages, special rules for	67
Woods, use of, in defence	103
Working parties and tasks	104
Working party table, example of	105
Wounded and sick, treatment of	232
„ men, disposal of	199
Wounds, treatment of	204
„ „ in horses	206

Printed under the authority of His Majesty's Stationery Office
By HARRISON and SONS,
PRINTERS IN ORDINARY TO HIS MAJESTY,
ST. MARTIN'S LANE, LONDON, W.C. 2.

Distinguishing Flag and Lamps

	Position of	Flag (by day)	Lamp (by night)
1	General Headquarters		
2	Hd. Qrs. of an Army		
3	Hd. Qrs. of a Division. Number in white; "C" in case of Cav. Div.		
4	Hd. Qrs. of a Brigade or Administrative District		
5	Hd. Qrs. Line of Communication		
6	Hd. Qrs. of a Post, Garrison or Base		
7	Ammunition Column		
8	Supply Depôt		

6365. 63/86. 7/8. 150,000, 4. 17.

At end of book

Plate 21

Distinguishing Flag and Lamps

Position of	Flag (by day)	Lamp (by night)
9	Hospital or Field Ambulance (The Geneva flag will be accompanied by the Union Jack)		
10	Ordnance Depôt		
11	Veterinary Hospital		
12	Telegraph Office		A telegraph office has no lamps as it will usually be with Divisional Headquarters at night.
13	Post Office		
14	Pay Office		
15	Latrine { British / Native		Note:- In India the Flag for British Latrines has a red centre.
16	Engineer Park India		

Malby & Sons. Lith.